NAZI POLICY ON THE EASTERN FRONT, 1941

Rochester Studies in East and Central Europe

Series Editor: Timothy Snyder, Yale University

(ISSN 1528-4808)

Post-Communist Transition: The Thorny Road
Grzegorz W. Kolodko

Globalization and Catching-up in Transition Economies
Grzegorz W. Kolodko

Polish Formalist School
Andrzej Karcz

Music in the Culture of Polish Galicia, 1772–1914
Jolanta T. Pekacz

*Between East and West:
Polish and Russian Nineteenth-Century Travel to the Orient*
Izabela Kalinowska

Ideology, Politics and Diplomacy in East Central Europe
M. B. B. Biskupski, Ed.

The Polish Singers Alliance of America, 1888–1998: Choral Patriotism
Stanislaus A. Blejwas

*A Clean Sweep?
The Politics of Ethnic Cleansing in Western Poland, 1945–1960*
T. David Curp

*Nazi Policy on the Eastern Front, 1941:
Total War, Genocide, and Radicalization*
Edited by Alex J. Kay, Jeff Rutherford, and David Stahel

NAZI POLICY ON THE EASTERN FRONT, 1941

TOTAL WAR, GENOCIDE, AND RADICALIZATION

Edited by
Alex J. Kay, Jeff Rutherford, and David Stahel

UNIVERSITY OF ROCHESTER PRESS

Copyright © 2012 by the Editors and Contributors

All Rights Reserved. Except as permitted under current legislation, no part of this work may be photocopied, stored in a retrieval system, published, performed in public, adapted, broadcast, transmitted, recorded, or reproduced in any form or by any means, without the prior permission of the copyright owner.

First published 2012
Transferred to digital printing and reprinted in paperback 2014

University of Rochester Press
668 Mt. Hope Avenue, Rochester, NY 14620, USA
www.urpress.com
and Boydell & Brewer Limited
PO Box 9, Woodbridge, Suffolk IP12 3DF, UK
www.boydellandbrewer.com

ISSN: 1528-4808
hardcover ISBN: 978-1-58046-407-9
paperback ISBN: 978-1-58046-488-8

Library of Congress Cataloging-in-Publication Data
  Nazi policy on the Eastern Front, 1941 : total war, genocide, and radicalization / edited by Alex J. Kay, Jeff Rutherford, and David Stahel.
      p. cm. — (Rochester studies in Central Europe, ISSN 1528-4808 ; vol. 8)
  Includes bibliographical references and index.
  ISBN 978-1-58046-407-9 (hardcover : alk. paper) 1. World War, 1939–1945—Campaigns—Eastern Front. 2. World War, 1939–1945—Atrocities—Eastern Front. 3. Germany—Armed Forces—History—20th century. 4. Germany—Military policy. 5. Soviet Union—History—German occupation, 1941–1944. 6. Total war. I. Kay, Alex J. II. Rutherford, Jeff. III. Stahel, David, 1975–
    D764.N393 2012
    940.54'2543—dc23

                                                                    2011047379

A catalogue record for this title is available from the British Library.

This publication is printed on acid-free paper.
Printed in the United States of America

Contents

List of Illustrations   vii

Foreword by Christian Streit   ix

Introduction   1
     Alex J. Kay, Jeff Rutherford, and David Stahel

1. Radicalizing Warfare: The German Command and the Failure of Operation Barbarossa   19
     David Stahel

2. Urban Warfare Doctrine on the Eastern Front   45
     Adrian E. Wettstein

3. The Wehrmacht in the War of Ideologies: The Army and Hitler's Criminal Orders on the Eastern Front   73
     Felix Römer

4. "The Purpose of the Russian Campaign Is the Decimation of the Slavic Population by Thirty Million": The Radicalization of German Food Policy in Early 1941   101
     Alex J. Kay

5. The Radicalization of German Occupation Policies: The *Wirtschaftsstab Ost* and the 121st Infantry Division in Pavlovsk, 1941   130
     Jeff Rutherford

6. The Exploitation of Foreign Territories and the Discussion of Ostland's Currency in 1941   155
     Paolo Fonzi

7. Axis Collaboration, Operation Barbarossa, and the Holocaust in Ukraine   186
     Wendy Lower

Contents

8   The Radicalization of Anti-Jewish Policies in
    Nazi-Occupied Belarus   220
    Leonid Rein

9   The Minsk Experience: German Occupiers and
    Everyday Life in the Capital of Belarus   240
    Stephan Lehnstaedt

10 Extending the Genocidal Program: Did Otto Ohlendorf
    Initiate the Systematic Extermination of Soviet "Gypsies"?   267
    Martin Holler

11 The Development of German Policy in Occupied France,
    1941, against the Backdrop of the War in the East   289
    Thomas J. Laub

Conclusion: Total War, Genocide, and Radicalization   314
    Alex J. Kay, Jeff Rutherford, and David Stahel

Appendix: Comparative Table of Ranks for 1941   321

Selected Bibliography   323

List of Contributors   341

Index   345

Illustrations

1.1	Dispositions of Army Group Center, July 26, 1941	30
3.1	The Commissar Order being implemented	89
4.1	*Staatssekretär* Herbert Backe wearing the insignia of an *SS-Gruppenführer*	104
6.1	Development of Germany's Clearing Debt, 1939–42	159
7.1	Hitler and Mussolini touring Ukraine in August 1941	191
7.2	German Order Police commanders and Ukrainian policemen shoot Jewish woman and child at close range	201
7.3	German Order Police commanders and Ukrainian policemen shoot a Jewish woman	201
7.4	Occupied Ukraine, September 1942	202
10.1	Otto Ohlendorf as defendant at the *Einsatzgruppen* Trial, October 9, 1947	270

Foreword

Christian Streit

The war against the Soviet Union brought National Socialist Germany the biggest single extension of its power and contributed decisively to its collapse. The number of dead that it cost exceeded those of the other fronts several times over. The reason for this is to be found in a radicalization of warfare on the German side unparalleled in history, which was accompanied by a systematic breech of international law and resulted not least in the civilizational rupture of the genocide against the Jews.

A decisive radicalizing thrust already occurred in the preparatory phase for the attack, between January and June 1941. At this point, Germany's political and military leadership resolved to wage the war beyond all boundaries of international law. The conflict was to be fought unscrupulously in every sense; the elites of the USSR were to be decimated, large parts of the Soviet population left to starve to death, and the rest condemned to an existence as helots. Even if in this campaign, in the view of the chief of the Army General Staff, *Generaloberst* Halder, "the troops [must] also fight the struggle of ideologies," it was still unclear on June 22 to what extent the conservative elites within the Wehrmacht, but also in the administration and the police, would support these radical policies or whether they would take advantage of the leeway remaining open to them to mitigate or even sabotage these policies.

We now know that the latter option only occurred in exceptional cases. In many areas, the measures ordered were already in the first weeks radicalized beyond what had been planned, and not only as a result of further intensifying directives from the political and military leadership but also repeatedly on the initiative of mid- and lower-level authorities. The megalomaniacal aims and assumptions of the plan of attack led within only a few weeks to a self-created state of emergency, which—regardless of any ideological convictions—in turn created an understanding for even more radical solutions. In the case of anti-Jewish policy, this process led to the most terrible consequences.

As early as 1976, Hans Mommsen identified the "cumulative radicalization" as a decisive trait of National Socialist policy. Historical scholarship has since shed light on this radicalization in various areas, though the entire radicalization process has yet to be systematically researched. The contributions in the present volume analyze a broad spectrum of developments and decision-making processes in the war in the east: in the waging of war, the planning for the exploitation of the occupied territories at the command level, the exploitation at the level of a division, the currency policy in the occupied east, the occupation policy and the policy of extermination toward Jews and Roma. The articles neither aim to nor can they substitute a systematic examination of the issue of cumulative radicalization, but they do contribute important material to this topic, many of them in an outstanding fashion. It is to be hoped that these stimuli will be taken up in further works on the subject.

The successful cooperation of eleven young historians from seven nations—Australia, Germany, Israel, Italy, Switzerland, the United Kingdom, and the United States—also calls attention to the fact that historians from the successor states to the Soviet Union have so far contributed few trendsetting impulses toward research into a war that brought such a degree of suffering to the peoples of the Soviet Union.

—Translated from the German by Alex J. Kay

Introduction

Alex J. Kay, Jeff Rutherford, and David Stahel

The year 1941 was a turning point both in the course of World War II and in the scope and magnitude of National Socialist Germany's policies. At the beginning of the year, Germany dominated continental Europe, having defeated the French in a stunning six-week campaign while at the same time forcing British troops to beat a hasty retreat back across the English Channel. To many contemporaries, it seemed as if the German army, utilizing a new doctrine of war termed "Blitzkrieg," was unstoppable. If Germany began 1941 in such a powerful position, however, it ended the year militarily on the back foot, waging a two-front, truly global war, its human and material resources severely stretched.

It is during these twelve months that the radicalization of Nazi policy, both in terms of an all-encompassing approach to warfare and the application of genocidal practices, can be seen most clearly. In this context, we understand the term "radicalization" to mean a willingness to contemplate, plan, and execute ever more extreme policies in order to achieve ever more far-reaching goals.[1] This was already hinted at with the expansion of the conflict to the Balkans by means of the invasion and occupation of Greece and Yugoslavia. In the former territory, rapacious economic policies unleashed by the German authorities led to widespread starvation, centered on Athens.[2] In Yugoslavia, the Wehrmacht itself initiated a brutal reprisal policy in which Jewish and Romani hostages were executed in "atonement" for partisan and other irregular attacks on army units and installations; within a year of the invasion, Serbia was declared *judenfrei* by the military authorities.[3] Even these operations, however, paled in comparison to the nature of the war against the Soviet Union. Not only was there a radical difference in the scale and the scope of the killings on Soviet territory, but more importantly the mass killings in Serbia were, at least at the beginning, reactionary and not part of a systematic program of extermination. Furthermore, it was only *after* the German invasion of the Soviet Union that the mass murder of Serbian Jews under the cover of reprisals in fact began.[4]

The unprecedented scale of the invasion of the Soviet Union, which included not only an enormous military effort but also an unrestrained and blatantly ideological conduct of war that culminated in genocide against Soviet Jewry and the decimation of the Soviet population through planned starvation and brutal antipartisan policies, distinguished Operation Barbarossa—the code name for the German invasion of the Soviet Union—from all previous military campaigns in modern European history. The genocide against Soviet Jewry in turn played its part in the process leading to the separate though linked decision to expand the killing to Jews in the rest of German-occupied Europe. By the end of 1941, the first of the six extermination camps in occupied Poland had begun operating, though death by poison gas in vast industrial killing centers was only one of several methods used to annihilate Europe's Jews. By this time, in fact, German units and their auxiliaries had already shot, clubbed, starved, and burnt to death as many as eight hundred thousand Jewish people in the occupied Soviet territories. On the home front, the magnitude of the Eastern campaign (and its continuation in the late autumn of 1941 following the realization that the Blitzkrieg had failed) quickly led to an overextension of the German economy to critical levels. Finally, 1941 ended with the expansion of the war beyond the European continent. Following the Japanese attack on Pearl Harbor in December 1941, Hitler declared war on the United States and transformed the conflict into a global struggle. These are all pertinent examples of the radical evolution of Nazi policy over the course of 1941, and they serve to highlight the centrality of the Soviet territories in the development of Germany's approach to the war.

Indeed, it was first and foremost Germany's decision to invade the Soviet Union that turned 1941 into the pivotal year of World War II. The invasion of the Soviet Union in June 1941 was what the late Andreas Hillgruber termed "Hitler's true war."[5] Certainly, increasingly brutal combat and occupation practices that violated international law had already appeared during the first two years of war. The Wehrmacht's invasion of Poland in 1939 and the subsequent partitioning of the country spoke to National Socialist population policies while simultaneously foreshadowing the increased levels of violence utilized by the German army and police forces in pacifying a given area.[6] German atrocities and ruthless forms of repression clearly reflected the Nazi tolerance, and even encouragement, of violent methods.[7] Even in the Western campaign, generally viewed as a *Normalkrieg*, German troops sporadically massacred black French colonial troops.[8] In these early campaigns, however, such actions were frequently enacted as ad hoc measures on the ground or limited to very specific and narrowly defined groups, and were by no means approved of unanimously by Germany's political and military leadership. Both the planning for and carrying out of the German invasion of the Soviet Union, by contrast, constituted not only a radical change in German policy, but also a watershed in modern European history. In both its unprecedented scale and unrivalled brutality, Operation Barbarossa stands as the focal point of World War II. The battles fought in the east were without comparison in the west until 1944. In 1941, the British Empire's main military effort was focused on the three German and seven Italian divisions in North Africa that threatened Egypt. In contrast, the Soviet Union was attacked by 160 German divisions with well over half a million supporting troops from Finland and the Axis allies. Accordingly, throughout the middle years of the war in Europe (1941–43), the fighting on the Eastern Front assumed a dominant role, a fact that has not always been reflected in Anglo-American historiography.

At the same time, Germany's parallel pursuit of a so-called war of annihilation in the east, in which the occupied territory would best be pacified by "shooting anyone who even looks askance,"[9] constituted its own watershed, fusing the racially inspired Nazi worldview with an environment where traditional legal norms counted for little or nothing. The circle of those targeted for removal in their entirety during the course of the war of annihilation in the east was constantly widened, both in the weeks and months prior to the military campaign being launched and in the aftermath of the invasion: the "Jewish-Bolshevik" intelligentsia, all Communist Party functionaries, everyone who demonstrated any form of passive or active resistance, all Jewish prisoners of war, Soviet Jewry root and branch. Radicalizing impulses emanated not only from above, from the center in Berlin, but also from below, on the ground in the killing fields of the east, as the incorporation of the Soviet *politruks* among the targeted victims of the notorious Commissar Order demonstrates, to cite just one example. Hundreds of thousands of Jews, as well as countless other Soviet civilians, fell victim to actions either carried out or incited by the occupying forces, especially during antipartisan raids that commenced mere days after the opening of hostilities, as well as to those led by local civilians who exploited the shift in the balance of power. This approach was soon applied to the entire Jewish population of the Soviet Union and paved the way for the Continental-wide annihilation of European Jewry.

The savagery of German security policies was complemented by an unprecedented campaign of exploitation in which some thirty million Soviet civilians were marked out for death by starvation to remove "useless eaters" and free up foodstuffs. The two largest victim groups in this respect were the Soviet urban population and Red Army soldiers taken prisoner. The siege of Leningrad and the subsequent horrors that occurred there on a daily basis during the winter of 1941/42, as well as the deaths of some 2.2 million Soviet prisoners of war by February 1942[10] have to be viewed within this context of economic thinking. This ravaging of the land was intended to provide Germany with the necessary resources to successfully fight a war of attrition against the Anglo-Saxon sea powers; the collapse of the home front that allegedly undermined imperial Germany's war effort in 1918 was thus to be avoided at all costs under the Nazi regime. Between 1941 and 1944, the Eastern Front constituted, therefore, the foremost theater of military operations, as well as, conversely, both Germany's principal hope for bolstering its economy and the main drain on German resources. The unexpected and—from the German viewpoint—unfavorable military developments in the east prevented German ambitions from being realized, while bleeding her armies white and weakening the Reich's economic potential and strategic maneuverability.

Despite all of this, the German-Soviet war in English-language historiography has followed a rather strange path. Due to the circumstances of the Cold War and the desire to integrate West Germany into the NATO bloc, early research into the savage war in the east frequently reduced it to purely operational histories. In these initial accounts, the German army's brilliant armored operations conquered Ukraine, laid siege to Leningrad, and reached the gates of Moscow before being defeated by a combination of factors that lay outside of its control: Hitler's interference in the conduct of the campaign; the weather, which alternately made the Soviet road network nothing more than a collection of muddy morasses and reduced the German army to a shivering mass of ill-clothed and ill-equipped men following the onset of winter; and finally, the overwhelming numbers of Soviet troops, who advanced in wave after wave, finally wearing down and halting the vaunted German Blitzkrieg.[11]

Operations received the lion's share of attention in English-language historiography for two reasons. First, American and British political and military leaders had no experience of fighting the Red Army and sought to learn as much as possible about their new enemy. After all, the Germans had fought an extremely bloody war against the Soviet Union for nearly four years. Second, many of these works relied almost exclusively on the memoirs and studies of former high-ranking German officers themselves. Obviously these men had very real reasons to obfuscate what had actually occurred during the war.[12] Such works led many to conclude that the German army had fought an essentially clean war and that any atrocities that had taken place had been perpetrated by the political soldiers of the SS. The myth of an honorable German army took firm root in the collective mind of the Western world.[13]

While some German historians began to question the validity of such an approach during the 1960s and 1970s,[14] English-language works examining German occupation policies in the east remained few and far between. Outside of Alexander Dallin's pioneering work *German Rule in Russia 1941–1945: A Study of Occupation Policies* (first published in 1957) and Gerald Reitlinger's *The House Built on Sand: The Conflicts of German Policy in Russia 1939–1945* (first published in 1960),[15] the most consequential works looking at the German experience of war on the Eastern Front were not published until the 1980s and 1990s. During this time period, Omer Bartov, Timothy Mulligan, and Theo Schulte produced important and innovative studies on the German army's complicity in committing atrocities on the Eastern Front.[16] New approaches to German occupation policy in the former Soviet Union have also more recently led to significant English-language works on both the occupation of Ukraine and the development of anti-Jewish policy in the Ukrainian region of Zhytomyr,[17] as well as on political and economic planning for German occupation policy during the preinvasion period, with particular emphasis on the priority given to the ruthless seizure of Soviet foodstuffs.[18] Increased focus on German antipartisan policy has furthermore led to new insights into another central aspect of the German war of annihilation directed against the Soviet Union and its population.[19] While all of these works have led to a much greater awareness of the imperial war waged with unprecedented ferocity by the Nazi state and its allies against the Soviet Union, they remain, despite their quality, the exception to the rule. Once again, English-language historiography significantly trails that of Germany.[20]

Yet it would be inaccurate to suggest that German historiography leads the field in every respect. With the exception of *Das Deutsche Reich und der Zweite Weltkrieg* and work produced by historians at the Research Institute for Military History,[21] the postwar German academic establishment has all but ignored military histories of the period, viewing operationally focused studies in particular as unworthy of serious attention.[22] The aforementioned Anglo-American operational accounts emerging from the 1950s to the 1970s, with their inherent limitations, have still not been comprehensively replaced by new histories addressing the campaign from the German point of view. Indeed, our understanding of this aspect of the war would be particularly poorly served were it not for the work of historians studying the war from the Soviet perspective.[23] It is these works that have provided a corrective in English-language historiography. As important as their insights have been in challenging the many myths established by the German postwar memoir literature, a great deal of work remains to be done concerning the German experience of war in the east.

Beyond the inherent importance of considering what David Glantz has correctly identified as the many "forgotten battles" of the Eastern Front,[24] there is also contemporary relevance in understanding the nature of Hitler's war and the applicability of the notion of a "total war."[25] Nazi Germany famously adopted total war in the spring of 1943 with Joseph Goebbels's speech in the *Sportpalast*, but in some ways this was only a formalization of what had already existed in Germany for years. The Hitler Youth and the Reich Labor Service included forms of paramilitary training, the war economy had made large inroads into the civilian sector, and not only did the state mobilize the domestic labor force, but it had also begun utilizing slave labor from its new empire. Yet total war also takes on another meaning, which can be applied just as equally to Germany's war in the east. Released in 1935, Erich Ludendorff's *Der totale Krieg*[26] established a new benchmark in understanding war when he wrote that a future conflict should aim for the annihilation not only of the enemy army but also of the enemy nation. Essentially, Ludendorff was blurring the distinction between combatants and noncombatants, thus creating the precondition for unrestrained violence directed indiscriminately against a civilian populace. The book's appearance merely publicized one strain of thinking that had developed within the German military leadership in the latter years of World War I and that became a significant influence on military thinking during the interwar period.[27] Though the radical officers who advocated a synthetic meshing of *Volkskrieg* and mechanized war never saw their vision completely accepted by the highest levels of the German armed forces, the establishment of the Nazi state—one that also drew on the lessons of World War I, particularly concerning the importance of the home front in this age of industrial war—accelerated and even radicalized such thinking within the ranks of the Wehrmacht. While the violence directed against Polish and French society during the military campaigns of 1939 and 1940 never reached this level, the Barbarossa operation was indeed based on the concept of total war. The German military, as well as other Reich institutions, utilized any and all means to destroy both the Red Army and the society from which it had emerged. Ludendorff's claim that "war and politics not only serve the survival of the people, but war is the highest expression of the racial will of life" certainly corresponded with the form of total war that drove Nazi policy in the east during 1941.[28]

Notwithstanding the lack of operational histories within German historiography, it remains the case that, during the past ten years or so, the German historical profession has produced extensive scholarship comprehensively exploring the political, economic, and ideological aspects of the German-Soviet war and the German occupation in particular. A new generation of historians such as Andrej Angrick, Christian Gerlach, Christian Hartmann, Johannes Hürter, Manfred Oldenburg, Christoph Rass, Dieter Pohl, Norbert Kunz, Felix Römer, and Bernhard Chiari, though not always in complete agreement, has advanced the state of existing knowledge concerning German occupation policy toward the Soviet Union in extremely important ways.[29] Unfortunately, their work is almost entirely inaccessible for English-language audiences.[30] The present volume aims to provide a bridge for English readers to the latest research on the German-Soviet war as well as present new perspectives with an emphasis on both the planning for the campaign and the first six months of the conflict itself.

In light of the pivotal role played by the German invasion of the Soviet Union in the development and radicalization of Nazi policy, it should not be surprising that the essays in this collection reflect the inherent tendency toward ever more extreme aims and approaches, which quickly came to symbolize the German war in the east as well as signaling the future path that Hitler's New Order in Europe would take. By focusing on the varied experiences of Nazi policy in the east, the volume illuminates the often diverse motivations and complex administrative structures that culminated in an increasingly ideological and violent occupation in the Soviet Union. This volume's collection of young historians present findings based on both their own recent archival research and the most recent historiographical developments in the field. Viewed separately, essays on urban warfare, food policy, Criminal Orders, genocide, and military strategy may seem disparate; presented and analyzed together, however, they deliver a comprehensive exploration of fundamental German objectives on the Eastern Front in 1941 in a way that a single-focus monograph cannot. This collection derives its importance from its weaving together of eleven diverse topics and its exploration of the motivations driving branches of the National Socialist state apparatus toward total war and total destruction through eleven different lenses. The volume also provides an up-to-date English-language synthesis of recent research on the Eastern Front. The scholarship contained here is not only new and thematically germane, but it also offers an international perspective on the events of 1941. The contributors come from the United States, the United Kingdom, Australia, Switzerland, Germany, Italy, and Israel.

From the military standpoint, David Stahel examines the evolution of the strategic approach to the Soviet campaign as a solution to the unyielding resistance of the Red Army. Hitler's war in the east was planned as a Blitzkrieg; major battles near the frontier were envisaged for the opening weeks of the war, but thereafter a rapid and relatively unopposed occupation of the western parts of the country was to follow. For this reason, fundamental differences of opinion between the Army High Command (OKH) and Hitler about the second phase of operations were allowed to pass unresolved during the planning phase. When the initial encirclements unexpectedly failed to break the back of Soviet resistance, the objectives for the second phase became a matter of vital importance. Toward the end of July, the increasingly heated debates became a strategic crisis as the generals of the OKH clashed openly with Hitler. At its root was the problem of how to defeat the Soviet state, but overshadowing the increasingly bitter disputes within the German command was the rapid exhaustion of the German panzer groups, upon which all future plans depended. The result was the failure of Operation Barbarossa, not in the autumn mud or early winter snow, but in the summer months of 1941.

Adrian E. Wettstein investigates the development of the German army's experience of urban warfare through an examination of changes at the tactical and strategic levels. The essay begins with an analysis of German experiences in urban fighting prior to Operation Barbarossa, especially during the 1939 campaign in Poland. With the opening of the campaign against the Soviet Union, German operations changed fundamentally. Ideologically and economically, Germany's objective was to destroy most of the big cities and their inhabitants by starvation. Militarily, on the other hand, the Wehrmacht looked for a rapid victory over the Soviet Union in a Blitzkrieg. This strategy forced German troops to occupy those cities—simultaneously junctions of the thin Soviet transportation system—that were needed for a rapid advance as well as for the supply of the troops. These areas provided strong defensive positions against tank attacks and this dramatically slowed the unprepared German armored forces, which lacked the infantry needed to overcome Soviet resistance. In costly battles, German forces were ground down. This process is shown by examining the battle for Dnipropetrovsk (August/September 1941).

Additionally, the evolution of the Wehrmacht's urban warfare doctrine is examined in the case of Leningrad, where German plans for starvation and the deployment of poison gas reached new levels of barbarity during the modern period.

Felix Römer's contribution looks at the involvement of the German army in the political aspects of the German-Soviet war in the form of the so-called Criminal Orders. Given their major impact on the conduct of war on the Eastern Front, these orders refer first and foremost to the Commissar Order and the Barbarossa Martial Jurisdiction Decree. The Commissar Order stipulated that all political officers in the Red Army were to be shot on the spot should they fall into German hands, which meant nothing less than the systematic murder of regular prisoners of war. The Barbarossa Martial Jurisdiction Decree allowed collective reprisals against whole villages and enabled each and every German officer to decide about matters of life and death regarding Soviet civilians. Römer provides an overview of his recent, groundbreaking research on how German troops viewed and dealt with the Criminal Orders. For the very first time, the records of all German ground forces fighting in the Eastern campaign were analyzed, including those of all armies, corps, divisions, and regiments deployed against the Red Army in 1941–42.

The vital importance within German objectives of the seizure of Soviet foodstuffs is reflected in the presence of two chapters on food policy in this volume, the first on high-level, preinvasion planning and the second on the implementation on the ground. Alex J. Kay's essay addresses high-level planning during the first half of 1941 for securing foodstuffs. At the beginning of the year, members of the Reich Ministry for Food and Agriculture and the Reich Food Estate made concrete proposals to obtain large quantities of foodstuffs for the benefit of the Wehrmacht and the German home front from the soon-to-be-occupied Soviet territories. These so-called surpluses were in fact to be created by forcibly reducing the consumption of the Soviet population. Between then and the launch of the military campaign in June of that year, interaction between the ministerial bureaucracy, Wehrmacht departments, and the political leadership led to a radicalization of proposals to seize Soviet foodstuffs and the reaching of a consensus among those involved to the effect that around thirty million Soviet citizens would starve to death as a result of this concept. As Hitler expected his planning staffs to work around problems and find solutions to difficulties confronting them, pessimistic assessments during the period in question did not result in a rejection of these proposals on the basis of their anticipated terrible consequences (and indeed utopian nature), but rather in a widening of the parameters of both what was acceptable and what was feasible, and, in this way, a radical departure from previous policy.

The contribution from Jeff Rutherford also explores the role played by economic considerations in the German invasion of the Soviet Union. In order to realize its economic goals there, the Reich established the Economic Staff East to systematically exploit the Soviet state's raw materials and natural resources. Once the invasion began, however, the economic authorities' objectives were increasingly frustrated by the actions of the German army itself. During its advance on Leningrad in 1941, the 121st Infantry Division—in accordance with the Wehrmacht's policy of living off the land—increasingly radicalized its food requisitioning, culminating in the organized plunder of the town of Pavlovsk. Such behavior hindered the Economic Staff East's mission, leading to real tension and competition between the two institutions. In the end, however, Soviet civilians paid the ultimate price as they suffered widespread hunger and starvation as a result of the application of German food policies at the local level.

Continuing the economic approach, Paolo Fonzi's chapter focuses on the German currency and finance crisis of 1941. On the one hand, the Soviet territories occupied by the German army were expected to yield great resources for the Reich and thereby alleviate the burden of the war effort on the German population. On the other hand, the war in the east enormously increased the needs of the German war machine and, consequently, the financial expenses incurred by the German state. The perception of a looming financial crisis caused by the war effort spread in the months following the beginning of the Eastern campaign and was a main point of debate among German economic *bureaucrats*. In the same period, a discussion began concerning the foundation of emission banks in the former Soviet territories, which was strongly influenced by the debate on the financial crisis. Two opposing strategies confronted each other: the first aimed at increasing exploitation with monetary means to solve the German budgetary problem; the second believed that the extension of exploitation would lead to an imminent collapse of the currencies in the new territories and, in the long run, make it impossible to pursue a policy of exploitation. Fonzi's contribution outlines this discussion and analyzes which principles were followed when the new Central Banks of Ukraine and Ostland were finally established.

The extensive research carried out on Nazi decision making and the origins of the "Final Solution" has established beyond doubt that the Nazi *Vernichtungskrieg* against the Soviet Union coincided with the physical extermination of all Soviet Jews and other so-called undesirables, and that we can no longer study the military history of the eastern campaigns and occupation policies without their genocidal components. One largely unexplored subject in this context is the focus of Wendy Lower's essay: Axis collaboration. Lower shows how Axis diplomacy and participation in the conquest and occupation of Soviet Ukraine contributed to the onset of the genocide. The diplomacy of the "Jewish Question" among Axis powers was an integral feature of Operation Barbarossa, which precipitated the Holocaust by mass shootings from Lviv to Kharkiv. Case studies of German collaboration with Hungarians, Romanians, and Slovakians reveal that perpetrator networks developed across occupation authorities and usually with local Ukrainians and ethnic Germans on hand to assist in the mass murder. The battles for Moscow and Stalingrad were major defeats for the Axis military, but in the rear areas of occupation another war against the nations or peoples of the Soviet Union, above all against the Jews, was advancing with success. This was the peace that Hitler and his non-German allies hoped to achieve in their racial reordering of Ukraine and the rest of Europe.

As Nazi anti-Jewish policy did not proceed uniformly in the occupied Soviet territories, Leonid Rein offers a companion chapter to Lower's on Ukraine by dealing with the radicalization of anti-Semitic measures in occupied Belarus in the course of 1941. This policy culminated in the total murder of virtually the entire Jewish population there. The persecution of Jews in Belarus began immediately with the isolation of the Jews and quickly progressed to outright murder. In the first two months of the German invasion, not only Jews in party and state positions but also entire Jewish male populations and sometimes even women and children were killed. August 1941 marked the transition to the systematic murder of entire Jewish communities. The expansion of the annihilation process manifested itself in ever-growing numbers of victims, in the widening of the circle of perpetrators, and also in the search for more effective killing methods, such as the gas van. By the end of 1941, practically the entire Jewish population of eastern Belarus and a large part of western Belarusian Jewry had already ceased to exist.

Staying with occupation policy in Belarus, Stephan Lehnstaedt analyzes why and to what extent German everyday life in Minsk in 1941 differed from life in Warsaw between 1939 and 1941. In doing so, he demonstrates with a case study how much more "total" the German approach to occupation in the Soviet Union in 1941 was in comparison with occupation in Poland during the period 1939 to 1941. His chapter begins by outlining the occupation of Belarus, which has been the focus of recent German research but has hardly been addressed in Anglo-Saxon countries. The second part of the chapter addresses not only crimes in

Minsk and their perpetrators, but also aspects of their everyday life in the city. It demonstrates how the perception of the town and its inhabitants as well as the perception of their own situation influenced the attitude of the *Herrenmenschen*. Their behavior, including crimes such as looting, rape, and murder, is investigated in the third part of the chapter. In its final part, Lehnstaedt demonstrates that feelings of superiority toward the Jewish and Belarusian peoples on the one hand, and the sense of being part of a small, besieged group of comrades on the other hand, led—compared to Poland at the same time—to more extreme forms of everyday life in which violence and even mass murder became an accepted and somewhat "logical" mode of conduct for the state and for the individual.

Addressing the much-neglected subject of the genocide perpetrated against Soviet Roma, Martin Holler considers the important role of Otto Ohlendorf, the commander of *Einsatzgruppe* D, in the radicalization of Nazi policy. As early as autumn 1941, units subordinate to Ohlendorf had already carried out the first mass shootings of Roma in the region of Nikolaev. The persecution in the Crimea took a particularly systematic course, where the extermination of "Gypsies" proceeded more or less parallel to the extermination of Jews and Krimchaks. In December 1941 the bigger cities of the peninsula, which had separate "Gypsy quarters," were "cleansed." By January 1942 the towns of Simferopol, Kerch, and Yevpatoria were considered to be *zigeunerfrei* (free of Gypsies). It is striking that, from the beginning, Ohlendorf's *Einsatzgruppe* D did not differentiate between sedentary and so-called itinerant "Gypsies." This approach differed from the other German-occupied Soviet territories, where the systematic obliteration of the whole Romani community did not begin until spring 1942. It is clear that Ohlendorf acted on his own authority when deciding to unite the fate of *all* Roma with that of Soviet Jewry. In doing so, the head of *Einsatzgruppe* D became to a certain extent the trailblazer for the complete "solution of the Gypsy question" on Soviet soil. Furthermore, it seems likely that his murderous activity influenced the decision-making process of the other *Einsatzgruppen* leaders in the sense that Ohlendorf's formal transgressions were evidently in no way restricted, either by the Reich Security Main Office or the German military.

Thomas J. Laub's essay follows on from Stephan Lehnstaedt's comparison of individual cities in Belarus and Poland by comparing aspects of Nazi policy vis-à-vis the Soviet Union with Western Europe, more specifically France. In doing so, he demonstrates that the operational and occupation policies pursued from the outset of Operation Barbarossa were not only far more severe and far reaching than anything that had gone before in France, but also that this very approach to the Soviet Union and its peoples led by the end of 1941 to policy in France becoming systematically more extreme. This affected the treatment of prisoners of war, reprisal measures against partisans and other members of the resistance, as well as the persecution of Jewish inhabitants of France.

The development of Nazi policy in the east during 1941 set the tone for the remaining three and a half years of the war: the pointless battle of attrition that Germany could not win; the single-minded pursuit of Jews throughout occupied Europe and the murder of those ensnared by the regime; the exceedingly violent and arbitrary response to partisan activity, in which innocent civilians were murdered in lieu of actual guerrillas; and the ruthless confiscation of foodstuffs that eventually led to the spread of famine into areas of Western Europe, such as the Netherlands, in the war's latter stages, were all phenomena witnessed on the Eastern Front in 1941. If Hitler and the German state stood at the pinnacle of their power as 1941 dawned, the Nazi regime found itself in a strategically untenable position as the curtain closed on the year. This collection of essays offers fresh appraisals of these fateful twelve months, a year that revealed just how far the Nazi regime was willing to go to achieve its terrible goals.

Notes

1. Mark Edele and Michael Geyer see in the German conduct of war in 1941 "a willful destructiveness at work that escalates relentlessly" and "a rapid escalation of the murderous aspects of the German conduct both from the bottom up and from the top down." Mark Edele and Michael Geyer, "States of Exception: The Nazi-Soviet War as a System of Violence, 1939–1945," in *Beyond Totalitarianism: Stalinism and Nazism Compared*, ed. Michael Geyer and Sheila Fitzpatrick (Cambridge: Cambridge University Press, 2009), 349–50, 356–60. On the radicalization of Nazi anti-Jewish policy, see Peter Longerich, *Der ungeschriebene Befehl: Hitler und der Weg zur "Endlösung"* (Munich: Piper, 2001). See also the discussion of the term "radicalization" in the chapter by Alex J. Kay in this volume.

2. Mark Mazower, *Inside Hitler's Greece: The Experience of Occupation, 1941–1944* (New Haven: Yale University Press, 1993); and Polymeris Voglis, "Surviving Hunger: Life in the Cities and Countryside during the Occupation," in *Surviving Hitler and Mussolini: Daily Life in Occupied Europe*, ed. Robert Gildea, Olivier Wieviorka, and Anette Warring (New York: Berg, 2006), 16–41.

3. Walter Manoschek, *"Serbien ist judenfrei!" Militärische Besatzungspolitik und Judenvernichtung in Serbien, 1941/42*, 2nd ed. (Munich:

Oldenbourg, 1995); Walter Manoschek, "Die Vernichtung der Juden in Serbien," in *Nationalsozialistische Vernichtungspolitik 1939–1945: Neue Forschungen und Kontroversen*, ed. Ulrich Herbert (Frankfurt am Main: S. Fischer, 1998), 209–34; and Ben Shepherd, "Bloodier Than Boehme: The 342nd Infantry Division in Serbia, 1941," in *War in a Twilight World: Partisan and Anti-Partisan Warfare in Eastern Europe, 1939–1945*, ed. Ben Shepherd and Juliette Pattinson (Basingstoke: Palgrave Macmillan, 2010), 189–209.

4. Dieter Pohl, *Die Herrschaft der Wehrmacht: Deutsche Militärbesatzung und einheimische Bevölkerung in der Sowjetunion, 1941–1944* (Munich: Oldenbourg, 2008), 79.

5. Andreas Hillgruber, *Hitlers Strategie: Politik und Kriegführung, 1940–1941*, 3rd ed. (1965; Bonn: Bernard & Graefe, 1993), 516n1.

6. On Poland, see Klaus-Michael Mallman and Bogdan Musial, *Genesis des Genozids: Polen, 1939–1941* (Darmstadt: Wissenschaftliche Buchgesellschaft, 2004); and Jochen Böhler, *Auftakt zum Vernichtungskrieg: Die Wehrmacht in Polen, 1939* (Frankfurt am Main: S. Fischer, 2006). On clashes between the army and the SS in implementing policy in Poland, see Helmut Krausnick and Hans-Heinrich Wilhelm, *Die Truppe die Weltanschauungskrieges: Die Einsatzgruppen der Sicherheitspolizei und des SD, 1938–1942* (Stuttgart: Deutsche Verlags-Anstalt, 1981), 80–81. A more general examination of this issue is found in Johannes Hürter, *Hitlers Heerführer: Die deutschen Oberbefehlshaber im Krieg gegen die Sowjetunion, 1941/42* (Munich: Oldenbourg, 2006), 181–90. On Nazi anti-Jewish policy in Poland, see Christopher R. Browning, *The Path to Genocide: Essays on Launching the Final Solution* (Cambridge: Cambridge University Press, 1992); and Christopher R. Browning, with contributions by Jürgen Matthäus, *The Origins of the Final Solution: The Evolution of Nazi Jewish Policy, September 1939–March 1942* (Lincoln: University of Nebraska Press, 2004).

7. On German atrocities in Poland, see Alexander B. Rossino, *Hitler Strikes Poland: Blitzkrieg, Ideology, and Atrocity* (Lawrence: University Press of Kansas, 2003), 227–35.

8. Raffael Scheck, *Hitler's African Victims: The German Army Massacres of Black French Soldiers in 1940* (New York: Cambridge University Press, 2006).

9. Words spoken by Hitler during the July 16, 1941, conference at Führer headquarters in East Prussia; see International Military Tribunal, ed., *Der Prozess gegen die Hauptkriegsverbrecher vor dem Internationalen Militärgerichtshof, Nürnberg, 14. November 1945–1. Oktober 1946*, vol. 38 (Nuremberg: Sekretariat des Gerichtshofs, 1949), 86–94, doc. 221-L, "Aktenvermerk," quote on p. 92.

10. See Christian Streit, *Keine Kameraden: Die Wehrmacht und die sowjetischen Kriegsgefangenen, 1941–1945*, 4th rev. ed. (1978; Bonn: Dietz, 1997). In spite of having first appeared nearly thirty-five years ago, Streit's

pioneering work on the treatment and fate of Soviet prisoners of war in German captivity remains the benchmark on the subject. The radicalization of Nazi policy is a recurring theme in his book.

11. Albert Seaton, *The Russo-German War, 1941–1945* (Novato: Presidio Press, 1971); John Keegan, *Barbarossa: Invasion of Russia, 1941* (New York: Ballantine, 1971); Ronald Seth, *Operation Barbarossa: The Battle for Moscow* (London: World Distributors, 1964); Ernest Lederrey, *Germany's Defeat in the East: The Soviet Armies at War, 1941–1945* (London: The War Office, 1955); George Blau, *The Campaign Against Russia (1940–1942)* (Washington, DC: Department of the Army, 1955); and Alan Clark, *Barbarossa: The Russian-German Conflict, 1941–1945* (New York: Hutchinson, 1965). Although it was originally published in German in 1963 under the title *Unternehmen Barbarossa: Der Marsch nach Rußland*, it is worth mentioning in this context Paul Carell [Paul Karl Schmidt], *Hitler's War on Russia* (London: Transworld, 1964).

12. See, for example, Elisabeth Wagner, ed., *Der Generalquartiermeister: Briefe und Tagebuchaufzeichnungen des Generalquartiermeisters des Heeres General der Artillerie Eduard Wagner* (Munich: Olzog, 1963); Walter Warlimont, *Im Hauptquartier der deutschen Wehrmacht, 1939 bis 1945*, vol. 1, *September 1939–November 1942* (Koblenz: Weltbild, 1990); Erhard Raus, *Panzer Operations: The Eastern Front Memoir of General Raus, 1941–1945*, comp. and trans. Steven H. Newton (Cambridge: Da Capo Press, 2005); F. W. von Mellenthin, *Panzer Battles* (New York: Ballantine, 1956); Erich von Manstein, *Lost Victories* (Novato: Zenith Press, 1958); Hans von Luck, *Panzer Commander: The Memoirs of Colonel Hans von Luck* (New York: Dell, 1989); Albert Kesselring, *The Memoirs of Field-Marshal Kesselring* (London: Greenhill, 1953); Wilhelm Keitel, *The Memoirs of Field-Marshal Keitel, Chief of the German High Command, 1938–1945*, ed. Walter Gorlitz (New York: Stein & Day, 1966); Hermann Hoth, *Panzer-Operationen: Die Panzergruppe 3 und der operative Gedanke der deutschen Führung Sommer, 1941* (Heidelberg: Vowinckel, 1956); Franz Halder, *Hitler als Feldherr* (Munich: Münchener Dom, 1949); Heinz Guderian, *Panzer Leader* (New York: Da Capo Press, 1952); Günther Blumentritt, *Von Rundstedt: The Soldier and the Man* (London: Odhams Press, 1952); and Alexander Stahlberg, *Bounden Duty: The Memoirs of a German Officer, 1932–1945* (London: Brassey's, 1990).

13. Ronald Smelser and Edward J. Davies II, *The Myth of the Eastern Front: The Nazi-Soviet War in American Popular Culture* (Cambridge: Cambridge University Press, 2008); Wolfram Wette, *Die Wehrmacht: Feindbilder, Vernichtungskrieg, Legenden* (Frankfurt am Main: S. Fischer, 2002); Oliver von Wrochem, *Erich von Manstein: Vernichtungskrieg und Geschichtspolitik* (Paderborn: Ferdinand Schöningh, 2006); and Omer Bartov, Atina Grossmann, and Mary Nolan, eds., *Crimes of War: Guilt and Denial in the Twentieth Century* (New York: The New Press, 2002).

14. See, for example, Norbert Müller, *Wehrmacht und Okkupation, 1941–1944: Zur Rolle der Wehrmacht und ihrer Führungsorgane im Okkupationsregime des faschistischen deutschen Imperialismus auf sowjetischem Territorium* (Berlin: Deutscher Militärverlag, 1971); and Roswitha Czollek, *Faschismus und Okkupation: Wirtschaftspolitische Zielsetzung und Praxis des faschistischen deutschen Besatzungsregimes in den baltischen Sowjetrepubliken während des zweiten Weltkrieges* (Berlin: Akademie, 1974).

15. Alexander Dallin, *German Rule in Russia, 1941–1945: A Study of Occupation Policies* (London: Macmillan; New York: St. Martin's Press, 1957); and Gerald Reitlinger, *The House Built on Sand: The Conflicts of German Policy in Russia, 1939–1945* (London: Weidenfeld & Nicolson, 1960).

16. Omer Bartov, *The Eastern Front, 1941–1945: German Troops and the Barbarisation of Warfare* (London: Palgrave Macmillan, 1985); Omer Bartov, *Hitler's Army: Soldiers, Nazis, and War in the Third Reich* (Oxford: Oxford University Press, 1991); Timothy Patrick Mulligan, *The Politics of Illusion and Empire: German Occupation Policy in the Soviet Union, 1942–1943* (New York: Praeger, 1988); and Theo J. Schulte, *The German Army and Nazi Policies in Occupied Russia* (Oxford: Oxford University Press, 1989).

17. Karel Berkhoff, *Harvest of Despair: Life and Death in Ukraine Under Nazi Rule* (Cambridge: Harvard University Press, 2004); Wendy Lower, *Nazi Empire-Building and the Holocaust in Ukraine* (Chapel Hill: University of North Carolina Press, 2005); and Ray Brandon and Wendy Lower, eds., *The Shoah in Ukraine: History, Testimony, Memorialization* (Bloomington: Indiana University Press, 2008).

18. Alex J. Kay, *Exploitation, Resettlement, Mass Murder: Political and Economic Planning for German Occupation Policy in the Soviet Union, 1940–1941* (New York: Berghahn, 2006).

19. Ben Shepherd, *War in the Wild East: The German Army and Soviet Partisans* (Cambridge: Harvard University Press, 2004); and Alexander Hill, *The War behind the Eastern Front: The Soviet Partisan Movement in North-West Russia, 1941–1944* (London: Frank Cass, 2005).

20. See, among others, Andrej Angrick, *Besatzungspolitik und Massenmord: Die Einsatzgruppe D in der südlichen Sowjetunion, 1941–1943* (Hamburg: Hamburger Edition, 2003); Christian Gerlach, *Krieg, Ernährung, Völkermord: Forschungen zur deutschen Vernichtungspolitik im Zweiten Weltkrieg* (Hamburg: Hamburger Edition, 1998); Christian Gerlach, *Kalkulierte Morde: Die deutsche Wirtschafts- und Vernichtungspolitik in Weißrußland, 1941 bis 1944* (Hamburg: Hamburger Edition, 1999); Hürter, *Hitlers Heerführer*; Manfred Oldenburg, *Ideologie und militärisches Kalkül: Die Besatzungspolitik der Wehrmacht in der Sowjetunion, 1942* (Cologne: Böhlau, 2004); Christoph Rass, *"Menschenmaterial": Deutsche Soldaten an der Ostfront. Innenansichten einer Infanteriedivision, 1939–1945* (Paderborn:

Ferdinand Schöningh, 2003); Pohl, *Die Herrschaft der Wehrmacht*; Norbert Kunz, *Die Krim unter deutscher Herrschaft, 1941–1944: Germanisierungsutopie und Besatzungsrealität* (Darmstadt: Wissenschaftliche Buchgesellschaft, 2005); Bernhard Chiari, *Alltag hinter der Front: Besatzung, Kollaboration, und Widerstand in Weißrußland, 1941–1944* (Düsseldorf: Droste, 1998); Felix Römer, *Der Kommissarbefehl: Wehrmacht und NS-Verbrechen an der Ostfront, 1941/42* (Paderborn: Ferdinand Schöningh, 2008); and Christian Hartmann, *Wehrmacht im Ostkrieg: Front und militärisches Hinterland, 1941/42* (Munich: Oldenbourg, 2009).

21. Militärgeschichtliches Forschungsamt, ed., *Das Deutsche Reich und der Zweite Weltkrieg*, 10 vols. (Stuttgart: Deutsche Verlags-Anstalt, 1979–2008); available in English as Research Institute for Military History, ed., *Germany and the Second World War*, 10 vols. (Oxford: Oxford University Press, 1991–).

22. Klaus Reinhardt, *Die Wende vor Moskau: Das Scheitern der Strategie Hitlers im Winter 1941/42* (Stuttgart: Deutsche Verlags-Anstalt, 1972) and the account by Ernst Klink in Horst Boog, Jürgen Förster, Joachim Hoffmann, Ernst Klink, Rolf-Dieter Müller, and Gerd R. Ueberschär, *Der Angriff auf die Sowjetunion*, vol. 4 of *Das Deutsche Reich und der Zweite Weltkrieg* (Stuttgart: Deutsche Verlags-Anstalt, 1983) are two of the very few serious studies on the course of the campaign in 1941. Much of the remaining German literature in the field was produced by and appealed to the German veteran community. The standard of these works was often low and their conclusions heavily biased, further strengthening the taboo against operational history in the eyes of German academia. For more on the scholarly rejection of military history in Germany, see David Stahel, *Operation Barbarossa and Germany's Defeat in the East* (Cambridge: Cambridge University Press, 2009), 25–29.

23. David M. Glantz, *Barbarossa: Hitler's Invasion of Russia, 1941* (Stroud: Tempus, 2001); David M. Glantz and Jonathan House, *When Titans Clashed: How the Red Army Stopped Hitler* (Lawrence: University Press of Kansas, 1995); Alexander Hill, *The Great Patriotic War of the Soviet Union, 1941–1945: A Documentary Reader* (London: Routledge, 2009); John Erickson, *The Road to Stalingrad: Stalin's War with Germany* (New York: Harper & Row, 1975); Chris Bellamy, *Absolute War: Soviet Russia in the Second World War* (New York: Vintage, 2007); Rodric Braithwaite, *Moscow, 1941: A City and Its People at War* (New York: Vintage, 2006); and Evan Mawdsley, *Thunder in the East: The Nazi-Soviet War, 1941–1945* (London: Hodder Arnold, 2005).

24. For an overview of forgotten battles from 1941 to 1944, see David M. Glantz, *Forgotten Battles of the German-Soviet War (1941–1945)*, vol.1, *The Summer-Fall Campaign (22 June–4 December 1941)* (privately published by David M. Glantz, 1999).

25. Past histories of World War II have made use of this term without seeking to explain its application or purpose. See: Gordon Wright, *The Ordeal of Total War, 1939–1945* (New York: Harper & Row, 1968); and Peter Calvocoressi, Guy Wint, and John Pritchard, *Total War: The Causes and Courses of the Second World War* (London: Penguin, 1989). For a first-rate introduction and contextualization, see Roger Chickering and Stig Förster, "Are We There Yet? World War II and the Theory of Total War," in *A World at Total War: Global Conflict and the Politics of Destruction, 1937–1945*, ed. Roger Chickering, Stig Förster, and Bernd Greiner (Cambridge: Cambridge University Press, 2005), 1–18, esp. 14–16.

26. Erich Ludendorff, *Der totale Krieg* (Munich: Ludendorffs, 1935).

27. Michael Geyer, "German Strategy in the Age of Machine Warfare, 1914–1945," in *Makers of Modern Strategy: From Machiavelli to the Nuclear Age*, ed. Peter Paret (Princeton: Princeton University Press, 1986), 543–72.

28. Ludendorff, *Totale Krieg*, 10.

29. See note 20 above.

30. The best guide to the vast amount of secondary literature in both English and German is Rolf-Dieter Müller and Gerd R. Ueberschär, *Hitler's War in the East, 1941–1945: A Critical Assessment*, 3rd rev. ed. (1997; New York: Berghahn, 2008); and Rolf-Dieter Müller and Gerd R. Ueberschär, *Hitlers Krieg im Osten, 1941–1945: Ein Forschungsbericht* (Darmstadt: Wissenschaftliche Buchgesellschaft, 2000).

CHAPTER 1

RADICALIZING WARFARE

The German Command and the
Failure of Operation Barbarossa

David Stahel

"Everything in war is very simple, but the simplest thing is difficult."[1] Thus remarked the renowned Prussian strategist Carl von Clausewitz in his seminal work *On War*. Casting a fleeting look at the respective strength of arms, experience, and professionalism of the Red Army and the Wehrmacht on the eve of Operation Barbarossa, one might be forgiven for thinking that on this occasion the ensuing war would indeed be very simple, even easy. Certainly many at the time thought so, yet deficient German planning and dogged Soviet resistance proved the virtue of Clausewitz's maxim. Indeed, from its very inception Operation Barbarossa was a problematic enterprise based on poor intelligence and an erroneous understanding of warfare in eastern Europe. Hitler's *Ostheer* (Eastern army) soon encountered problems, and a drastic cycle of improvisation forced a radicalization in tactical methods and strategic choices. At the tactical level, radicalization manifested itself in the increasingly arduous experience of warfare as dangerous materiel shortages, unceasing operational demands, and unprecedented losses overwhelmed units. At the strategic level, the radicalization stemmed from the failure of German plans to rapidly end Soviet resistance, leading to the command crisis over how best to continue the war. Certainly Hitler's war in the east was in many ways unique, but in military terms the Wehrmacht's problems were prefaced by past campaigns.

In his biography of Charles XII of Sweden, Voltaire noted that "there is no ruler who, in reading the life of Charles XII, should not be cured of the folly of conquest."[2] Arguably the best example of Charles XII's excesses in war was his invasion of Russia in 1708, which ended in disaster a year later at the battle of Poltava. Having invaded Russia from Poland with a formidable force marching toward Moscow, Charles's plans soon unravelled as he diverted his hapless army into Ukraine. There it was supposed to secure supplies and wait out the winter before continuing in 1709. Yet Charles's army withered and in the following year he was met by a reformed and numerically superior Russian opponent. At the pivotal battle of Poltava in June 1709, Charles's campaign came to a disastrous end. The corrosive effects of operating a foreign army in the hostile expanses of the Russian steppe made defeat ever more likely.[3]

Assessing Charles XII's ill-fated campaign one hundred years later, Napoleon Bonaparte ignored the dangers of sustaining an army in Russia and remained convinced that the Swedish king's cardinal error was not taking Moscow, which he believed was the key to the whole campaign.[4] Events were to prove the French emperor wrong. Napoleon took Moscow in his 1812 campaign, but it did him no good when the Russian tsar, Alexander I, refused to acknowledge defeat and simply continued the war. Confronting the grievous prospect of a winter deep inside Russia, Napoleon began his famous retreat, which ended in its own calamity. Yet the root of Napoleon's demise was not his delayed departure from Moscow, nor the unforgiving intensity of the Russian winter. It was his flawed understanding of the eastern theater of war, which from the beginning shunned or thwarted many of Napoleon's conventional conceptions of victory and conquest. A partial occupation was clearly insufficient to subdue Russia and yet its vast size hardly allowed for a more comprehensive subjugation. Time also favored the Russians, not simply because of the severe winter weather but also because of the high price to be paid by maintaining an army in the field. Throughout the march to Moscow in 1812 the Grande Armée lost men at a staggering rate. Indeed, advancing through the Russian theater was by far the single greatest peril for the armies of both Charles XII and Napoleon I. Diseases, exhaustion, heat stroke, dehydration, desertion, and even starvation cut swaths through the ranks and also decimated the vital horse population. Even Napoleon's bloody encounter at Borodino was dwarfed by losses on the march. Accordingly, the campaign cannot be understood simply through the sum of its major battles, as those alone would suggest a French victory that belies the dwindling strength of the invader.[5] By the time the French were encamped in Moscow, their unbeaten army had had its numerical superiority over the Russians slashed, and this was before the well-documented torments of their retreat. Clearly the bitter experiences of both Charles XII and Napoleon I set an ominous precedent for invaders of Russia.

Assessing Clausewitz's history of the 1812 campaign, Sir Michael Howard paraphrased the great strategist's conclusion "that battles are rather won by attrition, the slow exhaustion of reserves, than by either skilful manoeuvres beloved of military theorists or the 'shock' so dear to the hearts of fighting soldiers."[6] If this was true of Napoleon's day, it certainly retained its merit in 1941. The attrition of the invading German army was seen both on the battlefield and on the march, but as with past conquerors, the German command was largely oblivious to its effects. The implications had a distinctly radicalizing effect in two key areas.

At the strategic level, the premise of Operation Barbarossa's success—eliminating Soviet resistance through large-scale encirclements close to the German-Soviet border—proved excessively optimistic and necessitated further operations. These would have to be conducted at an ever increasing depth with rapidly diminishing resources, but because such stolid faith had been placed in the initial success of the campaign, little planning and no agreement had been reached on the continuation of the war. By the end of July, the war was being improvised on a day-to-day basis as Hitler and his commanders openly fought each other over which plan promised to deliver the final blow. Nothing decisive had been achieved at Minsk in June when the first great pocket was closed, nor was it achieved at Smolensk in July, nor at Uman in August, nor at Kiev in September, and hence still more plans were required; this led to the campaign becoming increasingly radicalized as time went on, compounded by the strenuous demands of successive operations as well as the scope and scale of Soviet resistance.

While the German command grappled with the unforeseen difficulties of finding an end to their war in the east, a parallel radicalization was taking place from below. At the tactical level, the severity of the combat and the remarkable rate of attrition among the German motorized forces led to a critical loss of momentum. This is made patently obvious from the war diaries and field reports of the panzer groups, but the problem remained a general one throughout the *Ostheer*. As operations extended, fallout rates grew to worrying levels, reducing the mobility, speed, and force with which offensive operations could be conducted. Taken together with the expanding funnel of the Soviet theater, Germany's shortage of military units, and the high causalities being sustained, momentum inevitably waned. Worst of all, this radicalization at the lower echelons was poorly appreciated at the top, meaning that new operations were being planned without a realistic understanding of what the forces, especially the panzer groups, could achieve.

While the radicalization of warfare in the east was a process that escalated throughout the summer and autumn of 1941, it was rooted in the planning of German operations and the many misconceptions upon which this was based. In the same dismissive manner that Napoleon rejected the experiences of Charles XII's ill-fated campaign, so too did

Hitler and his military commanders ignore 1812. Trusting in 129 years of technological advancement, as well as their own delusional notions of German racial superiority, the German command was remarkably impervious to doubts. The first serious discussion of a campaign against the Soviet Union came in the weeks following the astonishingly successful French campaign, which served to propagate the myth of German invincibility, first as a propaganda tool, but then as a widely embraced, self-styling image, readily adopted in the minds of the Nazi and Wehrmacht elite.[7] The grinding battles of the western front in World War I had now been overtaken by the power of technical innovation, restoring mobility to the battlefield and recovering the notion that bold operational maneuvers, accompanied by shock panzer tactics, could break even the strongest armies. Utilizing this formula, none of Hitler's senior commanders in the OKW (*Oberkommando der Wehrmacht*—High Command of the Armed Forces) or the OKH (*Oberkommando des Heeres*—Army High Command) doubted the outcome of a war against the Soviet Union.[8] As in Napoleon's case, the issue was not whether the Soviet armies could be defeated, but only a matter of how best to achieve that end. Accordingly, the German command paid only the most cursory attention to the unique problems of the Soviet theater and the difficulties that would arise from attempting deep mobile operations into its vast hinterland.

The first operational study for the OKH was produced by *Generalmajor* Erich Marcks and appeared only days after being commissioned. Astonishingly, no submissions on feasibility were sought from the army quartermaster general, and much of the information at Marcks's disposal was either dated or highly dubious. From the beginning it was simply assumed that the strategic objectives of the campaign could be met and that any difficulties would be ironed out at future stages of planning or by the field commanders during the campaign itself. Another operational study by *Oberstleutnant* Bernhard von Lossberg for the OKW concluded with similar results.[9] Thus, from its inception, the campaign's viability from a military point of view was regarded as absolute, and future planning was directed on that basis. Not surprisingly, such a dangerous premise left prodigious inconsistencies between what was being ordered and what was possible. For example, in November 1940 when the chief of the Army General Staff, *Generaloberst* Franz Halder, met with the army quartermaster general, *Generalmajor* Eduard Wagner, to discuss planning for the logistical support of the operation, Wagner's damning conclusions essentially undercut the basis of the whole invasion plan. Based on the premise of keeping some two million men, three hundred thousand horses, and five hundred thousand motor-vehicles supplied, Wagner frankly assessed that a maximum advance of between seven hundred and eight hundred kilometers would be possible. Such a distance was inconsistent with the objectives being assigned to the Army Groups, which in any case did not take into account the newly developed industrial zones in Siberia or the fact that the German invasion force would be far larger than Wagner anticipated.[10] Moreover, Wagner told Halder that supplies of foodstuffs and ammunition would suffice for only the first twenty days of the campaign.[11] Intelligence about the Red Army was another key failure; Germany grossly underestimated the imposing size of the Soviet Union's mobilization base, the quality of its weapons, and the robustness of its armaments industry. Though evidence to the contrary was at hand, it was simply not appreciated.[12] Thus, impervious to any doubts, Hitler, the OKW, and the OKH retained an indomitable faith in the success of Operation Barbarossa.

The OKH was charged with coordinating and conducting the war in the east, for which it set clear objectives. Army Group North would be directed toward Leningrad, Army Group Center to Moscow, and Army Group South toward the resource-rich Don Basin in eastern Ukraine. Reaching these distant objectives did not trouble the OKH, because it was firmly believed that in the initial border battles the bulk of the Red Army would be encircled and destroyed. The commander in chief of the army, *Generalfeldmarschall* Walther von Brauchitsch, gave a blunt assessment of the coming war in the east. Speaking in April 1941, Brauchitsch stated: "Fierce border battles anticipated, duration up to four weeks. Afterwards, only minor resistance is to be expected."[13] The emphasis was clearly on striking a decisive initial blow to cripple the Red Army and expose the rest of the country to occupation without large-scale fighting.

With the Eastern campaign expected to be both short and relatively trouble free, the OKH did not wish to confront Hitler directly when the dictator began to suggest that in the second phase of operations, after the initial encirclements, Army Group Center would swing north and march together with Army Group North on Leningrad. Hitler wanted to strike hard at the city he saw as the cradle of bolshevism and the ideological impetus behind the whole Soviet state. Halder and Brauchitsch did not agree. They wanted to use Army Group Center, which was by far the most powerful of the three invading army groups, against Moscow, as they believed the capital represented the linchpin of Soviet power. When this divergence of opinion first surfaced during a command conference on December 5, 1940, Halder was careful not to challenge Hitler directly over the matter and instead allowed it to pass without confrontation.[14] Hitler remained oblivious to the OKH's disaffection, to which he would not have reacted well given their recent history of heated disagreement over plans for the attack in the west. Perhaps it was for those same reasons that Halder and Brauchitsch opted against open dissent and instead adopted a course of silent duplicity, deferring to Hitler's view when in his presence, yet all the while informing Army Group Center's field commanders that they would be taking the road to Moscow. Conceivably, Halder calculated that the weight of the German blow would render arguments over a second phase redundant and, with the back of the Red Army broken, nothing would stop the German advance in all directions.[15] In any case, throughout the planning stages there was a stark difference of opinion between the OKH and Hitler as to the continuation of the war after the initial battles. According to *Generalleutnant* Friedrich Paulus, there existed "a sharp divergence of opinion between Supreme Headquarters (Hitler) and the Army General Staff regarding both the manner in which the operations should be conducted and the intermediate objectives that should be set."[16] Nor was the divergence limited to Leningrad. At the last major military conference, just a week before the invasion, Hitler made reference to the large Soviet concentrations in front of Army Group Center and then informed his audience, including Halder and Brauchitsch, that once these had been defeated Army Group Center would also have to reinforce Army Group South. Observing events, Hitler's Luftwaffe adjutant, Nicolaus von Below, noted that neither Halder or Brauchitsch raised a word of protest, yet Below suspected that the curious absence of discussion disguised a deeper friction. Summing up his observations over the preceding months, Below concluded:

> I had observed on various occasions an oppositional stance by Halder to Hitler's judgments and instructions, without the general voicing his differing views. I had the impression that Halder was forever eating something he didn't like, but swallowed anyway.
>
> Thus we embarked upon a truly massive offensive with a disjoined leadership and with leaders pulling in different directions. I saw this as a great danger for the success of the operation.[17]

The true extent of Below's ominous prescience when it came to Operation Barbarossa's lack of success must remain in question, but there is no doubt about the OKH's rejection of Hitler's plans, nor its attempt to circumvent his authority. Writing after the war, the commander of Panzer Group 3 in Army Group Center, *Generaloberst* Hermann Hoth, noted that "within Panzer Group 3 itself, everyone was driven by the thought that they were on the way to Moscow. One must understand, if the commander in chief of the army [Brauchitsch] would have been determined to fulfill Hitler's wishes, he would have informed the commander of the troops."[18] With the field commanders believing they were headed to Moscow, the generals at the OKH had to tread carefully. Halder and Brauchitsch had already experienced the futility of trying to forcefully change Hitler's mind, and the dictator bitterly resented them for having attempted to do so. Thus, they now tactfully adopted a more subtle approach. Their silence at the conference table prevented any formal commitment to Hitler's plans; at the same time it kept relations on a positive footing and earned them a revived measure of Hitler's confidence. When the campaign began Halder intended to use his position, as well as his improved standing, to supply Hitler with all the evidence that might result in a continued advance on Moscow. Only with the failure of this more subtle approach would more confrontational measures have to be contemplated.

In spite of their differences over strategy, the German command was firmly united by an ardent belief in victory. When the war began the most vital sector for the Germans was *Generalfeldmarschall* Fedor von Bock's Army Group Center. Here the Germans had concentrated two-thirds of their panzer strength[19] and the best elements of the Luftwaffe. These were the critical formations upon which much of the success of the campaign depended. The first strategic encirclement was closed in the area of Minsk, trapping the bulk of the Soviet Western Front in a giant caldron and effectively shattering the Soviet line. Feeling entirely justified in his predictions of a rapid victory, Halder recorded in his diary on July 3:

> On the whole one can already now say that the objective to destroy the mass of the Russian army in front of the Dvina and Dnieper [rivers] has been accomplished. I do not doubt ... that eastward of the Dvina and Dnieper we would only have to contend with partial enemy forces, not strong enough to hinder the realization of the German operational plan. Thus it is probably not an exaggeration when I claim that the campaign against Russia was won within fourteen days.[20]

On July 8, 1941, Army Group Center announced a figure of almost three hundred thousand Soviet POWs.[21] To the German command it was a modern-day Cannae and the harbinger of outright victory. The idea that the Red Army might patch up its front with reserves appeared absurd; and Bock's panzer groups were already continuing their advance eastward to cross the last defensive line anchored on the great rivers.

Although on the surface operations seemed to be going according to plan, there were many misconceptions about both the state of the Red Army and the capacity of the panzer groups to maintain their speed and power into the depths of the Soviet hinterland. Contrary to popular belief, the Soviet Western Front was not destroyed in the battle of Minsk. Soviet prewar planning called for a first strategic echelon, deployed between twenty and one hundred kilometers from the border, to counterattack and stop the enemy advance in order to facilitate a general Soviet offensive carried out by a second strategic echelon located well back from the frontier between one hundred and four hundred kilometers away.[22] Of even greater importance was the capacity of the Soviet Union to quickly raise reserves. On the eve of the German invasion, the Red Army possessed a mobilization base of some 14 million men. Only a week into the war some 5.3 million Soviet reservists had been called up, with further mobilizations following in succession. In July 1941 no less than thirteen new field armies appeared and in August another fourteen came into service.[23] Thus, while the Red Army certainly suffered appalling casualties at Minsk, the Soviet Union's force generation scheme was able to quickly replace its losses and dramatically expand the size of the Red Army.[24] On June 22, 1941, the Red Army numbered 5,373,000 men. By August 31, in spite of its losses, it had grown to 6,889,000 men, and by December 31, 1941, the army had reached an estimated 8 million men.[25]

On the other side, the linchpin of Germany's offensive success—the panzer groups—were suffering from an unsustainable rate of attrition. In the same way that Napoleon's army withered on the march through Russia, so too did the motorized divisions. Only six days into the campaign, the 7th Panzer Division, spearheading Hoth's thrust north of Minsk, reported a hefty 50 percent loss in its Mark II and Mark III tanks, while the Mark IV tanks had suffered 75 percent losses.[26] The fallout rate proved so high that the 7th Panzer Division could no longer obtain its objective and had to ask for reinforcements from the nearby 20th Panzer Division.[27] Nor was this an isolated problem. Two weeks into the campaign, *Generaloberst* Heinz Guderian's Panzer Group 2 reported an alarming rate of attrition in its divisions, which was eroding force strengths to critical levels. On July 7, the 18th and 3rd Panzer Divisions were at just 35 percent combat readiness; the 4th and 17th Panzer Divisions were at 60 percent strength; while the 10th Panzer Division, which had been in reserve, was strongest at 80 percent.[28] Such figures did not bode well given the enormous distances still to be traversed and the extent of Soviet reserves. Most of the losses were due to mechanical failure; while repairs were certainly possible, it would require precious time and the replacement parts were extremely limited. Moreover, as the advance continued, the number of tanks returned to service would constantly be offset by the continuing fallout rate. Indeed, the terrible road conditions constituted the single greatest impediment to the advancing panzer divisions, but it would also be wrong to dismiss the effect of Soviet resistance. In an ambush north of Zhlobin, twenty-two German tanks were destroyed in a single action on July 6.[29] Accordingly, even minor Soviet victories over the German panzer arm assumed disproportionate significance for depleting Germany's powerful, but very limited, mechanized weapons. While overall matériel losses for the German army at this point in the war remained low, the central importance of the tank and its alarming rate of attrition made its losses particularly critical. With production capacity in Germany still meager, and Hitler's determination to hold back all new production for future operations, the basis of Germany's battlefield mobility and striking power was threatened out of all proportion to the numerical strength of its other arms. Summing up the implications of such stark rates of attrition, *Generalmajor* Walther Nehring, the commander of the 18th Panzer Division, warned: "This situation and its consequences will become unbearable in the future, if we do not want to be destroyed by winning."[30]

Panzer losses were not the only fundamental threat to the German Blitzkrieg. Hoth and Guderian were dependent on motorized supply columns for fuel and munitions, and these were having to traverse increasing distances as the advance continued. Some of the trucks were purpose-built military vehicles, but the vast majority were either requisitioned from the civilian economy or seized from the occupied countries. The heavily loaded civilian vehicles, with lower ground clearance, frequently bottomed out on the rutted and uneven roads, causing severe damage to the transmission and oil sumps. Civilian vehicles also had weaker suspensions that were prone to snap, quickly leaving a trail of wreckage behind the German advance. Alexander Cohrs, assigned to a panzer division, gave a striking description of the perilous roads his unit traversed in the early summer. After referring to the "very bad roads, full of holes," his diary for July 5 continued:

> Some [vehicles] tipped over. Luckily none in our company. After eighteen kilometers of marching on foot I sat on an armored vehicle. It tipped so much that it balanced on two wheels, while the other two temporarily stood in the air; still it did not tip over. Along the way was a moor where the vehicles had to make a big detour ... one by one vehicles got stuck or even turned over, resulting in breaks and a slow tempo.[31]

Dust was another pervasive problem for all motorized transport, as it soon overwhelmed the inadequate air filters and infiltrated the engines. Initially this had the effect of greatly increasing oil consumption (of which army stocks were very low); ultimately the engines were immobilized altogether. Movement on roads all across the Soviet Union exacted a toll, as there were very few sealed roads and the conversion of the wide-gauge Soviet railways was inadequate. Claus Hansmann wrote that his motorized column drove "as if in a sandstorm," and he observed how "the wheels churned up fountains of sand that blackened out the sun."[32] On July 18, the 18th Panzer Division reported the devastating effect the terrible road conditions were having on the division's mobility. No less than 1,300 trucks were classed as total losses and a further 1,000 trucks remained under repair.[33] Another report from 47th Panzer Corps on August 4 made clear that the dust in the motors of its trucks doomed them to an early grave. Those of the 17th Panzer Division and the 29th Motorized Division were expected to last a further five hundred to eight hundred kilometers "without excessive operational demands," while the engines of the 18th Panzer Division were forecast to last only another two hundred to four hundred kilometers. The difference between the two estimates rested on the high number of inferior quality French vehicles in the 18th Panzer Division.[34] Although such lifespan projections were only made in the war diary of the 47th Panzer Corps, it may be assumed that the other panzer corps were similarly affected, spelling a foreseeable end to the mobility of the panzer groups.

As ominous as such developments should have been, the German command was stubbornly fixated on its success. In July, Hoth and Guderian were awarded the prestigious Oak Leaves to the Knight's Cross, and a number of their subordinate panzer commanders were issued with the Knight's Cross. Following the encirclement at Minsk, the continued advance broke through the Stalin defensive line built on the Dvina and Dnieper rivers and sought to encircle the remnants of the Soviet armies opposite Army Group Center. This called for a second ring to be closed east of Smolensk, but a month after the start of the war Army Group Center's offensive strength was waning. The panzer groups fought desperately for the last ten days of July attempting to close the ring, but they were operating in exclusion, having greatly outdistanced the supporting infantry of the Ninth and Second Armies. The result was not only hard fighting to cut off the Smolensk pocket. As more of the previously unknown Soviet reserve armies arrived, the overstretched panzer groups were also holding off large-scale Soviet counteroffensives from the east, at the same time as they were holding the line against breakouts from the pocket to the west. Bock's panzer groups were greatly overextended, short of munitions, and dispersed over such a wide area that the Soviet counterattacks, although ill coordinated, plunged many of the divisions into crisis.[35] The failure to foresee the latent Soviet strength in the hinterlands now cost the elite German formations dearly. There was no depth to German defensive lines and no reserves to meet local counterattacks or help at crisis points. At Yel'nya on July 26 Guderian's panzer group noted with alarm:

> At the fighting around Yel'nya the situation is especially critical. The corps has been attacked all day from strongly superior forces with panzers and artillery. The enemy achieved a breakthrough at Lipnja that has not yet been dealt with. ... Constant heavy artillery fire is inflicting heavy casualties on the troops. In addition there is the impact of enemy bombers. As a result of the artillery fire, the evacuation of the many wounded has so far not been possible. ... The corps has absolutely no reserves available. Artillery munitions have been so depleted that no shells remain for bombarding the enemy artillery. For the last few days the panzer brigade of the 10th Panzer Division has been immobilized because oil and fuel supplies are lacking. The corps can maybe manage to hold on to its position, but only at the price of severe bloodletting.[36]

It was against this background that the positive perception of the Eastern campaign began to change for the German command, and Bock's army group was not the only one in difficulty. Army Group North's progress was stalling as the depth of the advance and the length of its front increased. Army Group South likewise had its hands full facing the largest concentration of Soviet forces in the largest theater of operations. What was foreseen as a straightforward battle of annihilation followed by rapid conquest was turning into a hard-fought, sustained campaign. This was what the OKH had been hoping to avoid.

On July 19 Hitler issued War Directive No. 33 calling for the divergent north-south thrusts by Hoth and Guderian's panzer groups.[37] This was Hitler's solution to the continuing resistance of the Red Army, and one that he felt was consistent with prewar planning. With the battle of Smolensk still in its early stages, Halder hoped that rapid action by Army Group North would mollify Hitler on at least the question of Leningrad and prevent the diversion of Hoth's forces. Halder also flew to Army Group South on July 20 to see if the speed of operations there could be improved. On July 21 Halder's outlook remained confident and he told Brauchitsch and the OKH operations chief, *Oberst* Adolf Heusinger, that the advance on Moscow would suffice with just Hoth's panzer group and the two infantry armies of Army Group Center.[38] Brauchitsch, on the other hand, had become increasingly disheartened by the progress of the war and did not share Halder's upbeat assessment.[39] On July 22 Brauchitsch met with Hitler, and although records of what passed between them are vague, it seems that the commander in chief of the army expressed his doubts over the recent war directive, and he may even

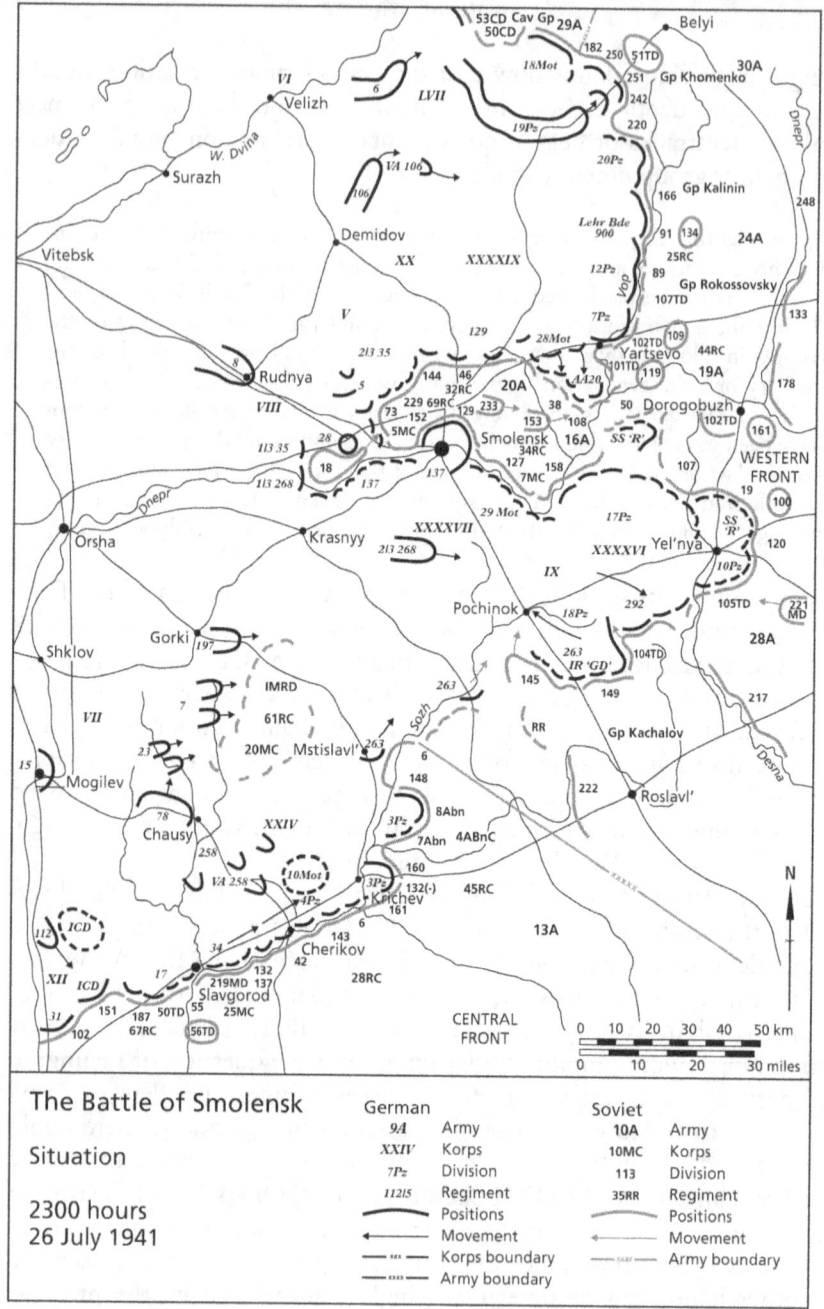

Figure 1.1. Dispositions of Army Group Center, July 26, 1941. Map first appeared in David M. Glantz, *Atlas of the Battle of Smolensk, 7 July–10 September 1941* (Carlisle, PA: printed by author, 2001), 55; and reprinted in David Stahel, *Operation Barbarossa and Germany's Defeat in the East* (Cambridge: Cambridge University Press, 2009), 310. Courtesy of Cambridge University Press.

have gone so far as to reveal the OKH's intention to attack Moscow. In any case, Hitler was incensed and his response was emphatic. He felt the matter was serious enough to issue a supplement to his previous war directive (known as War Directive No. 33a), which outlined in stern language what had essentially already been ordered in Directive No. 33. More than likely Hitler saw for the first time that the OKH had not been entirely honest with him about its strategic intentions, and if Brauchitsch had divulged anything relating to Halder's intention to attack Moscow with Hoth's units, Hitler may have correctly guessed he was being manipulated. Hitler already held a degree of instinctive suspicion toward the desk generals at the OKH, and with their turbulent past dispute over strategic matters seeming to rear its head again, Hitler had acted decisively.

When news of Directive No. 33a reached Brauchitsch and Halder there was consternation. The directive made clear that Army Group Center's two infantry armies were considered strong enough to eliminate all Soviet opposition east of Smolensk and capture Moscow. The panzer groups, it was stated, would be sent to the northern and southern flanks. Halder and Brauchitsch resolved to visit Hitler the following day (July 23) to confront him over the plans and argue for the Moscow alternative. In the event, Halder put the case strongly for attacking Moscow and even suggested that success on this front would lead to German troops on the Volga by the start of October—a belief Halder privately mocked.[40] As had been the case since the beginning, the chief of the General Staff was prepared to promise Hitler far more than was possible in order to gain his strategic preference, even if this necessitated outright dishonesty. Hitler's response to Halder's presentation was a lecture of his own on the wisdom of Directive No. 33a; there was no middle ground explored and no sense of a compromise. The lines of an open dispute were therefore drawn. Hitler's mind seemed to be made up, yet Halder was adamant in his resolve, and with the OKH nominally responsible for command on the Eastern Front, Halder was not about to concede on the single most important question of the war's continuation. The effect, Halder later noted, "was explosive."[41]

As the bitterness and recriminations of the infighting within the German command took hold, the lack of understanding for the diminishing offensive power of the *Ostheer* soon became pervasive. Neither Hitler nor his senior generals had an accurate picture of what was happening to the panzer groups or what would be required for a decisive victory over the Red Army. The source of this ignorance was in part a pervasive self-deception at many levels of the German chain of command that fostered a resilient ideological bias and superiority myth. Even in the face of the dismal reports coming up from below, this bias precluded a frank appraisal of the campaign's development. On the other hand, even among the more pragmatic minded commanders who could see how difficult the campaign was becoming, there was an inherent contradiction in making negative reports. The Nazi ideal of a tough, firebrand commanding officer who acted with iron resolve and forged ahead with the power of an indomitable will was incompatible with the dire, and sometimes panicked, warnings that circumstances necessitated. In this manner the flow of candid information, along with the open expression of opinion, was stunted at many levels of command.

At the strategic level the result was ruinous. The plan to win the war in the east had radicalized since the failure to destroy the Red Army in the first phase of the war. The encirclement at Minsk and the second underway at Smolensk were clearly not going to suffice. As a result, the German political and military commands were locked in an embittered dispute, forcefully backing rival alternatives. Yet in the combat units the parallel radicalization was also taking its toll, threatening to undercut both alternative plans. While in the opening days and weeks of the war the German forces operated with a clear tactical superiority, they were increasingly suffering from reduced maneuverability, physical fatigue, matériel losses, and a lack of supplies. In addition, vigorous Soviet counterattacks often had to be held by units operating in isolation over extensive battlefields without adequate flank protection. The result was that Soviet offensives, although often launched with depleted forces and a distinct lack of coordination, were now engaging a German enemy on a far more even playing field. The deadly German formula of concentrated strength and firepower, together with swift battlefield mobility, was much less evident and it was the vital motorized divisions that were being ground down. Clearly a watershed had been reached and the character of the war was changing as a result.

At the beginning of the campaign Guderian's Panzer Group numbered some 953 tanks of all models,[42] but five weeks later on July 29 only 286 tanks remained—a 70 percent loss of its original strength. As the Panzer Group's war diary noted, "this figure is <u>exceedingly low</u>."[43] More worrying still, of the remaining total only 135 tanks consisted of the modern Mark III and Mark IV designs, the other 128 tanks consisted of the obsolete Mark II. In Hoth's Panzer Group the situation was little better. One of his panzer corps was at 40 percent strength and the other at 30 percent. A report from Hoth's 57th Panzer Corps noted:

> It must be understood that without a rapid and <u>plentiful</u> supply of track rollers, track links and bolts for the Mark IV and track bolts for the [Pz.]Kpfw 38 (t),[44] the number of available panzers will sink further, so that the combat

strength of the panzer regiments will be greatly weakened. Still especially urgent is the delivery of fully operational motors, gearboxes, oil, and specialized panzer grease.[45]

Clearly, it was not only the fighting that was having an effect on the tank strengths. The overwhelmed logistics and the unavailability of spare parts (which Hitler was refusing to release to the front) were preventing even damaged tanks from returning to active service. Indeed, even as the encirclement at Smolensk ended in early August and a brief period of rest and refitting was undertaken in Army Group Center, it meant little without replacement motors and spare parts. Nor was it just the diminished number of available panzers that should have been worrying the German command. As Hoth noted on July 31, wheeled transport was also suffering badly. "A great number of the trucks," he wrote in a report, "now stand at the limit of their operational capacity and any further delay in their refitting will see a greatly increased total loss in a short period of time."[46] Mobility and striking power were the essential features of the panzer group's successes and with these having sunk so far, the danger implicit for the success of Operation Barbarossa was profound.

As the motorized divisions of Army Group Center looked to withdraw themselves from the front and attempt to restore some of their lost strength, the infantry divisions of the Ninth and Second Armies had to replace them. Yet the desperate race to catch up with the motorized divisions and provide them with urgently needed support in the battle of Smolensk had led to forced marches of up to fifty kilometres a day. This constituted an enormous physical burden for the men, as the commander of the 43rd Army Corps, *General* Gotthard Heinrici, wrote in his diary on July 11: "Yesterday one regiment marched 54, another 47 km. To do that once is possible. To do that having already had numerous marches of 30–40 km with more to come, that is something else, it makes it immense."[47] Infantryman Harald Henry wrote home of the terrible strain he was under after consecutive marches of over forty kilometers.

> We're wet through all over, sweat is running down our faces in wide streams—not just sweat, but sometimes tears too, tears of helpless rage, desperation, and pain, squeezed out of us by this inhuman effort. No one can tell me that someone who isn't an infantryman can possibly imagine what we're going through here.[48]

Likewise, August Sahm wrote in early July: "I am physically almost finished. Both feet are sore and suppurated."[49] Toward the end of July after a month of hard marching, many units were in a correspondingly worn-out condition. Yet far from simply occupying conquered territory, as had been the case in past campaigns, the infantry faced brutal defensive fighting. Army Group Center's infantry had to fan out into a great bulging semicircle, over distances that necessitated an excessive front allocation for each division. This allowed no depth to defensive lines and on some sectors of the front the Red Army enjoyed a numerical superiority as well as a preponderant advantage in artillery. From the end of July and throughout August, the infantry divisions, especially in the Ninth Army, were under enormous pressure. There were almost daily pleas for relief by the armored divisions, which were themselves worn out and desperately trying to juggle their attempts to refit with constant movements back into the line to repulse local breakthroughs or stave off a collapse of the front at crisis points like Yel'nya.

At the end of July, Hitler issued a new war directive that postponed the continuation of Army Group Center's operations in the east until such time as the rehabilitation period (projected to require just ten days) had passed.[50] To Halder's mind, it was a welcome breathing space allowing him time to muster the support of the field commanders whom he knew were in favor of the Moscow alternative. The directive was also an indication of Hitler's uncharacteristic hesitancy, which would become more apparent throughout the first half of August. Casting around for support, Hitler flew to Army Groups Center and South to canvass opinion and, he hoped, secure backing for his preference. The response, *Generalfeldmarschall* Wilhelm Keitel later noted contemptuously, was a united front against Hitler orchestrated by the OKH.[51]

To Halder's mind, Hitler's ardent determination to avoid taking the road to Moscow stemmed from an unwarranted fear of treading the same path as Napoleon, but if the French emperor's experience played any role in Hitler's decision it was more the Soviet capital's lack of decisive importance. Hitler argued for the attack into Ukraine both as an operational opportunity, to thrust into the exposed flank of the powerful Soviet South-Western Front, and as a strategic opportunity to open up the resource-rich eastern Ukraine. Unlike the generals at the OKH, Hitler concerned himself with economic matters, and he was aware that without direct access to raw materials Germany was in no position to wage a long war. Halder, on the other hand, was utterly convinced that the fall of Moscow would result in a victorious end to the war, whereby vital economic centers would consequently fall into Germany's lap. Yet the difficulty, from Halder's perspective, was convincing Hitler of this. Leaving no stone unturned, Halder approached the head of the Wehrmacht operations staff, *Generaloberst* Alfred Jodl, who was a known sympathizer to the plans of the army and a trusted figure in Hitler's inner circle. In a private meeting on August 7,

1941, they agreed to feed Hitler information that supported the attack on Moscow and give him the impression that objectives at Leningrad and in Ukraine could be attained by the northern and southern army groups, respectively. As Halder declared: "The question Moscow *or* Ukraine or Ukraine *and* Moscow must be answered with emphasis on the *and*."[52] It is not surprising, therefore, that Hitler was increasingly gripped by indecision as he resisted the chorus of opinion among his generals and the carefully selected flow of facts that crossed his desk. Hitler's army adjutant, *Major* Gerhard Engel, noted after the OKW military conference on August 8: "One notices immediately how irresolute the Führer is concerning the further direction of the operation. Constantly vacillating between ideas and objectives. From the situation conferences one comes out knowing nothing more than when one went in."[53]

That Halder would pervert the free flow of information to serve his own ends is no surprise, but attempting to present the Eastern Front in August 1941 as a continuous, forward-moving theater of attack was absurd. Yet Halder's twisting of the truth was not an entirely malicious act of deception. Halder, like many in the high command, had from the beginning perceived events with a significant degree of self-delusion, repeatedly overestimating what was possible. Now, as the momentum of German attacks slowed everywhere and positional warfare gripped increasing stretches of the front, Halder abruptly came to realize the extent to which the conflict had radicalized from the narrow parameters of prewar German plans. His bubble of optimism about Barbarossa's infallibility was finally burst when new information was reported by the intelligence department of Foreign Armies East. Until this time the perceived weakness of the Red Army was one of the central pillars sustaining Halder's belief in a foreseeable victory. Halder's diary entry for August 11 reveals his sudden loss of faith:

> Regarding the general situation, it stands out more and more clearly that we underestimated the Russian colossus.... This statement refers just as much to organizational as to economic strengths, to traffic management, above all to pure military potential. At the start of the war we reckoned with 200 enemy divisions. Now we already count 360. These divisions are not armed and equipped in our sense, and tactically they are inadequately led in many ways. But they are there and when we destroy a dozen of them, then the Russians put another dozen in their place. The time factor favors them, as they are near to their own centers of power, while we are always moving further away from ours.
>
> And so our troops, sprawled over an immense front line, without any depth, are subject to the incessant attacks of the enemy. These are sometimes successful, because in these enormous spaces far too many gaps must be left open.[54]

Halder was not exaggerating. On the same day (August 11) Guderian's 46th Panzer Corps reported a Soviet breakthrough across two and a half kilometers of its front,[55] and in the days following there was grave concern about a total collapse of the Yel'nya salient.

In the meantime, War Directive No. 34a was issued, which reflected a shift in Hitler's thinking toward the Moscow alternative. Army Groups North and South would not be reinforced from the center, but Army Group Center would have to extend its front in the north and deal with troublesome Soviet concentrations in the south. Halder was cautiously optimistic, but wary of the additional tasks Hitler was assigning to Army Group Center. Predictably, the fragile harmony of opinion did not survive long as a fresh crisis again changed Hitler's mind. A powerful Soviet offensive south of Staraya Russa had shattered the line of Army Group North's overextended 10th Army Corps, leading Hitler to demand that three motorized divisions from Hoth's panzer group be dispatched immediately to restore the situation. Halder and Bock were bitterly opposed. Halder claimed it was Hitler's "old mistake" of overreacting to local setbacks,[56] while Bock feared that with the loss of such units his Army Group would become bogged down. A revealing telephone conversation between Halder and Bock, recorded verbatim in Army Group Center's war diary, reveals the dire state of Germany's deteriorating war effort.

> Bock: In this case I don't know any more how I can move the Army Group forward. Today is the beginning of positional warfare!
> The units to be given up can only be moved in a partly finished condition [owing to their incomplete refitting]. I must make you aware that after the loss of this corps an attack by Strauss's army, except for the special action toward Velikie Luki, is no longer possible. The offensive intention of the Ninth Army is dead.
> Halder: In my opinion this goes for the Second Army too.
> Bock: Please inform the commander in chief of the army [Brauchitsch] that with this order any thought of an offensive posture by the Ninth Army, and as a result probably by the whole Army Group, ceases to exist. It is also to be borne in mind that going over to a defensive position is not possible given the current position. The existing line is not adequate for a lengthy defence. I have the intention to inform the Führer's chief adjutant [Schmundt] of the same thing.
> Halder: I don't know myself what I should do. I am utterly desperate and will try to save what there is to save.[57]

There was no disguising the scale of the calamity overtaking the war in the east, nor the dejection and melancholy this was feeding. The offensive strength of the panzer groups was shrinking from the constant fighting, while the continued absence of spare parts, particularly replacement engines, made it impossible to institute anything other than ad hoc, provisional repairs. Increasingly, the realization spread that the outcome of the present strategic crisis gripping the German command represented a last chance to win the war before the weather turned and the Wehrmacht's remaining offensive strength was decisively compromised.

At Hitler's headquarters publication of the Atlantic Charter, agreed upon by Churchill and Roosevelt and calling for "the final destruction of the Nazi tyranny," caused consternation. Hitler became convinced that another world war involving the United States was being fanned by what he called "international Jewry" and had become all but inevitable.[58] The implications had direct consequences for the Eastern Front. Hitler's pervasive uncertainty about the future course of the war now disappeared and he made up his mind to seize the vital Soviet economic centers in eastern Ukraine and the Caucasus. Hitler's new orders reached the OKH late on August 21 and struck, according to Heusinger, "like a bomb."[59] Halder was dumbfounded. He called Hitler's actions "unendurable for the OKH" and blamed Hitler alone for "the zigzag course" of German operations. He also proposed to Brauchitsch that they both resign their posts in protest, but in the event neither took such a radical step.[60]

Over the next month, Guderian's Panzer Group thrust down into Ukraine, trapping the Soviet South-Western Front together with elements from Army Group South's Panzer Group 1. The battle yielded a huge tally of Soviet POWs and captured war matériel, but existing histories have yet to fully consider its hard-fought progress as well as the cost to Germany's operational mobility, which was now nearing its end.[61] The two northern panzer groups were also kept busy. Hoth's Panzer Group 3 launched a renewed offensive to capture Velikie Luki, while in the area of Army Group North, *Generaloberst* Erich Hoepner's Panzer Group 4 made every effort to cut off Leningrad. Once isolated, a rash attempt was made to seize the city by storm. This proved a costly failure, and subsequent orders to redeploy the panzer units to the south for the coming offensive toward Moscow (Operation Typhoon) were to cut mobility and panzer strengths even further.

The 57th Panzer Corps provides an instructive example. On September 22 the only available figures for panzer strengths dated from before the corps had begun its redeployment to the south; even so, the 19th Panzer Division possessed only sixty-five combat ready tanks, while the 20th Panzer Division commanded just twenty. A limited number of replacement tanks had been dispatched from Germany, but the war diary of Panzer Group 4 made clear this would not restore anything approaching the corps's former strength. The 3rd Motorized Infantry

Division was ominously short of men and the limited replacements that had arrived were judged "almost useless." The average age of these men was between thirty-five and thirty-seven and they were without adequate training. More worrying still was the state of the wheeled transportation, which in the 20th Panzer Division was judged fit to last for only another three or four weeks.[62] Similarly, on September 27 Panzer Group 2, encompassing five panzer divisions, fielded just 7 to 9 obsolete Mark II panzers, 132 Mark III panzers, and 45 Mark IV panzers. A further 150 replacement panzers were due to be distributed among the divisions, but even for such understrength units the available fuel stocks were so low that the initial objectives of the coming operation could not all be reached.[63] The 24th Panzer Corps, for example, was ordered to simply advance as far as fuel permitted.[64]

In planning for Operation Typhoon, the German command quickly became convinced that one more major offensive would finally break the back of Soviet resistance. Yet logistical constraints loomed like a dark cloud over the whole operation. The tentative flow of supplies reaching Army Group Center hardly sufficed to meet its day-to-day needs much less allow for the build up of indispensable stockpiles necessary to sustain a major new offensive. Bock's forces required daily at least twenty-four trains to adequately maintain themselves; however less than half this number arrived in the first half of August, and later the number rose to only an average of eighteen trains per day. The other army groups were similarly affected. Army Group South required a minimum of twenty-four trains a day, but received only fourteen, while Army Group North had to make do with fifteen trains a day instead of the requisite eighteen deemed absolutely necessary.[65] It was not only the vital fuel, munitions, and to a lesser extent food that was lacking, but also the vast quantities of winter clothing that would very soon be required as temperatures dropped to just above freezing by the end of September. The men were still wearing their summer uniforms, many of which were tattered, and worn-out boots. The overall state of affairs led the Ninth Army to declare on September 14 that its transport "was insufficient to support the coming operations." Likewise, the commander of the Fourth Army, *Generalfeldmarschall* Günther von Kluge, wrote on September 13 that the tactical and supply situation did not allow for stockpiling. "The army," Kluge noted, "lives from hand to mouth, especially as regards the fuel situation."[66] It was an inauspicious foundation for an operation upon which Germany's last hopes of ending the war now rested. Yet it was also typical of the army command's propensity for impetuousness that all caution was thrown to the wind.

The dichotomy between the *Ostheer*'s diminished offensive strength and overextended logistical apparatus, measured against the manifest requirements of seizing Moscow, highlights the intractable difficulties of Operation Typhoon. The very limited fuel reserves and transportation capacity sufficed only for the initial encirclements centred on Viaz'ma and Bryansk, but no further. Yet the OKH ignored all evidence to the contrary and determined to rapidly drive on Moscow once the Soviet front had been destroyed. Their grandiose plans aimed for nothing less than the final defeat of the Soviet Union, but, as had so often been the case, there was no real appreciation of the state of the panzer divisions, the hopelessly long supply lines, or the worsening weather conditions. Nor were the prominent field commanders willing to forsake the allure of conquering Moscow for a more pragmatic strategy that addressed the alarming shortfalls and losses of the field units. The difficulties facing the German army were exemplified by Bock on September 15 when he criticized the initial encirclements at Viaz'ma and Bryansk as too small. "Narrow-mindedness is becoming an art!" he wrote in his diary. "And after the battle we will again be facing the enemy's reserves."[67] Bock's concerns proved well founded, and yet by advocating a much larger maneuver the commander of Army Group Center made evident his excessive faith in the strength of his army. Indeed, the German offensive had been running out of steam for weeks and the imposing scale of what Operation Typhoon sought to achieve reinforces the delusional tendencies gripping the whole German command.

Even beyond the prohibitive weaknesses of the *Ostheer*, there is no evidence that the Red Army was on the verge of collapse, nor that Moscow's capture, had it been a possibility, would have ended the war. As the number of men in the Red Army continued to rise throughout 1941, the Soviet Union also produced more tanks than Germany,[68] 66 percent of these consisting of the newer T-34 and KV-1 variety.[69] Soviet industry also turned out more aircraft and a great deal more artillery pieces than Germany, which helped to meet the most immediate needs of the Red Army.[70]

Far from achieving the demise of the Soviet Union, the first months of Hitler's war in the east reveal an emergent colossus awoken in the east. While no one could yet predict the Red Army in Berlin, time clearly favored the Soviet war effort and, by the end of the summer of 1941, Barbarossa had without doubt failed in what it set out to do. Expedient operations, organized as stopgap measures and improvised on a shoestring of resources, were the only solution left to German commanders. Typhoon was not an operation stemming from Germany's overriding dominance and power, but rather one of increasing desperation, necessitated by past failures to force an end to the conflict. By the autumn of 1941, the German campaign against the Soviet Union had become a wayward venture, having long since expended its slender chance of success. The continual radicalization of Germany's approach to the war did not change the fundamental problem that operational successes did not equal strategic victory. A prolonged campaign had become inevitable, a parallel that had not favored Charles XII or Napoleon I and promised little more hope for Adolf Hitler.

Notes

1. Michael Howard and Peter Paret, eds., *Carl von Clausewitz: On War* (New York: Alfred A. Knopf, 1993), 138.
2. Adam Zamoyski, *1812: Napoleon's Fatal March on Moscow* (London: HarperCollins, 2004), 92.
3. William C. Fuller Jr., *Strategy and Power in Russia, 1600–1914* (New York: Free Press, 1992), 41–42, 80–83.
4. Zamoyski, *1812*, 92.
5. Howard, *Carl von Clausewitz*, 569.
6. Michael Howard, foreword to *The Campaign of 1812 in Russia*, by Carl von Clausewitz (New York: Da Capo Press, 1995), xii.
7. Karl-Heinz Frieser's research demonstrates how the Germans misunderstood the reasons for their victory over France in 1940. See Karl-Heinz Frieser, *Blitzkrieg-Legende: Der Westfeldzug 1940* (Munich: Oldenbourg, 1996); Karl-Heinz Frieser, *The Blitzkrieg Legend: The 1940 Campaign in the West* (Annapolis: Naval Institute Press, 2005).
8. That Nazi Germany's underestimation of the Soviet Union was not a uniquely German phenomenon can be seen from British and American intelligence assessments prior to Barbarossa. See Andreas Hillgruber, *Der Zenit des Zweiten Weltkrieges, Juli 1941* (Wiesbaden: Steiner, 1977), 26–27; Gerd R. Ueberschär, "Das Scheitern des Unternehmens 'Barbarossa': Der deutsch-sowjetische Krieg vom Überfall bis zur Wende vor Moskau im Winter 1941/42," in *"Unternehmen Barbarossa": Der deutsche Überfall auf die Sowjetunion, 1941; Berichte, Analysen, Dokumente*, ed. Gerd R. Ueberschär and Wolfram Wette (Paderborn: Ferdinand Schöningh, 1984), 150–51; and H. F. Hinsley, "British Intelligence and Barbarossa," in *Barbarossa: The Axis and the Allies*, ed. John Erickson and David Dilks (Edinburgh: Edinburgh University Press, 1998), 72.
9. For an overview of early planning for Operation Barbarossa, see David Stahel, *Operation Barbarossa and Germany's Defeat in the East* (Cambridge: Cambridge University Press, 2009), chap. 1.

10. The actual figures of German strength on June 22, 1941, proved much higher: 3 million men, 625,000 horses, and 600,000 motor vehicles.

11. Franz Halder, *Kriegstagebuch: Tägliche Aufzeichnungen des Chefs des Generalstabes des Heeres, 1939–1942*, vol. 2, *Von der geplanten Landung in England bis zum Beginn des Ostfeldzuges (1.7.1940–21.6.1941)*, ed. Hans-Adolf Jacobsen (Stuttgart: W. Kohlhammer, 1963), 176 (November 12, 1940).

12. Robert Gibbons, "Opposition gegen 'Barbarossa' im Herbst 1940: Eine Denkschrift aus der deutschen Botschaft in Moskau," *Vierteljahrshefte für Zeitgeschichte* 23 (1975): 332–40.

13. International Military Tribunal, ed., *Der Prozess gegen die Hauptkriegsverbrecher vor dem Internationalen Militärgerichtshof, Nürnberg, 14. November 1945–1. Oktober 1946*, vol. 26 (Nuremberg: Sekretariat des Gerichtshofs, 1947), 400. Thanks to Alex J. Kay for passing on this reference.

14. Percy Ernst Schramm, ed., *Kriegstagebuch des Oberkommandos der Wehrmacht (Wehrmachtführungsstab) 1940–1945*, vol. 1, *1. August 1940–31. Dezember 1941*, ed. Hans-Adolf Jacobsen (Bonn, 1965; repr., Munich: Bernard & Graefe, 1982), 981–82, doc. 41 (December 5, 1940).

15. Christian Hartmann, *Halder Generalstabschef Hitlers, 1938–1942* (Paderborn: Ferdinand Schöningh, 1991), 234.

16. Walter Görlitz, *Paulus and Stalingrad* (London: Citadel Press, 1963), 106.

17. Nicolaus von Below, *Als Hitlers Adjutant, 1937–1945* (Mainz: Pour le Mérite, 1999), 278–80.

18. Hermann Hoth, *Panzer-Operationen: Die Panzergruppe 3 und der operative Gedanke der deutschen Führung Sommer 1941* (Heidelberg: Vowinckel, 1956), 48.

19. Not only did Army Group Center have two of the four panzer groups deployed on the Eastern Front, but Hoth and Guderian's panzer groups were also numerically stronger than their counterparts in the north and the south.

20. Franz Halder, *Kriegstagebuch: Tägliche Aufzeichnungen des Chefs des Generalstabes des Heeres 1939–1942*, vol. 3, *Der Russlandfeldzug bis zum Marsch auf Stalingrad (22.6.1941–24.9.1942)*, ed. Hans-Adolf Jacobsen and Alfred Philippi (Stuttgart: W. Kohlhammer, 1964), 38. (July 3, 1941); hereafter cited as Halder, KTB.

21. Fedor von Bock, "Tagebuchnotizen Osten I, 22.6.1941 bis 5.1.1942," July 8, 1941, N-22/9, fol. 20, Bundesarchiv-Militärarchiv, Freiburg im Breisgau (hereafter BA-MA).

22. Jacob W. Kipp, "Barbarossa, Soviet Covering Forces, and the Initial Period of War: Military History and Airland Battle," published online by the Foreign Military Studies Office (Fort Leavenworth, 1989), 7–8.

23. David M. Glantz and Jonathan House, *When Titans Clashed: How the Red Army Stopped Hitler* (Lawrence: University Press of Kansas, 1995), 67–68.

24. Michael Geyer, "German Strategy in the Age of Machine Warfare, 1914–1945," in *Makers of Modern Strategy: From Machiavelli to the Nuclear Age*, ed. Peter Paret (Oxford: Oxford University Press, 1999), 591.

25. David M. Glantz, *Barbarossa: Hitler's Invasion of Russia 1941* (Stroud, Gloucestershire: Tempus, 2001), 68.

26. Along with the StuG III (a mobile assault gun), the Mark III and IV were, in the summer of 1941, the best tanks in Germany's arsenal. They far surpassed the obsolete Mark I and II, which were also deployed in the Soviet Union, as well as the somewhat more versatile Czech Pz Kpfw 38 (t).

27. "Kriegstagebuch Nr. 3 der 7. Panzer-Division Führungsabteilung, 1.6.1941–9.5.1942," June 28, 1941, RH 27-7/46, fol. 21, BA-MA.

28. "KTB Nr. 1, Panzergruppe 2, vom 22.6.1941 bis 21.7.41," July 7, 1941, RH 21-2/927, fol. 149, BA-MA.

29. Department of the US Army, ed., *Small Unit Actions during the German Campaign in Russia* (Washington, DC: Center for Military History, 1953), 91–92.

30. Omer Bartov, *Hitler's Army: Soldiers, Nazis, and War in the Third Reich* (Oxford: Oxford University Press, 1992), 20.

31. Walter Kempowski, ed., *Das Echolot Barbarossa '41: Ein kollektives Tagebuch* (Munich: Albrecht Knaus, 2004), 238 (July 5, 1941).

32. Claus Hansmann, *Vorüber—Nicht Vorbei: Russische Impressionen, 1941–1943* (Frankfurt: Ullstein Sachbuch, 1989), 119.

33. "Kriegstagebuch Nr. 2, XXXXVII. Pz. Korps., Ia 25.5.1941–22.9.1941," July 19, 1941, RH 24-47/2, BA-MA.

34. Ibid., August 4, 1941.

35. Tactically panzer divisions were poorly disposed toward sustained defensive operations because of their inadequate infantry component as well as the fact that tanks, as an instrument of war, are considerably less effective in static defense.

36. "KTB Nr. 1, Panzergruppe 2, Bd. II, vom 22.7.1941 bis 20.8.41," July 26, 1941, RH 21-2/928, fols. 49–50, BA-MA.

37. Hugh R. Trevor-Roper, ed., *Hitler's War Directives, 1939–1945* (London: Pan, 1964), 139–42.

38. Halder, KTB, 3:100 (July 21, 1941).

39. Ibid., 98 (July 20, 1941).

40. Ibid., 107–8 (July 23, 1941).

41. Franz Halder, *Hitler als Feldherr* (Munich: Münchener Dom, 1949), 42.

42. Burkhart Müller-Hillebrand, *Das Heer, 1933–1945*, vol. 3, *Der Zweifrontenkrieg: Das Heer vom Beginn des Feldzuges gegen die Sowjetunion bis zum Kriegsende* (Frankfurt am Main: Mittler & Sohn, 1969), 205.

43. Underlining in the original. "KTB Nr. 1, Panzergruppe 2, Bd. II, vom 22.7.1941 bis 20.8.41," July 29, 1941, RH 21-2/928, fol. 78, BA-MA.

44. The Panzerkampfwagen 38 (t) was a formerly Czech-built tank.
45. Underlining in the original. "Panzerarmeeoberkommandos Anlagen zum Kriegstagesbuch 'Berichte, Besprechungen, Beurteilungen der Lage,' Bd. IV, 22.7.41–31.8.41," July 27, 1941, RH 21-3/47, fols. 99–100, BA-MA.
46. Ibid., July 31, 1941, fol. 126.
47. Johannes Hürter, ed., *Ein deutscher General an der Ostfront: Die Briefe und Tagebücher des Gotthard Heinrici, 1941/42* (Erfurt: Sutton, 2001), 67 (July 11, 1941).
48. Walter Bähr and Hans Bähr, eds., *Kriegsbriefe gefallener Studenten, 1939–1945* (Tübingen: Rainer Wunderlich, 1952), 71 (July 4, 1941).
49. Christiane Sahm, ed., *Verzweiflung und Glaube: Briefe aus dem Krieg, 1939–1942* (Munich: Don Bosco, 2007), 41 (July 2, 1941).
50. Trevor-Roper, ed., *Hitler's War Directives, 1939–1945*, 145–48.
51. Walter Gorlitz, ed., *The Memoirs of Field-Marshal Keitel: Chief of the German High Command, 1938–1945* (New York: Stein & Day, 1966), 150–51.
52. Italics in the original. Halder, KTB, 3:159.
53. Hildegard von Kotze, ed., *Heeresadjutant bei Hitler, 1938–1943: Aufzeichnungen des Majors Engel* (Stuttgart: Deutsche Verlags-Anstalt, 1974), 108.
54. Halder, KTB, 3:170 (August 11, 1941).
55. "KTB Nr. 1, Panzergruppe 2, Bd. II, vom 22.7.1941 bis 20.8.41," August 11, 1941, RH 21-2/928, fol. 209, BA-MA.
56. Halder, KTB, 3:178 (August 15, 1941).
57. "Kriegstagebuch Nr. 1 (Band August 1941) des Oberkommandos der Heeresgruppe Mitte," August 15, 1941, RH 19II/386, BA-MA, 328–29.
58. Tobias Jersak, "Die Interaktion von Kriegsverlauf und Judenvernichtung: Ein Blick auf Hitlers Strategie im Spätsommer 1941," *Historische Zeitschrift* 268 (1999): 350.
59. Georg Meyer, *Adolf Heusinger: Dienst eines deutschen Soldaten, 1915 bis 1964* (Berlin: Mittler & Sohn, 2001), 156.
60. Halder, KTB, 3:193 (August 22, 1941).
61. The author has recently completed a new history of the Battle of Kiev in August and September 1941.
62. "Anlage zum KTB Panzer Gruppe, 4.20.9.41–14.10.41," September 22, 1941, RH 21-4/34, fols. 119–21, BA-MA.
63. "Kriegstagebuch Nr. 1, Panzergruppe 2, Band 2, vom 21.8.1941 bis 31.10.41," September 27, 1941, RH 21-2/931, fol. 323, BA-MA.
64. Ibid., fol. 319.
65. Klaus Schüler, "The Eastern Campaign as a Transportation and Supply Problem," in *From Peace to War: Germany, Soviet Russia, and the World, 1939–1941*, ed. Bernd Wegner (New York: Berghahn, 1997), 213nn7–8.

66. Martin van Creveld, *Supplying War: Logistics from Wallenstein to Patton* (Cambridge: Cambridge University Press, 1984), 170–71.

67. Fedor von Bock, *Generalfeldmarschall Fedor von Bock: The War Diary, 1939–1945*, ed. Klaus Gerbet (Atglen, PA: Schiffer Military History, 1996), 313.

68. Table 1: Soviet and German wartime production, 1941–1945, in Richard Overy, *Russia's War: A History of the Soviet War Effort, 1941–1945* (London: Penguin, 1997), 155.

69. Table 7: Production of New Weapons, in M. R. D. Foot, "USSR," in *The Oxford Companion of the Second World War*, ed. I. C. B. Dear and M. R. D. Foot (Oxford: Oxford University Press, 1995), 220.

70. Table 1: Soviet and German wartime production, 1941–1945, in Overy, *Russia's War*, 155.

CHAPTER 2

URBAN WARFARE DOCTRINE ON THE EASTERN FRONT

Adrian E. Wettstein

Eight days after the German invasion of Poland opened World War II, spearheads of the German 4th Panzer Division reached the Polish capital of Warsaw.[1] In the mistaken assumption that Warsaw had been declared an open city, tanks pushed unsupported into the city. They were abruptly stopped by street barricades and heavy Polish fire from every window and door at point-blank range, causing the loss of some twenty armored vehicles. The German units pulled back and established a defensive position outside of the city. During the night, artillery moved into position and additional infantry was brought to the frontline. On the next day, the division repeated its attack. It quickly became clear that the Germans did not possess enough strength to break Polish resistance in this well-fortified area. The division commander, *Generalmajor* Hans Reinhardt, prevented a third attack that had been scheduled in the afternoon by his superior, *General der Kavallerie* Erich Hoepner. The 4th Panzer Division then went on the defensive and blocked Warsaw from the southwest until it was replaced by the 31st Infantry Division during the following days.[2] As this first attack of World War II on a major city made clear, a coup de main with tanks could turn into a costly operation.

By September 20, 1939, German forces had encircled Warsaw completely. While the Eighth Army (south and west of the Vistula River) was heavily involved in the battle at the Bzura, there were only minor forces encircling the city in their sector.[3] On the northern and eastern side of the Vistula, the Third Army advanced from East Prussia and closed the ring. German victory in the battle at the Bzura led to the final decision in the Polish campaign. While motorized troops pursued the beaten Polish army eastward, strong infantry forces under the command of the Eighth Army prepared for the assault on Warsaw. Heavy artillery, including two 305-millimeter mortars, and pioneers from the Tenth and Fourteenth Armies were also allocated to the assault. A special assault pioneer detachment and more specialized equipment such as flamethrowers were flown to Warsaw.[4] Preparatory fire started on September 23, 1939, and hit the city hard. *Generalleutnant* Conrad von Cochenhausen, commander of the 10th Infantry Division wrote: "From our position above, the image of a blazing metropolis was powerful and stirring. Although it was a clear, sunny day, it looked as though a heavy storm was in the sky. Huge fires smouldered in the city; the ascending smoke overshadowed the city more and more."[5] The fire was restricted to so-called vital establishments such as electrical power stations, gas and water works, and communication centers.[6]

There was also a prolonged discussion about bombing the city. In the end, notions of military necessity limited the use of airpower.[7] Similar thoughts motivated German policy toward civilian fugitives. The Germans announced their attack through the use of leaflets, which caused a massive refugee exodus from the city. Eighth Army command feared that the Polish army would use the fugitive columns as a cover for operations and ordered that civilians be stopped and returned to the city, by the use of rifle fire if necessary. This also led to a prolonged discussion, since the Army Group did not want to take responsibility for such measures. In both cases, it wanted Hitler to make the final decision and hence assume responsibility for these actions.[8] Army guidelines for house fighting, as manifested in the 10th Infantry Division's files, ordered the "avoidance of all cruelty against the civil population."[9] The assault on the beleaguered and burning city started on September 25, 1939. All units involved in the operation were soon engaged in heavy street fighting. They were shot at from all sides and blocked by barricades. Even though the Germans had a massive superiority in artillery, they found themselves under precise Polish artillery fire more than once, as it proved difficult to find and destroy the Polish batteries. Indeed, as all German reports indicated, such superiority in artillery and air force had little impact on the street fighting. Opposing them were Polish regulars, cadets of the Polish Military Academy, and civilians. Some of the latter were shot on the spot by the Germans, including several women.[10] In the heat of combat, especially in the confusing situation of urban warfare, it seems possible that German troops mistook quickly mobilized Polish soldiers for irregulars and treated them as such. Finally, at 9:00 a.m. on September 27, 1939, Warsaw capitulated. But this did not mean that all combat had ended. Due to communication problems, German forces exchanged messages about encounters with Polish forces throughout the day.[11]

There was never any doubt that Warsaw would fall. The question, however, was at what price: How many casualties would the Germans suffer? How many resources would be wasted? How much of the city would be destroyed and how many Polish civilians would lose their lives?

By the end of September, the Polish command opted to end the suffering of its citizens as it became obvious that the Germans would extract victory at any price.

At this point a brief examination of the development of German urban warfare doctrine is necessary. German regulations, especially the main tactical regulation, described a doctrine for fighting in built-up areas under the name *Ortsgefecht*, or locality fighting. Its origins date to the immediate aftermath of the Franco-Prussian War, when the Germans were confronted by this type of fighting for the first time.[12] A doctrine was not codified, however, until the publication of the Army Regulation of 1906. During World War I, this doctrine was improved owing to the experiences of trench warfare. Villages in the frontline area were integrated into the trench system and often became pillars of the defensive line.[13] In the interwar period, army regulation 487 of the Reichswehr and 300 of the Wehrmacht made only minor changes. The latter regulation dedicated only six ciphers to locality fighting.[14] As was typical of most German regulations, they provided more description of the nature of village fighting than actual rigid rules of engagement. But was such a doctrine suitable for urban warfare?

In the first of these six ciphers, one finds for both the first and last time the use of the word "city": "Cities and large cities could become combat areas as well."[15] A look at the individual ciphers makes clear that German doctrine was focused on small villages. Cipher no. 553, for example, stated that localities draw fire on themselves because of the ease with which they could be identified. Though this is true for both villages and cities, the effect of artillery fire on each was very different. While an artillery battery or a battalion could completely shell a village, a larger city would require enormous numbers of guns and vast quantities of artillery to saturate it with fire. Locating troops inside a city was also difficult, especially if they could maneuvre in undetected ways, such as through subways or sewers. German regulations also recommended bypassing localities. While a village is easy to go around, avoiding a city is potentially much more difficult.[16] These guidelines also noted in cipher no. 554 three important points: the rapid depletion of forces committed to close combat in larger communities, the short combat distances within towns and cities, and the importance of independent action by the lower levels of leadership.[17] In dedicating one-third of the text to the attack, the regulation also recognized the difficulties inherent in attacking villages and towns. This proved even more so in large cities, where a defender had far better chances of recovering after a tactical defeat. For such an operation, the order stressed reconnaissance and "constant shelling" of the locality.

Troops entering the city needed to be directly supported by their heavy weapons, and single artillery guns were to follow right on the heels of the raiding patrols. Forces were then to push straight through to the other side of the locality; obviously in large cities this was frequently not possible. At its core, street fighting degenerated into a question of "cold steel and the hand grenade."[18]

Two rather noticeable omissions from the guidelines concern the presence of civilians and the importance of intelligence. In villages, neither are as important as in cities. In cities, entire combat groups could get lost owing to ignorance of the area, while command and control of units could be seriously impaired by the presence of thousands of civilians trying to survive. As this discussion makes clear, German doctrine on fighting in urban areas was more focused on smaller locales than on cities—a result of their experiences in the Franco-Prussian War and World War I.

In the campaigns following the Polish war, German forces did not meet serious resistance in cities. In the Scandinavian campaign, all major cities easily fell to the Wehrmacht. The same is true for the majority of the campaign in the west in May and June 1940. Paris, for example, was declared an open city and seized without combat by the German 87th Infantry Division on June 14, 1940.

Only Rotterdam witnessed urban fighting.[19] German planning for the west called for a quick strike against the Netherlands with dual objectives: to draw Allied troops northward and pin them down in Belgium, as well as to mislead the Allied command about the primary German advance. In the so-called Fortress Holland, a system of natural and artificial obstacles, the Dutch command hoped to hold their position until Allied support arrived. The German High Command wanted to crack the fortress through a combination of paratroopers and fast-moving panzer units. The paratroopers had to take several bridges, the last over the Maas in Rotterdam, thereby permitting a rapid advance of the German armored spearhead into the fortress. Other units were to directly attack the residence of the queen, government buildings, and the war ministry in the hope of paralyzing Dutch resistance. Both objectives lay in built-up areas.

Already by 12:00 a.m. on May 10, 1940, it became clear that the coup de main against the Dutch government had failed, and German paratroopers were forced onto the defensive in the Dordrecht area. On the plus side, all bridges necessary for the rapid break into the fortress were under German control, including the two in Rotterdam. But here the city's garrison, strengthened by several arriving infantry battalions, offered stiff resistance.

On the northern end of the bridge, there was a stalemate between a well-entrenched but small (only two platoons with fifty-eight men) German force and the Dutch, who, while lacking the power to crack this small bridgehead, were able to effectively cut it off from the remainder of the German forces. This defense drew German attention to Rotterdam, since it prevented the linkup with the paratroopers in the Dordrecht area and the cracking of Fortress Holland, tying down the entire German Eighteenth Army. At noon on May 13, 1940, when the German armored spearhead of the 39th Army Corps reached the Rotterdam area, they sent out emissaries for capitulation negotiations. *General der Artillerie* Georg von Küchler, commander of the Eighteenth Army, sent the following message to the corps: "Resistance in Rotterdam is to be broken with all means, the destruction of the city is to be threatened and carried out if necessary."[20] While negotiations dragged on as the Dutch played for time, the Germans prepared a massive air strike for May 14, 1940. This information was passed on to the Dutch commander, who waited on a decision from his superior. While the Germans directly threatened to destroy the city, Küchler sent another message to the 39th Army Corps on the morning of May 14, 1940, demanding that everything possible be done to avoid spilling the blood of the Dutch civilian population. The Germans expected that the threat, in combination with the knowledge of what had transpired in Warsaw, would force the Dutch city commander to come to terms. When this finally occurred on May 14, 1940, at 3:00 p.m., communication problems ensured that the already airborne bombers could not be completely stopped. Sixty percent of the bombers scheduled to take part in the operation dropped their payloads (between sixty and ninety tons) on the old city, causing nine hundred civilian deaths and massive destruction due to raging fires. As in Warsaw, the Wehrmacht did not kill civilians as an end in itself, as was later to be the case in the Soviet Union, but it was ready to use its firepower to break the opponent's resistance if necessary, thereby taking into account civilian casualties. But it was the ultima ratio, and field commanders in both battles seemed to hope that the threat of such a bombing would bring the defenders to terms. At the same time, it is clear that the Germans' opponents were not prepared to accept massive civilian casualties and destruction, so they capitulated when they realized that the Wehrmacht would use any and all means to achieve victory. Neither the Polish nor Dutch governments saw any purpose in sacrificing their civilian population and cultural centers to a German military prepared to take such steps. This would change radically with the opening of the Eastern Front.

The Planning and Opening of Operation Barbarossa

On the Herculean task of planning history's largest land campaign, the British historian Evan Mawdsley writes: "Operation Barbarossa was one of history's most carefully premeditated and planned invasions, developed by the German staff officers over eight or nine months, and thought about even longer.... Nevertheless, the German planning for the attack on the Soviet Union contained fatal flaws."[21] Among the flaws were the different objectives of Adolf Hitler and the German High Command, especially *Generaloberst* Franz Halder, chief of the General Staff of the Army High Command (OKH), and the German army's near total ignorance concerning the Soviet Union. This included not only the strength, training, and morale of Soviet armed forces, but also questions about armament capacities and production sites, extending even to simple geographical issues.[22] As if this were not enough, the German High Command operated in a groupthinklike process, ignoring all negative incoming information.[23] Further pressure on the planning came from the necessity to conduct a Blitzkrieg-style campaign. The Third Reich simply lacked the resources for a prolonged struggle with the Soviet Union. It was already at war with Great Britain, and the Soviet Union's resources were required by the Nazi state for the final fight for global supremacy against the Anglo-Saxon sea powers.[24] Another lacuna in the army's planning concerned the possibility of urban combat and the consequences of this for German strategy.[25] An additional important factor for the further development of the war in the east was that the German leadership planned it as a war of annihilation. This ensured that there was, in addition to economic factors, not only no interest in the cities and their inhabitants, but also a plan to completely erase them. This meant that German forces paid no attention to the civil population in their conception or conduct of the fighting. Orders to avoid unnecessary cruelty against civilians as mentioned above for Warsaw and Rotterdam simply did not exist in the east. Herein lay the first step toward a radicalization of urban warfare doctrine.

Cities became strategic objectives during the planning process, but more in a geographical sense than from an operational perspective.[26] Army Group North's primary objective was Leningrad (originally seen as even more important than Moscow); Army Group Center's final goal was Moscow; and after taking Kiev, Army Group South's final objectives were Stalingrad and the Caucasus region. In both the planning studies as well as in the final deployment orders, no mention or thought was given to the possibility of a prolonged fight around or especially within these cities. There are three reasons for this: First, as detailed above, the Wehrmacht's previous experiences gave no reason for such planning—there were only minor urban engagements during the initial campaigns of the war. Second, the German battle plan called for quick strikes to encircle and destroy the mass of the Red Army westward of the Dnieper and the Dvina in a classic battle of annihilation.[27] This meant that by the time the German armies reached the cities of Leningrad and Moscow, resistance would be minimal as the bulk of the Red Army should have been already destroyed. Third, the Soviet potential for resistance was completely underestimated. Because of a combination of National Socialist propaganda and older (World War I) and more recent (the Soviet-Finnish Winter War) combat experiences, the High Command, as well as the average German officer and soldier, underestimated Soviet combat morale and ability and consequently expected a quick Soviet collapse. This strengthened the German expectation that they would not encounter large-scale urban combat.

When the Wehrmacht launched Operation Barbarossa in the early morning of June 22, 1941, the extent of its miscalculation regarding Soviet combat power quickly became evident. While the Wehrmacht enjoyed almost unbelievable success in the first stage of Barbarossa, frontline troops soon realized that Soviet soldiers were tenacious opponents. Alarming reports of grim resistance reached headquarters, and it became apparent that Red Army numbers as well as German casualties had been calculated far too optimistically. Almost from the outset of Operation Barbarossa, German troops met ferocious Soviet resistance in built-up areas, including small villages and cities. In the first weeks this resistance was unorganized and thereby quickly overcome by German troops. But even then, it took time for the troops to "cleanup"[28] the conquered cities to avoid lingering combat in urban rear areas. Since this task was mainly carried out by infantry forces, the gap between the fast-moving panzer divisions and the marching infantry divisions increasingly widened. The further the operation progressed, however, the more determinedly and tenaciously the Red Army defended urban areas, even when only second-line units were at hand.

This became especially evident after the rapid advance of the first three weeks, when the German spearheads crashed into the second Soviet echelon. When Panzer Group 2 (*Generaloberst* Heinz Guderian) reached the Dnieper, it failed to take the bridges in Rogatchev and Mogilev by surprise attacks. To avoid a direct attack on the heavily defended Russian bridgeheads around Rogatchev, Mogilev, and Orsha, Guderian decided to cross the river in between these Soviet positions. An attack on the cities would have cost him time, as he would have required infantry to be successful and the mass of these units were at least two marching days away. The operation succeeded, but it cost time and precious bridging material. Perhaps more important, it made the supply of those forces across the river difficult, since the crossing point was not conveniently located near the supply lines.[29]

Smolensk fell relatively easily to the Germans on July 16, 1941—but even here the 29th Motorized Infantry Division needed two days to break Soviet resistance. Remnants of the Soviet 34th Rifle Corps, supported by NKVD units and hastily mobilized militia battalions, defended the city. Soviet forces barricaded streets and fortified houses. In order to avoid at least some heavy street fighting, the German forces moved around the city, destroyed several heavy artillery batteries south of it, and finally attacked from the southeast, catching the Soviets off balance. On the second day, with massive support by assault guns, flamethrowing tanks, and antiaircraft guns all firing at point-blank range, the assault troops reached the northern part of the city after heavy fighting in the industrial district. Even after this apparent victory, however, the city still had to be "cleansed" of Soviet defenders.[30]

It was a much harder fight at Mogilev. Home to one hundred thousand inhabitants, Mogilev also contained a large railway repair shop, important sections of the Soviet silk industry, and one of the few bridges over the Dnieper in that area. A month into the invasion, it was already far behind German lines and defended by three rifle divisions of the Thirteenth Soviet Army. By July 20, 1941, the 7th German Corps had enveloped the city. The 23rd Infantry Division directly attacked, but could not break into the city and suffered heavy losses in the confusing landscape of houses and orchards. The 11th company of the 67th Infantry Regiment lost all of its officers and two-thirds of its men. On July 26, 1941, the Soviets blew up the bridge and thereby destroyed their last avenue of escape. They held out for an additional day, until the pressure of the 7th, 15th, 23rd and 78th German Infantry Divisions became too much for the defenders. During this gruelling battle, the Germans suffered enormous losses: the 23rd Infantry Division alone left 264 dead on the field; 83 men were missing and another 1,088 were injured.[31]

These are only some examples of city combat during the opening stages of Operation Barbarossa. The frequency of such combat was due to three factors. First and foremost, the Soviet traffic system was focused on communication lines (streets and railways) between cities. There were few connections between these main arteries, and bypasses around cities simply did not exist. The crossings over large rivers, for example railway bridges, were also generally within cities. Consequently, if the Germans were going to make full use of this thin traffic network, they needed to control these intersections. This was especially necessary for the rapid advance that was demanded by the planned German Blitzkrieg strategy as well as for the supply of this advance.

Second, Stalin was prepared to use any means to stop the German attack. Such thinking was reflected by the hundreds of thousands of soldiers who died or became prisoners during the first months of the campaign due to the "stand fast" orders issued by Stalin.[32] Such a strategy, however, also included cities: the Red Army defended cities even at the price of massive destruction of their infrastructure and heavy civilian losses. Though this was not one of Stalin's strategic intentions at the beginning, it quickly became a common feature of the war as the Red Army's mobilization points were concentrated in urban areas. During the opening weeks, partly mobilized troops were often surprised by German armored spearheads and were forced to fight with any and all means at hand. The same was true for the hastily raised militia units (*Narodnoe opolcheniye*)[33] and worker battalions.[34] The ruthless will with which the Red Army chose to resist German forces, including the conscious sacrifice of civilians, is best exemplified in the mining of cities. The most wellknown example of this was in Kiev; here the Soviets used all kinds of explosive devices, including both time fuses and remote controlled detonators.[35] It took units of the 29th Corps five days to get the resulting fires under control, and sections of at least two infantry divisions searched for further explosive devices for upward of a week.[36] A few days before explosions rocked Kiev, the Finns underwent the same type of experience in Viborg with heavy losses. It was actually the Finns who warned the Germans of the possible use of delayed-action bombs by the Soviets.[37] This marked a further step in the radicalization process, as it was the Red Army who carried out the demolitions. From the Soviet perspective, such destruction was worth the cost, since parts of several German divisions were held up by the fires. By tenaciously defending cities, the Red Army traded blood and devastation for the resource it most needed and that the Germans could least afford to lose: time. No combat area provided more advantages to the defender than a city, and within such a landscape, even poorly trained and lightly equipped infantry units could seriously delay German operations.

Such combat brought one of the great weaknesses of the German army to the forefront: its "semi-modernity."[38] This was the third factor that caused the German army to struggle with urban combat. The core of the German army was some twenty panzer and motorized infantry divisions.

These were all fully motorized, fast moving units manned by younger and better-trained soldiers. Marching infantry divisions constituted the overwhelming bulk of the army, and because they possessed only a few vehicles they relied on horse-drawn supply and artillery. The differing rates of speed for these two different transport forces within the German army became a problem in the early operations of the war, and this phenomenon was also found during Operation Barbarossa. It was significantly aggravated in the east by the vast area in which the campaign took place. The panzer divisions quickly reached Soviet cities, but if they failed to seize them by a coup de main, they were forced into a full-scale fight for the city, a task they were simply not equipped for. Due to an endemic lack of vehicles, German motorized troops did not have the usual complement of nine infantry battalions. Instead, a motorized division could field only six (and sometimes just four) battalions, and panzer divisions possessed only four. These mobile divisions thus lacked the most important troops needed for urban warfare. The main strength of mechanized units—their mobility—was also negated by the terrain of urban areas, as the defender could easily stop or canalize vehicles into killing zones through the use of street barricades, mines, and other obstacles. Fire and rubble that resulted either from the fighting itself or from preliminary bombardment also constrained mobile units. Such things would continually break the German advance and bring the mechanized units to a halt, forcing them to wait for the infantry to close the gap. When this happened, Soviet defenders gained valuable time needed to rally themselves, strengthen their defences, and bring reinforcements to the area.

All these issues came to a head in the battle for Dnipropetrovsk.[39] Following the conclusion of the encirclement at Uman, *Generaloberst* Ewald von Kleist's Panzer Group 1 raced eastward to the Dnieper River. Its objective was to gain bridgeheads over this river, which could otherwise become a massive obstacle to the army's continued advance. The 3rd Motorized Army Corps, one of Panzer Group 1's spearheads, was directed toward Dnipropetrovsk. The city contained three large bridges, among them a very important railway bridge.[40] It also functioned as an important railway junction and industrial center.[41] On August 24, 1941, after eight days of heavy fighting, the attack was stopped within sight of Dnipropetrovsk by a tenacious Soviet defense strengthened by heavy Soviet tanks.[42] As German forces approached the city, they were surprised by its immense size. Dnipropetrovsk went through a period of massive growth during the interwar years; its population ballooned from one hundred thousand in the 1920s to some five hundred thousand inhabitants by 1939 as a consequence of Stalin's crash industrialization process. It was impossible for the Germans to reconcile the behemoth in front of them with their outdated maps from the early 1920s. The maps were rendered even more ineffective by their scale—at only 1:100,000—which made orientation as well as command and control inside the city impossible.[43] Only the intelligence officer of the 3rd Motorized Corps had two so-called military-geographical plans of the city, which were more accurate guides to the area.[44]

The 13th Panzer and 60th Motorized Infantry Divisions were chosen to lead the attack into the city and toward the bridges on August 25, 1941. The Germans found only minor resistance inside the city and were able to push rapidly on to the important Dnieper bridges. All of them, however, were blown up by Soviet forces before the Germans could reach them. Nevertheless, in the chaotic situation the Soviet command neglected to destroy a small pontoon bridge, which vehicles up to three tons and foot soldiers could use. One German *Kampfgruppe* was able to seize the crossing, and the commander of the battle group, *Oberst* Eberhard Rodt, demonstrated the effectiveness of German doctrine. Rodt, who was on the spot, decided at 10:50 a.m. to take the chance and drive unsupported over the crossway. He then communicated his decision to the division in order to get reinforcements. At this moment, the commander of the 3rd Corps, *General der Kavallerie* Eberhard von Mackensen, appeared on the riverside and supported Rodt's decision. The corps commander instructed the commander of the 120th Motorized Infantry Regiment[45] to assemble his forces and follow Rodt's battle group. A mere two and a half hours later, the 66th Rifle Regiment with its two battalions had crossed the river, followed by the 43rd Motorcycle Battalion[46] and soldiers of the 120th Motorized Infantry Regiment. Rodt's Command Staff also quickly crossed over the pontoon bridge, ensuring that he could exercise command and control over these units. At 2:15 p.m. *Oberst* Traugott Herr, CO of the 13th Panzer Division's Rifle Brigade, crossed the river, assuming command of all forces in the bridgehead regardless of what divisional unit they belonged to. This example demonstrates the two guidelines of the successful German tactical leadership: forward command and mission-oriented leadership. In other words, this was a textbook application of German *Auftragstaktik*.[47]

While the Germans continued to reinforce their units in the bridgehead, the Soviet command regained its balance and assembled strong forces. During the night of August 26, 1941, a fierce Soviet counterattack nearly cracked the bridgehead. From this point on, the battle for the bridgehead became a race between the Soviets, who attempted to prevent further forces from crossing the river by shelling and bombing the pontoon bridge and the ferry docks, and the German engineers, who furiously repaired the crossing and transported across reinforcements and supply goods. During this engagement, the Red Army enjoyed both air and artillery superiority. The combination of these two factors led to a significant loss of valuable specialists from the engineers as well as bridging material. Inside the bridgehead, chaos reigned as German troops were running low on ammunition and wounded soldiers could not be evacuated; extremely heavy Soviet artillery and grenade launcher fire cost the units of the 60th Motorized Infantry Division alone up to two hundred men daily. Panzer Group 1 pumped further forces into the bridgehead—at first elements of the SS Viking Division, then men from the 198th Infantry Division. Artillery from several divisions, as well as from the corps and army pools, was concentrated in the area, until there were twenty-five battalions in action; this was one of the strongest concentrations of artillery during the entirety of Operation Barbarossa.[48] By September 10, 1941, all attacks and counterattacks in the sector had ceased—both sides were completely exhausted. No reinforcements were available and the troops in the frontline, which still ran through sections of the suburbs, could no longer actively fight. Attention on both sides had shifted to the Kremenchuk area, where Panzer Group 1 attacked northward to meet Guderian's Panzer Group 2 to encircle Kiev. The situation remained at a stalemate until the end of September 1941, when Panzer Group 1 finally secured the bridgehead and began pushing in the direction of Rostov.

As we have seen, combat inside cities led to a radicalization of warfare. The Wehrmacht viewed these urban centers as merely operational and economically valuable points filled with civilians who could be killed during or after the war with the Soviet Union. The Soviet leadership also looked at the cities as primarily military and economic objectives. There was no evacuation beyond that which was stipulated by economic necessity, nor were any measures adopted to avoid fighting inside these densely populated areas. There was no overt Soviet intention to kill their own people deliberately; however, the Soviet leadership was not averse to massive civilian casualties if they stopped or held up the German invasion. The mining of populated areas was beyond all reasonable military necessity and must be seen as a desperate attempt to strike at the German forces. The experience of Kiev helped the Nazi leadership to implement a harder course of action, since it radicalized field commanders and troops. This is most evident in the massacre of 33,771 Jews at Babi Yar, in which elements of the German army such as engineers, military police, and even regular infantry units supported the leading *Sonderkommando* 4a.[49]

Field commanders as well as subordinated units now also tried to avoid assaults on cities more than before, and in the case of Leningrad they actively supported a siege strategy. But even then, field commanders from Army Group North hoped to stay away from the extermination of Leningrad's civil population by accepting a capitulation of the besieged city, gaining the prestige and leaving the dirty work to rear units or SS troops.[50] The special nature of fighting within cities, however, further radicalized combat. Urban terrain was fragmented and confusing. This led to a much higher frequency of close range combat that generally caused higher losses and increased stress. The latter condition was exacerbated by the permanent fear engendered by the confusing landscape and the possibilities for ambushes. The fragmented area often led to the loss of command and control since radio contacts were frequently disrupted and messengers failed to reach their objective. The lack of a general orientation caused by such miserable maps led to a bewildering situation that frequently culminated with troops mistakenly crossing the frontline. Such uncertainty was only compounded by overrun Soviet groups that continued fighting behind German lines.[51] The frustration and fear caused by these conditions led to increased aggression and violence. The loss of control meant not only that incidences of cruelty were more common, but also that errors such as friendly fire were widespread. The presence of large numbers of civilians left to their fate by the Soviet state, which focused on economic evacuation, and attacked by German forces that took no steps to minimize civilian losses, meant that the usual separation between civilians and soldiers evaporated within cities. Civilians suffered in a variety of ways. Blamed for military failures, they were sometimes shot as hostages, though they were generally ignored as humans beings, as the shelling or mining of their houses demonstrated. Culturally valuable objects, such as churches, old towns, and museums, shared a similar fate: the Germans only looked to save objects with economic value.[52]

A look at the battle of Dnipropetrovsk illustrates many of these processes. The Soviet regime placed a premium on evacuating industrial resources and skilled workers, but not the civilian population as a whole. Once the German bridgehead was established, the Red Army poured down massive fire on it as well as on all of its lines of communication. This led not only to high German losses, but also to civilian losses in the area. The Soviets focused on shelling ferry points, areas they recognized or expected to be used as rear service positions and supply routes. Since most of these targets were inside the city, the shelling also caused civilian casualties. Those artillery attacks also hit hospitals and collection points for wounded soldiers.[53] Such continuous fire frustrated German troops, who could not respond to it in an effective manner. When the Germans realized that the fire was guided by Soviet observers behind German lines,[54] their proposed reaction was grim: the clearance of all people within a five hundred meter strip on both riverbanks. Every civilian that German troops found there after the evacuation was to be shot immediately. But since the 3rd Corps lacked the forces needed for such an operation, it instead proposed to take hostages and shoot them in response to further Soviet artillery fire.[55]

German documentation indicates that they suffered heavy casualties during the fight for Dnipropetrovsk. Some of the units inside the bridgehead had seen continuous action for ten days *before* the fight for the bridgehead. Nearly every report of the 60th Motorized Infantry Division to the corps mentioned this very point, and the continual combat and shelling inside the bridgehead brought men to the verge of collapse.[56] On August 26, 1941, troops in the bridgehead received Pervitine, a methamphetamine compound, in an attempt to increase their attentiveness. The constant fighting and resulting combat fatigue led to a much higher rate of losses. Tired soldiers were much more careless, and wounded soldiers frequently succumbed to minor wounds due to their level of exhaustion. This led to a death rate of up to 30 percent of soldiers fighting in the city instead of the usual 10 to 15 percent.[57] The higher rate of casualties also made excessive demands on the medical services. The combination of these various factors decimated the German divisions fighting in the city. Between August 25 and September 2, 1941, the 60th Motorized Infantry Division lost 28 officers and 1,020 NCOs and soldiers.[58] The 198th Infantry Division lost no less than 35 officers and 990 men (238 dead) in only three days of combat.[59] Perhaps even more noteworthy, some 450 engineers lost their lives trying to maintain the pontoon bridge and continuing to ferry traffic across the river up to September 8, 1941.[60]

This constant flow of wounded proved too much for the German medical system.[61] German medical units had been in action since August 13, 1941; this meant that they were already exhausted by the time the real battle for Dnipropetrovsk began. Due to the constricted size of the bridgehead, it was impossible to establish a casualty station on the eastern bank of the river during the first week. This meant that all of the wounded had to be transported across the river, which was possible only under cover of darkness, since the crossing points were under constant Soviet artillery fire. The consequence was that the wounded soldiers were able to reach the field hospitals only during the second half of the night, which, according to modern labor studies, is the period of time in which individuals tend to increase the number of mistakes they make.[62] Soon the hospital personnel were so fatigued that surgical teams had to stop work for full days to recover, even as loads of wounded continued to arrive. Two surgeons in the 198th Infantry Division had to be withdrawn after being diagnosed with acute articular rheumatism.[63] To ensure the availability of elementary needs such as water and electricity, several medical posts were established inside the city; these, inevitably, were damaged by Soviet shelling.

Another problem faced by the hospitals was a lack of clean water, which caused gastric diseases. To cope with up to two hundred wounded soldiers arriving daily at the medical stations, evacuation out of the aid stations in the bridgehead was needed. Since vehicles designated for exclusive medical use were rare,[64] medic units had to fall back on regular trucks, which were in constant demand by other German units, especially the artillery. The concentration of up to twenty-five artillery battalions within the bridgehead necessitated prodigious quantities of ammunition. Supplying these guns with shells became a major task, one that was only complicated by the number of different guns in German use.[65] The troops inside the bridgehead also needed enormous quantities of munitions (especially for heavy infantry weapons), as they were under nearly constant Soviet attack. As the battle dragged on, divisional officers were forced to decide when individual guns would be fired; such micromanagement pointed to the desperate supply situation faced by the Germans.[66]

The problem at Dnipropetrovsk specifically, and for the campaign more generally, was that the German logistic system could not keep pace with the rapid advance. In the original plans for Operation Barbarossa, the Germans believed that a break in the advance at the Dnieper would be necessary to refit units and stockpile goods necessary for the next stage of the advance. During the actual operation, when Panzer Group 1 reached the Dnieper it was involved in a major battle. There was no possibility for refitting or stockpiling: on the contrary, the quartermaster of Panzer Group 1 claimed that his forces used no less than forty thousand tons of ammunition during the battle of Dnipropetrovsk up to September 6, 1941.[67] This situation was exacerbated by a higher number of German trucks breaking down than expected and by a railway system that proved incapable of transporting the necessary amount of supplies. Panzer Group 1's logistics officer graphically described the problem: "The Panzer Group, reduced to 60 percent of its normal supply columns, still had to supply, in addition to [its] nine motorized and armored divisions, the 44th Army Corps, the Italian Expeditionary Corps, and the Hungarian Mobile Corps. The distance from the railhead in Bialacerkiev . . . is 350 km. Under these circumstances, the quartermaster can no longer guarantee a smooth supply."[68] He made this claim *before* the battle had even started, and the deteriorating situation prompted him to conclude: "The quartermaster is forced to appeal to the quartermaster of the III Army Corps by explaining the munitions situation, in order that he urges that the tactical use of his artillery be reconciled with the possibilities of supply."[69] Such a demand in the operationally focused German army was extraordinary.

Further pressure on the logistical system resulted from the semi-modern nature of the German forces. Since infantry units had not kept pace with the advance after Uman, the attacking armored forces lacked the necessary boots on the ground to hold conquered territory against fierce Soviet counterattacks. Panzer Group 1 reacted by ordering a total of two hundred vehicles from the 16th Panzer Division and the *SS-Leibstandarte*[70] to transport all combat elements of the 198th Infantry Division to Dnipropetrovsk. Such an action was required as rear-area units did not possess sufficient functioning vehicles and the 198th Infantry Division lacked its own organic transportation, and this only placed a further strain on the Germans' already overstretched logistics.[71]

The consequences of this prolonged battle should not be underestimated. The divisions involved were not only unable to rest and refit, but indeed had also suffered severely from the fighting. This included two of the precious motorized divisions. Enormous quantities of resources, especially munitions, were wasted during the fight, for only moderate benefit. Finally, the Wehrmacht lost nearly a month as its forces in central and southern Ukraine made only incremental progress. This gave the Soviet Union the time to regain its balance as it embarked on a program of mobilizing more forces and evacuating as many industrial goods and machines as possible from the Kharkiv and Donets Basin areas. Dnipropetrovsk itself was destroyed during the fighting, and this included the important rail bridge and the majority of its industrial capacity.

A Further Step: Leningrad and Moscow

Leningrad was one of the primary objectives of Hitler himself, as he believed that the total destruction of the city would be a death blow against international bolshevism. In addition to such ideological reasoning, Leningrad was also an important industrial area.[72] After the beginning of Operation Barbarossa, Hitler confirmed his desire for a quick seizure of Leningrad. On June 30, 1941, he was considering the use of parts of Army Group Center's armored units to rapidly take the

"Leningrad industrial center."[73] On July 8, 1941, when Barbarossa seemed to be proceeding well, Hitler made clear *"that he wanted to raze Moscow and Leningrad to the ground."*[74] This was to be carried out by the Luftwaffe, but it was not to influence ground operations.[75]

On July 17, 1941, Hitler expressed for the first time his idea to cut Leningrad off from the remainder of the Soviet Union through the use of forces from Army Group Center,[76] only to demand four days later during a visit to Army Group North "a quick seizure of Leningrad."[77] He hoped to stop Soviet submarine attacks directed against ships transporting iron ore from Sweden. He expected tenacious Soviet resistance south of Leningrad (but not inside the city), since the Soviet government had to defend this "symbol of the Revolution"; its loss, he believed, could lead to a quick Soviet collapse. During this visit, Hitler gave no indication that he was considering an encirclement of the city. On July 25, 1941, during a visit to Army Group Center with *Generalfeldmarschall* Keitel, he discussed his "further plans": "Leningrad must be quickly cordoned off and starved out."[78] On both July 28[79] and August 4, 1941,[80] this was affirmed, marking a turn in strategy, though not a definitive one. The longer Operation Barbarossa lasted, the clearer the German underestimation of Soviet potential resources became. As a consequence, Hitler and Halder cut back the more ambitious objectives of Barbarossa. After a long, contentious period of debate between Hitler and the OKH, the northern thrust fell down the list of priorities, as it became clear that it would be impossible to achieve decisive results across the entirety of the front.[81]

This decision, however, was not communicated clearly to frontline commanders.[82] On August 21, 1941, Army Group North ordered its subordinate formations to encircle Leningrad as closely as possible. In the same order, the Army Group demanded that motorized units avoid street fighting "inside the city."[83] Lower levels of command within the Army Group were also in the dark as to the change in plans: when the 41st Motorized Corps, the spearhead of the drive on Leningrad, was relieved in September 1941 and shifted to Army Group Center for Operation Typhoon, its CO, *General der Panzertruppen* Hans Reinhardt, complained about being held back in his assault on Leningrad. He believed that his units would have seized what he assumed to be an undefended city in September.[84] Here German frontline commanders thought much more in military than political terms. They wanted to take the city, since they believed that a prolonged siege would tie down numerous troops, while conquering the city and destroying its defenders would raise German morale and cause a massive blow to the Soviet cause.

But how realistic was Reinhardt's idea? How close were the Germans to taking Leningrad? When the forces of Army Group North finally reached the outskirts of the city, the Red Army and the local party organizations had turned Leningrad into a fortress; there were several defense lines before the city as well as numerous barricades and strong points within it. In addition, several militia units were raised in the city. While they were later destroyed in combat with German forces in the open field, where their lack of training cost them heavily, inside the city these lightly armed soldiers could have caused substantial damage to a German attacking force, especially since they knew the city's terrain very well. Viewed from this perspective, a raid on the city would have certainly turned into large-scale urban combat with all of its unpredictability.[85]

The belief that an engagement in the city was possible certainly played a role in the shift to a siege strategy, since many frontline commanders were wary of becoming involved in street fighting. This siege strategy was, especially in the highest echelon, supported by the ideas of the hunger strategy. The hunger strategy was part of the war of annihilation and aimed at the starvation of up to thirty million Soviets in the wooded regions of Belarus and northern Russia as well as in the cities. Its success would supply continental Europe's inhabitants with the foodstuffs they would otherwise have to import from overseas, making continental Europe—in other words, German-occupied Europe—immune from naval blockade and thereby preparing the German sphere of control for the looming confrontation with the Anglo-Saxon powers.[86] Several possibilities were discussed, including occupation or a narrow closure with or without gates for the population to leave Leningrad. Each of these proposals had serious disadvantages produced by the question of alienating two million people. A fourth possibility lay in leaving the whole question to the Finns, who unofficially wanted the Neva as a frontier, "but Leningrad had to disappear" in their eyes too. Since the Finns were not able to handle the population question, it was clear that the Germans needed to carry out this task. The issue boiled down to a question of how: "There is no satisfactory solution," wrote *General der Artillerie* Alfred Jodl. "When it comes down to it, Army Group North must have an order that can actually be carried out."[87]

Up to mid-October, Army Group North and its commander, *Generalfeldmarschall* Wilhelm Ritter von Leeb, wanted to occupy the city, especially if the defenders were to capitulate.[88] Already on September 25, 1941, von Leeb doubted that the starvation strategy would work, especially if the narrow encirclement option was not utilized.[89] He favored the bombing and shelling of the city until it was "ripe for capitulation."[90]

It took several orders (with the last issued on October 12, 1941) from Hitler to make the decision to encircle Leningrad clear to Army Group North.[91] While Hitler's mind was made up, those of the different commanders in Army Group North were not. It seems that even the OKH was still thinking about seizing the city: on October 17, 1941, the Army High Command ordered Army Group North to inform it of any Soviet capitulation offers, since no final decision within the German camp had been made regarding such offers.[92] Such thoughts continued even during the last week of October, when Army Group North still discussed Leningrad's seizure.[93]

The Tichvin operation between October 16 and December 27, 1941, marked the point when Army Group North finally dropped all ideas of taking the city and accepted the siege strategy.[94] But at this point it was already clear that the defeat of the Soviet Union would require a second German campaign. The case of Leningrad was again brought up and a new alternative was introduced to the discussion. This marked the climax of radicalization in terms of urban warfare. A paper written on November 27, 1941, by *Major* Zimmermann, the specialist for munitions supply questions within the General Quartermaster Section Army Supply, anticipated the end of Blitzkrieg and the ascent of positional warfare. Such a transition, he believed, would cause a massive rise in the use of ammunition.[95] To relieve pressure on the tense munitions situation, he proposed the use of chemical weapons, which were viewed as more effective than regular weapons. Even if the document points to positional warfare, it is no accident that Leningrad was chosen as a case study for such an attack. German reconnaissance had clearly recognized the frantic work that had transformed Leningrad into a bristling fortress. This, combined with the German experiences of summer and autumn 1941, in which conquering defended cities turned into prolonged battles of attrition with an enormous waste of resources, human as well as material, led to notions of using chemical weapons. From the German perspective, poison gas could break the enemy's will to resist quickly and thereby conserve resources. Since the munitions question was one of the main reasons for considering poison gas, it must be concluded that battles like the one for Dnipropetrovsk significantly influenced the development of such plans. In addition, poison gas would kill large numbers of civilians, thereby also contributing to the aim of the hunger strategy. This can be seen by the objective given in the case study: "Elimination of resistance by troops and civilian population. The city has to be taken."[96] Poison gas was to be used for the breakthrough and for flank security; more important, it was to completely contaminate some 200 square kilometers of the city center of Leningrad. For this last purpose, Zimmerman calculated that 1 million light field howitzer shells and 350,000 heavy field howitzer shells filled with the highly effective "Lost" gas were needed.[97] Since the Germans did not possess enough shells filled with gas, or have enough guns to fire such a large quantity of shells, Zimmerman believed that the air force should carry out the attack. This was necessary for two reasons: first, German field artillery could not reach the city, and second, the use of the Luftwaffe would enable the delivery of gas with a much smaller use of resources. In comparison to artillery shells, aerial bombs had a higher ratio of poison gas to overall weight. But even if there were some questions about the carrying out of such an operation, this paper marks the climax of German thinking regarding urban warfare, since not only would the city have been captured but it would have occurred in a way that targeted the civilian population as well.[98] With such an attack, the Germans would have killed two birds with one stone: conquered the city and massively reduced the civilian population. The way would then have been clear to raze the city to the ground, as Hitler wished.

In terms of urban warfare, radicalization worked like a spiral.[99] Even in the period before Operation Barbarossa, the Wehrmacht was ready to use any means at hand to break enemy resistance in cites. During the early stages of World War II, threats, in combination with events such as those witnessed in Warsaw, were frequent enough to bring the defenders to terms. In the rare cases when the Germans had to storm a city, they generally tried to avoid unnecessary civilian casualties. This changed in the Soviet Union. Fierce Soviet resistance drew the German forces into prolonged urban combat that cost them both manpower and resources and significantly delayed the German advance, as seen in Dnipropetrovsk. For both sides, the life of the civilian population often had no value except, in some cases, for economic reasons. The mining of cities such as Kiev by the Soviets in September 1941 turned them into death traps for both the Germans and the local population. Together with the recognition that the Blitzkrieg campaign had failed, this catalyzed the implementation of German plans for mass starvation. Before the start of Operation Barbarossa, those plans were made with a short campaign in mind, so that their main impact would come *after* the victory over the Soviet Union. With the jarring thought of a prolonged conflict with the Soviet Union, these plans were now integrated into the campaign, as seen in the siege of Leningrad. To ensure quicker results for both the military campaign and the starvation plan, the use of poison gas was considered by at least a small group of officers in the highest echelons of the army. Even if all other bonds of civilization and international military law were broken on this front to a much higher degree than on other fronts, the use of weapons of mass destruction against densely populated places never occurred. In strictly military terms, "conventional" urban warfare continued with terrible losses to both soldiers and civilians on all sides up to the very last days of the war and the Soviet attack on Berlin.

Notes

1. For the following, see: 4. Panzer-Division/Ia, War diary entries for September 8 and 9, 1939, RH 27-4/197, Bundesarchiv-Militärarchiv, Freiburg im Breisgau (hereafter BA-MA); Panzer-Regiment 35/Cdr., Kriegstagebuch Polenfeldzug, September 8–9, 1939, RH 39-372, BA-MA; and divisional orders for September 8 and 9, 1939, in RH 27-4/1, BA-MA. See also: Hans Reinhardt, "Die 4. Panzer-Division vor Warschau und an der Bzura, vom 9.–20.9.1939," in Wehrkunde 5 (1958): 237–47.

2. Reinhardt, "Die 4. Panzer-Division," 239. See also: 31. Infanterie-Division/Ia, War diary entries for September 12–16, 1939, RH 26-31/1, BA-MA.

3. The reduced 31st Infantry Division covered the approaches to Warsaw on a forty kilometer sector. 31. Infanterie-Division/Ia, War diary entry September 13, 1939, RH 26-31/1, BA-MA.

4. AOK 8/A.Pi.Fhr., Pioniere der 8. Armee im Feldzug gegen Polen, September 1–October 7, 1939, January 1940, RH 20-8/251, fols. 6–7, BA-MA.

5. Die 10. Infanterie-Division im polnischen Feldzug, RH 20-8/52, fols. 36–37, BA-MA.

6. AOK 8/Ia, Armeebefehl für den Angriff auf Warschau, September 22, 1939, RH 20-8/306, BA-MA.

7. The bombing, especially with incendiaries, hampered artillery control, and already before the attack started friendly fire incidents had become so numerous that Third and Eighth Army demanded a complete cessation of air attacks. See AOK 8/Ia, War diary entries for September 23–25, 1939, RH 20-8/11, BA-MA.

8. AOK 8/Ia, War diary entries for September 24 and 25, 1939, RH 20-8/11, BA-MA.

9. 10. Infanterie-Division/Ia, Richtlinien für den Häuserkampf, September 23, 1939, RH 26-10/477, BA-MA.

10. Already during the attacks on September 8 and 9, 1939, German sources claimed that civilians were shooting at them. On September 14, a German officer observed "women with rifles" fighting against the Germans. 31. Infanterie-Division/Ia, War diary entry for September 14, 1939, RH 26-31/1, BA-MA.

11. Die 10. Infanterie-Division im polnischen Feldzug, RH 20-8/52, fols. 38–40, BA-MA.

12. Geoffrey Wawro, *The Franco–Prussian War: The German Conquest of France in 1870–1871* (Cambridge: Cambridge University Press, 2003), 213. Wawro does not mention this special fact, but he describes several examples of village fighting.

13. A good overview of the first cases of village fighting as well as doctrinal changes is provided in Immanuel Friedrich, "Der Kampf um und in Ortschaften: Kriegstechnische Betrachtungen aus der neuesten Kriegsgeschichte," *Kriegstechnische Zeitschrift*, nos. 7, 8 (1916): 145–64.

14. Generalstab, *Heeresdienstvorschrift 300*, 2 vols. (Berlin: Offene Worte, 1936), 225–28.

15. Ibid., 225.

16. One should keep in mind, for example, that Stalingrad and its suburbs in 1942 formed a belt stretching forty kilometers along the Volga.

17. Generalstab, *Heeresdienstvorschrift 300*, 226.

18. Ibid., 227.

19. For details, see Hans-Adolf Jacobsen, "Der deutsche Luftangriff auf Rotterdam (14. Mai 1940), Versuch einer Klärung," *Wehrwissenschaftliche Rundschau* 5 (1968): 257–85. This article is still the best scholarly examination of the battle for Rotterdam. For a Dutch approach and one that is more tactical, see D. A. Van Hilten, "A Rotterdam en mai 1940," *L'Armée/La Nation*, no. 5 (1948): 17–21.

20. Radio message from Eighteenth Army/Ia to the 39th Corps on May 13, 1940, quoted in Jacobsen, "Der deutsche Luftangriff," 275.

21. Evan Mawdsley, *Thunder in the East: The Nazi-Soviet War, 1941–1945* (London: Hodder Arnold, 2005), 53.

22. This can be seen by the fact that many war diaries up to the summer of 1942 mention the lack of useful maps. For a detailed approach to the military, logistical, and political planning for Operation Barbarossa, see Horst Boog, Jürgen Förster, Joachim Hoffmann, Ernst Klink, Rolf-Dieter Müller, and Gerhard R. Ueberschär, *Der Angriff auf die Sowjetunion*, vol. 4 of *Das Deutsche Reich und der Zweite Weltkrieg* (Stuttgart: Deutsche Verlags-Anstalt, 1983), hereafter, *DRZW 4*; and Mawdsley, *Thunder*, 3–54.

23. Groupthink is a theoretical concept first used by Irving L. Janis, *Victims of Groupthink* (Boston: Houghton Mifflin, 1972). For the planning atmosphere inside the German High Command, see Geoffrey P. Megargee, *Inside Hitler's High Command* (Lawrence: University Press of Kansas, 2000).

24. *DRZW 4*, 25–28; and Mawdsley, *Thunder*, 6–9.

25. Discussed in more depth in Adrian Wettstein, "Operation 'Barbarossa' und Stadtkampf," *Militärgeschichtliche Zeitschrift* 66, no. 1 (2007): 21–44.

26. Jörg Ganzenmüller, *Das belagerte Leningrad, 1941–1944: Die Stadt in den Strategien von Angreifern und Verteidigern* (Paderborn: Ferdinand Schöningh, 2005), 13.

27. Mawdsely, *Thunder*, 41–54.

28. Beyond antipartisan actions, the term "cleanup" was also extensively utilized in urban warfare reports. The term on its own provides evidence of the often problematic nature of fighting inside cities.

29. Heinz Guderian, *Erinnerungen eines Soldaten* (Stuttgart: Motorbuch, 1994), 151–57. As is typical for the German approach, there is no mention of these logistical consequences—only the operation as such counted. In the same phase of Barbarossa, *Generaloberst* Hermann Hoth's Panzer Group 3 failed to take Vitebsk in a coup de main. The city fell by a forceful attack of four divisions. *DRZW 4*, 456–58.

30. Mawdsley, *Thunder*, 66–69. See also the war diary of the 29th Motorized Infantry Division: 29. Motorisierte Infanterie-Division/Ia, War diary, July 13–18, 1941, RH 26-29/6, BA-MA.

31. Only the apologetic and tendentious work of Paul Carell [Paul Karl Schmidt], *Unternehmen Barbarossa: Der Marsch nach Russland* (Frankfurt am Main: Ullstein, 1963), 79–80 mentions the battle. For a detailed approach to the battle, see VII. Armee-Korps/Ia, War diary entry July 18–27, 1941, RH 24-7/40, BA-MA, and the after-action reports from the operations section ("Die Erstürmung des befestigten Brückenkopfes Mohilew," August 15, 1941, RH 24-7/43, BA-MA), and from the quartermaster section (Gefechtsbericht über "Die Schlacht um Mogilew," July 31, 1941, RH 24-7/48, BA-MA). See also 23. Infanterie-Division/Ia, Gefechtsbericht über die Schlacht um Mogilew, July 29, 1941, RH 24-7/48, BA-MA.

32. Mawdsley, *Thunder*, 60–65, 78.

33. Ibid., 64. For Leningrad, especially with detailed numbers, see David M. Glantz, *The Battle for Leningrad, 1941–1944* (Lawrence: University Press of Kansas, 2002), 39–40, 125–29.

34. When fighting inside cities, these units had at least minor combat value by simply defending fortified positions to the death in places where the Germans could not make full use of their superiority in maneuver and air support. Because of leadership errors, however, these units were often enough used in open field battles with predictable results.

35. *DRZW 4*, 514–15.

36. XXIX. Armee-Korps/Ia, War diary entry September 24–29, 1941, RH 24-29/9, BA-MA. See also XXIX. Armee-Korps/Ic, Tätigkeitsbericht, September 20–30, 1941, RH 24-29/77, BA-MA.

37. See XXIX. Armee-Korps/Ic, Betr.: Fernzündungen, September 17, 1941, RH 24-29/29, BA-MA. See also XXIX. Armee-Korps/Ic, Tätigkeitsbericht, September 16, 1941, RH 24-29/76, BA-MA.

38. The term originates with Theodor Ropp; see Karl-Heinz Frieser, *Blitzkrieg-Legende: Der Westfeldzug, 1940* (Munich: Oldenbourg, 1995), 37.

39. Literature on this battle is rare, since it took place during the much more examined Kiev campaign. Most standard works do not even mention the battle. *DRZW 4*, 512 gives only a minor assessment. The best analysis

can be found in the newer divisional history: Dieter Hoffmann, *Die Magdeburger Division: Zur Geschichte der 13. Infanterie- und 13. Panzer-Division, 1939–1945* (Hamburg: Mittler & Sohn, 2001), 132–37. For a more detailed examination of the battle, see Wettstein, "Operation 'Barbarossa' und Stadtkampf," 31–43.

40. In the remaining months of 1941, but also for the 1942 summer campaign (Case "Blau"), Dnipropetrovsk became the eye of the needle as a result of this bridge being blown up. Until the very end of 1942, when the Germans finally repaired the bridge, all supply goods had to be unloaded and ferried across the river and loaded on to trains again.

41. Dnipropetrovsk was one of the centers of Soviet aluminium production.

42. Hoffmann, *Magdeburger Division*, 133.

43. III. Armee-Korps (mot.)/Ia, Karten zur Operation "Barbarossa," RH 24-3/63k, BA-MA; 13. Panzer-Division/Ia, Karten zum KTB Nr. 5 Abt. Ia, RH 27-13/47k, BA-MA; 60. Infanterie-Division (mot.)/Ia, Karten zu KTB, RH 26-60/50k, BA-MA; 198. Infanterie-Division/Ia, Karten zum KTB Nr. 6 Abt. Ia, RH 26-198/12k, BA-MA.

44. III. Armee-Korps (mot.)/Ic, Anlagen zum Tätigkeitsbericht Nr. 1 (Mappe Dnjepropetrowsk), RH 24-3/140, BA-MA. The one for the northeastern riverside is an arranged aerial photograph.

45. This unit was part of the 60th Motorized Infantry Division.

46. This was the "Fifth" Infantry Battalion of the 13th Panzer Division.

47. German terms are "Führen von Vorne" and "Führen durch Auftrag," better known as "Auftragstaktik." Frieser, *Blitzkrieg-Legende*, 421–24.

48. Panzer-Gruppe 1/O.Qu., War diary entry September 5, 1941, RH 21-1/327, BA-MA.

49. On Babi Yar, see Christian Hartmann, *Wehrmacht im Ostkrieg: Front und militärisches Hinterland, 1941/42* (Munich: Oldenbourg, 2009), 297–303; Wolfram Wette, *Die Wehrmacht: Feindbilder, Vernichtungskrieg, Legenden* (Frankfurt am Main: S. Fischer, 2002), 115–28; Dieter Pohl, *Die Herrschaft der Wehrmacht: Deutsche Militärbesatzung und einheimische Bevölkerung in der Sowjetunion, 1941–1944* (Munich: Oldenbourg, 2008), 259–261; and Klaus-Jochen Arnold, "Die Eroberung und Behandlung der Stadt Kiew durch die Wehrmacht im September 1941: Zur Radikalisierung der Besatzungspolitik," *Militärgeschichtliche Mitteilungen* 58 (1999): 23–63.

50. In 1942 and 1943, plans for taking the city by assault were renewed, suggesting that the commanders on the spot never fully accepted the extermination by siege, often for operational—not humane—reasons, or tried to avoid taking responsibility for this crime.

51. See I./Schützen-Regiment 66/Kdr., Gefechtsbericht des I. Bataillon/Schützenregiment 66 vom 25. und 26.8.1941, RH 27-13/46, fol. 4, BA-MA.

52. The German navy, for example, demanded the preservation of the shipyards at Leningrad.

53. The Red Army relied heavily on grenade launchers, well supported with ammunition. German units reported up to more than half of their losses to grenade launchers; several fire raids were carried out daily, each with four hundred to five hundred grenades. See Kradschützen-Bataillon 160/Kdr., Gefechtsbericht über den Einsatz des Btl. im Brückenkopf Dnjepropetrowsk vom 28.8.–10.9.41, RH 26-60/39, BA-MA, 2.

54. Pionier-Bataillon 160/Kdr., Betr. Lenkung des feindl. Art.-Feuers durch Spione hinter der Front, RH 21-1/214, BA-MA.

55. Letter Ic III. A.K. (mot.) to the Commander of the Rear Area of Army Group South of September 21, 1941, RH 24-3/135, BA-MA.

56. See weekly reports in RH 26-60/37, BA-MA.

57. See divisional medic files of the 60th Motorized Infantry Division in RH 26-60/71, BA-MA. Loss statistics can be reconstructed by daily reports of the 198th Infantry Division to the 3rd Motorized Army Corps; see RH 26-198/93, BA-MA.

58. 60. Infanterie-Division (mot.)/Ia, daily reports September 2, 1941, RH 26-60/37, BA-MA.

59. See 198. Infanterie-Division/Ib, Täglicher Versorgungslagebericht Nr. 30–32, September 2–4, 1941, RH 26-198/93, BA-MA.

60. Situation report by *Oberst* [Kurt] Zeitzler to [*Generalfeldmarschall* Walther von] Brauchitsch on September 8 [1941], RH 21-1/51, 14–15, BA-MA.

61. The information is based on three reports: 60. Infanterie-Division/IVb, Tätigkeitsbericht für die Zeit vom 11.–25.8.41, Anlage 377; Tätigkeitsbericht für die Zeit vom 26.8.–17.11.41, Anlage 375; and Bergung, Versorgung und Abtransport im Brückenkopf Dnjepropetrowsk, Anlage 376; all in RH 26-60/71, BA-MA.

62. Simon Folkard and Philip Tucker, "Shift Work, Safety, and Productivity," *Occupational Medicine* 53 (2003): 95–101.

63. 198. Infanterie-Division/IVb, Tätigkeitsbericht 15.8–31.10.41, RH 26-198/94, BA-MA.

64. German medic units were low on the priority list for equipment. They felt more than other services the lack of vehicles and often received older ones. This led to an above average breakdown rate, and since they already possessed a lower number of vehicles it frequently resulted in a temporary paralysis.

65. An artillery map of the 60th Motorized Infantry Division from September 2, 1941, indicated at least seven different types of artillery guns.

66. 198. Infanterie-Division/Ib, Munitionswesen, RH 26-198/91, BA-MA.

67. Panzer-Gruppe 1/0.Qu., War diary entry for September 6, 1941, RH 21-1/327, BA-MA. The number looks extremely high and is to be questioned. But all units reported enormous use of ammunition. The 13th Panzer Division alone used 661.9 tons of munitions between August 19 and September 7, 1941, see 13. Panzer-Division/W.u.G., Tätigkeitsbericht 18.8.–7.9.41,

RH 27-13/128, BA-MA. The equipment staff officer (Ib/W.u.G.) of the 60th Motorized Infantry Division mentioned that the use of ammunition was five to six times as high as expected. 60. Infanterie-Division (mot.)/W.u.G., Betr. Beitrag zum Kriegstagebuch (Anlage 369), RH 26-60/71, BA-MA.

68. Panzer-Gruppe 1/Ib, War diary entry for August 20, 1941, RH 21-1/327, BA-MA.

69. Ibid., September 6, 1941.

70. A Waffen-SS division formed from Hitler's bodyguard.

71. This was not a singular action. On August 27, 1941, the 13th Panzer Division had to send a column to Bialacerkiev to collect a replacement battalion, and four days later the division again had to free up 144 vehicles to bring up an engineer battalion. See 13. Panzer-Division/Ib, War diary entries for August 27 and 31, 1941, RH 27-13/126, BA-MA.

72. Glantz, *Battle for Leningrad*, 9. The industrial potential of the Leningrad area can also be seen from the production number for the period from June 22 to December 31, 1941: beyond an unknown number of small arms production, the Leningrad area provided 3 million shells and mines, 40,000 multiple rocket launcher rounds, 42,000 bombs, but also 491 tanks from the Kirov factory and 317 artillery pieces (Glantz, *Battle for Leningrad*, 130).

73. Percy Ernst Schramm, ed., *Kriegstagebuch des Oberkommandos der Wehrmacht (Wehrmachtführungsstab) 1940–1945*, vol. 1, *1. August 1940– 31. Dezember 1941*, ed. Hans-Adolf Jacobsen (Bonn, 1965; repr., Munich: Bernard & Graefe, 1982), 1020 (hereafter OKW war diary).

74. Ibid., 1021.

75. This clearly contradicts Ganzenmüller, who asserts that it meant no ground operation against Leningrad; see *Das belagerte Leningrad*, 33. The "Sonderakte" of the OKW diary mentions: "Army Group North will presumably with its forces at hand fulfill its mission to push to Leningrad." OKW war diary, 1:1021. Ganzenmüller bases his analysis on Halder's reception ("Tanks must not be employed for it"), but even this is not a clear indication against ground operations, since the German army had had negative experiences with the use of tanks inside cities (e.g., Warsaw).

76. Führererwägung am 17.7.1941, OKW war diary, 1:1029. According to Ganzenmüller, Halder mentioned the mission of encircling Leningrad on July 15, 1941. But he made no reference to any official order (53).

77. Besuch des Führers bei Heeres-Gruppe Nord am 21. Juli 1941, OKW war diary, 1:1029–30.

78. Besprechung des Chefs OKW mit Oberbefehlshaber der Heeresgruppe Mitte am 25. Juli 1941, OKW war diary, 1:1034. This was the first time that plans for "starving out" Leningrad were mentioned in operational circles, though the intention to starve out both Leningrad and Moscow had already been recorded in comprehensive economic policy guidelines issued by the agricultural section of the Economic Staff East on May 23, 1941. See

"Wirtschaftspolitische Richtlinien für Wirtschaftsorganisation Ost, Gruppe Landwirtschaft," Doc. 126-EC, May 23, 1941, in International Military Tribunal, ed., *Der Prozess gegen die Hauptkriegsverbrecher vor dem Internationalen Militärgerichtshof, Nürnberg, 14. November 1945–1. Oktober 1946*, vol. 36 (Nuremberg: Sekretariat des Gerichtshofs, 1949), 135–57, here 138, 141, 145.

79. Erwägungen und Anordnungen des Führer am 28. Juli 1941, OKW war diary, 1:1036.

80. Besprechung gelegentlich Anwesenheit des Führers und Obersten Befehlshabers der Wehrmacht bei Heeresgruppe Mitte am 4. August 1941, OKW war diary, 1:1042.

81. For a detailed approach, see *DRZW* 4, 540–54; and David Stahel, *Operation Barbarossa and Germany's Defeat in the East* (Cambridge: Cambridge University Press, 2009); see also Ganzenmüller, *Das belagerte Leningrad*, 30–32.

82. The most detailed study on the frontline command in the Leningrad area, the Eighteenth Army, is still Johannes Hürter, "Die Wehrmacht vor Leningrad: Krieg und Besatzungspolitik der 18. Armee im Herbst und Winter 1941/42," *Vierteljahreshefte für Zeitgeschichte* 49, no. 3 (2001): 377–440. See also Jörg Friedrich, *Das Gesetz des Krieges: Das deutsche Heer in Russland, 1941 bis 1945: Der Prozess gegen das Oberkommando der Wehrmacht* (Munich: Piper, 1993), 424–25.

83. Heeresgruppe Nord/Ia, Heeresgruppen-Befehl Nr. 3 für die Fortführung des Angriffs, August 21, 1941, RH-19 III/562, BA-MA. The order points out that the final decision about the "continuation of the attack against Leningrad lay with the Führer," which meant that there was still no definitive decision about whether to attack or besiege the city. Eight days later, in a further army group order, the occupation force for the city was already mentioned. Heeresgruppe Nord/Ia, Heeresgruppen-Befehl Nr. 1 für die Einschliessung der Stadt Leningrad, August 29, 1941, RH-19 III/562, BA-MA. This can be seen as evidence that the Army Group command did not expect a long siege, but rather a quick capitulation.

84. Ganzenmüller, *Das belagerte Leningrad*, 24–26. This was the same General Reinhardt who tried to storm Warsaw on September 8 and 9, 1939.

85. See also Ganzenmüller, *Das belagerte Leningrad*, 25–27.

86. Alex J. Kay, *Exploitation, Resettlement, Mass Murder: Political and Economic Planning for German Occupation Policy in the Soviet Union, 1940–1941* (New York: Berghahn, 2006); *DRZW* 4, 989–1022; and Christian Gerlach, *Krieg, Ernährung, Völkermord: Forschungen zur deutschen Vernichtungspolitik im Zweiten Weltkrieg* (Hamburg: Hamburger Edition, 1998), 13–17.

87. Abteilung Landesverteidigung, Vortragsnotiz Leningrad, September 21, 1941, RW 4/578, BA-MA. On this document see also: *DRZW* 4, 551–52.

88. Heeresgruppenkommando Nord/Ia, Fernschreiben an AOK 18, October 17, 1941, RH-19 III/562, BA-MA.

89. Fernspruch HGR Nord an OKH/Op.Abt., September 25, 1941, 19:45 Uhr, RH 19 III/766, BA-MA.

90. See, for example, Heeresgruppenkommando Nord/Ia, Beurteilung der Lage, September 20, 1941, RH-19 III/766, BA-MA. Hunger is mentioned here too; not in the sense of the hunger strategy, but more as a last resort to bring the defenders to terms.

91. Heeresgruppenkommando Nord/Ia, War diary entry October 12, 1941, RH-19 III/168, BA-MA. "The Führer has again decided that a capitulation of Leningrad is not to be accepted."

92. *DRZW 4*, 552. This discussion is completely missing in Ganzenmüller.

93. See *DRZW 4*, 843–44.

94. *DRZW 4*, 555–59. Such plans were discussed for Moscow too in October and November 1941. But it seems much more unrealistic that such a strategy could have been implemented, because of the very different traffic situation of Leningrad and Moscow. Leningrad was for the German advance in a peripheral position, whereas Moscow was a traffic center. The supplying of siege forces around Moscow without possession of the urban traffic network would have become a very difficult task. Beyond that, the final German siege line would have laid within the city, causing all kinds of control problems. See: *DRZW 4*, 589.

95. Generalquartiermeister, Abteilung Heeresversorgung. Gellermann reproduces in full the so-called Leningrad file: Günther W. Gellermann, *Der Krieg, der nicht stattfand: Möglichkeiten, Überlegungen, und Entscheidungen der deutschen Obersten Führung zur Verwendung chemischer Kampfstoffe im Zweiten Weltkrieg* (Koblenz: Bernard & Graefe, 1986), 234–41. For a different position, see Olaf Groehler, *Der lautlose Tod* (Berlin: Rowohlt, 1984).

96. Gellermann, *Krieg*, 239.

97. This is the German military term for mustard gas, originating from the names of LOmmel and STeinkopf, who first proposed the military use of sulphur mustard to the imperial army in World War I. Gellermann, *Krieg*, 24–26.

98. It is interesting to note that Gellermann as well as Ganzenmüller followed the sources in not stressing this point further. Gellerman, *Krieg*, 146–49; and Ganzenmüller, *Das belagerte Leningrad*, 71–72.

99. The spiral of radicalization is also described in Hartmann, *Wehrmacht im Ostkrieg*, 250–423.

CHAPTER 3

THE WEHRMACHT IN THE WAR OF IDEOLOGIES

The Army and Hitler's Criminal Orders on the Eastern Front

Felix Römer

With the attack of the German Eastern Army on the Soviet Union at daybreak on June 22, 1941, the "most monstrous war of conquest, enslavement, and annihilation that modern history has known" began.[1] The war on the Eastern Front ultimately devoured about twenty-seven million human lives on the Soviet side and became the scene of significant stages within the Holocaust and further unprecedented crimes in which the army played a primary role from the outset. The repercussions ultimately struck back at the invaders themselves and contributed in this way to making the Eastern Front the central theater of World War II, in which the Wehrmacht suffered its most costly and, in the end, most decisive defeats.[2] The course set in spring 1941, which already prior to the start of Operation Barbarossa committed the German Eastern Army to the most radical and criminal waging of war imaginable, seems in hindsight all the more grave. The decision for this can be traced back to Hitler himself, who had instructed that the "crusade against bolshevism" be waged as an unlimited "conflict of annihilation." At the same time, Hitler's demands put the Wehrmacht's conception of itself to the test. Never before had the German armed forces been issued orders, as happened shortly after, that amounted to blatant, systematic breaches of the law. It now remained to be seen whether the Wehrmacht was rightly mistrusted by the National Socialist rulers as a "gray rock in the brown tide" or not.[3]

The planning for the war of ideologies was initiated in March 1941 through a series of meetings at the highest level, at which the supreme commander of the Wehrmacht prepared his generals for the coming campaign as not a conventional recourse to arms but rather a "conflict of two ideologies"[4] which, therefore, made the application of the "most brutal means necessary."[5] Shortly after, Hitler also swore the troop commanders of the Eastern Army in on "assisting in the struggle of ideologies."[6] In his formative speech in Berlin's Reich Chancellery on March 30, 1941, which was attended, among others, by all army group and army commanders of the Eastern Army, Hitler established that the war against the Soviet Union would be a "struggle for survival" that would have to diverge from the previous "pattern."[7] In the struggle against the Soviet Union, the army would have to "move away from the position of soldierly camaraderie"—even the military opponent was "beforehand no comrade and afterward no comrade" (*vorher kein Kamerad und nachher kein Kamerad*).[8] Hitler's demands also included the radicalization of martial jurisdiction in the occupied territories: military justice toward all "criminals" in the conquered territories had been "too humane" and "protected them instead of killing them."[9] The rigorous elimination of any impulse to resist, however, was "no question of courts-martial"; rather, the formations at the front would have to take matters into their own hands: "The troops must defend themselves with those means with which they are attacked."[10] In order to justify the premeditated, radical approach against Soviet political officers, the supreme commander presented to his generals the "crimes of the Russian commissars" and concluded that they "deserve no mercy." Hitler commissioned the army's front formations themselves with the "annihilation of the Bolshevist commissars":[11] "Not to be court-martialed, but eliminated immediately by the troops. Not to be sent to the rear."[12]

When the troop commanders gathered in the Reich Chancellery failed to disagree with the intended criminal waging of war, a time of reckoning had struck for the German military. The compliance of the branches of the Wehrmacht could also be seen in the central offices of the High Command of the Wehrmacht (*Oberkommando der Wehrmacht*, or OKW) and the High Command of the Army (*Oberkommando des Heeres*, or OKH), where shortly after the meeting work on written orders was taken up in order to realize Hitler's instructions. The initiative for this presumably came from the Army General Staff and its chief, *Generaloberst* Franz Halder.[13] Between the beginning of May and the beginning of June 1941, the General Staff officers and Wehrmacht lawyers in Berlin eventually finalized both "Führer decrees" that would later go down in history as the Criminal Orders (*verbrecherische Befehle*): the "Decree on the Exercise of Martial Jurisdiction in the Area 'Barbarossa' and Special Measures of the Troops" (*Erlaß über die Ausübung der Kriegsgerichtsbarkeit im Gebiet 'Barbarossa' und über besondere Maßnahmen der Truppe*) from May 13, 1941 (the Martial Jurisdiction Decree), and the "Guidelines for the Treatment of Political Commissars" (*Richtlinien für die Behandlung politischer Kommissare*) from June 6, 1941 (the Commissar Order).[14] Also belonging to the complex of orders were further decrees, leaflets, and directives, which had likewise been produced in order to transform the imminent German-Soviet War into an ideological "struggle of annihilation," as demanded by Hitler. The "Regulations on the Deployment of the Security Police and the SD in Army Formations" (*Regelung des Einsatzes der Sicherheitspolizei und des SD im Verbande des Heeres*), adopted on April 28, 1941, sealed the Wehrmacht's cooperation with the *Einsatzgruppen* of the Reich Security Main Office (*Reichssicherheitshauptamt*, or RSHA) and cleared the way for the annihilation of Soviet Jewry.[15] The "Guidelines for the Conduct of the Troops in Russia" (*Richtlinien für das Verhalten der Truppe in Russland*) from May 19, 1941, committed the troops to a "ruthless and energetic clampdown on Bolshevist agitators, guerrillas, saboteurs, Jews and [the] complete removal of all active and passive resistance," and contributed in this way to the incitement of the troops at the front.[16] The leaflets released on Hitler's instructions by the front staffs, which warned the combat formations of the alleged "cruelty" and "perfidiousness" of the Red Army and gave the troops carte blanche to carry out measures of retribution, fulfilled a similar purpose.[17] At the center of the complex of orders, however, were the Martial Jurisdiction Decree and the Commissar Order, which for the first time demanded that the army itself commit murder, and became in this way symbols for the "involvement of the Wehrmacht in the National Socialist policy of extermination."[18]

In place of the henceforth annulled traditional military justice over the civilian population in the occupied territories, the Martial Jurisdiction Decree allowed the troops to take action themselves.[19] The primary clause stated that "offences committed by enemy civilians" were to be removed from the "responsibility of the courts-martial and military courts until further notice." Any "elements suspected of criminal action" (*tatverdächtige Elemente*) taken prisoner should be summoned to the nearest officer, who was to decide promptly as to "whether they are to be shot." The capture and detainment of "suspect perpetrators" (*verdächtige Täter* [!]) was "expressly forbidden." In the event that following attacks on the troops no perpetrators could be seized, the Jurisdiction Decree granted furthermore all troop commanders from battalion commander upward the right to initiate "collective violent measures" (*kollektive Gewaltmaßnahmen*). The OKH recommended for the practical implementation of these reprisals to immediately "shoot thirty men" in the locality concerned.[20] In the second section of the Jurisdiction Decree, the obligatory criminal prosecution of "offences committed by members of the Wehrmacht" against the Soviet civilian population was annulled. Provided that it did not relate to actions resulting from "sexual abandon" or "a criminal disposition," the responsible judge, as a rule a divisional commander, could leave it at a disciplinary penalty in place of court-martial proceedings. Before the decree was passed on to the Eastern Army, the commander in chief of the army, *Generalfeldmarschall* Walther von Brauchitsch, added comments on May 24, 1941, that primarily met widespread concerns that the order could abet "arbitrary excesses of *individual* members of the army" and ultimately lead to a "brutalization of the troops."[21] These remarks, however, altered nothing when it came to the radical provisions of the Martial Jurisdiction Decree. At meetings held by those responsible in the OKW and the OKH in May and June 1941 in order to peruse the issued Führer decrees with representatives of the Eastern Army, additional accentuations were even added. The most consequential innovation of the Jurisdiction Decree remained, however, the introduction of executions without legal proceedings. According to the hitherto existing legal regulations, the sentencing of irregulars necessitated proceedings before a court-martial, of which there were only around a dozen in a typical Wehrmacht division, military courts of the regimental commanders included. In contrast, after the Martial Jurisdiction Decree came into effect all officers, the number of which in a full strength division amounted to over five hundred men, could henceforth make decisions concerning life and death. This universalization of executive power, the envisaged reprisals on the basis of mere suspicion, and the creation of a lawless region through the abolition of obligatory criminal prosecution made the Martial Jurisdiction Decree a deeply radical order that was to form the basis of German tyranny in the occupied Soviet Union.

The Commissar Order enjoined the systematic murder of regular, uniformed prisoners of war on the German front troops. They were directed at those Soviet political officers who were integrated into the Red Army in order to supervise the units. The central provision stated that all political commissars—who could be identified on the basis of their insignia, the "red star with golden woven hammer and sickle on the sleeves"—falling into German captivity were to be segregated "already on the battlefield" from the remaining prisoners of war and subsequently to be executed promptly: "These commissars are not to be recognized as soldiers; the protection due to prisoners of war under international war does not apply to them. Once they have been separated out, they are to be finished off."[22] For the nonmilitary "commissars," that is, the functionaries of the Soviet party and civil administration, the same fate was not necessarily foreseen. First of all, it had to be verified whether they were "guilty of a hostile action" or were "suspected of such." The procedure with the civilian functionaries ultimately, however, remained at the discretion of the troop officers, on whom the decision as to the "question of 'guilty or not guilty'" was incumbent.

Behind the Criminal Orders were both ideological and pragmatic considerations. The Commissar Order constituted an ideologically motivated program of murder that pursued first and foremost a radical end in itself in accordance with the intended "annihilation of bolshevism." Since both Nazis and many soldiers considered bolshevism a Communist tyranny dominated by Jews, and the party functionaries in the Red Army were thus commonly suspected of being of Jewish origin, the Commissar Order also relied on widespread German anti-Semitism, even if these allegations were not mentioned in the decree itself. Simultaneously, the systematic suppression of the "bearers of resistance" in the Red Army also served the aim of accelerating the military collapse of the Soviet Union. The Martial Jurisdiction Decree, on the other hand, on the basis of an ideologically distorted image of Russia, acted on the premise that the troops in the Soviet Union would encounter an "incited" and "bolshevized" civilian population that would make "special measures" urgently necessary. At the same time, the radicalization of occupation policy was also regarded as a military necessity. In order to safeguard the envisaged trouble-free progress of operations, it seemed essential to quickly bring the rear under control. The condition of "combat at the front, quiet in the rear" (*vorn Kampf, hinten Ruhe*)[23] should be established as soon as possible and with all force: the motto was deterrence through terror, particularly as the enormous expansion of the theater of war seemed to urge radical solutions that promised maximum benefit with minimum effort.[24] In this way, the Criminal Orders were a part of Hitler's ludicrous colonial plans for the conquest of living space (*Lebensraum*) and the associated racial-ideological annihilation policy. Simultaneously, they were conceived as catalysts for the Blitzkrieg strategy, a commitment to the military aim of more quickly bringing about the downfall of the Soviet colossus.

In the postwar period, veterans and apologists vehemently disputed that the Criminal Orders had ever been disclosed to the formations of the Eastern Army, let alone carried out. In this respect, the Federal German Republic's "politics addressing the past" (*Vergangenheitspolitik*) of the 1940s and 1950s was only ruptured in the late 1970s and early 1980s, when the first studies appeared that demonstrated, through the use of a broad range of sources, that large numbers of German combat units on the Eastern Front had indeed carried out executions of captured Soviet political officers and countless civilians.[25] Even these pioneering studies, however, could only rely on a sample from the files of the Eastern Army; a complete analysis of all records from the Eastern Front was yet to be carried out until very recently. The less than exhaustive research on this topic allowed for the question of how German formations in the Soviet Union dealt with the Commissar Order and the Martial Jurisdiction Decree to remain one of controversy. In spite of numerous research results to the contrary, a standard textbook that addressed the Commissar Order still stated in 2004 that merely "several hundred prisoners" had been "shot on the order of individual officers,"[26] although almost one thousand execution reports had already been cited in the relevant literature and it was beyond all question that even these figures by no means reflected the entire extent of the murders. The comprehensive evaluation of the records of all 12 armies and panzer groups, the more than 40 corps, and all of the almost 150 divisions that were deployed on the Eastern Front in 1941–42, which was recently carried out, however, has now been able to achieve far-reaching clarity on the handling of the Criminal Orders in the Eastern Army.

The application of the Criminal Orders already began when the weapons were still silent. During the final phase of preparations for the campaign, the transmission of the Führer decrees to the front formations moved on to the agenda, so that the first situation emerged in which the troop leaders had to decide how they would deal with the orders. Aside from minor differences, the transmission of the decrees to all commands followed roughly the same pattern. The Martial Jurisdiction Decree was sent on May 31, 1941, to the high commands of the army groups, the armies, and the panzer groups, and in most cases during the first half of June it was passed on in written form down as far as the divisional staffs. The Commissar Order had been circulated on June 8, 1941, though it may have been passed on below army level only orally. During the week of June 12 to 19, 1941, the army high commands informed the staffs of all subordinate corps and divisions about the guidelines. After the decrees had been received by the divisional staffs, the divisional commanders addressed the subject at the closing deployment meetings with the commanders of the regiments and battalions. The noncommissioned officers and the enlisted men in the companies were, as a rule, only on the day before the attack instructed by their unit commanders on the provisions of the Criminal Orders that were relevant for them. In all armies and panzer groups, the form and framework of the issuing of the orders was the same. In the army high commands, both the responsible intelligence officers and the army judges, whose departments were also affected, held central meetings with the relevant departmental heads of the subordinate corps and divisions. To some extent, the commanders of the armies and corps exerted their authority in order to personally disclose the decrees to their subordinates. Thus, the issuing of the Criminal Orders to the troop formations of the Eastern Army took place simultaneously via several parallel chains of command with remarkable bureaucratic routine. In total, clear evidence exists for almost 60 percent of all command authorities of the Eastern Army that the criminal Führer decrees were transmitted to their troops, as ordered: a high percentage in light of the gaps in the records, the concentration of files on the later events of the war, and the tendency to omit these incidents from the records.[27]

In their dealings with the Führer decrees, most commanders assumed a standpoint that was decidedly consistent with the orders. In more than a few staffs, the orders were even unreservedly approved of. Thus, the commander of the 134th Infantry Division, *Generalleutnant* Conrad von Cochenhausen, instructed his subordinates during a deployment meeting on June 16, 1941, on the core provisions of the Martial Jurisdiction Decree:

> Only strength impresses the opponent. Courts-martial and military courts are abolished. Whoever even attempts to resist, even passively, will be shot without further ado. Every officer is permitted to immediately pass a sentence of death. This is an order from the Führer that is to be made known to the enlisted men. In old Germany, such an order would not have been possible, for no one would have had the courage to issue it.[28]

The Commissar Order guidelines also had their resolute advocates. The commander of the Eighteenth Army, for example, *Generaloberst* Georg von Küchler, regarded the Soviet political commissars and party functionaries as criminals and hoped that the policy of annihilation against them would also bring a military benefit: "When it becomes known that we immediately put the political commissars and GPU people in front of military courts, it is to be hoped that the Russian troops and the populace liberate themselves from this servitude. In any case, we want to apply these means. It saves German blood and we make swift progress."[29] Some commanders even expanded the program of murder. Thus, the commander of the Eleventh Army, *Generaloberst* Eugen Ritter von Schobert, ordered not only all captured political officers of the Red Army but also all "political commissars of the civil administration to be shot without further ado" as a matter of course, although the guidelines in no way required this.[30] Such independent, radicalizing stimuli attest particularly strikingly that the Commissar Order was in no way accepted merely out of opportunism, but was met rather with express approval by significant sections of the Eastern Army.

While the majority of the troop leaders accepted the Criminal Orders without hesitation and some even expressly endorsed them, criticism of the planned radical measures stirred among a minority of commanders. As a result of their reservations, some commanders even made the decision to intervene by independently modifying the regulations of the Führer decrees. Thus, on the day before the attack, the leadership of the 296th Infantry Division under *Generalmajor* Wilhelm Stemmermann released rules for the "treatment of enemy civilians" that in essence concurred with the "harsh measures" foreseen by the Martial Jurisdiction Decree but deviated from them when it came to the details.[31] The division altered in a decisive point paragraph I.4 of the decree, which stated: "Where such measures were neglected or were not initially possible, *persons suspected of criminal action will be brought at once before an officer. This officer will decide whether they are to be shot*," and instead ordered its troops: "If such measures were neglected or were not initially possible, *persons suspected of criminal action* are to be brought at once before an officer with the powers of a dependent battalion commander. This officer will decide whether the suspect is to be shot or released."[32] While according to the original regulations, every single one of the roughly five hundred officers present in a full-strength division could initiate shootings at their own discretion, according to the construction of the 296th Infantry Division only the few departmental, battalion, and regimental commanders, who numbered not even two dozen officers, were entitled to do so. With this alteration, the divisional leadership had admittedly not invalidated the Martial Jurisdiction Decree, but at least they considerably toned it down in respect of a decisive point. The Commissar Order guidelines were also met in some staffs with such strong reservations that some commanders decided to alter the command status. Thus, *Generalleutnant* John Ansat, the commander of the 102nd Infantry Division, was up in arms about his soldiers being "no hangman's assistants" and curtailed the guidelines with regulatory annexes to the order.[33] He forbade his troops to carry out shootings of captured commissars themselves. At the same time, however, he ordered that political officers should at least be separated out and delivered to "other units" such as the field gendarmerie or the SS commandos, who should assume the executions. As in this case, the limited interventions by critics of the Commissar Order generally took the form of work-sharing procedures that in the end changed nothing regarding the ultimate goal of the policy of annihilation and in fact eased its realization by means of the atomization of the course of action and responsibility for it.

The objections to the Criminal Orders were based partly on military-functional concerns and partly on moral-traditional reluctance. The most weighty and widespread reservation consisted of the pragmatic concern about negative repercussions on military discipline within the troop formations. No provision aroused so much skepticism as the abolition of obligatory criminal prosecution in the case of violent acts by Wehrmacht soldiers against civilians, as contained in the Martial Jurisdiction Decree. The empowerment of the troops to carry out independent executions, whether of civilians or commissars, was also met with concern. The criticism was largely limited to anxiety about a brutalization (*Verwilderung*) of the soldiers and did not exclude a fundamental concurrence with the principles of the Criminal Orders. Even a hardliner like *Generalfeldmarschall* Walter von Reichenau, who revealed himself particularly early to be a decided advocate of the radical Führer decrees, warned that the troops could fall into a "delirium of shooting" and get out of control.[34] Most commanders met these concerns by combining the announcement of the Criminal Orders with insistent calls for the maintenance of military discipline, but which otherwise did not question the provisions of the decrees. Behind the stereotypical appeals for the observance of male discipline (*Wahrung der Manneszucht*) was the fear of a reduction in the military effectiveness of the formations, which from the point of view of the success-orientated troop leaders had to be given top priority. Possible humanitarian empathy with the suffering civilian population, which many Wehrmacht generals in any case viewed with racist contempt, appeared in contrast to be clearly secondary. The aversion to uncontrolled, arbitrary acts and independent excesses, however, was due not least to the traditional self-perception of the Wehrmacht and related notions of honor. This manifested itself particularly clearly in the isolated cases of proven criticism of the Commissar Order guidelines, which not only aroused concern for military discipline but at the same time ran contrary in some units "to soldierly feelings."[35] The established ethics of the Wehrmacht articulated themselves above all in that the planned procedure against political officers within the military was resented first and foremost because they were very evidently regular combatants, whilst the measures directed at civilian functionaries were commonly met with hardly any protest.

The very target and scope of the modifications applied to the Criminal Orders by some troop leaders reveal, however, that the concerns of the commanders revolved around their own troops rather than the victims. The interventions in the guidelines merely led to a special and institutional shifting of the program of murder and served above all to relieve the front troops, who nevertheless continued as a rule to make an essential contribution to the selection of the political officers. The alterations to the Martial Jurisdiction Decree were not aimed at a complete revision of the policy of violence, but rather first and foremost at a higher degree of control over the application of reprisals. Hardly any commander thought of completely avoiding any participation in the realization of the Criminal Orders. This was not only the result of an absolute duty to obey and loyalty toward the Führer. Approval of the Führer decrees arose above all from the widely shared consensus on the necessity of the campaign against the Soviet Union and the goal of the extermination of bolshevism. Militant anticommunism was already deeply rooted in the socialization of the Wehrmacht elite and had received an additional radicalizing stimulus as a result of the experience of military defeat and revolution in the years 1918–19. Thus, barely any of the deeply anti-Bolshevist troop leaders in the Eastern Army doubted that the forthcoming war was to be an existential conflict with an unscrupulous deadly enemy in which all and every means were justified; indeed special measures even appeared essential. The identification with the ideological premises of Operation Barbarossa manifested itself particularly clearly in the widespread concurrence with the demonic concept of the Soviet commissars that was at the center of the strategy of legitimizing the annihilation policy directed against them. The advocacy of the uncompromising concept of pacification that was contained in the Martial Jurisdiction Decree resulted furthermore from an identification with the Blitzkrieg strategy, for the success of which a radicalization of the occupation regime seemed indispensable. Similar expectations banded together with the Commissar Order because it was directed against the alleged mainstays of the Red Army, so that there seemed to be very rational reasons for concurring with the policy of violence.

The acceptance of the Criminal Orders was furthered by their partial location in the continuity of earlier practices and conceptual traditions dating back a long way to the previous century. Thus, the Martial Jurisdiction Decree was at least in part covered by international law and could furthermore draw on a long prehistory. At the latest since the confrontation with the *franc-tireurs*, during the Franco-Prussian War of 1870–71, a fixed understanding had existed within the German military regarding the strict rejection of this form of warfare and the uncompromising suppression of all irregular combatants. This manifested itself anew during World War I, when a "guerrilla psychosis" emerged and massive reprisals were carried out against the civilian population not only during the advance westward but also in the southeastern and eastern theaters.[36]

Many of the later Wehrmacht generals had furthermore experienced the brutal Freikorps battles in the Baltic at the end of World War I and were therefore all the more receptive to the motto that in eastern Europe and the Soviet Union "there can only be a successful clampdown if practices are applied with eastern methods."[37] The idea of the legitimacy of eastern fighting methods[38] was based, however, not only on the immediate experiences of unrestricted violence in this theater of war, but also arose from the widespread racist conviction of the alleged inferiority of the eastern peoples (*Ostvölker*). This distorted perception of the eastern region and its alleged uniqueness also seemed to affirm the validity of the Commissar Order. For the battles of the Freikorps and the Russian Civil War had at the same time created a precedence for the radical course of action against Bolshevik functionaries and military commissars, including a bleak concept of the enemy that could again be seized on in the summer of 1941. Executions without due process and collective reprisals against the enemy civilian population were thus no longer something entirely new in spring 1941. These practices were flanked by the doctrine of total war, which had found its way into the thinking of the military during the interwar period and expressly legitimated the bending of the law as long as it could be justified with military necessity. How effective these traditions were was demonstrated at the beginning of World War II, when the Polish campaign of 1939 as well as the Balkan campaign of 1941 already anticipated aspects of the policy of violence later practised on the Eastern Front.

With the transmission of the Criminal Orders to their troops during the preparatory phase of the campaign, the commanders of the Eastern Army had given proof of their intention to put the decrees into practice. The consequences were logical: both the Martial Jurisdiction Decree and the Commissar Order were ubiquitously implemented in all sections of the Eastern Front from the first day of Operation Barbarossa on. The occupation terror that the formations unfurled on the basis of the Martial Jurisdiction Decree was in no way limited, however, to a "partisan war without partisans."[39] It is true that the cohesive rising of the populace against the invaders called for by Stalin at the beginning of July 1941 failed to materialize, but the beginnings of a Soviet partisan movement did develop during the first year of the war on the Eastern Front. In the first weeks of Operation Barbarossa it was above all dispersed Soviet soldiers, who had fallen behind the front following the destruction of their formations during the course of the German penetration and initially just struggled to survive there, who made up the nucleus of the partisan groups. The radical approach of German formations to the dispersed groups and the civilian population then led until autumn 1941 to a distinct "growth of the partisan movement."[40] Despite or perhaps because of the rigorous retaliatory measures of the German leadership, which responded with "new harsh order[s],"[41] the partisans, supported by the Soviet leadership, received a further influx during the turn of the year 1941/42 and by spring 1942 evidently had a six-figure number of combatants at their disposal.[42] Even if some formations of the Eastern Army again witnessed a virulent "guerrilla psychosis"[43] during the initial phase of the campaign, the threat from illegal combatants in the Soviet theater of war was not always imaginary and their suppression not a priori illegal. Even the death penalty for irregulars was covered by contemporary international law, although court-martial proceedings were mandatory. The threshold to a criminal waging of war was crossed, however, at the moment when the invaders took an expanded concept of "guerrillas" as the basis for their violent measures and carried out executions merely on the basis of suspicion and without legal proceedings, as was prescribed in the Martial Jurisdiction Decree and the supplementary instructions of the senior leadership. The break with international law consisted above all in German reprisals from the outset being directed not only against irregulars but also all too often toward uninvolved villagers, civilians who had been picked up or dispersed Red Army soldiers, who were declared in arbitrary acts of substitution to be "partisan suspects,"[44] "partisan helpers,"[45] or other "suspicious elements"[46] and called to account for "the increasing precariousness"[47] of the occupied territories.

Just how comprehensively the Martial Jurisdiction Decree was implemented on the Eastern Front is demonstrated by the files of the German front formations. There is hardly a division and no corps or army in whose records evidence of executions of Soviet civilians and real and alleged partisans without legal proceedings cannot be found. Thus, for all forty-three corps that lined up on June 22, 1941, for the attack on the Soviet Union, evidence exists for such violent acts.[48] Samples demonstrate that a similarly homogenous picture emerges at a divisional level. Thus, for all divisions of Panzer Group 2, for which a largely intact record of files has been preserved, there is evidence for reprisals carried out on the basis of the Jurisdiction Decree.[49] The systematic evaluation of German file material shows with great clarity that the Martial Jurisdiction Decree was as a rule complied with in the formations of the Eastern Army. Countless reports from the Eastern Army prove with which compliance and ruthlessness the provisions of the order were implemented in the formations. Thus, "eight Russians" were "whacked in short order" (*kurz umgelegt*) by a rifle battalion on the second day of the war because they had allegedly "attempted to carry out sabotage."[50] Another infantry battalion reported two days later to its superior regimental headquarters that during the course of a combing operation "forty-one guerrillas" (*Freischärler*) had been taken prisoner and then "finished off as ordered" (*befehlsgemäss erledigt*).[51] Within a few days after the beginning of operations, "a proportion of civilians had already been shot" by artillery units.[52] It was by no means unusual for troop outfits to observe during the advance in the summer of 1941 that "very often ... corpses of shot civilians [lay] in the streets."[53] The Sixth Army declared at the beginning of December 1941 that in its own section already "several thousand [had] been publicly hanged and shot."[54] One of its infantry divisions reported within three weeks in autumn 1941 alone almost four hundred executions.[55] The "shooting of fifty snipers" by one infantry regiment could occur on a single day.[56]

Even if the Barbarossa Decree was in essence implemented by most troop formations, the practical implementation did vary in its details. Not all formations carried it out with the same resoluteness. Thus, it was not rare for units to circumvent the application of the Martial Jurisdiction Decree by marching off civilians they had picked up to prison installations, although it was expressly forbidden by the Martial Jurisdiction Decree "to *safeguard* suspects." Many command authorities energetically opposed the practice of "shunting those brought forward from one military post to another or bringing them to a prisoner collection point"[57] and forbade their troops "to simply pass on civilian suspects and in this way shift the responsibility."[58] Other staffs, on the other hand, ultimately granted their troops the right to hand over captured civilians to prisoner facilities in order that examinations could be carried out by members of the Secret Field Police (*Geheime Feldpolizei*, or GFP) or the SD. The original alternative of "shooting or release"[59] was, therefore, soon supplemented in part by an additional option: "shooting, prisoner camp, or release."[60] As a result, the troops were admittedly given the option of circumventing the carrying out of reprisals themselves. With the capture and transfer of civilian suspects, however, they continued to make an indispensable contribution to the realization of the policy of reprisals, which also explains why the staffs sometimes yielded and turned a blind eye to the ban on safeguarding.

The freedom offered by the Eastern Front allowed the command authorities to partially reshape the command status. Similarly to what had happened during the preparatory phase for the campaign, some staffs, on the basis of their experiences, resolved during the course of operations in favor of diluting corrections to the orders. The leadership of the 8th Infantry Division, for example, considerably curtailed the statutes of the Führer decree by ordering that the carrying out of death sentences against civilians could take place "only on the order of commanders with at least the disciplinary penal power of a battalion commander and only following an interrogation by the division," although the Martial Jurisdiction Decree had categorically granted this right to all officers.[61] Aside from this, some command authorities also deemed it necessary to additionally regulate the rules for carrying out collective violent measures. The need for action here had evidently also arisen from a much too excessive application in many cases of this provision. As more than a few staffs soon recognized that "with collective measures exactly the opposite"[62] of that intended was achieved, they instructed their units to apply penal measures as prudently as possible, though admittedly without dispensing with this method altogether. Hardly anyone went as far in this respect as the commander of the 4th Mountain Division, who de facto took away from the leaders of his regiments and battalions the right to apply collective reprisals by ordering at the beginning of August 1941: "For the implementation of such collective violent measures, my authorization is to be strictly obtained."[63] However, the pendulum could also be swung in the other direction. Above all during the radicalizing impulses of autumn and winter 1941/42, ever more rigorous basic orders and inflammatory appeals were issued that urged the troops to proceed "mercilessly against every civilian suspect."[64] By February 1942 at the latest, the staff of the 29th Army Corps, for instance, had authorized all company commanders to order collective measures such as "for example shooting of hostages, burning down of villages," although such decisions were exclusively reserved for battalion commanders and senior troop leaders according to the clear regulations of the Martial Jurisdiction Decree.[65]

Both the command authorities and the troop units had scope for discretion when it came to interpreting the Martial Jurisdiction Decree. In the run-up to the war, the much-discussed abolition of obligatory criminal prosecution was also handled very differently by the staffs of the Eastern Army. Countless formations implemented the far-reaching amnesty for acts of violence committed by their own soldiers against civilians in that, "considering the abolition of obligatory criminal prosecution, offences by soldiers against Russian nationals ... [were] as a rule disciplinarily punished."[66] Other command authorities, on the other hand, much more often made use of the possibilities available for further instituting court-martial proceedings against delinquent soldiers, which primarily served to uphold discipline, but also testified to isolated efforts to maintain certain ethical standards. At the lower levels of the command hierarchy, there developed divergent types of proceedings when it came to the practical application of the Martial Jurisdiction Decree. Whilst an initial suspicion was sufficient for some company chiefs to justify the shooting of a civilian, other unit leaders left the decision to their superior commanders by transferring the prisoners to the next command post. In addition to this, the tolerance levels that had to be reached in order for units to resolve on retaliatory measures also differed. The assessment of the reprisals with which the formations sanctioned comparable incidents likewise fluctuated. In the vastness of the Eastern Front, the implementation of the Jurisdiction Decree was dependent to a large extent on the arbitrariness of the mid- and lower-level troop commanders and unit leaders, who were in a position to take advantage in all directions of the considerable freedom of action available in the area of operations.

There existed between the commanders and the troops extensive agreement on the fundamental justification for the hard line in the occupied Soviet territories, even if by no means every member of the Eastern Army personally came into contact with the violent measures. The dogmatization of the oft-apostrophized "security of the troops" (*Sicherheit der Truppe*), which counted among the central objectives of the Criminal Orders, had to be of vital interest, however, to the ordinary soldiers as well, especially as the troops in most cases already regarded irregular resistance as illegitimate and considered themselves to be in the right when it came to their rigorous course of action against "the cruel and malicious sniper war."[67] Within the formations reprisals were, therefore, commonly regarded as "harsh but necessary and just punishment[s]!"[68] Carrying out the reprisals was nonetheless "difficult even for the hardest soldier."[69] That the violence against the civilian population was not, despite everything, taken for granted, and roused scruples among ample numbers of soldiers that required effort to overcome, was also noted by the command staffs, as demonstrated by, among other things, reports written by field chaplains. Nevertheless, the strategies of legitimization communicated by the leadership and the ideological images of the enemy, the defensive attitude toward country and people that was fuelled by the seemingly omnipresent feelings of menace and racism toward the population, as well as the pressure to conform and the ideology of camaraderie in the formations proved to be stronger than any misgivings and counted among the most influential factors for ensuring that the Martial Jurisdiction Decree was adhered to in the Eastern Army.

The Commissar Order guidelines were also implemented comprehensively on the Eastern Front. The executions began on the very first day of Operation Barbarossa. Even a diplomat like *Legationsrat* Josef

Schlemann, who experienced the campaign as a representative of the Foreign Office on the staff of the Ninth Army, could see this for himself. After the first five days of war he summed up as follows: "The question of the political commissars is being thoroughly settled. All captured pol[itical] commissars are immediately shot."[70] By the beginning of August 1941, the intelligence officer of Panzer Group 3, *Major* Lindner, had already entered in his records 170 shootings of commissars by the subordinated divisions, and noted: "The implementation did not constitute a problem for the troops."[71] This also arose in Infantry Regiment 27, when a reconnaissance patrol of the I Battalion picked up an armed civilian and a political commissar at the end of June. One of the officers present observed the scene without emotion, whereby the battalion commander had "both shot immediately": "The Russian remains stoically calm; the commissar falls to his knees and whimpers. But it's of no use to him."[72] The German source material shows that these were not isolated cases. For almost all formations that fought on the Eastern Front, there is evidence of their adherence to the Commissar Order. Reports of executions of captive Soviet political officers exist for all 13 armies, all 44 army corps, and more than 80 percent of the almost 150 German front divisions.[73] Following the inclusion of additional cases where there are indications to this effect, the proportion at divisional level increases to over 90 percent; this is a disenchanting discovery, considering that the hitherto available sources had provided much lower quotas. Until now, shootings of Soviet political officers were only proven for 80 percent of the army corps and less than half of the divisions.[74] The complete evaluation of the German source material now shows that the idea of a merely sporadic implementation of the Commissar Order can definitively no longer be sustained.

In total, at least 3,430 executions of Soviet political officers and functionaries are on record in the files of the Eastern Army; when taking into account several hundred additional cases where there are indications to this effect, the number increases to almost 4,000 instances.[75] This secured minimum figure clearly exceeds all estimates thus far made. The actual number of victims must, however, be set much higher, as a considerable proportion of the obligatory confirmation reports has not been retained in the written record; to some extent shootings were not even documented. The results from the well-documented front sections argue in favor of the total number of victims of shootings amounting in fact to a high four-digit figure, though probably not a five-digit one, or, if so, then only just. As murderous as this balance sheet appears, from the point of view of the originators of the annihilation policy, it was in fact,

Figure 3.1. The Commissar Order being implemented. The caption on the reverse of the photograph reads: "A Jewish commissar digs his own grave." Date and location of the execution are unknown. Courtesy of Deutsch-Russisches Museum, Berlin-Karlshorst.

if anything, meagre. The program of murder ultimately encompassed little more than around every tenth Soviet political officer deployed on the Eastern Front. However, this in no way means that the German troops consciously safeguarded the remaining proportion of the commissars, as is sometimes assumed in the historiography on the Criminal Orders.[76] The relative failure of the policy of annihilation stemmed rather from the fact that the German troops simply did not get hold of most of the political officers of the Red Army. As the formations in almost all front sections reported, the Soviet political officers only seldom fell into German hands alive. Many of them eluded the grasp of the invaders in good time, fought to the end in hopeless situations, or even committed suicide. This was all the more the case once the shootings quickly became known on the Soviet side, which was the case in some sections of the front already after the first week of the war. Thus, even a formation like the Waffen-SS division *Reich* had to report after almost two months of war that "Communist commissars [could] not yet [be] captured by the division," as they had "either fled" or "fought until their annihilation."[77] Those political officers who nevertheless fell into German captivity disposed of their insignia and personal papers in time, "so that they cannot be distinguished from the ordinary soldier," as the intelligence officer of a panzer division complained as early as July 1941.[78] Many commissars had at least temporary success with this survival strategy. The increasingly overextended and decimated German front formations did not possess the capacity to locate the political officers in the amorphous masses of prisoners. In any case, it did not contravene existing orders when the combat formations left this laborious task to other authorities in the rear. The Commissar Order had in fact explicitly forbidden the front troops to initiate such "search and purge operations" in order that they were not distracted from their original tasks. Thus, a considerable proportion of the captured commissars only met their fate in the rearward prisoner camps, where counterintelligence officers and SS commandos carried out thorough selections.

The fact that the German army leadership realized at the beginning of August that the captured political officers were "for the most part detected only in prisoner camps,"[79] rested in no way, therefore, on a self-determined decision to circumvent the implementation of the Commissar Order. More important was the shrinking practicability of the annihilation policy, as the window of opportunity for the scheduled implementation of the program of murder was open merely during the first weeks of the war. Thus, the prerequisites for being able to summarily execute captured political officers in the front area only existed for a short time. The capture of Soviet commissars was in any case a rather uncommon occurrence, with which many soldiers were never confronted. Herein lies a grain of truth in the protestations of the veterans that they never obeyed the Commissar Order; many units never had the opportunity to do so because no Soviet political officers fell into their hands.

It was a different matter entirely, however, when units succeeded in capturing commissars. This is demonstrated not least by the logic of the execution statistics, which developed at significant time intervals.[80] The highest execution figures occurred during the phases of the biggest military victories, which were connected with the capture of a correspondingly higher number of prisoners. When the troops were on the offensive and captured larger numbers of prisoners, the figures for shootings rose. As soon as the prerequisite of larger numbers of prisoners was fulfilled, the probability that political officers were among them also increased. As soon as the advance stagnated, however, and the formations were forced on to the defensive and unable to take prisoners, the execution figures correspondingly dropped off. Alongside the mode of application, the place of application also proved to be decisive. The farther forward the units fought and the heavier the battles that they experienced, the higher as a rule their murder balance sheet. The troops of the panzer corps, which advanced farthest and were involved in the bloodiest battles, also as a rule exceeded the formations of the infantry corps in their implementation of the Commissar Order. The average execution figures attained by the panzer corps of the Eastern Army during Operation Barbarossa amounted to more than seventy-three shootings, whilst the infantry corps averaged only around thirty-one executions.[81] The unmistakeable correlation between offensives and shooting statistics prove how much the policy of annihilation depended on its situational practicability. At the same time, this rhythm testified to an automatism in the behavior of the troops. As a rule, every time the external prerequisites were fulfilled and the units were actually in the position of having to apply the Commissar Order, did they decide to do so.

Only a few officers defied the murder order of the Führer. For instance, the commandant of a prisoner camp in the rear area of Army Group Center protected several admitted political officers at the beginning of the campaign. Contrary to the myth of superior orders (*Befehlsnotstand*), however, this earned him nothing more than the reprimand of his superiors, who criticized that the mildness displayed was out of place.[82] This was admittedly the only camp commandant in this section who was reproached in this manner—as in this case, those in the Eastern Army who otherwise refused to carry out orders constituted an infinitesimal minority. To whomsoever was unable to overcome his scruples, alternatives were in any case open that were consistent with objectives and allowed participation in the policy of annihilation without having to assume the burden of executions. A work-sharing modus emerged during the first phase of the campaign that was tolerated and in part fostered by the command authorities and permitted captured political officers to be shunted off to headquarters, police units, or prisoner installations that assumed the interrogation and execution of the doomed men. In the area of the 9th Army Corps, for instance, an alternative arrangement had already been authorized prior to the beginning of the war that allowed the captured political commissars "to be separated off from the remaining prisoners, transferred to the divisional prisoner collection points, and there—also by field gendarmerie—eliminated."[83] This led, for example in the case of the subordinate 292nd Infantry Division, to all commissar shootings during the initial phase of the campaign being carried out in the divisional prisoner installations.[84]

The division of labor allowed a moral burden sharing that eased the tasks for all involved. Scarcely anybody who identified with the aim of the extermination of bolshevism was still able to refuse to make a minimal contribution to the realization of the murder program with the selection and delivery of the political officers.

The fact that the complete rejection of the Commissar Order in the Eastern Army remained the exception also stemmed from the plan to apply special measures against the Soviet commissars meeting in principle with broad agreement within the formations. The willingness to contribute to the policy of annihilation was based not only on blind obedience but also arose to a significant extent from the widely shared demonizing image of the political officers, which functioned for the soldiers as a justification for the shootings. In the eyes of the invaders, the commissars were agitators, oppressors, and executioners, and personified not only the oppressive Bolshevik regime, including its supposedly Jewish influences, but also the horror of the Eastern Front.[85] The tenacious, allegedly perfidious fighting style of the Red Army soldiers was ascribed to incitement and terror on the part of the political officers.[86] Many therefore even blamed the commissars for the unprecedented German losses, as propaganda lies and draconian methods of violence on the part of the political officers were seen as the cause of the fierce resistance of the Red Army, which was brushed off as senseless and illegitimate. Not least, the commissars were also suspected as being the driving forces (*treibende Elemente*) behind all Soviet breaches of international law.[87] On the basis of such blanket accusations, the Soviet political officers became the target of the growing frustration on the part of the invaders. The shootings of commissars thus served to compensate for the adverse developments on the Eastern Front, the enormous losses, and the emotions that arose from the heavy engagements waged mercilessly by both sides. The more the troops perceived the shootings of commissars as legitimate acts of retaliation, the more the sense of wrongdoing regarding the murders diminished. The strategies of legitimizing the annihilation policy and the psychosocial dynamics of the violence enabled the soldiers to commit war crimes without feeling like criminals.[88]

The program of murder at the front only ended in June 1942 when Hitler yielded to the repeated pressure of his generals to cancel the commissar decree. However this did not mean a rediscovery of conscience, but merely the carrying out of an opportunistic U-turn. The shootings of commissars were counterproductive: they had further strengthened the already heavy resistance of the Red Army and contributed to propelling German casualty rates to record highs. The policy of annihilation proved to be a severe burden that yielded far more loss than benefit. The cancellation of the Commissar Order came about at the instigation of the army, yet neither the importance of the action nor the possibilities of the Wehrmacht leadership for influencing the policies of the Nazi regime should be overestimated. The preceding interventions in this matter by the front staffs in autumn 1941 had all failed, and the generals had not been able to bring themselves to independently suspend the annihilation policy. Not the army leadership but external circumstances, the decisive failure of Operation Barbarossa in the winter of 1941/42, had finally convinced Hitler of the necessity of a course correction.

The Commissar Order did not represent the most serious crime of the Wehrmacht. Its participation in the Holocaust, the reprisals against the civilian population, and its assistance in the mass mortality of Soviet prisoners of war quantitatively dwarfed the murder of commissars. In hardly any other area, however, did the Wehrmacht operate so directly, actively, and comprehensively in the realization of the National Socialist annihilation policy as in the implementation of the Commissar Order. Compared to the Martial Jurisdiction Decree, the Commissar Order represented the more blatant breach of law, for hardly any contravention of international law was more obvious than the systematic murder of regular, uniformed prisoners of war. The Martial Jurisdiction Decree, however, proved to be by far the more momentous order, because in contrast to the Commissar Order, whose repercussions were largely limited to the comparatively narrowly defined circle of political officers and functionaries, it affected far more people, namely, the entire Soviet civilian population. Moreover, the German generals at the front, in contrast to their later opposition to the Commissar Order, made no attempt to abolish the Martial Jurisdiction Decree. The strategy of "taking action against hostile elements ... with unhesitating severity"[89] remained unaltered, even if the German staffs came to the conclusion at the latest following the failure of the Blitzkrieg in the winter of 1941/42 that in the future "a good relationship with the populace [was] necessary"[90] and urged the troops to differentiate "between the partisans and the ... populace."[91] Despite such attempts at a partial revision of the policy of violence, the radical principles of the Martial Jurisdiction Decree remained in force until the end of the German occupation regime in the Soviet Union. According to recent estimates, a total of at least half a million people fell victim to the antipartisan operations and reprisals of the German occupiers in the Soviet Union.[92]

The willingness of both the Wehrmacht leadership and the front commanders to implement Hitler's Criminal Orders testified not only to the moral and professional "deformity"[93] of this elite but also demonstrated at the same time how deeply the Wehrmacht had integrated itself in the Nazi state and how far its concepts of the enemy overlapped with the ideology of the regime. As a result of the considerable possibilities to shape events on the Eastern Front, however, the troop leaders made a significant contribution to molding the waging of war against the Soviet Union. It is characteristic of the attitude of the front commanders of the Eastern Army that, all in all, only very few of them used the far-reaching freedom of action available to at least gradually dilute the Criminal Orders. The handling of the Führer decrees in violation of international law on the part of the German troop leaders thus demonstrates once more that the Wehrmacht elite supported the criminal waging of war on the Eastern Front by no means reluctantly but for the most part from conviction.[94]

—*Translated from the German by Alex J. Kay*

Notes

1. Ernst Nolte, *Der Faschismus in seiner Epoche: Die Action française, der italienische Faschismus, der Nationalsozialismus* (Munich: Piper, 1963), 436–37.

2. See Catherine Merridale, *Iwans Krieg: Die Rote Armee, 1939 bis 1945*, trans. Hans Günter Holl (Frankfurt am Main: S. Fischer, 2006), 148–54, 161–64, 167, who describes "how only the atrocities of the Germans allowed the Soviets to hold out."

3. This piece is based on the studies of the author on the so-called Criminal Orders. See Felix Römer, *Der Kommissarbefehl: Wehrmacht und NS-Verbrechen an der Ostfront, 1941/42* (Paderborn: Ferdinand Schöningh, 2008); and Felix Römer, "'Im alten Deutschland wäre solcher Befehl nicht möglich gewesen': Rezeption, Adaption, und Umsetzung des Kriegsgerichtsbarkeitserlasses im Ostheer 1941/42," *Vierteljahrshefte für Zeitgeschichte* 56, no. 1 (2008): 53–99.

4. Percy Ernst Schramm, ed., *Kriegstagebuch des Oberkommandos der Wehrmacht (Wehrmachtführungsstab) 1940–1945*, vol. 1, *1. August 1940–31. Dezember 1941*, ed. Hans-Adolf Jacobsen (Bonn: Bernard & Graefe, 1965), 340–42 (entry for March 3, 1941).

5. Franz Halder, *Kriegstagebuch: Tägliche Aufzeichnungen des Chefs des Generalstabes des Heeres 1939–1942*, vol. 2, *Von der geplanten Landung in England bis zum Beginn des Ostfeldzuges (1.7.1940–21.6.1941)*, ed. Hans-Adolf Jacobsen (Stuttgart: W. Kohlhammer, 1963), 320 (entry for March 17, 1941). Already in February, Göring had mentioned the envisaged measures against Bolshevik functionaries in a meeting with General Thomas. See Georg

Thomas, *Geschichte der deutschen Wehr- und Rüstungswirtschaft* (Boppard am Rhein: Harald Boldt, 1966), 18.

6. Halder, *Kriegstagebuch*, 2:399 (entry for May 6, 1941).

7. Aufzeichnungen des Befehlshabers der Panzergruppe 3, Generaloberst Hoth, von Hitlers Rede in der Reichskanzlei am 30.3.1941, RH 21-3/40, fol. 32, Bundesarchiv-Militärarchiv, Freiburg im Breisgau (hereafter BA-MA).

8. Halder, *Kriegstagebuch*, 2:336–37 (entry for March 30, 1941).

9. Aufzeichnungen des Befehlshabers der Panzergruppe 3, Generaloberst Hoth, von Hitlers Rede in der Reichskanzlei am 30.3.1941, RH 21-3/40, fol. 32, BA-MA.

10. Halder, *Kriegstagebuch*, 2:336–37 (entry for March 3,1941): "Die Truppe muß sich mit den Mitteln verteidigen, mit denen sie angegriffen wird."

11. Ibid.

12. "Nicht an Kriegsgericht, sondern sofort durch die Truppe beseitigen. Nicht nach hinten abschieben." Aufzeichnungen des Befehlshabers der Panzergruppe 3, Generaloberst Hoth, von Hitlers Rede in der Reichskanzlei am 30.3.1941, RH 21-3/40, fol. 32, BA-MA.

13. The emergence of the Criminal Orders has been researched in detail. See Jürgen Förster, "Das Unternehmen 'Barbarossa' als Eroberungs- und Vernichtungskrieg," in Horst Boog, Jürgen Förster, Joachim Hoffmann, Ernst Klink, Rolf-Dieter Müller, and Gerd R. Ueberschär, *Der Angriff auf die Sowjetunion*, vol. 4 of *Das Deutsche Reich und der Zweite Weltkrieg* (Stuttgart: Deutsche Verlags-Anstalt, 1983), 426–40; Johannes Hürter, *Hitlers Heerführer: Die deutschen Oberbefehlshaber im Krieg gegen die Sowjetunion, 1941/42* (Munich: Oldenbourg, 2006), 247–65; and Helmut Krausnick, "Kommissarbefehl und 'Gerichtsbarkeitserlaß Barbarossa' in neuer Sicht," *Vierteljahrshefte für Zeitgeschichte* 25, no. 4 (1977): 682–738.

14. The decrees are reproduced in Gerd R. Ueberschär and Wolfram Wette, eds., *Der deutsche Überfall auf die Sowjetunion: "Unternehmen Barbarossa," 1941*, new ed. (Frankfurt am Main: S. Fischer, 1991), 252–53, 259–60.

15. The decree is reproduced in ibid., 249–50.

16. See "Richtlinien für das Verhalten der Truppe in Russland," reproduced in ibid., 258: "rücksichtsloses und energisches Durchgreifen gegen bolschewistische Hetzer, Freischärler, Saboteure, Juden und restlose Beseitigung jedes aktiven oder passiven Widerstandes."

17. See "Merkblatt über Abwehr von heimtückischer Kriegführung," evidently from Army High Command (*Armeeoberkommando*, or AOK) 9, RH 24-23/52, BA-MA. See the leaflet "Sieh Dich vor" from AOK 6, RH 20-6/489, fol. 326, BA-MA. See the leaflet "Kennt Ihr den Feind?" from the area of Army Group Center, RH 21-3/746, BA-MA.

18. Christian Streit, *Keine Kameraden: Die Wehrmacht und die sowjetischen Kriegsgefangenen, 1941–1945*, 4th rev. ed. (1978; Bonn: Dietz, 1997), 45.

19. This is how General for Special Purposes (*General zur besonderen Verwendung,* or *General z.b.V.*) of the OKH Eugen Müller characterized the purpose of the order at a meeting in Allenstein on June 10, 1941, RH 19-III/722, fol. 87, BA-MA.

20. Protokoll von der Besprechung beim Generalquartiermeister des OKH in Wünsdorf am 16.5.1941, RH 20-11/334, BA-MA.

21. See Brauchitsch's comments on the order from May 24, 1941, reproduced in Ueberschär and Wette, *Der deutsche Überfall auf die Sowjetunion,* 253–54.

22. "Diese Kommissare werden nicht als Soldaten anerkannt; der für Kriegsgefangene völkerrechtlich geltende Schutz findet auf sie keine Anwendung. Sie sind nach durchgeführter Absonderung zu erledigen." Ueberschär and Wette, *Der deutsche Überfall,* 259–60.

23. Protokoll von der Besprechung beim Generalquartiermeister des OKH in Wünsdorf am 16.5.1941, RH 20-11/334, BA-MA.

24. See Römer, "Im alten Deutschland," 75–81.

25. See Streit, *Keine Kameraden*; and Jürgen Förster, "Die Sicherung des 'Lebensraumes,'" in Boog et al., *Der Angriff auf die Sowjetunion,* 1030–78.

26. Rolf-Dieter Müller, *Der Zweite Weltkrieg, 1939–1945* (Stuttgart: Klett-Cotta, 2004), esp. 125–37.

27. See Römer, *Kommissarbefehl,* 197–98. See the overview of the supporting evidence in Müller, *Der Zweite Weltkrieg,* 571–76.

28. Schlussansprache des Kommandeurs der 134. Infanteriedivision v. 16.6.1941, RH 26-134/5, Anlage 7, BA-MA.

29. Rede des Oberbefehlshabers der 18. Armee v. 25.4.1941, RH 20-18/71, fols. 20–34, BA-MA: "Wenn bekannt wird, daß wir die politischen Kommissare u. G.P.U.-Leute sofort vor ein Feldgericht stellen u. aburteilen, so ist zu hoffen, daß sich die russ. Truppe u. die Bevölkerung selbst von dieser Knechtschaft befreien. Wir wollen das Mittel jedenfalls anwenden. Es spart uns deutsches Blut u. wir kommen schnell vorwärts." The GPU (*Gosudarstvennoe Politicheskoe Upravlenie,* or State Political Administration) was the Soviet secret police between 1922 and 1934.

30. Kriegstagebuch der 239. Inf.Div. zur Besprechung beim AOK 11 v. 18.6.1941, RH 26-239/17, BA-MA.

31. Anlage 6 zum Befehl der 296. Inf.Div./Abt. Ia Nr. 1309/41 geh. v. 21.6.1941, RH 26-296/14, BA-MA.

32. Ibid. "Wo Maßnahmen dieser Art versäumt wurden oder zunächst nicht möglich waren, werden *tatverdächtige Elemente sogleich einem Offizier vorgeführt. Dieser entscheidet, ob sie zu erschießen sind.*" "Soweit Maßnahmen vorstehender Art versäumt wurden oder zunächst nicht möglich waren,

sind *tatverdächtige Elemente* sogleich einem Offizier *mit den Befugnissen eines nichtselbst[ändigen]. Bat[ail]l[ons].K[omman]deurs.* vorzuführen. Dieser entscheidet, ob die Verdächtigen zu erschiessen oder freizulassen sind." (Emphasis in the original.)

33. Protokoll zur Besprechung bei der 102. Inf.Div. am 10.6.1941, Appendix 21, RH 26-102/6, BA-MA.

34. Besprechung des Oberbefehlshabers der 6. Armee v. 28.4.1941, RH 24-17/41, fols. 26–27, BA-MA.

35. See Tätigkeitsbericht (Ic) der 78. Inf.Div. v. 1.–22.6.1941, RH 26-78/64, BA-MA.

36. See Oswald Überegger, "'Verbrannte Erde' und 'baumelnde Gehenkte': Zur europäischen Dimension militärischer Normübertretungen im Ersten Weltkrieg," in Sönke Neitzel and Daniel Hohrath, eds., *Kriegsgreuel: Die Entgrenzung von Gewalt in kriegerischen Konflikten vom Mittelalter bis zum 20. Jahrhundert* (Paderborn: Ferdinand Schöningh, 2008), 241–78.

37. Protokoll der Besprechung des Generalquartiermeisters des OKH v. 16.5.1941, RH 20-16/1012, fol. 72, BA-MA: "erfolgreich nur durchgegriffen werden kann, wenn ein Kriegsbrauch mit östlichen Mitteln angewandt wird."

38. Ausführungsbestimmungen des AOK 6/Abt. Ic/AO Nr. 209/41 g.Kdos. v. 16.6.1941, RH 20-6/96, fols. 153–56, BA-MA.

39. See the obsolete thesis of Hannes Heer, "Die Logik des Vernichtungskrieges: Wehrmacht und Partisanenkampf," in Hannes Heer, and Klaus Naumann, eds., *Vernichtungskrieg: Verbrechen der Wehrmacht, 1941–1944* (Hamburg: Hamburger Edition, 1995), 119.

40. Eintrag im Tätigkeitsbericht (Ic) des XX. Armeekorps v. 27.9.1941, RH 24-20/74, BA-MA.

41. Ibid.

42. See Hürter, *Hitlers Heerführer*, 418–19.

43. Kriegstagebuch (Ia) der 35. Inf.Div. v. 23.6.1941, RH 26-35/35, fol. 29, BA-MA.

44. Befehl der 17. Inf.Div./Abt. Ic, betr. Partisanenbekämpfung, geh. v. 17.11.1941, RH 26-17/72, BA-MA: "Elements suspected of being partisans are to be shot ruthlessly" (Partisanenverdächtige Elemente sind rücksichtslos zu erschießen).

45. Kriegstagebuch (Ia) des Befehlshaber rückwärtiges Heeresgebiet Mitte v. 7.4.1942, RH 22/229, fol. 58, BA-MA.

46. Ic-Morgenmeldung des VI. AK an das AOK 9 v. 10.8.1941, RH 24-6/241, fol. 6, BA-MA: "Two suspicious elements, against whom nothing can be proven, are shot" (Zwei verdächtige Elemente, denen nichts nachgewiesen werden kann, werden erschossen).

47. Kriegstagebuch (Ia) der 99. lei. Inf.Div. v. 26.6.1941, RH 26-99/2, BA-MA, 30.

48. See the supporting evidence in Römer, "Im alten Deutschland," 84–85.

49. See ibid., 85.
50. Tagebuch des Truppenarztes des I./Schützenregiment 394 v. 23.6.1941, MSg 2/5354, BA-MA, 3.
51. Meldung des II./Infanterieregiment 202 an das Inf.Rgt. 202 v. 26.6.1941, 11 a.m., RH 26-75/110, BA-MA.
52. Kriegstagebuch der I./Artillerieregiment 19 v. 27.6.1941, RH 41/1207, BA-MA: "Actually they should all be whacked" (Eigentlich sollte man sie alle umlegen).
53. Tagebuch des Lt. Kurt M., Art.Rgt. 34, v. 24.6.1941, MSg 1/619, BA-MA, 14.
54. Befehl des AOK 6/Abt. Ia/Ic/AO/Abw. III. Nr. 3609/41 geh. v. 9.12.1941, RH 20-6/495, fol. 200, BA-MA.
55. Ic-Abendmeldung der 75. Inf.Div. v. 12.11.1941, RH 26-75/117, BA-MA.
56. Ia-Tagesmeldung der 257. Inf.Div. v. 28.6.1941, RH 26-257/9, Anlage 94, BA-MA.
57. Befehl des VI. AK/Abt. Ic Nr. 506/41 geh. v. 21.7.1941, RH 24-6/237, fols. 124–25, BA-MA.
58. Divisionsbefehl der 132. Inf.Div./Kdr. v. 5.8.1941, RH 26-132/36, Anlage 70, BA-MA.
59. Vortrag des Gen. z.b.V. in Allenstein v. 10.6.1941, RH 19-III/722, fol. 87, BA-MA.
60. Befehl des XX. AK/Abt. Ic Nr. 5732/41 geh. v. 7.12.1941, RH 26-292/53, BA-MA, Appendix 38.
61. Befehl der 8. Inf.Div./Abt. Ic, betr. Befriedung der Bevölkerung, v. 12.9.1941, RH 26-8/73, Anlage 33, BA-MA: "nur auf Befehl von Kommandeuren mit mindestens der Disziplinarstrafgewalt eines Bat[ai]l[lons].-K[omman]deurs. und erst nach Vernehmung durch die Division."
62. Feindnachrichtenblatt der 56. Inf.Div./Abt. Ic v. 5.10.1941, RH 26-56/22b, Anlage 143, BA-MA.
63. Befehl der 4. Gebirgsdivision/Kdr./Abt. Ic Nr. 312/41 geh. v. 3.8.1941, RH 28-4/45, Anlage 6, BA-MA: "Für die Durchführung derartiger kollektiver Gewaltmaßnahmen ist grundsätzlich meine Genehmigung einzuholen."
64. "Parolen des Tages" der 4. Panzerdivision v. 18.1./4.2.1942, in der Anlage zum Schreiben der 4. Pz.Div. an das XXXXVII. AK v. 20.3.1942, RH 24-47/113, BA-MA.
65. Befehl des XXIX. AK/Abt. Ic, betr. Partisanenbekämpfung, v. 27.2.1942, RH 24-29/48, Anlage 226, BA-MA.
66. Tätigkeitsbericht (III) der 217. Inf.Div. v. August 1940–Februar 1942, RH 26-217/54, BA-MA.
67. Tagebuch des Unteroffiziers Paul M., II./Inf.Rgt. 154, v. 27.6.1941, RH 37/2787, BA-MA.
68. Ibid., entry for July 28, 1941.

69. Merkblatt über Partisanenbekämpfung des XXXXVIII. AK v. 17.11.1941, RH 24-48/201, Anlage 81, BA-MA.
70. "Die Frage der politischen Kommissare findet eine gründliche Erledigung. Alle festgenommenen pol. Kommissare werden sofort erschossen." Hürter, *Hitlers Heerführer*, 397.
71. Tätigkeitsbericht (Ic) der Pz.Gr. 3 v. 1.1.–11.8.1941, RH 21-3/423, BA-MA, 30: "Die Durchführung bildete kein Problem für die Truppe."
72. Tagebuch des Oberleutnants Theo Habicht, Chef 4./Inf.Rgt. 27, v. 28.6.1941, MSg, 1/2311, BA-MA: "Der Russe hält stoische Ruhe dabei, der Kommissar geht in die Knie und winselt. Aber es hilft ihm nicht."
73. See Römer, *Kommissarbefehl*, 399–400. See the overview of the supporting evidence (ibid., 586–629).
74. Detlef Siebert, "Die Durchführung des Kommissarbefehls in den Frontverbänden des Heeres: Eine quantifizierende Auswertung der Forschung," unpublished manuscript, 2000.
75. See Römer, *Kommissarbefehl*, 359–60.
76. See Christian Hartmann, "Verbrecherischer Krieg—verbrecherische Wehrmacht? Überlegungen zur Struktur des deutschen Ostheeres, 1941–1944," *Vierteljahrshefte für Zeitgeschichte* 52, no. 1 (2004): 48–49.
77. Einsatzbericht der SS-Div. "Reich"/Abt. Ia v. 20.7.1941, RS 3-2/5, BA-MA, 181.
78. Ic-Meldung der 3. Pz.Div. an das XXIV. AK v. 29.7.1941, RH 24-24/331, BA-MA.
79. Franz Halder, *Kriegstagebuch: Tägliche Aufzeichnungen des Chefs des Generalstabes des Heeres 1939–1942*, vol. 3, *Der Russlandfeldzug bis zum Marsch auf Stalingrad (22.6.1941–24.9.1942)*, ed. Hans-Adolf Jacobsen and Alfred Philippi (Stuttgart: W. Kohlhammer, 1964), 139 (entry for August 1, 1941).
80. See Römer, *Kommissarbefehl*, 367–97.
81. See ibid., 389.
82. TB (Ic) der 403. Sicherungsdivision für den Juli 1941, Abschnitt "Abwehr," RH 26-403/4a, BA-MA.
83. See Aktennotiz der 292. Inf.Div./Abt. Ic über die mündliche Weisung des Stabschefs des IX. AK v. 21.6.1941, RH 26-292/53, BA-MA, Appendix 1: "abgesondert von den übrigen Gefangenen—in die Div.-Gefangenensammelstellen überführt und dort—auch durch Feldgendarmerie—beseitigt werden."
84. Meldung des Sonderführers Arndt an den Ic der 292. Inf.Div. v. 12.7.1941 über eine Kriegsgefangenenmeldung der Abt. Ib und zehn Exekutionen an gefangenen sowjetischen Politoffizieren, RH 26-292/55, BA-MA.
85. See Römer, *Kommissarbefehl*, 275–317.
86. See, as exemplary, the report of the adjutant of an antitank unit: "Im Osten 1. Teil (26. Juni 41–1. Okt. 41)," from October 2, 1941, RH 39/426, BA-MA.

87. Bericht der 168. Inf.Div./Abt. Ia, "Erfahrungen während der Kämpfe ostw. Kiew," October 1, 1941, RH 26-299/123, Anlage 425, BA-MA.

88. See Harald Welzer, *Täter: Wie aus ganz normalen Menschen Massenmörder werden* (Frankfurt am Main: S. Fischer, 2005), 38.

89. Korpsbefehl des LV. AK/Abt. Ia Nr. 1919/41 v. 20.10.1941, RH 26-100/40, fol. 219, BA-MA.

90. Armeebefehl des Pz.AOK 2/Abt. Ic/AO Nr. 83/42 geh. v. 3.3.1942, RH 21-2/867a, fol. 304, BA-MA.

91. Armeebefehl des Pz.AOK 2 Nr. 1102/42 geh. v. 19.6.1942, RH 23/29, fol. 189, BA-MA.

92. See Hartmann, "Verbrecherischer Krieg," 25.

93. Hürter, *Hitlers Heerführer*, 615.

94. I am very grateful to Alex J. Kay for translating this chapter from German into English.

CHAPTER 4

"The Purpose of the Russian Campaign Is the Decimation of the Slavic Population by Thirty Million"

The Radicalization of German Food Policy in Early 1941

Alex J. Kay

Over the course of six months between the end of 1940 and June 1941, German planning staffs developed a concept that envisaged the seizure of substantial amounts of grain from the occupied Soviet territories at the cost of tens of millions of Soviet lives. This concept was the brainchild of the number two person in the Reich Ministry for Food and Agriculture (*Reichsministerium für Ernährung und Landwirtschaft*, RMEL), *Staatssekretär* Herbert Backe, and was referred to internally as the Backe plan or some variation of this.[1] What began in the RMEL ultimately became state policy advocated by Germany's military leadership, ministerial bureaucracy, and political elites. This piece will trace and analyze the radicalization[2] of German food policy vis-à-vis the Soviet territories and their inhabitants during the period in question.

The "Severity of the Food Situation"

Proposals for a military campaign against the USSR were being heard in the corridors of power as early as July 1940,[3] and *Staatssekretär* Backe was informed of Hitler's intentions toward the Soviet Union no later than November 6, 1940.[4] The official directive to commence preparations for an invasion of the Soviet Union, Directive No. 21: Case Barbarossa, was issued a month and a half later, on December 18, 1941. An early occupation of the Donets Basin, a major source of coal, was stressed, and the capture of "the important transport and armaments center" of Moscow was described as constituting "politically and economically a decisive success."[5] Beyond this, however, there was little reference to the economic gain to be had from the Soviet territories, and no reference at all to agricultural produce.

During the Christmas holidays, just a few days after the issuing of Directive No. 21, Backe redrafted the annual report of the RMEL on the food situation in Germany. This was the third draft of the memorandum, as Backe felt that neither the first nor the second version, drawn up in November and December 1940, respectively, had sufficiently reflected "the severity of the food situation." On January 9 Backe passed the revised report, bearing the same date, to his immediate superior, Reich Minister Richard Walther Darré, for the latter's signature.[6] That same day Darré forwarded the report, just as he did every year, to Hitler via the head of the Reich Chancellery, Dr. Hans-Heinrich Lammers.[7]

Already before the beginning of the war, Germany had not been autarkic; 17 percent of its annual food requirements had to be imported from overseas.[8] Continental Europe required imports of twelve to thirteen million tons of grain a year, which equated to the food requirements of over twenty-five million people.[9] This was bound to increase in wartime due to loss of efficiency and Germany's inability to import from the Western Hemisphere as a result of the British sea blockade. Indeed, by the end of 1940, the grain deficit for continental Europe—much of which was under German occupation—had already risen significantly.[10] Thus the need, in the eyes of the German leadership, to take decisive action to combat Germany's and German-occupied Europe's lack of self-sufficiency was becoming ever more pressing.

In addition to the report on the food situation for the economic year 1940–41, Backe—without the assistance of other members of the ministry—also produced a description of the likely food situation in the coming third year of the war, which provided the basis for the revisions to the annual report. Backe then presented his findings to a combined session of the RMEL and the Reich Food Estate (*Reichsnährstand*, RNSt), the latter organization being responsible for the supervision of all aspects of rural life in Germany, from production to distribution.[11] According to Backe, all those present voiced their full agreement with the findings of his account.[12]

The "Occupation of Ukraine Would Liberate Us from Every Economic Worry"

On January 13, four days after his submission of the RMEL's annual report on the food situation, *Staatssekretär* Backe gave a joint presentation together with *Staatssekretär* in the Office of the Four-Year Plan (*Vierjahresplanbehörde*, VJPB) Erich Neumann on the same subject to Plenipotentiary for the Four-Year Plan Hermann Göring, in which they recommended that meat rations be reduced. Prior to the presentation, Neumann had already prepared a corresponding decree for approval by Göring.[13] The decree was circulated the same day among all Reich ministers, all NSDAP *Gauleiter*, and various other representatives of the state and the party. It announced that, because of the disappointing harvest in the second year of the war and uncertainty as to how long the war would last, various combative measures would have to be taken, including the reduction of meat rations in the summer.[14]

During a presentation on January 22, *General der Infanterie* Georg Thomas, chief of the War Economy and Armaments Office (*Wehrwirtschafts- und Rüstungsamt*, Wi Rü Amt) in the High Command of the Wehrmacht (*Oberkommando der Wehrmacht*, OKW), informed Chief of the OKW *Generalfeldmarschall* Wilhelm Keitel that his office was in the process of preparing a study addressing its misgivings with regard to the planned operations against the Soviet Union.[15] It was this very pessimism, however, that led to the realization on Thomas's part that only a more radical approach would enable Germany to achieve its economic objectives.[16] A two-and-a-half-hour meeting on January 29 between Göring and ministerial representatives, including Backe and Thomas, addressed eastern questions and would have given Thomas the opportunity to explore other perspectives within the field of civilian economic planning and, if he did not know already, learn about Backe's proposals.[17] It was probably at this meeting that Thomas learned of an earlier meeting between Backe and Hitler, which may feasibly have come about as a result of Hitler's having read or been briefed on Backe's annual report on the food situation from January 9. A day after the January 29 meeting, Thomas was in any case in a position to inform members of his staff: "*Staatssekr[etär]* Neumann has an expert for Russia, with whom we should work. *St[aats]s[ekretär]* Backe is supposed to have told the Führer that the occupation of Ukraine would liberate us from every economic worry. In reality, however, Backe is supposed to have said that if any territory can be of use to us then it could only be Ukraine. Ukraine alone is a surplus territory; the whole of European Russia, however, is not."[18]

Four Million Tons of Grain

These new developments were reflected in calculations made by the Reich Food Estate in early February: "Reich Food Estate estimates the shortfall

Figure 4.1. *Staatssekretär* Herbert Backe wearing the insignia of an *SS-Gruppenführer*, photo dated June 2, 1942. Reproduced with permission from Bundesarchiv (Bild 183-J02034 / N.N.).

of Germany and the territories controlled by Germany to be 5 million tons [of grain]. By means of a 10% reduction of Russian consumption, around 4 million tons can be obtained from Russia."[19] Four million tons compared very favorably with the normal Soviet surplus of 1 million tons and even with the amount of 2.5 million tons promised by the Soviets in accordance with the German-Soviet trade agreement of January 10, 1941.[20] According to the Soviets, it was only possible to achieve a surplus of 2.5 million tons of grain by falling back on the national grain reserves.[21]

The study Thomas had mentioned to Keitel in January was sent to Keitel on February 20, who in turn submitted it to Hitler. Göring received a second copy.[22] In perhaps the most important section of his study, which was entitled "The Effects on the War Economy of an Operation in the East," Thomas suggested that the German grain deficit could be offset at the expense of the Soviet population:

> Even if it appears uncertain as to whether M.T.S. [Machine and Tractor Stations] and supplies can be protected from destruction in large amounts, if, moreover, as a result of the effects of war, a harvest of 70% at the most can be expected, it must be considered that the Russian is accustomed to adapting his needs to poor harvests and that with a population of 160 million, even a *small reduction* of the consumption per head would free up considerable quantities of grain.
>
> Under these circumstances, it could be possible to meet the German *shortfall* for 1941 and 1942.[23]

On February 26 Thomas presented his paper to Göring in person, who gave it his approval. Göring himself had already received Hitler's approval for his assumption of control over the entire economic administration in the Soviet territories to be occupied. Evidently impressed with Thomas's paper, Göring in turn transferred responsibility to him for the preparation of an economic organization to exploit the said territories and emphasised that Thomas would have a "completely free hand" in the matter. This transfer of responsibility had been authorized by Hitler in advance. Already at the meeting itself, Thomas was able to respond to Göring's commission by informing him that the relevant preparations were underway and that he would shortly be able to present Göring with an organizational draft.[24]

By February the quartermaster general of the army, *Generalmajor* Eduard Wagner, was also privy to the planning underway, as demonstrated by the results of a war game that month in St. Germain outside Paris.[25] A paper drawn up on the basis of the war game stipulated: "The supplies must be limited through extensive exploitation of the land, [and] the capture must be tightly controlled. The country's stocks are not to be utilized through indiscriminate pillaging, but rather through seizure and collection according to [the] well thought-out plan."[26] Wagner's reference here to a well thought-out plan indicates his knowledge of Backe's starvation policy. Indeed, by the end of February Backe had received a "special commission" in the food sector.[27] One of the appendixes to the paper on the February war game formed the basis of the "Special Instructions for Provisioning, Part C" issued on April 3 in the name of Commander in Chief of the Army *Generalfeldmarschall* Walther von Brauchitsch and signed by Chief of the General Staff of the Army *Generaloberst* Franz Halder.[28] Halder and Wagner had discussed the results of the February war game on March 4 and the forthcoming "Special Instructions" ten days later.[29] These special instructions made clear: "Securing the major transport routes and exploiting the land for the requirements of the troops in order to relieve the supply is of decisive importance for the operations. It is therefore a question of all army forces in the rear areas being deployed exclusively for these tasks."[30]

8.7 Million Tons of Grain

On March 12, Thomas visited Backe and obtained his agreement for the incorporation of agriculture into the economic organization that Thomas was in the process of setting up.[31] A week later, Göring declared himself "fully in agreement" with Thomas's organizational draft. The War Economy and Armaments Office would be responsible for the executive. *Staatssekretär* Körner, *Staatssekretär* Backe, *Unterstaatssekretär* in the Reich Economics Ministry *Generalleutnant* Hermann von Hanneken, *Staatssekretär* in the Reich Forestry Office Friedrich Alpers, and Thomas himself would be on the organization's Command Staff.[32] On March 25, *Generalleutnant* Dr. Wilhelm Schubert of the Luftwaffe assumed the leadership of the organization,[33] which was provisionally called the Planning Staff Oldenburg (*Arbeitsstab Oldenburg*), but later became the Economic Staff East (*Wirtschaftsstab Ost*, Wi Stab Ost).

Three days later, on March 28, the Staff Office of the Reich Farming Leader (*Stabsamt des Reichsbauernführers*) completed a study entitled "Production and Consumption of Foodstuffs and Fodder in the USSR." The study concluded that in the event of a reduction in the consumption of foodstuffs per head from 250 kg to 220 kg annually, that is, a reduction of 12 percent, a grain surplus of 8.7 million tons could be achieved.[34]

This study constituted without doubt a limited but clear radicalization of German food policy vis-à-vis the Soviet territories. The 10 percent reduction in Soviet consumption proposed by the Reich Food Estate in early February had now been increased to 12 percent. Like the Reich Ministry for Food and Agriculture and the Reich Food Estate, the Staff Office of the Reich Farming Leader was clearly operating under the aegis of Backe during this planning phase. Richard Walther Darré, the nominal head of all three organizations and Backe's superior, knew nothing of the planning, as is evident from a series of letters exchanged between Backe, Darré, and Göring after the military campaign had begun.[35]

A further meeting between Thomas and Backe took place on March 31 and was attended by Schubert, Hanneken, *Ministerialdirektor* in the RMEL Dr. Hans-Joachim Riecke, and *Ministerialrat* in the Office of the Four-Year Plan Dr. Friedrich Gramsch, among others.[36] A day later, Körner had lunch with *Reichsführer-SS* Heinrich Himmler and the two of them may well have discussed the starvation plans in which Körner was deeply involved.[37] On April 12, a "secret" decree (*Geheimerlaß*) signed by Körner conferred additional powers on Backe for the implementation of the "special task" concerning Barbarossa assigned to Göring by Hitler. The task resulting from this authorization and all related organizational preparations were, "on the order of the Führer," to remain strictly secret under all circumstances, from which it can be assumed that these powers related to the starvation policy.[38] The total bypassing of Backe's nominal superior, Darré, and the appointment of Backe for the implementation of these tasks was one way of promoting the radicalization of food policy vis-à-vis the Soviet civilian population.

"Tens of Millions of People Will Doubtlessly Starve to Death"

The implications of the proposals developed over the course of the previous few months were stated unmistakably clearly at a meeting on May 2 between Thomas, Schubert, and the *Staatssekretäre* of the various ministries involved in the economic planning for Barbarossa. This meeting was in all likelihood an official session of the Economic Command Staff East (*Wirtschaftsführungsstab Ost*, Wi Fü Stab Ost).[39] A memorandum recorded the results of the discussion:

> 1. The war can only continue to be waged if the entire Wehrmacht is fed from Russia during the 3rd year of the war.

2. As a result, if what is necessary for us is extracted from the land, tens of millions of people will doubtlessly starve to death.[40]

In an incredibly matter-of-fact way, the participants declared that tens of millions of people in the soon-to-be-occupied territories of the Soviet Union would have to starve to death if Germany was to win the war. It was envisaged that starvation on this scale would create a surplus of foodstuffs in the occupied east that would be used first and foremost to feed Germany's armed forces during the third year of the war (i.e., September 1941 to August 1942), above all those three million soldiers serving on the Eastern Front.[41] Eliminating the necessity of supplying three million men with particularly high rations directly from the Reich would ease the pressure placed on the existing transport routes between Germany and the Soviet territories for the (anticipated) duration of the war in the east, as well as on food stocks in Germany and German-occupied Europe as a whole, thereby simultaneously bolstering the home front and contributing to Germany's economic capacity to fight the expected war of attrition against the Anglo-Saxon powers. From the point of view of those who conceived of it, the importance of this ruthless approach in the occupied east cannot be overestimated. Three days later, in notes pertaining to issues still requiring a decision from Hitler or Göring, Thomas stressed the urgency of providing for the fighting troops, agriculturally exploiting the Soviet territories, and strengthening the transport system.[42] These were all integral components of the starvation policy.

By early May at the latest,[43] rumors were circulating—even among those not directly involved in the planning—to the effect that Hitler had decided on the destruction of Soviet cities. The Austrian military diplomat *Generalleutnant* Edmund Glaise von Horstenau recorded the following information obtained during a meeting with *SS-Oberführer* Dr. Franz Walter Stahlecker on May 5: "In Russia, all cities and cultural sites including the Kremlin are to be razed to the ground; Russia is to be reduced to the level of a nation of peasants, from which there is no return."[44] It is reasonable to assume that Stahlecker, as designated chief of *Einsatzgruppe* A,[45] would have been well informed.

On the same day as Glaise's conversation with Stahlecker, Backe gave a presentation at a gathering of the leading representatives of the party, the *Reichsleiter* and *Gauleiter*, after which Reich Minister for Public Enlightenment and Propaganda Dr. Joseph Goebbels recorded in his diary: "If only this year's harvest is good. And then we want to line our pockets in the east."[46] Goebbels had been treated to a private presentation by Backe five days earlier, on which occasion Backe had informed

Goebbels that meat rations would be reduced by 100 g per week from June 2. Goebbels demonstrated his faith in Backe by noting in his diary: "Backe presides over his department, by the way, in masterly fashion. He'll do whatever is at all possible."[47] Two days after his presentation for the *Reichsleiter* and *Gauleiter*, Backe met with the designated head of a civil administration in the occupied Soviet territories, Alfred Rosenberg,[48] who conferred with *Staatssekretär* Körner a day later.[49] A letter from Chief of the Wi Stab Ost Schubert to his superior in the Wi Fü Stab Ost, Thomas, on a meeting that had taken place between Schubert and Army Quartermaster General Wagner on May 12, shows that the two men explicitly discussed the starvation policy. They agreed on the "phenomenal importance of the area of operations" for their economic work and the necessity of beginning with this work as soon as operations commenced. The fact that Schubert's request for an office next to Wagner's was immediately granted is testament to the close working relationship of their respective organizations.[50]

Liaison between the different departments involved in developing the starvation policy also took place at a lower level. Two days after Schubert and Wagner had met, a discussion took place in Berlin between *Ministerialdirigent* Dr. Julius Claussen of the RMEL and an official in the Wi Rü Amt.[51] Claussen described the food situation as "strained and difficult." The reduction in meat rations planned for the beginning of June would hit not only normal consumers but also all other sections of the population, including the troops, three million of whom would be deployed in the Soviet Union as of June 22. In the event of a longer-lasting war, a substantial reduction in fat rations from 270 g to 200 g (almost 26 percent) was also foreseen by the RMEL. As almost all European countries had a significant grain deficit, those territories under German occupation had for the most part to be supplied by Germany.[52] One European state that could be of greater assistance in terms of food supplies, continued Claussen, was the Soviet Union, more specifically Ukraine, "the granary of Russia [sic]." According to Claussen, Ukraine produced 40 million tons of grain annually, 40 percent of the entire Soviet harvest of 100 million tons. Germany, on the other hand, without the newly incorporated Polish territories, had produced 23.5 million tons the previous year. Claussen then claimed that the Ukrainian population could make do with 10 to 15 million tons of grain, so that Ukraine constituted a major surplus territory. He did not need to spell out what would happen to the remaining 25 to 30 million tons produced by Ukraine.[53]

Ukraine may have produced 40 percent of the Soviet Union's grain, but its population constituted only around a fifth of the entire Soviet population,[54] which meant that the territory also supplied other parts of the Soviet Union. Thus the Germans would be removing grain that was intended for Soviet citizens, not for export. It was not a surplus, as Claussen claimed; it was required in order to feed part of the Soviet population. The figure of 25 to 30 million tons of grain per year to be plundered by the invaders appears to be the largest amount mentioned by anyone involved in these preparations, dwarfing as it did the earlier figures of 4 and 8.7 million tons calculated by the Reich Food Estate and the Staff Office of the Reich Farming Leader, respectively. It was admittedly uncommon for the economic planners to set the target quite so high, indicating that even in their inflated view of what was possible, Claussen's colleagues were aware that such an expectation was completely unrealistic. By this stage in the preparations, the figure cited was more often than not around a third of that given by Claussen.

In a letter dated May 14, Backe reminded Keitel of the importance for the economy of the "complete feeding of the army from [the] occupied territories" and added that he would be "exceedingly grateful" to be granted as soon as possible the opportunity to speak to Keitel in person on a matter that was "very important" for the food sector: "It is regarding the balancing of provisioning for the troops."[55] A mere five days later, the OKW issued Special Instructions to Directive No. 21 (Case Barbarossa), in which it was stated: "The exceptional conditions in the area 'Barbarossa' necessitate the *comprehensive and tightly conducted exploitation of the land* for supplying the troops, especially in the food area. The troops must realize that *every reduction in supplies*, particularly in food, increases the scope of the operations."[56]

On May 23 the notorious Economic Policy Guidelines for Economic Organization East produced by the agricultural section of the Economic Staff East appeared.[57] Exactly who penned the guidelines is unknown. The head of the agricultural section of the Economic Staff East was Dr. Hans-Joachim Riecke, *Ministerialdirektor* in the RMEL and Backe's right-hand man. The guidelines constituted the most explicit elucidation of the starvation policy known:

> As Germany and Europe require [grain] surpluses under all circumstances, consumption [in the Soviet Union] must be reduced accordingly. . . . In contrast to the territories occupied so far, this reduction in consumption can indeed be implemented because the main surplus territory is spatially starkly separated from the main deficit territory. . . . The surplus territories are located in the black earth territory (i.e., in the south and the southeast) and in the Caucasus. The deficit territories are located predominantly in the wooded zone of the north (Podsol soils). Thus a sealing off of the black earth territories must make

more or less large surpluses in these territories available to us at all costs. The consequence is the nondelivery of the entire wooded zone, including the important industrial centers of Moscow and [St.] Petersburg. . . . The population of these territories, in particular the population of the cities, will have to face the most terrible famine. . . . Many tens of millions of people in this territory will become superfluous and will have to die or migrate to Siberia. Attempts to rescue the population there from death through starvation by obtaining surpluses from the black earth zone can only be at the expense of the provisioning of Europe. They prevent the possibility of Germany holding out until the end of the war; they prevent Germany and Europe from resisting the blockade. With regard to this, absolute clarity must reign.[58]

Among other things, the guidelines confirmed the accuracy of rumors circulating since the beginning of May to the effect that Russian cities were to be destroyed and their inhabitants starved to death. The guidelines also contained the explicit endorsement of Hitler and the rest of the German leadership: the strategy had received "the approval of the highest authorities" (*die Billigung der höchsten Stellen*).[59] On May 16, one week before the guidelines were issued, Backe had held a presentation for Hitler at the latter's mountain retreat on the Obersalzberg.[60] Although the subject of Backe's presentation is not known, work on the guidelines would by that time have been at an advanced stage and Backe's meeting with Hitler would have provided him with an opportunity to report on them. That the guidelines received Hitler's approval demonstrates that the starvation policy was not devised in order to provide arguments for an "a priori fixed policy of annihilation" on Hitler's part.[61] It had in fact been conceived long before other criminal policies vis-à-vis the Soviet civilian population, such as the Wehrmacht's so-called Criminal Orders or the deployment of the *Einsatzgruppen* of the Security Police and the SD.[62]

The "Decimation of the Slavic Population by Thirty Million"

As part of the Folder for District Agricultural Leaders (*Kreislandwirtschaftsführermappe*), Backe issued his "12 Commandments" (*12 Gebote*) on June 1.[63] The eleventh commandment served as a reminder, if one was needed, of the intention to starve large sections of the Soviet population: "The Russian has already endured poverty, hunger, and frugality for centuries. His stomach is elastic, hence no false sympathy. Do not attempt to apply the German standard of living as your yardstick and to alter the Russian way of life."⁶⁴ These words were very similar to the terminology used by Thomas in his study of February 1941, quoted earlier. This should come as no surprise, particularly in light of their close cooperation during the planning phase and their shared points of view, as expressed at the beginning of May. As early as 1984, Rolf-Dieter Müller identified Backe and his "partner" Thomas as the "two men" who—"in absolute agreement"—set up a new economic organization and "formulated its objectives."⁶⁵ A number of experts in the field have since subscribed to Müller's assessment of Thomas's role as the chief exponent of the starvation policy alongside Backe.⁶⁶

At the beginning of June, the reduction of meat rations announced in January came into effect.⁶⁷ Just over a week later, on June 10, Backe visited *Reichsführer-SS* Himmler to discuss agriculture in the Soviet territories.⁶⁸ A postwar statement by the designated higher SS and police leader for Russia-Center, *SS-Gruppenführer* Erich von dem Bach-Zelewski, indicates that the two men may have discussed the starvation policy. In any case, Himmler was aware of it by this time at the latest. Between June 12 and 15, Himmler hosted a gathering of a dozen senior SS leaders at his Westphalian castle, the Wewelsburg.⁶⁹ Bach-Zelewski, who was among those present, recalled Himmler saying that "the purpose of the Russian campaign" was "the decimation of the Slavic population by thirty million."⁷⁰ Coincidence or not, thirty million was the amount by which the Soviet population—exclusively the urban population—had grown between the beginning of World War I in 1914 and the beginning of World War II in 1939.⁷¹ According to the economic policy guidelines of May 23, it was "in particular the population of the cities" that would "have to face the most terrible famine."⁷² The references to the death from starvation of "tens of millions" at the May 2 meeting and to "many tens of millions" in the economic policy guidelines of May 23 had by mid-June at the latest been concretized; the murder of thirty million Soviet citizens was envisaged.

The explicit reference to the decimation of the Slavic population during the campaign against the USSR demonstrates that although economic motivations lay at the core of proposals to starve millions of Soviet citizens to death, racial considerations shaped the discourse when it came to what was deemed possible or not. It is barely imaginable that the starvation policy would have met with such a consensus within Germany's military and political elite had it been directed against, for example, the French or the Norwegian populace.⁷³

According to postwar testimony by the designated higher SS and police leader for Russia-South, *SS-Obergruppenführer* Friedrich Jeckeln, it was Bach-Zelewski, as higher SS and police leader for Russia-Center, whom Himmler had tasked with the "annihilation of 20 million Soviet citizens" in Belarus and the territories further east, a fact Bach-Zelewski had neglected to mention in his statement at Nuremberg.[74] This was confirmed by comments made during a visit to the headquarters of Army Group Center during July 1941 by the chief of the Advance Commando Moscow (*Vorkommando Moskau*) of *Einsatzgruppe* B, Professor Dr. Franz Alfred Six:

> Hitler intends to extend the eastern border of the Reich as far as the line Baku-Stalingrad-Moscow-Leningrad. Eastward of this line as far as the Urals, a "blazing strip" will emerge in which all life is to be erased. It is intended to decimate the around thirty million Russians living in this strip through starvation, by removing all foodstuffs from this enormous territory. All those involved in this operation are to be forbidden on pain of death to give a Russian even a piece of bread. The large cities from Leningrad to Moscow are to be razed to the ground; the SS-Leader von dem Bach-Zelewski will be responsible for the implementation of these measures.[75]

Clearly, the SS aimed to play a central role in the fulfillment of the starvation policy.

On June 16, less than a week before the launch of operations, the Guidelines for the Management of the Economy in the Soviet territories were issued in Göring's name.[76] These instructions, known as the Green Folder (*Grüne Mappe*) because of the color of their binding, constituted the official economic handbook for the occupation troops and served first and foremost to orientate those in the highest leadership and command positions down as far as divisional level.[77] In his preamble to the guidelines, the chief of the OKW, *Generalfeldmarschall* Wilhelm Keitel, stated that it was of exceptional importance for the continuation of the war that the economic exploitation of the Soviet territories be carried out "immediately and to the greatest extent possible."[78] The Green Folder itself stated that the first task in the area of food and agriculture was to ensure as soon as possible that the German troops were completely fed from the occupied territory in order to relieve Europe's food situation and to unburden the transportation routes. The outflow of the most important foodstuffs, oil crops and grain, from the southern territories into the agricultural deficit territories of central and northern Russia was to be ruthlessly suppressed.[79]

These instructions constituted the explicit endorsement of the strategy described in the economic policy guidelines from May 23. It is thus no wonder that Leningrad, Moscow, and the territory east of them were described in the Green Folder as constituting a "difficult problem" with regard to the treatment of the population, as the million-strong cities required substantial food subsidies.[80] The guidelines from May 23 had already made clear what fate awaited the inhabitants of these cities. The Green Folder had been compiled by *Oberst* Hans Nagel of the Wi Rü Amt,[81] who was Thomas's liaison officer with Göring,[82] and was approved by Rosenberg's staff prior to its release.[83] The contents of the Green Folder confirm that the starvation strategy was communicated in written form to the troops themselves down as far as divisional level. Corresponding instructions would conceivably have been passed further down the chain of command in oral form.

Two days before the launch of operations, Rosenberg held a speech in which he signalled his approval of the starvation policy:

> During these years, the feeding of the German people stands without doubt at the top of German demands in the east, and here the southern territories and northern Caucasus will have to balance out German food requirements. By no means do we acknowledge the obligation to feed the Russian people as well [as ourselves] from these surplus territories. We know that that is a harsh necessity that is beyond any emotion. A very extensive evacuation will without doubt be necessary, and very difficult years will certainly be in store for the Russian people.[84]

By the time German troops crossed the border on June 22, Germany's leading military and political institutions had all contributed to formulating the starvation policy or signalled their explicit endorsement of it. It had become state policy.

A "Real Possibility If One is Militarily Able to Keep the Central Russians from Their Fields": Implementation and Consequences of the Starvation Policy

In referring during his testimony at Nuremberg to the decimation of the Slavic population by thirty million, Bach-Zelewski stated: "I am of the opinion that these methods really would have led to the annihilation of thirty millions if they had in this way been pursued further and if the situation had not been completely altered due to changes in circumstances."[85] The consultant for eastern questions in the Office of the Four-Year Plan, *Leutnant* Dr. Friedrich Richter, was of the same opinion. In a letter from the front written in the spring of 1943, Richter commented on some of the reasons for invading the Soviet Union two years earlier:

Economic interests and the predicament, as a result of the isolation of Europe, of having to obtain yet more grain and oil crops and oil from our own sphere of influence also brought about for many an affirmation of the campaign on economic grounds, although experts at the time pointed out that Russia already in peacetime could only fulfill German treaty demands at the greatest cost to itself, much less so after disruption of the transportation routes and the economic cycle there. [*Oberregierungsrat* Dr. Otto] Donner and my house [i.e., the VJPB] also pointed at the time to this expected deterioration.

Out of this situation, the Backesian thesis [*Backesche These*] developed [that] one must separate the western and southern Russian territories, as main producers, from their consumer territories in central Russia and incorporate them once more into the European supply zone; a real possibility if one is militarily in a position to keep the central Russians from their fields for a long period of time and if one wins over the inhabitants of the occupied territory.[86]

It should come as no surprise, however, that the starvation policy could not be implemented to the extent to which the preinvasion planners had envisaged. It soon became clear that the military campaign was not going according to plan. With insufficient numbers of security troops and a military situation that rapidly began to deteriorate, it proved impossible to cordon off whole regions and simply bring about the death of millions of people through starvation. In the event, countless Soviet civilians took to the country roads in search of food, and trade on the black market thrived.

Nevertheless, one should by no means conclude from the failure to bring about the death from starvation of thirty million Soviets that the implementation of this policy was not attempted. The occupation authorities on the spot knew how they were to treat the indigenous population. During a speech held in 1942, Plenipotentiary for Labor Deployment Fritz Sauckel recalled that during a visit to Ukraine in late autumn 1941, all German authorities there were convinced that in the winter of 1941/42 "at least ten to twenty millions of these people will simply starve to death."[87] During a discussion in Berlin in late November 1941, Göring told the Italian foreign minister, Count Galeazzo Ciano, that certain peoples had to be decimated and twenty to thirty million inhabitants of the Soviet Union would starve during 1941.[88] The acquisition of agricultural surpluses to the detriment of the indigenous population remained, indeed, the primary aim of German occupation policy in the Soviet Union right through to 1944.[89]

As a result of the unexpected course taken by the military campaign, it was the Soviet prisoners of war who constituted the largest group among the victims of the starvation policy. It was clear to the Wehrmacht on exactly what scale they could expect to capture Soviet troops and yet they neglected to make the requisite preparations for feeding and sheltering the captured soldiers,[90] who were viewed by the economic planners and the military leadership alike as the German troops' direct competitors when it came to food. The obvious limitations on their freedom of movement and the relative ease with which large numbers could be segregated and their rations controlled were crucial factors in the death of over 3 million of them, the vast majority directly or indirectly as a result of starvation and undernourishment.[91] The most reliable figures for the death rate among Soviet POWs in German captivity reveal that 3.3 million died from a total of 5.7 million captured between June 1941 and February 1945.[92] Of these 3.3 million, 2 million had already died by the beginning of February 1942.[93] Among Soviet civilians, it was—as intended—primarily the urban population that succumbed to the effects of this conscious policy of starvation. Although Leningrad was ultimately besieged instead of conquered and razed to the ground, as had been the preinvasion intention, at least 800,000 and probably well over a million civilians starved to death during the almost nine-hundred-day siege.[94] Urban centers that, unlike Leningrad, German forces did succeed in occupying, such as the Ukrainian cities of Kiev and Kharkiv, also suffered a horrendous loss of human life.[95] All in all, the starvation policy cost the lives of millions of Soviet citizens.[96]

Concluding Remarks: Starvation Policy and Radicalization

In discussing the starvation policy pursued by Germany during the war against the Soviet Union, the German historian Jörg Ganzenmüller recently commented that prior to the campaign the view within the political and military elites that it could only be won with the utmost ruthlessness, and that this was therefore legitimate, had already hardened into a doctrine. All problems that posed themselves during the war were thus met with a radicalization of methods. Alternative suggestions for solutions were regarded as defeatist and excluded from the discourse. In this way, the decision not to feed the Soviet civilian population during the war became a dogma. The radicalization process was therefore predetermined by a discourse of radicalism, yet this did not progress of its own accord or in any way unavoidably. It was in fact again and again accelerated anew, accepted or at least countenanced.[97] This appraisal applies in the same measure to the preinvasion planning process that set the scene for the actual occupation policy pursued from June 22, 1941, onward.

Notes

1. Letter from Dr. Wilhelm Schubert to Georg Thomas, "Betr. Studie Südost," May 13, 1941, signed Wilhelm Schubert, fol. 272: "Backesian plan" (Backe'scher Plan), RW 19/739, fols. 272–73, Bundesarchiv-Militärarchiv, Freiburg im Breisgau (hereafter BA-MA); and "Auszug aus einem Feldpostbrief von Leutnant Dr. Friedrich Richter, Referent für Ostfragen vom Vierjahresplan, vom 26.5.1943," fol. 1: "Backesian thesis" (Backesche These), R 6/60a, fols. 1–4, Bundesarchiv, Berlin-Lichterfelde (hereafter BAB).

2. Here the term "radicalization" is understood to mean the "cumulative radicalization" inherent within the National Socialist regime (see Hans Mommsen, "Der Nationalsozialismus: Kumulative Radikalisierung und Selbstzerstörung des Regimes," in Bibliographisches Institut, ed., *Meyers Enzyklopädisches Lexikon*, vol. 16, rev. ed. (Mannheim: Lexikonverlag, 1976), 785–90) rather than the concept of a radicalization resulting from a combination of the German response to Soviet crimes, Hitler's manipulation of a supposedly reluctant German military, and so-called economic necessity and deteriorating circumstances (e.g., as applied by Klaus Jochen Arnold), which is used as an apologetic explanation for atrocities committed by German troops in the east. On this, see Christian Gerlach's review of Klaus Jochen Arnold, *Die Wehrmacht und die Besatzungspolitik in den besetzten Gebieten der Sowjetunion. Kriegführung und Radikalisierung im "Unternehmen Barbarossa"* (Berlin: Duncker & Humblot, 2005), in *Zeitschrift für Ostmitteleuropa-Forschung 55*, no. 2 (2006): 295–97.

3. See Alex J. Kay, *Exploitation, Resettlement, Mass Murder: Political and Economic Planning for German Occupation Policy in the Soviet Union, 1940–1941* (New York: Berghahn, 2006), 27–31.

4. Georg Thomas, *Geschichte der deutschen Wehr- und Rüstungswirtschaft (1918–1943/45)*, ed. Wolfgang Birkenfeld (Boppard am Rhein: Harald Boldt, 1966), 261.

5. "Weisung Nr. 21: Fall Barbarossa," doc. 21, December 18, 1940, signed Adolf Hitler, reproduced in Walter Hubatsch, ed., *Hitlers Weisungen für die Kriegführung, 1939–1945*, 2nd ed. (Koblenz: Bernard & Graefe, 1983), 84–88, here 86–87. Leningrad was also to be occupied.

6. "Geheime Reichssache!," letter from Herbert Backe to Richard Walther Darré, February 9, 1941, R 3601/3371, fols. 16–20, BAB. According to Backe, he had made these revisions in the presence of *Ministerialdirektor* Dr. Alfons Moritz of the RMEL (see fol. 19).

7. "Betr.: Bericht über die Versorgungslage Getreide, Fleisch, und Fett im Wirtschaftsjahr 1940/41," letter from Darré to Dr. Hans-Heinrich Lammers, January 9, 1941, R 3601/3371, fols. 28–31, BAB. Although Darré did pass on the report, he apparently did not sign it because Backe's revisions to

the report had been made *after* the departments subordinated to Backe had already signed the report (see R 3601/3371, fol. 19).

8. Herbert Backe, *Um die Nahrungsfreiheit Europas: Weltwirtschaft oder Großraum*, 2nd ed. (Leipzig: Goldmann, 1943), Darstellung 1, inside front cover.

9. Götz Aly and Susanne Heim, *Vordenker der Vernichtung: Auschwitz und die deutschen Pläne für eine neue europäische Ordnung* (Hamburg: Hoffmann & Campe, 1991), 366.

10. Ibid., 366n2. An RMEL report from December 14, 1940, titled "The First Wartime Harvest in Europe" put continental Europe's annual grain deficit at 21.7 million tons, the equivalent of food requirements for almost fifty million people.

11. William Carr, *Arms, Autarky, and Aggression: A Study in German Foreign Policy, 1933–1939* (New York: W. W. Norton, 1973), 53–54.

12. R 3601/3371, fol. 19, BAB.

13. "Geheime Reichssache!," letter from Dr. Alfons Moritz to Darré, February 13, 1941, R 3601/3371, fols. 6–7, BAB; "Geheime Reichssache," letter from Darré to Moritz, February 12, 1941, R 3601/3371, fol. 8, BAB; and Terminkalender Hermann Göring, fol. 7, entry for January 13, 1941, ED 180/5, Archiv des Instituts für Zeitgeschichte, Munich (hereafter IfZ-Archiv). *Staatssekretär* in the Office of the Four-Year Plan Paul Körner was also present.

14. "Rundschreiben," January 13, 1941, signed Hermann Göring, R 3601/3371, fol. 10, BAB.

15. "Vortrag Amtschef bei GFM Keitel," January 22, 1941, RW 19/164, fol. 111, BA-MA.

16. Christian Gerlach, *Kalkulierte Morde: Die deutsche Wirtschafts- und Vernichtungspolitik in Weißrußland, 1941 bis 1944* (Hamburg: Hamburger Edition, 1999), 66–68; and Kay, *Exploitation, Resettlement, Mass Murder*, 50–53, 56–57.

17. Terminkalender Hermann Göring, fol. 15, entry for January 29, 1941, ED 180/5, IfZ-Archiv. The meeting was also attended by Körner; Neumann; *Staatssekretär* in the Reich Labor Ministry, Friedrich Syrup; *Unterstaatssekretär* in the Reich Economics Ministry, *Generalleutnant* Hermann von Hanneken; Reich minister for armaments and munitions, Dr. Fritz Todt; head of the research and development department in the Office of the Four-Year Plan, Carl Krauch; and commander of the Replacement Army, *Generaloberst* Fritz Fromm. Thomas had attended a two-hour meeting two days earlier at which Göring, Körner, Neumann, and Hanneken were also present (see Terminkalender Hermann Göring, fol. 14, entry for January 27, 1941, ED 180/5, IfZ-Archiv).

18. See "Vortrag Hauptmann Emmerich beim Amtschef," January 30, 1941, RW 19/164, fol. 126, BA-MA: "Staatssekr. Neumann hat einen Fachmann

für Rußland, mit dem zusammengearbeitet werden soll. Sts. Backe soll dem Führer gesagt haben, daß der Besitz der Ukraine uns von jeder wirtschaftlichen Sorge befreien würde. In Wirklichkeit soll Backe aber gesagt haben, daß, wenn überhaupt ein Gebiet uns nützen kann, es dann nur die Ukraine sein könnte. Die Ukraine allein Überschußgebiet, das ganze europäische Rußland aber nicht."

19. "Vortrag Obstlt. Matzky, Major Knapp, Hptm. Emmerich beim Amtschef," February 12, 1941, RW 19/164, fol. 150, BA-MA: "Reichsnährstand schätzt den Zuschußbedarf Deutschlands und der von Deutschland beherrschten Gebiete auf 5 Mill. t. Durch eine 10%ige Senkung des russischen Verbrauchs glaubt man etwa 4 Mill. t. aus Russland zu bekommen."

20. RW 19/164, fol. 150, BA-MA. The text of the German-Soviet trade agreement of January 10, 1941, is reproduced in *Akten zur deutschen auswärtigen Politik, 1918–1945, Serie D: 1937–1945*, vol. 11/2 (Bonn: Gebr. Hermes, 1964), 887–89 (doc. 637, "Wirtschaftsabkommen zwischen dem Deutschen Reich und der Union der Sozialistischen Sowjet-Republiken vom 10. Januar 1941").

21. See RW 19/164, fol. 150, BA-MA.

22. "Vortrag Hptm. Emmerich beim Amtschef," February 19, 1941, RW 19/164, fol. 171, BA-MA. A total of fifty-five copies were made (see Thomas, *Geschichte*, 515).

23. For the full text of the study, see Thomas, *Geschichte*, 515–32, "Die wehrwirtschaftlichen Auswirkungen einer Operation im Osten," dated February 13, 1941, here 517: "Wenn es auch ungewiß erscheint, ob es gelingt, M.T.S. und Vorräte in großem Umfange vor der Vernichtung zu bewahren, wenn außerdem infolge der Einwirkungen eines Krieges im Höchstfalle eine 70%ige Ernte erwartet werden kann, so muß man doch berücksichtigen, daß der Russe gewöhnt ist, seinen Verbrauch schlechten Ernten anzupassen, und daß bei einer Bevölkerung von 160 Mill. auch eine *kleine Senkung* des je Kopf-Verbrauchs erhebliche Getreidemengen freimacht. Unter diesen Voraussetzungen könnte es möglich sein, den deutschen *Zuschußbedarf* für 1941 und 1942 zu decken."

24. "Vortrag Amtschef beim Reichsmarschall," February 26, 1941, RW 19/164, fol. 180, BA-MA; and "Aktennotiz über Vortrag beim Reichsmarschall am 26.2.1941," February 27, 1941, RW 19/185, fol. 171, BA-MA.

25. Franz Halder, *Kriegstagebuch: Tägliche Aufzeichnungen des Chefs des Generalstabes des Heeres 1939–1942*, vol. 2, *Von der geplanten Landung in England bis zum Beginn des Ostfeldzuges* (Stuttgart: W. Kohlhammer, 1963), 271–72, entries for February 4 and 5.

26. Quoted in Christian Gerlach, "Militärische 'Versorgungszwänge,' Besatzungspolitik, und Massenverbrechen: Die Rolle des Generalquartiermeisters des Heeres und seiner Dienststellen im Krieg gegen die Sowjetunion,"

in *Ausbeutung, Vernichtung, Öffentlichkeit: Neue Studien zur nationalsozialistischen Lagerpolitik*, ed. Norbert Frei, Sybille Steinbacher, and Bernd C. Wagner (Munich: K.G. Saur, 2000), 184: "Der Nachschub muß durch weitgehende Ausnutzung des Landes eingeschränkt, das Erfassungswesen straff geregelt werden. Nicht durch wahlloses Zugreifen, sondern durch Beschlagnahme und Beitreibung nach wohldurchdachtem Plan sind die Bestände des Landes nutzbar zu machen."

27. See Nuremberg document (hereafter Nbg. Doc.) 1317-PS, "Aktennotiz Besprechung beim Herrn Amtschef, General der Inf. Thomas am 28.2.41," March 1, 1941, signed *Hauptmann* Dr. Hamann, printed in International Military Tribunal, ed., *Der Prozess gegen die Hauptkriegsverbrecher vor dem Internationalen Militärgerichtshof, Nürnberg, 14. November 1945–1. Oktober 1946* (hereafter *IMG*), vol. 27 (Nuremberg: Sekretariat des Gerichtshofs, 1948), 170.

28. Gerlach, *Kalkulierte Morde*, 73. Gerlach misdates the second meeting to March 13. A discussion between Halder and Wagner did take place on March 13 (see Halder, *Kriegstagebuch*, 2:311, entry for March 13), though not the one in question.

29. Halder, *Kriegstagebuch*, 2:301, 312, entries for March 4 and 14.

30. Norbert Müller, ed., *Okkupation, Raub, Vernichtung: Dokumente zur Besatzungspolitik der faschistischen Wehrmacht auf sowjetischem Territorium, 1941 bis 1944* (Berlin: Militärverlag der DDR, 1980), 35–42, doc. 4, "Anordnung des Oberbefehlshabers des Heeres über Organisation und Aufgaben des militärischen Okkupationsregimes in den zu erobernden Gebieten der UdSSR (Besondere Anordnungen für die Versorgung, Teil C)," April 3, 1941, signed Franz Halder: "Die Sicherung der großen Verkehrswege und die Ausnützung des Landes für die Bedürfnisse der Truppe zur Entlastung des Nachschubs ist von ausschlaggebender Bedeutung für die Operationen. Es kommt daher darauf an, daß alle im rück. Gebiet eingesetzten Kräfte des Heeres ausschließlich für diese Aufgaben eingesetzt werden" (35).

31. "Besprechung Amtschef bei Staatssekretär Backe," March 12, 1941, RW 19/164, fol. 213, BA-MA.

32. "Vortrag bei Reichsmarschall Göring am 19.3.41," March 20, 1941, RW 19/164, fol. 228, BA-MA.

33. Rolf-Dieter Müller, ed., *Die deutsche Wirtschaftspolitik in den besetzten sowjetischen Gebieten, 1941–1943: Der Abschlußbericht des Wirtschaftsstabes Ost und Aufzeichnungen eines Angehörigen des Wirtschaftskommandos Kiew* (Boppard am Rhein: Harald Boldt, 1991), 43.

34. See Nbg. Doc. 126-EC, "Wirtschaftspolitische Richtlinien für Wirtschaftsorganisation Ost, Gruppe Landwirtschaft," May 23, 1941, Wirtschaftsstab Ost, Gruppe La, printed in *IMG*, vol. 36 (Nuremberg: Sekretariat des Gerichtshofs, 1949), 137–38. For the date of the study ("Erzeugung

und Verbrauch von Nahrungs- und Futtermitteln in der UdSSR") see Gerlach, *Kalkulierte Morde*, 67–68.

35. "Geheime Reichssache!," letters from Backe to Darré, June 25 and 26, 1941, N 1094/II 20, Mappe III, Bundesarchiv, Koblenz (hereafter BAK); "Geheime Reichssache," letter from Darré to Göring, June 27, 1941, N 1094/II 20, Mappe II, BAK; letter from Chief of the Staff Office of the *Reichsmarschall* of the Greater German Reich *Ministerialdirektor* Dr. Erich Gritzbach to Darré, July 17, 1941, N 1094/II 20, Mappe II, BAK; "Geheime Reichssache," letter from Darré to Gritzbach, July 22, 1941, N 1094/II 20, Mappe II, BAK. See also entry in Darré's diary for March 5, 1941, N 1094/I 65a, fol. 123, BAK; Kay, *Exploitation, Resettlement, Mass Murder*, 53.

36. "Aktennotiz über Besprechung am 31.3.," April 2, 1941, RW 19/165, fol. 2, BA-MA.

37. Peter Witte, Michael Wildt, Martina Voigt, Dieter Pohl, Peter Klein, Christian Gerlach, Christoph Dieckmann, and Andrej Angrick, eds., *Der Dienstkalender Heinrich Himmlers, 1941/42* (Hamburg: Christians, 1999), 143 (entry for April 1, 1941).

38. "Geheime Reichssache!," letter from Körner to Backe, April 12, 1941, N 1094/II 20, Mappe III, BAK. For use of the term "secret decree," see "Geheime Reichssache!," letter from Backe to Darré, June 25, 1941, N 1094/II 20, Mappe III, BAK.

39. Alex J. Kay, "Germany's *Staatssekretäre*, Mass Starvation and the Meeting of 2 May 1941," *Journal of Contemporary History* 41, no. 4 (2006): 690–91.

40. Nbg. Doc. 2718–PS, "Aktennotiz über Ergebnis der heutigen Besprechung mit den Staatssekretären über Barbarossa," May 2, 1941, printed in *IMG*, vol. 31 (Nuremberg: Sekretariat des Gerichtshofs, 1948), 84: "(1) Der Krieg ist nur weiter zu führen, wenn die gesamte Wehrmacht im 3. Kriegsjahr aus Rußland ernährt wird. (2) Hierbei werden zweifellos zig Millionen Menschen verhungern, wenn von uns das für uns Notwendige aus dem Lande herausgeholt wird." On the May 2 meeting, see Kay, "Germany's *Staatssekretäre*"; Alex J. Kay, "Revisiting the Meeting of the *Staatssekretäre* on May 2, 1941: A Response to Klaus Jochen Arnold and Gert C. Lübbers," *Journal of Contemporary History* 43, no. 1 (2008): 93–104; Alex J. Kay, "Verhungernlassen als Massenmordstrategie: Das Treffen der deutschen Staatssekretäre am 2. Mai 1941," *Zeitschrift für Weltgeschichte* 11, no. 1 (2010): 81–105.

41. See also Nbg. Doc. 126-EC, "Wirtschaftspolitische Richtlinien für Wirtschaftsorganisation Ost, Gruppe Landwirtschaft," printed in *IMG*, 36:148–50, 154.

42. Rolf-Dieter Müller, "Industrielle Interessenpolitik im Rahmen des 'Generalplans Ost': Dokumente zum Einfluß von Wehrmacht, Industrie und SS auf die wirtschaftspolitische Zielsetzung für Hitlers Ostimperium,"

Militärgeschichtliche Mitteilungen 29 (1981): 118, doc. 4, "Auszug aus einer geheimen Aufzeichnung von General Thomas vom 5. Mai über von Hitler bzw. Göring noch zu entscheidende Fragen," May 5, 1941.

43. During a discussion with journalists in February 1942, Hans-Joachim Riecke claimed to have pointed out as early as two months before the beginning of operations, that is, in late April 1941, that "with regard to food, the problem of supplying Leningrad cannot be solved" (see Aly and Heim, *Vordenker der Vernichtung*, 384–85).

44. Peter Broucek, ed., *Ein General im Zwielicht: Die Erinnerungen Edmund Glaises von Horstenau*, vol. 3, *Deutscher Bevollmächtigter General in Kroatien und Zeuge des Untergangs des "Tausendjährigen Reiches"* (Vienna: Böhlau, 1988), 107–8: "In Rußland sollen alle Städte und Kunststätten samt dem Kreml dem Erdboden gleichgemacht, Rußland auf das Niveau eines Bauernvolkes herabgedrückt werden, aus dem es keinen Aufstieg gibt" (108). For contradictory statements on whether Hitler intended *before* the campaign to raze large Soviet cities to the ground, see Dieter Pohl, *Die Herrschaft der Wehrmacht: Deutsche Militärbesatzung in der Sowjetunion, 1941–1944* (Munich: Oldenbourg, 2008), 152, 183.

45. It remains unclear, however, exactly when Stahlecker was appointed chief of *Einsatzgruppe* A. See Michael Wildt, *Generation des Unbedingten: Das Führungskorps des Reichssicherheitshauptamtes*, rev. ed. (Hamburg: Hamburger Edition, 2003), 189; Christian Gerlach, "Die Einsatzgruppe B 1941/42," in *Die Einsatzgruppen in der besetzten Sowjetunion 1941/42: Die Tätigkeits- und Lageberichte des Chefs der Sicherheitspolizei und des SD*, ed. Peter Klein (Berlin: Edition Hentrich, 1997), 64n5; and Helmut Krausnick, "Die Einsatzgruppen vom Anschluß Österreichs bis zum Feldzug gegen die Sowjetunion: Entwicklung und Verhältnis zur Wehrmacht," in Helmut Krausnick and Hans-Heinrich Wilhelm, *Die Truppe des Weltanschauungskrieges: Die Einsatzgruppen der Sicherheitspolizei und des SD 1938–1942* (Stuttgart: Deutsche Verlags-Anstalt, 1981), 143.

46. Elke Fröhlich, ed., *Die Tagebücher von Joseph Goebbels. Teil 1, Aufzeichnungen 1923–1941*, vol. 9, *Dezember 1940–Juli 1941* (Munich: K. G. Saur, 1998), 293–94, entry for May 6, 1941: "Wenn nur die diesjährige Ernte gut wird. Und dann wollen wir uns ja im Osten gesundstoßen."

47. Ibid., 283–84, entry for May 1, 1941: "Backe beherrscht übrigens sein Ressort meisterhaft. Bei ihm wird getan, was überhaupt nur möglich ist."

48. "Termine am Mittwoch, dem 7. Mai 1941," N 1075/9, BAK.

49. "Aktennotiz über die Unterredung mit Staatssekretär Körner," May 8, 1941, Nbg. Doc. PS 1018, fols. 64–73, IfZ-Archiv. Rosenberg's permanent representative, *Gauleiter* Dr. Alfred Meyer, also attended the meeting.

50. Letter from Schubert to Thomas, "Betr. Studie Südost," May 13, 1941, signed Wilhelm Schubert, RW 19/739, fol. 272, BA-MA.

51. "Dr. Claussen über die Ernährungslage," May 14, 1941, signed Eicke, RW 19/473, fols. 177–79, BA-MA.

52. RW 19/473, fols. 177–78, BA-MA. See also "Kriegswirtschaftlicher Lagebericht Nr. 21, Mai 1941," June 10, 1941, signed Georg Thomas, RW 19/177, fol. 19, BA-MA, where the phraseology used is almost identical.

53. RW 19/473, fol. 178, BA-MA. For a figure of 120 million tons for the entire Soviet grain harvest, see "Die sowjetische Landwirtschaft," May 21, 1941, Volkswirtschaftliche Abteilung, Deutsche Reichsbank (for 1940), R 2/30921, BAB. On Claussen, see Gotthilf Hempel, "Dr. Julius Claussen zum siebzigsten Gebürtstag," *Berichte der Deutschen Wissenschaftlichen Kommission für Meeresforschung* 20, no. 3/4 (1969): 177–78; and Gotthilf Hempel, "Der erste Streich," *Der Spiegel*, August 26, 1964, 32–33.

54. "Zur Möglichkeit, den großdeutschen Fehlbedarf an Getreide in Höhe von jährlich 3 Millionen t aus Sowjetrußland sicherzustellen," June 13, 1941, Referat A 4, Dr. Storm, R 2501/7007, fols. 233–56, here fols. 241, 253, 255, BAB (31 million from 170.5 million in 1939, 40.3 million from 193.2 million in 1940); and R 2/30921, BAB (31 million from 169 million in 1937). The second of these reports states that Ukraine produced as of 1937 only 20 percent of the entire grain harvest of 120 million tons. Compare these figures with Enrico Insabato, "Die Ukraine: Bevölkerung und Wirtschaft," Sammlung politischer und wirtschaftlicher Studien geleitet von Luigi Lojacono, n.d. (1940?), NS 43/41, fols. 130–41, here fols. 130–31, BAB, which states that the population of Ukraine was 33.5 million and that of the Soviet Union 173 million (also around a fifth).

55. Letter from Backe to Keitel, May 14, 1941, RW 19/739, fols. 124–25, BA-MA: "welche Bedeutung ... der restlosen Versorgung des Heeres aus besetzten Gebieten zukommt"; "Es handelt sich um die Bilanzierung der Truppenverpflegung."

56. N. Müller, ed., *Okkupation, Raub, Vernichtung*, 45–54, doc. 7, "Besondere Anordnungen Nr. 1 des Chefs des OKW zur Weisung Nr. 21 mit Anlagen über: Gliederung und Aufgaben der im Raum 'Barbarossa' einzusetzenden Wirtschaftsorganisation (1); Beute, Beschlagnahme, und Inanspruchnahme von Dienstleistungen (2); Verhalten der deutschen Truppen in der Sowjetunion (3)," May 19, 1941, signed Wilhelm Keitel: "Die besonders gelagerten Verhältnisse im Raum 'Barbarossa' machen die *umfassende und straff geleitete Ausnutzung des Landes* für die Versorgung der Truppe gerade auf dem Verpflegungsgebiet erforderlich. Die Truppe muß sich bewusst sein, daß *jede Einsparung im Nachschub*, besonders von Verpflegung, die Reichweite der Operationen vergrößert" (45).

57. Nbg. Doc. 126-EC, "Wirtschaftspolitische Richtlinien für Wirtschaftsorganisation Ost, Gruppe Landwirtschaft," May 23, 1941, Wirtschaftsstab Ost, Gruppe La, printed in *IMG*, 36:135–57.

58. Ibid., 138, 141, 145: "Da Deutschland bezw. Europa unter allen Umständen Überschüsse braucht, muß also der Konsum entsprechend herabgedrückt werden.... Dieses Herabdrücken des Konsums ist im Gegensatz zu den bisherigen besetzten Gebieten auch durchführbar deshalb, weil das Hauptüberschußgebiet von dem Hauptzuschußgebiet räumlich scharf getrennt ist.... Die Überschußgebiete liegen im Schwarzerdegebiet (also im Süden, Südosten) und im Kaukasus. Die Zuschußgebiete liegen im wesentlichen [sic] in der Waldzone des Nordens (Podsolböden). Daraus folgt: Eine Abriegelung der Schwarzerdegebiete muß unter allen Umständen mehr oder weniger hohe Überschüsse in diesen Gebieten für uns greifbar machen. Die Konsequenz ist die nicht Belieferung der gesamten Waldzone einschließlich der wesentlichen Industriezentren Moskau und Petersburg.... Die Bevölkerung dieser Gebiete, insbesondere die Bevölkerung der Städte, wird größter Hungersnot entgegensehen müssen.... Viele 10 Millionen von Menschen werden in diesem Gebiet überflüssig und werden sterben oder nach Sibirien auswandern müssen. Versuche, die Bevölkerung dort vor dem Hungertode dadurch zu retten, daß man aus der Schwarzerdezone Überschüsse heranzieht, können nur auf Kosten der Versorgung Europas gehen. Sie unterbinden die Durchhaltemöglichkeit Deutschlands im Kriege, sie unterbinden die Blockadefestigkeit Deutschlands und Europas. Darüber muß absolute Klarheit herrschen."

59. Ibid., 140. It is unclear why Christopher Browning and Jürgen Matthäus regard this reference to "the highest authorities" as too vague (see Christopher R. Browning, with contributions by Jürgen Matthäus, *The Origins of the Final Solution: The Evolution of Nazi Jewish Policy, September 1939–March 1942* (Lincoln: University of Nebraska Press, 2004), 487n120). Speaking to a colleague in December 1941, Dr. Wilhelm Stuckart, *Staatssekretär* in the Reich Ministry of the Interior, stated: "The treatment of the evacuated Jews is based on a decision from the highest authority (*von höchster Stelle*)." Commenting on this, Wilhelm Lenz concludes: "It should be beyond dispute that with 'highest authority' Stuckart can only have meant Hitler." See Wilhelm Lenz, "Die Handakten von Bernhard Lösener, 'Rassereferent' im Reichsministerium des Innern," in *Archiv und Geschichte: Festschrift für Friedrich P. Kahlenberg*, ed. Klaus Oldenhage, Hermann Schreyer, and Wolfram Werner (Düsseldorf: Droste, 2000), 693.

60. Letter from Backe to Darré, October 9, 1941, N 1094/II 20, Mappe III, BAK. According to an entry in the diary of Backe's wife, Ursula, for May 30, 1941, Backe and Hitler met on May 15 in the presence of Lammers, Keitel, and head of the Party Chancellery Martin Bormann. See Gesine Gerhard, "Food and Genocide: Nazi Agrarian Politics in the Occupied Territories of the Soviet Union," *Contemporary European History* 18, no. 1 (2009): 57. Gesine Gerhard is currently working on a biography of Herbert Backe.

61. As claimed in Rolf-Dieter Müller, "Die Konsequenzen der 'Volksgemeinschaft': Ernährung, Ausbeutung, und Vernichtung," in *Der Zweite Weltkrieg: Analysen, Grundzüge, Forschungsbilanz*, ed. Wolfgang Michalka (Munich: Piper, 1989), 244.

62. On this see Gerlach, *Kalkulierte Morde*, 68–74, esp. 68–69.

63. Nbg. Doc. 089-USSR, "12 Gebote," June 1, 1941, signed Herbert Backe, printed in *IMG*, vol. 39 (Nuremberg: Sekretariat des Gerichtshofs, 1949), 367–71.

64. Ibid., 371: "Armut, Hunger und Genügsamkeit erträgt der russische Mensch schon seit Jahrhunderten. Sein Magen ist dehnbar, daher kein falsches Mitleid. Versucht nicht, den deutschen Lebensstandard als Maßstab anzulegen und die russische Lebensweise zu ändern."

65. Rolf-Dieter Müller, "Das 'Unternehmen Barbarossa' als wirtschaftlicher Raubkrieg," in *"Unternehmen Barbarossa": Der deutsche Überfall auf die Sowjetunion, 1941; Berichte, Analysen, Dokumente*, ed. Gerd R. Ueberschär and Wolfram Wette (Paderborn: Ferdinand Schöningh, 1984), 180–83.

66. Gerlach, *Kalkulierte Morde*, 68; Johannes Hürter, *Hitlers Heerführer: Die deutschen Oberbefehlshaber im Krieg gegen die Sowjetunion, 1941/42* (Munich: Oldenbourg, 2006), 243, 493; Adam Tooze, *The Wages of Destruction: The Making and Breaking of the Nazi Economy* (London: Allen Lane, 2006), 478; Kay, *Exploitation, Resettlement, Mass Murder*, 51–63; and Kay, "Revisiting the Meeting of the *Staatssekretäre*," 96–97.

67. RW 19/473, fol. 177, BA-MA. The date of June 1 given here, on May 14, by Claussen, diverges slightly from the date Backe announced to Goebbels on April 30, namely June 2 (see Fröhlich, ed., *Die Tagebücher von Joseph Goebbels, Teil 1, Band 9*, 283, entry for May 1, 1941).

68. Letter from Himmler to *SS-Brigadeführer* Ulrich Greifelt, head of the Staff Main Office of the Reich Commissar for the Strengthening of German Nationhood, June 11, 1941, NS 19/3874, fol. 9, BAB.

69. Witte et al., *Der Dienstkalender Heinrich Himmlers*, 172, entry for June 12, 1941; and postwar testimony of Erich von dem Bach-Zelewski in Nuremberg from January 7, 1946, printed in *IMG*, vol. 4 (Nuremberg: Sekretariat des Gerichtshofs, 1947), 542.

70. Postwar testimony of Erich von dem Bach-Zelewski in Nuremberg from January 7, 1946, printed in *IMG*, 4:535–36. Karl Wolff, the chief of Himmler's personal staff, who organized the gathering and also attended, qualified Bach-Zelewski's assertion by claiming that Himmler had "only spoken of millions of people who would lose their lives during this campaign." See Jochen von Lang, *Der Adjutant Karl Wolff: Der Mann zwischen Hitler und Himmler* (Munich: Herbig, 1985), 50–51.

71. Backe, *Um die Nahrungsfreiheit Europas*, 162; and Nbg. Doc. 126-EC, "Wirtschaftspolitische Richtlinien für Wirtschaftsorganisation Ost, Gruppe Landwirtschaft," printed in *IMG*, 36:136. These are the figures the

German planners were working with and believed to be true, and their accuracy is indeed confirmed by recent German and English research. See Hans-Heinrich Nolte, *Kleine Geschichte Rußlands* (Stuttgart: Reclam, 2003), 235; and Walter G. Moss, *A History of Russia*, vol. 2, *Since 1855* (New York: McGraw-Hill, 1997), 303. See also Peter Gatrell, "Economic and Demographic Change: Russia's Age of Economic Extremes," in *The Cambridge History of Russia*, vol. 3, *The Twentieth Century*, ed. Ronald Grigor Suny (Cambridge: Cambridge University Press, 2006), 399.

72. Nbg. Doc. 126-EC, "Wirtschaftspolitische Richtlinien für Wirtschaftsorganisation Ost, Gruppe Landwirtschaft," printed in *IMG*, 36:141.

73. Gerlach, *Kalkulierte Morde*, 630; Kay, *Exploitation, Resettlement, Mass Murder*, 120–21; and Hürter, *Hitlers Heerführer*, 501n250.

74. Postwar testimony of Friedrich Jeckeln in Riga from January 2, 1946, ZM 1683, vol. 1, fol. 105, Bundesarchiv-Zwischenarchiv, Dahlwitz-Hoppegarten.

75. Rudolf-Christoph Freiherr von Gersdorff, *Soldat im Untergang* (Frankfurt am Main: Ullstein, 1977), 93: "Hitler beabsichtige, die Ostgrenze des Reiches bis zur Linie Baku-Stalingrad-Moskau-Leningrad vorzuschieben. Ostwärts von dieser Linie werde bis zum Ural ein 'Brandstreifen' entstehen, in dessen Bereich alles Leben ausgelöscht werden würde. Man wolle die in diesem Streifen lebenden etwa dreißig Millionen Russen durch Hunger dezimieren, indem man alle Nahrungsmittel aus dem riesigen Gebiet entfernte. Allen an dieser Aktion Beteiligten werde bei Todesstrafe verboten werden, einem Russen auch nur ein Stück Brot zu geben. Die großen Städte von Leningrad bis Moskau sollten dem Erdboden gleichgemacht werden; der SS-Führer von dem Bach-Zelewski werde für die Durchführung dieser Maßnahmen verantwortlich sein." On the identity of the visitor, see Gerlach, *Kalkulierte Morde*, 53–54n98.

76. For the first print run of one thousand copies, issued on June 16, see "Richtlinien für die Führung der Wirtschaft (Grüne Mappe), Teil 1: Aufgaben und Organisation der Wirtschaft," Berlin, June 1941, 223rd copy, F 500/1703, Militärgeschichtliches Forschungsamt, Potsdam; for the second print run of two thousand copies, issued the following month, see "Richtlinien für die Führung der Wirtschaft in den neubesetzten Ostgebieten (Grüne Mappe), Teil 1 (2. Auflage): Aufgaben und Organisation der Wirtschaft," Berlin, July 1941, R 26 IV/33a, BAB.

77. "Vortragsnotiz über die Besprechung betr. Vorbereitungen Barbarossa am 29.4. nachmittags," May 9, 1941, RW 19/739, fol. 77, BA-MA.

78. "Richtlinien für die Führung der Wirtschaft (Fall 'Barbarossa')," June 16, 1941, signed Wilhelm Keitel, in "Richtlinien für die Führung der Wirtschaft in den neubesetzten Ostgebieten (Grüne Mappe)," R 26 IV/33a, BAB. For almost identical expressions in the Green Folder itself, see p. 3 of the guidelines.

79. Ibid., 4.

80. Ibid., 18.

81. "Niederschrift zur 4. Sitzung des Wirtschafts-Führungsstabes Ost unter Vorsitz von Staatssekretär Körner vom 26. Mai 1941," signed *Regierungsrat* (retired) Dr. Joachim Bergmann, RW 19/739, fol. 135, BA-MA.

82. Postwar testimony of Hans Nagel in Nuremberg from September 8, 1948, 99 US 7/1110, fol. 176, BAB; and Nbg. Doc. 003-EC, "Wirtschaftsaufzeichnungen für die Berichtszeit vom 15.8. bis 16.9.1941," September 16, 1941, signed Hans Nagel, printed in *IMG*, 36:105–6, 109.

83. "Niederschrift zur 4. Sitzung des Wirtschafts-Führungsstabes Ost unter Vorsitz von Staatssekretär Körner vom 26. Mai 1941," RW 19/739, fol. 135, BA-MA.

84. Nbg. Doc. 1058-PS, "Rede des Reichsleiters A. Rosenberg vor den engsten Beteiligten am Ostproblem am 20. Juni 1941," printed in *IMG*, vol. 26 (Nuremberg: Sekretariat des Gerichtshofs, 1947), 610–27: "Die deutsche Volksernährung steht in diesen Jahren zweifellos an der Spitze der deutschen Forderungen im Osten, und hier werden die Südgebiete und Nordkaukasien einen Ausgleich für die deutsche Volksernährung zu schaffen haben. Wir sehen durchaus nicht die Verpflichtung ein, aus diesen Überschussgebieten das russische Volk mit zu ernähren. Wir wissen, dass das eine harte Notwendigkeit ist, die ausserhalb jeden Gefühls steht. Zweifellos wird eine sehr umfangreiche Evakuierung notwendig sein und dem Russentum werden sicher sehr schwere Jahre bevorstehen" (622).

85. Postwar testimony of Erich von dem Bach-Zelewski in Nuremberg from January 7, 1946, printed in *IMG*, 4:539: "Ich bin der Ansicht, daß diese Methoden wirklich zur Vernichtung von dreißig Millionen geführt hätten, wenn sie so weiter fortgeführt worden wären, und wenn nicht durch die Entwicklung der Lage sich die Situation ganz geändert hätte."

86. "Auszug aus einem Feldpostbrief von Leutnant Dr. Friedrich Richter, Referent für Ostfragen vom Vierjahresplan, vom 26.5.1943," R 6/60a, fol. 1, BAB: "Wirtschaftliche Interessen und die Zwangslage, infolge der Isolierung Europas noch mehr Getreide und Ölsaaten und Öl aus dem eigenen Machtbereich zu schaffen, haben bei vielen eine auch wirtschaftliche Bejahung des Feldzuges bewirkt, obwohl Fachleute damals darauf hinwiesen, daß Rußland schon friedensmäßig nur unter schwersten eigenen Opfern die deutschen Vertragsforderungen erfüllen könne, wieviel weniger erst nach Störung der Verkehrswege und des wirtschaftlichen Kreislaufes. Auch Donner und mein Haus haben damals auf diese zu erwartende Verschlechterung hingewiesen. Aus dieser Lage hat sich die Backesche These entwickelt, man müsse die west- und südrussischen Gebiete als Haupterzeuger von ihren Abnehmergebieten im zentralen Rußland trennen und wieder in die europäische Versorgung einbauen; eine reale Möglichkeit, wenn man auf lange Zeit militärisch in der Lage ist, die zentralen Russen von ihren Äckern fernzuhalten, und wenn man die Bewohner des besetzten Gebietes für sich gewinnt."

87. Quoted in R.-D. Müller, ed., *Die deutsche Wirtschaftspolitik*, 56n63: "alle deutsche Dienststellen auf der Überzeugung bestanden, daß im kommenden, also im vergangenen Winter, mindestens zehn bis zwanzig Millionen dieser Leute einfach verhungern werden."

88. See Czesław Madajczyk, *Die Okkupationspolitik Nazideutschlands in Polen, 1939–1945* (Berlin: Akademie, 1987), 92. There is no explicit mention in Ciano's diary of this exchange, though Göring did inform Ciano of conditions in the prisoner of war camps (including cases of cannibalism) and compared the Soviet POWs to "a herd of ravenous animals" (*una mandria d'animali famelici*). See Galeazzo Ciano, *Diario 1939–1943. Volume secondo, 1941–1943* (Milan: Rizzoli, 1946), 98, entry for November 24–26, 1941.

89. Christian Gerlach, "Deutsche Wirtschaftsinteressen, Besatzungspolitik, und der Mord an den Juden in Weißrußland, 1941–1943," in *Nationalsozialistische Vernichtungspolitik, 1939–1945: Neue Forschungen und Kontroversen*, ed. Ulrich Herbert (Frankfurt am Main: Fischer Taschenbuch, 1998), 273.

90. Christian Streit, *Keine Kameraden: Die Wehrmacht und die sowjetischen Kriegsgefangenen, 1941–1945*, 4th rev. ed. (1978; Bonn: Dietz, 1997), 76; and Gerlach, *Kalkulierte Morde*, 783.

91. Streit, *Keine Kameraden*, 137–90, 249–53; and Gerlach, *Kalkulierte Morde*, 788–855 (for Belarus).

92. For the calculations, see Streit, *Keine Kameraden*, 128–37, 244–49, esp. 244–46. Almost thirty-five years since its first publication, Streit's pioneering work remains the benchmark on the subject. See also Gerlach, *Kalkulierte Morde*, 857–58.

93. Streit, *Keine Kameraden*, 128, 357n5.

94. Peter Jahn, "Sowjetische Kriegsgefangene und die Zivilbevölkerung der Sowjetunion als Opfer des NS-Vernichtungskrieges," in *Dimensionen der Verfolgung: Opfer und Opfergruppen im Nationalsozialismus*, ed. Sybille Quack (Munich: Deutsche Verlags-Anstalt, 2003), 158–59; Jörg Ganzenmüller, *Das belagerte Leningrad, 1941 bis 1944: Die Stadt in den Strategien von Angreifern und Verteidigern* (Paderborn: Ferdinand Schöningh, 2005), 238–39; and Hürter, *Hitlers Heerführer*, 500.

95. As of mid-August 1941, the intention had been to destroy Kiev by means of incendiary bombs and artillery fire. See "Ergänzung der Weisung 34," doc. 34 a, August 12, 1941, signed Wilhelm Keitel, reproduced in Hubatsch, ed., *Hitlers Weisungen für die Kriegführung*, 148–50, here 148; and Franz Halder, *Kriegstagebuch: Tägliche Aufzeichnungen des Chefs des Generalstabes des Heeres, 1939–1942*, vol. 3, *Der Rußlandfeldzug bis zum Marsch auf Stalingrad (22.6.1941–24.9.1942)*, ed. Hans-Adolf Jacobsen and Alfred Philippi (Stuttgart: W. Kohlhammer, 1964), 186 and 189 (entries for August 18 and 20). According to Christian Steit, this plan could not be

realised because of a lack of ammunition required for the envisaged five-day bombardment (see Streit, *Keine Kameraden*, 369n199). On Kiev, see Karel C. Berkhoff, *Harvest of Despair: Life and Death in Ukraine under Nazi Rule* (Cambridge: Harvard University Press, 2004), 164–86. Berkhoff is mistaken in viewing the starvation of the inhabitants of major Soviet cities as "the default option" to razing these cities to the ground (164–65). The starvation of most or all of the inhabitants of major Soviet cities was an integral part of the preinvasion intention to raze these cities. On Kharkiv, see Norbert Kunz, "Das Beispiel Charkow: Eine Stadtbevölkerung als Opfer der deutschen Hungerstrategie 1941/42," in *Verbrechen der Wehrmacht: Bilanz einer Debatte*, ed. Christian Hartmann, Johannes Hürter, and Ulrike Jureit (Munich: C. H. Beck, 2005), 136–44. The civilian population of Kharkiv was cordoned off by the local German military commander, resulting in the death from starvation of many thousands of the city's inhabitants, 1,202 alone in the first half of May 1942 (see Kunz, "Das Beispiel Charkow," 140, 144).

96. Timothy Snyder, for example, puts the figure at 4.2 million. See Timothy Snyder, *Bloodlands: Europe between Hitler and Stalin* (New York: Basic, 2010), 411. Dieter Pohl's claim that "hundreds of thousands" died of starvation under German occupation rather than millions, is untenable. See Pohl, *Die Herrschaft der Wehrmacht*, 199, 342–43.

97. Ganzenmüller, *Das belagerte Leningrad*, 51.

CHAPTER 5

THE RADICALIZATION OF GERMAN OCCUPATION POLICIES

The *Wirtschaftsstab Ost* and the 121st Infantry Division in Pavlovsk, 1941

Jeff Rutherford

In 1963, Ernst Nolte characterized the German-Soviet War as "the most monstrous war of conquest, enslavement, and annihilation" in European history.[1] Fifty years of further research has not only confirmed Nolte's assessment, but indeed has also amplified his contention. The ruthless ideological war waged by the Nazi state against the Soviet Union manifested itself in a myriad of ways, from the German army's murder of Red Army commissars and Soviet Roma, to its vicious treatment of partisans, both real and imagined, and, most horrifically, in the extermination of millions of Jews by the SS and other German institutions.[2] During the 1980s and 1990s, this emphasis on ideology drove the historiography of German aims and actions during the war with the Soviet Union; such an approach found its most prominent and controversial expression in the Hamburg Institute for Social Research's travelling exhibition *Verbrechen der Wehrmacht*.[3]

Recent research has begun to shift the focus from ideology to economics as the fundamental underlying basis of the war.[4] This research, however, has tended to emphasize either the prewar planning for such economic exploitation or how the process worked in the rear areas. This chapter will examine a relatively neglected aspect of the German economic exploitation of the Soviet Union: how two of the primary institutions of German aggression—the army and the *Wirtschaftsstab Ost* (*Wi Stab Ost* or Economic Staff East)—carried out their dual missions of military conquest and economic exploitation during Operation Barbarossa and the subsequent Winter Crisis of 1941/42 by focusing on the German occupation of Pavlovsk, located outside of Leningrad. In this relatively small town, the 121st Infantry Division radicalized its food requisitioning policy to such an extent during the winter of 1941/42 that even the local branch of the Economic Staff East pleaded for a more measured program, one that took at least some notice of the surrounding population's plight. This chapter looks first at the establishment of the Economic Staff East and the mission entrusted to it by the German leadership. The second section will examine the 121st Infantry Division within the context of Army Group North's advance toward Leningrad in the summer and autumn of 1941 and how the army's policy of "living off the land" affected both Soviet civilians and the *Wi Stab Ost*. While the former entered a seven-month period of hunger, misery, and ultimately starvation, the latter found its responsibilities increased and made more complex. The cooperation and competition between the army and the Economic Staff East in the town of Pavlovsk constitutes the third section of the essay. As the Blitzkrieg sputtered to a halt in Pavlovsk, the radicalization of the 121st Infantry Division's policies only increased, leading to widespread suffering. Despite being established by the Reich for the express purpose of exploiting the Soviet Union's resources, the *Wi Stab Ost* attempted to act as a brake on the army's depredations during the occupation. Unfortunately for the Soviet civilians in the 121st Infantry Division's area of operations, food requisitioning and outright plunder only increased in severity as the year advanced, and it was these civilians who paid the ultimate price.

German Aims in the Soviet Union and the Creation of the Economic Staff East

Following the successful conclusion of the French campaign and the subsequent failure of the Luftwaffe to destroy the Royal Air Force, the German Reich faced a strategic Gordian knot. Though France lay prostrate before it, Great Britain remained defiant and the Reich's new-found ally, the Soviet Union, pursued an aggressive foreign policy in the Balkans that clashed with German interests.[5] Even more importantly, the German economy was unable to shoulder the burden of maintaining a large field army and ensuring that the living standards of the Reich remained high. It became clear to experts in both economic and military circles that one potential way of solving both the strategic and economic issues facing Germany was to invade the Soviet Union, eliminate it as a potential ally of Great Britain, and exploit the country's abundant agricultural resources and raw materials.[6] Though such an approach seemed a simple way to solve the real problems facing the Reich, Germany's economy was ill prepared for a long campaign, as it had neither the ability to equip its army for a sustained war of attrition nor the resources to feed both a large standing army and its population at the same time.[7] One way of escaping this seemingly insoluble problem was to develop an organization that would exploit the industrial and agricultural resources of the Soviet Union for the German war effort. During early 1941, Hitler tasked Hermann Göring, head of the Four-Year Plan, with establishing such an organization, and Göring then turned to *General der Infanterie* Georg Thomas, chief of the War Economy and Armaments Office section of the *Oberkommando der Wehrmacht* (OKW). Thomas saw the creation of a "war-economy apparatus" as the "most important task" of the War Economy and Armaments Office for the forthcoming campaign.[8] This was the beginning of the Economic Staff East, though it did not receive such a designation until June 9, 1941.[9]

This new economic organization, code named "Oldenburg," was finally established on February 21, 1941.[10] Subordinated to Göring's Four-Year Plan, it was responsible for "everything concerned with the war economy" with the exception, at least initially, of food supplies; this meant that it was tasked with seizing raw materials, equipment (such as tractors), and factories during the opening weeks of the invasion.[11] In a development familiar to the turf battles that plagued the Nazi state during the entirety of its existence, this organization would be independent from the field army, though it was charged with maintaining close cooperation with the army. Despite the dominance of military officers in the upper echelons of Oldenburg (and it was indeed part of the OKW), the majority of its members were chosen from various civilian ministries, and this ensured that the organization never functioned exclusively within the military's hierarchy.[12] Such an organizational split took on great importance during the campaign, as the two institutions, particularly at the local level, clashed over scant resources.[13] This bureaucratic infighting only increased during the Winter Crisis of 1941/42, and it led to horrific results for Soviet civilians.

By mid-March 1941, the planning and construction of this organization had taken more concrete shape and its responsibility increased as the invasion date neared. "Not only ... the war economy, but now the entire economy" fell under the Economic Staff East's umbrella.[14] In addition to securing the industrial resources necessary for the Reich's war economy, it was now also to help "supply the troops off the land." This obviously greatly increased the scope of the organization's responsibilities. *Generalmajor* Hans Nagel, one of the founding members of the Economic Staff East, later wrote about this shift in policy: "Economic goals [now] needed to be differentiated between long-term economic polices and the use of the land for the *war economy*."[15] The latter aim became its primary function during Operation Barbarossa, as its other tasks were seen as objectives that could be fulfilled once the blitz campaign had ended.[16] Such a modification of policy had dramatic effects on the Soviet civilian population. Now two organizations were devoted to ensuring that the invading Germans found adequate sustenance in the Soviet Union, and since the availability of foodstuffs in this country was a zero-sum game in 1941, it was clear that those who possessed the rifles would eat at the expense of those who did not.

Once the invasion began, 5 Economic Inspections (*Wirtschaftsinspektionen*) were to be spread throughout the country; directly subordinate to these were 23 Economic Commandos (*Wirtschaftskommandos*).[17] An additional 12 commandos were established in areas of particular economic concern to the Germans, generally in the rear areas. The Economic Commandos were charged with working closely with Wehrmacht forces in the area and making those decisions that required a detailed knowledge of the local situation. Despite being given such a large and important task in such an enormous country, only 6,485 people initially staffed the Economic Staff East.[18] While the size of the organization increased as the conflict degenerated into a war of attrition, reaching 19,000 by December 1942, the organization never had enough manpower to consistently fulfill its mission.[19]

For Holstein, the name given to the branch of the *Wi Stab Ost* in Army Group North's area of operations, five Economic Commandos were planned: Vilna (Vilnius), Riga, Reval (Tallinn), Leningrad, and Murmansk.[20] Only two of these were located in Russia proper and this pointed to the Germans' rather low expectations for this area in terms of resources. While the Leningrad area itself contained one of the Soviet Union's highest concentrations of industry, its agricultural production was frighteningly low. This had been the case since the founding of the city during the eighteenth century, and the frenetic industrialization of the 1930s had only increased the region's dependence on grain shipments from Ukraine.[21] German prewar planning recognized this fact and consigned the Leningrad region to starvation. The economic-political guidelines for the exploitation of the Soviet Union published by the Economic Staff East in late May made such thinking explicit.[22] For the purpose of economic exploitation, the Soviet Union was divided into two sections: surplus and deficit areas. The former centered on the black-soil region of Ukraine. Here, more foodstuffs were produced than the area required, and the surpluses were shipped to the central and northern regions of the Soviet Union. These areas, which included cities such as Leningrad and Moscow, were termed deficit or forest zones, in that they were forced to import food. Food produced in Ukraine and normally shipped to the deficit areas was to be used primarily to supply the advancing German army, and any excess sent back to the German home front. The deficit zones were to be rapidly deindustrialized and their populations decimated through starvation. This was made quite clear in directions for the agricultural exploitation of the region. In the deficit zones, "outside of supply for the German troops stationed there, there was no German interest in maintaining the productive power of the region." The guidelines continued by noting that "the population of the forest zone, especially in the cities, will have to suffer from widespread starvation ... this starvation is not to be stopped." While the area's dairy and beef production was foreseen as providing some alleviation for the German home front, "the essential agricultural-economic objective in this region consisted of the security of the troops' supply."[23] This rather desultory view of the resources of northwestern Russia was confirmed in Nagel's history of the *Wi Stab Ost*. While the Baltic States were viewed as possessing important agricultural resources as well as minerals and other raw materials needed for the war economy, Russia proper merited only brief comments about industrial potential and some raw materials.[24] Alex J. Kay's description of the Economic Staff East as "nothing more than a gigantic organization for the plundering of the Soviet Union" certainly rings true for the organization as a whole; for Holstein, however, the question remained what exactly one could plunder in northwestern Russia.[25]

While economic thinking constituted the basis for German starvation plans for large Soviet cities, racism also played an important role. From the beginning, some sections of the German leadership tried to differentiate between ethnic Russians and other Slavic groups living under Soviet rule; the former were targeted for much more severe treatment.[26] It was thus no accident that cities such as Moscow and Leningrad as well as Smolensk and Bryansk were targeted to starve.[27] While Nazi ideological tenets prominently linked bolshevism to Judaism, both political and military authorities also conflated bolshevism with ethnic Russians and this, mixed with the Reich's toxic racism and plans for plunder, consigned urban Russians to a horrific fate.[28]

The 121st Infantry Division and the Advance on Leningrad

As the 121st Infantry Division prepared to invade the Soviet Union, the 2nd Corps reminded it that "senseless plundering" as well as a "desire for destruction" was explicitly forbidden because of the army's need to both exploit captured resources and placate the indigenous population.²⁹ These acts were to be "punished with the heaviest penalties."³⁰ Such orders, however, did little to stop the troops from looting the populace from the very beginning of the campaign. Members of the 7th Company, II/407th Infantry Regiment embarked on a campaign of robbery and plundering that especially targeted Jews. On the second day of the invasion, they discovered several Jews and wagons loaded with goods that had been hidden by their owners. A platoon leader cryptically stated that the Jews were "taken care of" and the company continued the advance, loaded down with booty.³¹ Such behavior became routine for members of this unit; one can assume that such practices occurred throughout the division as a whole. When the 7th Company entered a small Lithuanian village and took a quick break from the advance,

> many simple [biedere] soldiers went off in search of items of food and clothing. Oh, that was not all that was claimed that day. Radios, cloth. Lemonade, Seltzer-water, pickles, heaps of canned fish. Cigarettes, chocolate, and many other things.... Someone brought me numerous photos autographed by actors. War booty according to the *Landser*'s way.³²

During the first three weeks of July, both the Sixteenth Army and the 2nd Army Corps issued orders demanding that the men stop practices such as issuing illegible receipts to Russian peasants and stealing a family's last cow, as these only exacerbated relations between the Wehrmacht and the civilian population.³³ The 2nd Corps described such behavior as plundering and warned that it would be treated as such.³⁴

On July 27, a mere three weeks after threatening its men with punishment for such actions, the corps reversed track, declaring that the supply situation had reached a "breaking point."³⁵ It ordered its subordinate formations, including the 121st Infantry Division, to "exhaust all means" to supply themselves. Christian Gerlach's observation that "only two to four weeks after the beginning of the invasion, the organized plundering of the occupied territories for food was declared a primary objective of German divisions" certainly rings true for the 121st Infantry Division.³⁶

As historians have noted, Operation Barbarossa was planned on a logistical shoestring that generally failed to take into account the primitive road network within the country.³⁷ The division, however, did not seem to feel the pinch of supplies. One soldier wrote that "our supply functions reasonably well," though the troops did supplement their rations with vegetables and livestock taken from the surrounding countryside.³⁸ Another soldier wryly noted that "many hens found in hidden corners were forced to give up their lives for Germany's Wehrmacht," but he also added that the field kitchens usually provided the troops with nourishment every evening.[39] Despite this seemingly functioning supply system, the division received the order to feed itself (and its horses) every second day.[40] Once the prohibition of requisitioning had been lifted, the division as a whole became much more proactive in scouring the countryside. One soldier vividly described the process:

> Mounted troops swarm like the Huns to the right and left of the route of advance, searching for hay, pigs, calves, [and] chickens in villages kilometers away. There is, however, little there, and when we are gone there is nothing left.[41]

The 121st Infantry Division now began living off the land as planned by the Nazi state's political and military leadership.

The addition of Army Group North and its twenty-seven subordinate formations—approximately 350,000 men—severely disrupted the economic basis of the northwestern Soviet Union.[42] The Wehrmacht's insatiable appetite for foodstuffs led *Einsatzgruppe* A to report already in August that large sections of northwestern Russia were experiencing "economic anarchy."[43] This chaos was caused by both German depredations and Soviet scorched earth tactics that attempted to destroy or evacuate anything of economic value.[44] By the autumn of 1941, the situation threatened to turn into catastrophe as the Army Group's military mission changed. Instead of storming Leningrad, Army Group North's armor was stripped and sent to Army Group Center, and its remaining infantry armies settled into a siege of the city.[45] As the Army Group prepared its long-term permanent positions, it began to more systematically scour the countryside for foodstuffs. Police units reported in late September that

> the entire Russia proper area that has been occupied by Army Group North presents a uniform picture of economic and cultural misery.... In several areas, for example near Luga and Lake Samra, nearly all cattle herds and horses have been carried off. German troops have requisitioned nearly the entire chicken population, so that the food situation is extraordinarily difficult for the civilian population.[46]

A few weeks later, a Soviet source confirmed that "in the occupied districts, where there has been a German presence, all domestic poultry has been seized ... leaving very little livestock. The population eats in general only potatoes."[47]

In early October, the 38th Army Corps was already asking for instructions concerning the starving population in its area of operations. The response from *General der Artillerie* Eduard Wagner, Chief Quartermaster of the German Army, was that "every supply train out of the *Heimat* cuts down on stocks in Germany. It is better if our people have something and the Russians starve."⁴⁸ While rural areas in northwestern Russia felt the sting of German forced requisitioning first hand, urban areas suffered the most. Cut off from Ukraine's grain and unable to bring in foodstuffs from the surrounding countryside, the cities of northwestern Russia faced widespread starvation during the subsequent winter months.

The fate of Leningrad during its nine-hundred-day siege is well known in the West.⁴⁹ Its tremendous suffering, however, has overshadowed the crisis faced by those cities and towns, such as Pushkin and Pavlovsk, that fell within the German siege line. German units seized and occupied these suburbs in October 1941, and their inhabitants almost immediately faced the specter of large-scale starvation.⁵⁰ In the city of Pushkin, the 50th Army Corps notified the Eighteenth Army in early October that "20,000 people, most of whom are factory workers, are without food. Starvation is expected." Eighteenth Army's quartermaster noted in reply that "the provision of food for the civilian population by the troops is out of the question."⁵¹ This attitude toward the civilian population mirrored that of other commands in Army Group North.

In a meeting between members of the Sixteenth Army and 28th Army Corps on October 29, the corps received instructions to leave civilians to their own devices regarding their sustenance: "the feeding of the civilian population is completely out of the question." Sixteenth Army then ordered the establishments of evacuated zones behind the front lines, with the civilians shipped to labor camps.⁵² Eighteenth Army also began to view evacuation as a means to get around the problem of starving civilians in its midst: its commander in chief, *Generaloberst* Georg von Küchler, ordered the removal of all civilians from the forward area of operations in response to his corps commanders' fears of epidemics and the effects on the troops' discipline caused by watching starving women and children.⁵³ Less than two weeks later, eighteen thousand civilians had been evacuated out of the forward combat area and a further ten thousand were scheduled to follow shortly thereafter.⁵⁴ By May 1942, more than seventy-five thousand civilians had been deported from the forward combat lines and sent to Army Group North's rear area; this, however, did not lead to a satisfactory solution to the food issue.⁵⁵ It merely shifted the problem onto the shoulders of rear-area officers and led, as aptly described by Johannes Hürter, to a "ghetto-like refugee reservation."⁵⁶

German transportation capacity, however, was insufficient to carry out a complete evacuation of the civilian population, and those who remained in the cities and towns ringing Leningrad faced an increasingly desperate struggle for survival. The 50th Army Corps complained to the Eighteenth Army that the population's situation has deteriorated to such an extent that it is intolerable for the troops' morale to continually have to see such misery. For example, women and children come to the troops' local headquarters and beg for food. They suggest that they would rather be shot immediately than be abandoned to an excruciating death by starvation.[57]

The sight of "pitiful [civilians] feeding themselves on dead horses, potatoes and cabbage that are still found in the fields, or from food begged from the troops" led the 28th Army Corps to request a new policy for supplying civilians with sustenance.[58] At the lower levels of the German army, the plight of civilians caused numerous officers and men to question official policies.

The Wehrmacht's response to the growing starvation was encapsulated in *Generalfeldmarschall* Walter von Reichenau's infamous order issued on October 10. Reichenau, commander of the Sixth Army operating in Ukraine, neatly summed up the ideological motivations behind the war with this directive. Hitler saw it as mirroring his own thinking and had it distributed to other *Ostheer* units. The 121st Infantry Division received the directive on November 6. Regarding the food situation in the occupied territories of the Soviet Union, Reichenau stated that

> the feeding from troop kitchens of native inhabitants and prisoners of war who are not in the service of the Wehrmacht is the same misconstrued humanity as is the giving away of cigarettes and bread. What the *Heimat* has spared, what the command has brought to the front despite great difficulties, should not be given by the troops to the enemy, even when it comes from war booty. This is a necessary part of our supply.[59]

The 28th Army Corps attached its own formulation to Reichenau's directive. Stating that the general situation required that "soldiers must be educated to be extremely tough," it then "stressed" the following points:

> 1. Every piece of bread that is given to the civilian population is one taken from the *Heimat*.
> 2. Every civilian, including women and children, who wants to cross through our encirclement ring around Leningrad is to be shot. The fewer eaters there are in Leningrad increases the resistance there, and every refugee tends toward spying or being a partisan; all of this costs the lives of German soldiers.[60]

Küchler's thinking on the food issue converged with these orders. He ordered the strict separation of the Russian population from the occupying German soldiers, in part because of espionage dangers and in part "so that the soldiers aren't continually tempted to give their food to the inhabitants." During a visit to the SS-*Polizei* Division in late November, Küchler emphasized that "under no circumstances could food be given to the civilian population," utilizing the familiar slogan that such misplaced acts of charity were costing the German home front food.[61] The views of Eighteenth Army's commander on this question were certainly echoed by other members of the German High Command.[62]

On November 4, Wagner distributed a directive to all army and panzer groups that stated that the Economic Staff East and not the Wehrmacht was responsible for feeding Soviet civilians.[63] He then categorically forbade the provisioning of foodstuffs to the surrounding population, ordering local commandants to merely supervise the distribution of food in villages and towns. A similar line was taken at the meeting of *Generaloberst* Franz Halder, chief of the German General Staff, and the commanders and quartermasters of the Eastern Army at Orsha on November 13, 1941. According to the notes of Eighteenth Army's chief of staff, *Oberst* Gerhart Hasse, "the food question is especially worrying."[64] Since winter deliveries could not be sufficiently sent to the front, "it [was] of especial importance that the troops do everything possible to live off the land for as long as possible." The plight of the civilian population was then considered:

> The question of feeding the civilian population is catastrophic. To reach some sort of solution, one needs to proceed toward a classification system. It is clear that within this classification, the troops and their needs stand at the highest level. The civilian population will only be allowed a minimum necessary for existence.... The question of feeding the large cities is unsolvable. There is no doubt that especially Leningrad will starve, as it is impossible to feed this city. The commanders' only objective can be to keep the troops as far as possible away from this and its associated occurrences.

A further meeting between the corps quartermasters and Eighteenth Army quartermaster in December neatly summed up the prevailing attitude: it was decided that when it came to the civilian population, "feeding was a crime."[65] With such agreement at the highest levels of the German army, the deaths due to starvation of Russian civilians in Leningrad's occupied suburbs only increased during the winter of 1941/42.

During the autumn and winter of 1941, the Economic Staff East faced two pressing problems. First, the organization's systematic approach to collecting and utilizing Soviet resources was upset by the German army's rather cavalier short-term approach to the occupied territories. This clash of interests, however, did not impair its primary mission of supplying the field army. One of the reserve Economic Commandos working in Army

Group North's rear area reported in November that it had delivered, among other foodstuffs, one million kilograms of rye and over three million kilograms of potatoes to the army since the outbreak of war.[66] The dairy and beef herds of the region ensured that Holstein also provided sufficient meat to the army.[67] Second, Wagner's previously cited order of November 4 placed the burden of feeding Soviet civilians on the shoulders of the Economic Staff East; this stretched the organization's already thin resources to the breaking point. This merely codified an already existing state of affairs in which the field army pressured economic authorities to deal with starving civilians.[68] While the *Wi Stab Ost* grudgingly accepted this state of affairs, it indicated that it would do so only "so long as it was possible not to interfere with German interests."[69] The tension created by having such a weakly staffed organization supply the army and assist civilians led to insoluble problems throughout the region during the winter of 1941/42.

Holstein reported that "the difficulties [in feeding the civilian population] were so considerable that immediate measures need to be taken."[70] The largest issue facing economic authorities was the stream of refugees flowing from the front to the rear area. The *Wirtschaftskommando* located at Krasnogvardeisk reported that the constant influx of bedraggled and hungry people into the area made the "food situation increasingly difficult."[71] Similar concerns plagued the Economic Commando in Opotschka, where 11,550 refugees had been evacuated.[72] The command staff of Holstein estimated that 40,000 to 45,000 refugees had been added to the already 3.5 million civilians it had unceremoniously been made responsible for by the army. These refugees "constituted a noticeable burden in terms of the food situation" and the competition for scant resources led to increasing hostility on the part of the civilian population. Food was so scarce that "the majority of the population was starving and sections of it could not even leave their beds due to weakness."

From the perspective of the Economic Staff East, the humanitarian crisis created in Army Group North's area of operations was due to the army's misguided and mismanaged policies. Instead of an orderly evacuation, civilians simply wandered to the rear through forests and swamps, avoiding German sentries posted on the main roads. This made the process "simply uncontrollable."[73] Not only did the situation degenerate into near chaos, but it also seemed that various levels of the army actually encouraged this:

> The urge to wander in the rear areas is consequently much more noticeable, and this cannot be stopped as on the one hand the wanderers use back roads and on the other the commanders, especially of the frontline troops, have supported and

encouraged this wandering through certain measures because they don't want the sight of civilians' starvation to be a strain on the nerves of the troops.[74]

The army's systematic forced requisitioning had both short-term and long-term consequences. First, as already noted, starvation spread rapidly throughout the region. Second, various diseases, such as typhus, ravaged the malnourished population, and children and the elderly were most likely to fall victim to these epidemics. These deaths obviously had an extremely negative effect on the morale of survivors; the view of Germans as liberators failed to survive the winter.[75] Third, the general weakening of the population only increased the difficulty that the Economic Staff East had in jump-starting the economy in the rear area. Fourth, and perhaps most detrimental to the Germans' desire to yoke Russian agriculture to the Reich, the looting of foodstuffs led civilians and their animals to consume the seeds for the next harvest. This, in combination with the "catastrophic fodder situation," created a crisis in which nothing remained to plant in the spring and there were no animals left to plough; it was frighteningly clear to German economic authorities in the area that very little, if anything, could be expected from this region in the near future.[76]

The 121st Infantry Division and the Economic Staff East in Pavlovsk

The situation in Pavlovsk neatly fit into this general picture of civilian famine and misery as well as that of the Wehrmacht's self-imposed logistical crisis. Though the 121st Infantry Division's supply system functioned reasonably well during the drive on Pavlovsk, once the advance stopped, the supply of cattle dried up and the men were forced to rely upon deliveries from the army's butcher station in Krasnogvardeisk.[77] A general lack of transport capacity limited the Wehrmacht to deliveries of either ammunition or food; this created a situation in which one or the other was invariably in short supply.[78] Insufficient stores or stocks in the Russian interior aggravated these problems. One soldier reported that when such establishments were found, "they were either ransacked or burned down, as nearly every village is" by either the retreating Soviet forces or the pursuing German units.[79] All of this contributed to the scourge of wild requisitioning that various German authorities correctly saw as threatening to destroy the fragile relationship between the Wehrmacht and Russian civilians. The Economic Staff East complained that the department finds itself . . . in a difficult and just as hopeless defensive struggle against the "organizing" of the individual man as well as that of entire units and finds a thankful understanding for its tasks from only a few units. The guilt lies less with the men, and more with . . . the higher leadership, which partly has no real understanding and which partly has exclusively focused on specific ideas, none of which are either sound or reasonable.[80]

The 28th Army Corps instructed its subordinate units that the following actions all contributed to the increasing bitterness of the civilian population toward the Wehrmacht: the forceful requisitioning of cattle without compensation, especially when children were present; the taking of a farmer's last grain or cow without payment; and rummaging through a house and confiscating items used daily by the inhabitants. It then ordered an outright ban on wild requisitions.[81]

Though such requisitions were theoretically banned, the organized plunder of Pavlovsk received official sanction. Soon after their arrival in the town, soldiers and other German officials confiscated all food stocks in warehouses and markets as well as those held by individuals in their houses.[82] This, in the words of the Soviet Extraordinary State Commission, "created a situation of incredible hunger in the city, the result of which caused the intentional death of the population."[83] Over six thousand inhabitants of the town died of starvation and the various diseases that accompany hunger.[84] In one of the most tragic cases of organized starvation, 387 children between the ages of three and thirteen died during the winter of 1941/42 while staying in an orphanage established by the Germans. According to witnesses, the death of 10 to 15 children due to hunger on a single day occurred more than once.[85]

In an attempt to survive, many civilians resorted to crimes of desperation. In Pushkin, an ethnic German killed his aunt in order to trade her jewelry for food; he was arrested and shot.[86] The disappearance of a dozen children and adolescents in Pushkin led to the arrest of a man whose home contained various female body parts. He had been selling human flesh as pork at the local market.[87] In Pavlovsk, a married couple was hanged for cannibalism in February 1942. Apparently they had killed one of their grandfathers and, after using part of his remains at home, sold the rest at market as rabbit meat. The couple then murdered three children and disposed of their bodies in the same manner as that of the elderly man. They were finally apprehended while in the midst of dismembering a fifth victim—a nine-year-old girl.[88] An investigation into the disappearance of several children led German police units to the apartment of yet another woman in April. Finding human flesh there, they arrested her and brought her in for questioning. While admitting to having eaten five children, she claimed to have killed no one; rather she maintained that she had disinterred them from the town's cemetery. Neither members of the Russian auxiliary police nor the German Security Police believed the woman and she was executed.[89] Such acts highlighted the desperation felt by Soviet citizens under the boot of German occupation.

Members of the staffs of Army Group North and the Eighteenth Army viewed these developments with resignation. The ranking medical officer in the Eighteenth Army, after visiting Pavlovsk to check on the possibility of an outbreak of dysentery, told Küchler that

> there is no epidemic . . . the primary cause of all of the population's sickness is hunger and the general weakness caused by this. The population will be medically watched as far as this is possible. Medicine is in short supply, as the materials needed for it are in short supply. They just suffice for the needs of the troops. . . . Nothing can be done for the population.[90]

Despite the efforts of some members of the 121st Infantry Division to alleviate the suffering in their midst, the relentless plundering by the Germans created unbearable scenes of despair and misery.[91] One German medic in the greater Pavlovsk area described the situation in late December 1941:

> A man is lying on the street, a civilian or a prisoner of war. He is completely broken down by exhaustion in the freezing weather, and steam rises off his still warm head. In general, ragged and starving civilians. They stagger and drag themselves till [their death], in –40 degree weather. Their houses are destroyed, either by the Bolsheviks or by us. No one can help them. With weakened arms, they try to hack pieces out of frozen horse cadavers. Many children are dying in the villages, one sees many with prematurely aged faces and with bloated stomachs. Children and women look through the horse excrement on the street . . . in the hope of making something edible.[92]

Begging became an everyday occurrence in the region and it became such a widespread event that the army issued an order in February forbidding German troops from providing civilians with food, tobacco, and even fuel.[93] Soviet authorities also recognized that German troops generally acted sympathetically toward women and children; they instructed female agents to approach German field kitchens and beg, as "many German soldiers have children at home and can't stand to watch the misery of children in this country."[94] SD units also believed that Wehrmacht soldiers played an important role in assisting numerous civilians in surviving the winter, reporting that "it must be assumed that the population was able to beg food from Wehrmacht units ... Wehrmacht camps have alleviated the worst of the emergency situation by making foodstuffs available to the civilian population." *Einsatzgruppe A* noted that the troops slaughtered horses during the winter and gave at least some of the meat to civilians.[95] While the members of the 121st Infantry Division certainly enforced many of the Wehrmacht's most severe and criminal directives, individual soldiers did what they could to assist the helpless in their midst.

In addition to the confiscation of foodstuffs, the division's men also turned to the civilian population for winter clothing; the largest problem from the individual soldier's point of view concerned the delivery of clothing and equipment. According to the division's own report on winter equipment, numerous items were in short supply, including coats, boots, and woollen underclothes.[96] By late November, only 50 percent of the gloves and 5 percent of the felt boots required by the Eighteenth Army (to which the 121st Infantry Division was subordinated) had been delivered to the men.[97] Soldiers were reduced to asking their relatives and friends at home for such items.[98] Another means of securing warm clothing was to find it in the Soviet Union itself. With one unit working under the slogan "prepare yourself in any way!" German soldiers frequently looted fallen Soviet soldiers, not only for the prized waterproof boots, but also for any other clothing that could help them survive the dropping temperatures.[99] By early December, the division ordered its troops to purchase the necessary items from the civilian population. If the native inhabitants refused to sell these items to the soldiers, division superiors empowered the *Landser* to force Russian communities to sell clothing and boots.[100] Once superior officers effectively gave the troops free reign to acquire clothing, it seems extremely likely that when ordered to collect these goods, forced requisitioning and outright robbery became standard practices.

Just as the Economic Staff East had complained of the army's requisitioning of food, it was also critical of its taking of clothing and other such goods. The Command Staff of Holstein complained that "the ordered confiscation of the civilian population's protective winter clothing appears to be a heavy strain on their mood as well as a questionable success, in that their ability to work will be reduced." It added that the continued seizing of "essential private property" from Soviet civilians was perhaps the largest cause in turning the "most obliging" civilian into the "most irreconcilable enemy" of the German army.[101] From the perspective of the *Wi Stab Ost*, army policy was self-defeating: not only was it creating enemies among the surrounding population, but it was also sabotaging the long-term economic goals in the occupied Soviet territories. Without a productive labor force, transforming this region into a functioning part of the Nazi New Order was bound to fail.

Just as the Economic Staff East provided the army with food during 1941, so it was able to produce some cold weather clothing for the division in Pavlovsk. It reopened various enterprises in the city (though the earlier forced evacuations of able-bodied males predictably led to a labor shortage), and this led to frequent contact between the two organizations.[102] The division even reported that relations between it and the economic authorities were "close and profitable," and representatives from the division requested labor from the Economic Staff East on several occasions.[103] One example of this relationship took place in January 1942 when the 121st Infantry Division placed an order for twenty felt blankets needed for wounded soldiers. The commander of the *Wi Stab Ost* branch agreed, but stipulated that such work could only be completed if the soldiers provided sustenance for the workers. The division promised to deliver dead horses to the workshop and the matter was settled.[104] This example typified the relationship between the division and the Economic Staff East as the latter "continually provided labor" for the former.[105] In addition to establishing a factory to produce badly needed Russian felt boots for the troops, the division resurrected a mechanical repair shop in Pushkin that built three motors and performed numerous smaller repairs for the troops.[106] Pushkin also housed a knitting factory that produced upwards of 40 sweaters and 450 pieces of warm winter headgear for the troops.[107] By late February 1942, over 1,300 civilians worked for the occupiers, the majority coming under the direct control of the Economic Staff East.[108]

As the preceding discussion indicates, the 121st Infantry Division and the Wehrmacht as a whole were prepared to sacrifice the civilian population in the greater Leningrad area on the altar of what it perceived as military necessity.[109] In order to ensure the combat efficiency of its troops, the Wehrmacht confiscated winter clothes and boots, commandeered dwellings, and requisitioned all of the food it could lay its hands on. Such actions had a twofold effect: An individual soldier could rightly claim that Pavlovsk was "not the worst position!" as the troops found the town relatively hospitable.[110] For civilians, however, these policies, in the words of Geoffrey Megargee, "amounted to nothing less than death sentences."[111] Here the radicalization of German food policy led to horrific scenes of hunger and despair. At the beginning of the war, the 121st Infantry Division was warned to requisition materials in an organized manner and that failure to do so would result in punishment. By the end of July, however, the division was ordered to find its sustenance in the fields and barns of the Soviet Union, and this typified its behavior for the remainder of its advance. Once the war shifted from one of movement to positional warfare, the 121st Infantry Division radicalized its requisitioning of foodstuffs, as it knew it could no longer move on to virgin soil to feed its needs. While the advance of the Wehrmacht in the summer and autumn of 1941 led to hunger throughout northwestern Russia, the region's cities literally starved during the winter, the fate of Pavlovsk symptomatic of the general misery that accompanied German occupation.

The evolution of German operations led to a somewhat paradoxical result. The Economic Staff East, despite being created with the specific purpose of exploiting the economic and food resources of the Soviet Union, found its mission significantly complicated by the army's behavior. Though it was generally able to fulfill its short-term objective of supplying the army with foodstuffs and some cold weather gear, its longer-term goals proved much more difficult to achieve. While Soviet scorched earth policies certainly played a role here, the primary culprit was the German army itself. Instead of working within the systematic and planned requisitioning policy developed by the *Wi Stab Ost*, the army instead consumed resources without any sort of foresight. This led to several major problems. First, the division's ruthless requisitioning caused a complete breakdown in the area's economy, which resulted in widespread starvation among the civilian population. These starving people left the cities in large numbers—through deportations by the army and on their own initiative. Already understaffed, the Economic Staff East was in no position to gather all of the area's resources before the refugees consumed them. Second, the decision taken by the German High Command to place the responsibility for feeding Soviet civilians on the Economic Staff East placed an unmanageable burden on the organization. As the example of Pavlovsk illustrates, Holstein needed the army to provide civilians with food; it simply did not have the resources to do so on its own account. Third, the army's continual depredations against the civilian population turned possible collaborators into implacable enemies, and this only complicated the task of maintaining a sufficient labor reserve. Radicalization of the 121st Infantry Division's food requisitioning policies during 1941 not only caused innumerable problems for the Economic Staff East, but also led to widespread misery and starvation in its area of operations, including Pavlovsk.

Notes

1. Ernst Nolte, *Der Faschismus in seiner Epoche: Die Action française, der italienische Faschismus, der Nationalsozialismus* (Munich: Piper, 1963), 436.
2. See the contributions by Felix Römer, Wendy Lower, Leonid Rein, and Martin Holler in this volume.
3. See the catalog for the first and most controversial version of the exhibition: Hamburger Institut für Sozialforschung, ed., *Vernichtungskrieg: Verbrechen der Wehrmacht 1941–1944* (Hamburg: Hamburger Edition, 1996).
4. See Rolf-Dieter Müller, "Von der Wirtschaftsallianz zum kolonialen Ausbeutungskrieg," and "Das Scheitern der wirtshaftlichen 'Blitzkriegstrategie,'" in Horst Boog, Jürgen Förster, Joachim Hoffmann, Ernst Klink, Rolf-Dieter Müller, and Gerd R. Ueberschär, *Der Angriff auf die Sowjetunion*, vol. 4 of *Das Deutsche Reich und der Zweite Weltkrieg* (Frankfurt am Main: Fischer Taschenbuch, 1996), 141–245, and 1116–1226; Rolf-Dieter Müller, "Das 'Unternehmen Barbarossa' als wirtschaftlicher Raubkrieg," in *Der deutsche Überfall auf die Sowjetunion: "Unternehmen Barbarossa," 1941*, ed. Gerd R. Ueberschär and Wolfram Wette, new ed. (Franfurt am Main: S. Fischer, 1991), 125–57; Christian Gerlach, *Kalkulierte Morde: Die deutsche Wirtschafts- und Vernichtungspolitik in Weißrußland, 1941 bis 1944* (Hamburg: Hamburger Edition, 1999); and Alex J. Kay, *Exploitation, Resettlement, Mass Murder: Political and Economic Planning for German Occupation Policy in the Soviet Union, 1940–1941* (New York: Berghahn, 2006).
5. Gabriel Gorodetsky, *Grand Delusion: Stalin and the German Invasion of the Soviet Union* (New Haven: Yale University Press, 1999), 23–114.
6. Andreas Hillgruber, *Hitlers Strategie: Politik und Kriegsführung 1940–1941*, 2nd rev. ed. (Bonn: Bernard & Graefe, 1993).
7. On the army's equipment problems, see "Grundlagen für eine Geschichte der deutschen Wehr- und Rüstungswirtschaft," doc. 2353-PS, in International Military Tribunal, ed., *Der Prozess gegen die Hauptkriegsverbrecher vor dem Internationalen Militärgerichtshof, Nürnberg, 14. November 1945–1. Oktober 1946* (hereafter IMG), vol. 30 (Nuremberg: Sekretariat des Gerichtshofs, 1948), 260–80. On the food situation, see Kay, *Exploitation, Resettlement, Mass Murder*, 38–42; and R.-D. Müller, "Von der Wirtschaftsallianz," 169.
8. "Grundlagen für eine Geschichte der deutschen Wehr- und Rüstungswirtschaft."
9. Gerlach, *Kalkulierte Morde*, 143.
10. Ibid.

11. "Aktennotiz, Besprechung beim Herrn Amtschef, General der Inf. Thomas am 28.2.41," doc. 1317-PS, *IMG*, vol. 27 (Nuremberg: Sekretariat des Gerichtshofs, 1948), 169–71.

12. Dieter Pohl, *Die Herrschaft der Wehrmacht: Deutsche Militärbesatzung und einheimische Bevölkerung in der Sowjetunion, 1941–1944* (Munich: Oldenbourg, 2008), 108.

13. For a discussion of this bureaucratic rivalry that included not only the Economic Staff East and the army but also SS-police forces and civil administrators, see R.-D. Müller, "Von der Wirtschaftsallianz," 174.

14. "Besprechung mit den Wehrmachtteilen am Dienstag, den 29. April 1941," doc. 1157-PS, *IMG*, 27:32–38.

15. Rolf-Dieter Müller, *Die deutsche Wirtschaftspolitik in den besetzten sowjetischen Gebieten, 1941–1943: Der Abschlußbericht des Wirtschaftsstabes Ost und Aufzeichnungen eines Angehörigen des Wirtschaftskommandos Kiew* (Boppard am Rhein: Harald Boldt, 1991), 24. Emphasis in the original.

16. Gerlach, *Kalkulierte Morde*, 143.

17. "Besprechung mit den Wehrmachtteilen am Dienstag, den 29. April 1941." The remainder of the paragraph is based on this document unless otherwise noted.

18. R.-D. Müller, "Von der Wirtschaftsallianz," 173.

19. Gerlach, *Kalkulierte Morde*, 146.

20. "Besprechung mit den Wehrmachtteilen am Dienstag, den 29. April 1941." The commando planned for Vilnius was later established in Kaunas; see R.-D. Müller, *Die deutsche Wirtschaftspolitik*, 45.

21. Gerhart Hass, "Deutsche Besatzungspolitik im Leningrader Gebiet," in Babette Quinkert, ed., *"Wir sind die Herren dieses Landes": Ursachen, Verlauf und Folgen des deutschen Überfalls auf die Sowjetunion* (Hamburg: VSA, 2002), 66–67.

22. "Allgemeine wirtschaftspolitische Richtlinien für die Wirtschaftsorganisation Ost, Gruppe Landwirtschaft, vom 23.5.1941," reproduced in Ueberschär and Wette, *Der deutsche Überfall auf die Sowjetunion*, 323–25.

23. Alexander Hill has noted that the region, with the exception of Leningrad and its suburbs, was primarily a rural area in which dairy farming and the raising of livestock were quite important; see *The War behind the Eastern Front: The Soviet Partisan Movement in North-West Russia, 1941–1944* (London: Routledge, 2005), 28.

24. R.-D. Müller, *Die deutsche Wirtschaftspolitik*, 37–38.

25. Kay, *Exploitation, Resettlement, Mass Murder*, 59.

26. A good overview of this issue is found in Mark Mazower, *Hitler's Empire: How the Nazis Ruled Europe* (New York: Penguin, 2008), 144–57.

27. Pohl, *Die Herrschaft der Wehrmacht*, 183.

28. Karel Berkhoff has persuasively argued that prisoners deemed Russian by German soldiers and administrators received far worse treatment

than those identified by other ethnic designations, owing in part to a belief that bolshevism was inextricably linked to Russians; see *Harvest of Despair: Life and Death in Ukraine under Nazi Rule* (Cambridge: Harvard University Press, 2004), 89–113, esp. 90–91. Such a differentiation between ethnic Russians and other nationalities in the Soviet Union also proves extremely important in explaining the evolution of Army Group North's increasingly brutal and violent policies during its campaign that began in the Baltic States and ended at the gates of Leningrad.

29. "Besprechung Unterabschnitt Ostpreußen I am 26.5.41," RH 26-121/6, Bundesarchiv-Militärarchiv, Freiburg im Breisgau (hereafter BA-MA). Members of the division staff were present at this meeting.

30. Generalkommando II Armeekorps, Studie Barbarossa, June 8, 1941, RH 24-2/460, BA-MA.

31. "Der Todesmarsch nach Leningrad," Msg 2/2580, 40–43, BA-MA.

32. Ibid.

33. Armee Oberkommando 16, Armeetagesbefehl Nr. 17, July 14, 1941, RH 24-2/83, BA-MA; and Generalkommando II. Armeekorps, Abt. Qu., Besondere Anordnungen für die Versorgung des II A.K. Nr. 22, July 18, 1941, RH 24-2/462, BA-MA. One German official noted that peasants frequently were given receipts that stated "paid for by the love of God" or, less eloquently, "kiss my ass"; see R.-D. Müller, *Die deutsche Wirtschaftspolitik*, 595.

34. Der Kommandierende General des II. Armeekorps, Korpstagesbefehl, July 3, 1941, RH 24-2/83, BA-MA.

35. Generalkommando II. Armeekorps, Abt. Qu., Besondere Anordnungen für die Versorgung des II A.K. Nr. 30, July 26, 1941, RH 24-2/462, BA-MA.

36. Gerlach, *Kalkulierte Morde*, 255.

37. On the logisitic problems facing the Wehrmacht during Operation Barbarossa, see Müller, "Das Scheitern der wirtschaftlichen 'Blitzkriegstrategie,'" in Boog et al., *Der Angriff auf die Sowjetunion*, 1138–68; on those facing Army Group North in particular, see Wilhelm Ritter von Leeb, *Tagebuchaufzeichnungen und Lagebeurteilungen aus zwei Weltkriegen*, ed. Georg Meyer (Stuttgart: Deutsche Verlags-Anstalt, 1976), entry for July 12, 1941, 293.

38. Tagebuchartige Aufzeichnungen des Lt. E., Btl. Adj., July 13, 1941, RH 37/3095, BA-MA.

39. "Der Todesmarsch nach Leningrad," Msg 2/2580, 74, 112, BA-MA.

40. KTB, Abt. Ib, Divisionsintendant 121. Inf. Division 10.3.1942, Tätigkeitsbericht für die Zeit vom 20.6.41 bis 20.9.41, RH 26-121/65, BA-MA. The division's quartermaster reported that the division moved so quickly during the first three months of war that it never had time to systematically live off the land.

41. Tagebuchartige Aufzeichnungen des Lt. E., Btl. Adj., July 20, 1941, RH 37/3095, BA-MA.

42. Army Group North commanded nineteen infantry, two motorized, two panzer, and three security divisions, as well as one Waffen-SS formation; see "Schematische Kriegsgliederung vom 27.6.41 abends," in Percy Ernst Schramm, ed., *Kriegstagebuch des Oberkommandos der Wehrmacht (Wehrmachtführungsstab) 1940–1945*, vol. 1, *1. August 1940–31. Dezember 1941*, ed. Hans-Adolf Jacobsen (Bonn, 1965; repr., Munich: Bernard & Graefe, 1982), 1137.

43. "Ereignismeldung UdSSR Nr. 53," August 15, 1941, T 175, Roll 233, National Archives and Records Administration, Washington, DC (hereafter NARA).

44. Hill identifies several instances of such behavior in the Leningrad region; see *War behind the Eastern Front*, 26–30.

45. On this decision-making process, see Jörg Ganzenmüller, *Das belagerte Leningrad, 1941–1944: Die Stadt in den Strategien von Angreifern und Verteidigern* (Paderborn: Ferdinand Schöningh, 2005), 20–32.

46. "Ereignismeldung UdSSR Nr. 94," September 25, 1941, T 175, Roll 233, NARA.

47. Quoted in Hill, *War behind the Eastern Front*, 54.

48. Quoted in Johannes Hürter, "Die Wehrmacht vor Leningrad: Krieg und Besatzungspolitik der 18. Armee im Herbst und Winter 1941/42," *Vierteljahrshefte für Zeitgeschichte* 49, no. 3 (2001): 409.

49. In addition to classic works such as Harrison Salisbury, *The 900 Days: The Siege of Leningrad* (New York: Harper & Row, 1969), and Leon de Goure, *The Siege of Leningrad* (Stanford: Stanford University Press, 1962), see the recent studies by Cynthia Simmons and Nina Perlina, *Writing the Siege of Leningrad: Women's Diaries, Memoirs, and Documentary Prose* (Pittsburgh: University of Pittsburgh Press, 2002); David M. Glantz, *The Siege of Leningrad 1941–1944: 900 Days of Terror* (London: Cassell, 2004); and Ganzenmüller, *Das belagerte Leningrad*.

50. Pohl dates the beginning of mass starvation throughout the Soviet Union to October 1941; see *Die Herrschaft der Wehrmacht*, 185–86.

51. AOK18, Kriegstagebuch Oberquartiermeister, October 5, 1941, reproduced in Peter Jahn, ed., *Blockade Leningrads—Blokada Leningrada* (Berlin: Ch. Links, 2004), 126.

52. XXVIII AK, KTB, October 29, 1941, RH 24-28/20, BA-MA. At this time, there were approximately forty thousand civilians in the 28th Corps's area of responsibility. See XXVIII AK, Tätigkeitsbericht Teil III, October 23–24, 1941, RH 24-28/109, BA-MA.

53. Hürter, "Die Wehrmacht vor Leningrad," 411. As Hürter notes, "instead of feeding the civilians, the idea developed to separate them from the troops and evacuate them" (410). The local branch of the Economic Staff East

also viewed these evacuations as positive measures because of the "increasingly worsening food situation"; Wi.Kdo. Görlitz, Gef.St.Krasnogwardeisk, Lagebericht (Monat Dezember 1941), RW 31/948, BA-MA.

54. Heeresgruppenkommando Nord, Ib Nr. 7991/41 geheim. 21.10.41, Betr.: Behandlungen der Zivilbevölkerung aus den Vorstädten von Leningrad, T-312, Roll 766, NARA.

55. Ganzenmüller, *Das belagerte Leningrad*, 76.

56. Hürter, "Die Wehrmacht vor Leningrad," 413.

57. Generalkommando L AK, Abt. Qu. 29.11.41, Betr.: Flüchtlingsverkehr, T-312, Roll 766, NARA.

58. Johannes Hürter, "Konservative Mentalität, militärischer Pragmatismus, ideologisierte Kriegführung: Das Beispiel des Generals Georg von Küchler," in *Karrieren im Nationalsozialismus: Funktionseliten zwischen Mitwirkung und Distanz*, ed. Gerhard Hirschfeld and Tobias Jersak (Frankfurt am Main: Campus, 2004), 245.

59. Armeebefehl des Oberbefehlshabers der 6. Armee, Generalfeldmarshall von Reichenau, vom 10.10.1941, reproduced in Ueberschär and Wette, *Der deutsche Überfall auf die Sowjetunion*, 285–86.

60. Generalkommando XXVIII AK, Tätigkeitsbericht Teil II, November 6, 1941, RH 24-28/108, BA-MA.

61. Quoted in Hürter, "Konservative Mentalität," 246.

62. This is not to say that there were no critics of Eighteenth Army's occupation policies. *Generalmajor* Hans Knuth, commandant of the rear army area, wrote Küchler's headquarters: "one gives the people something to eat, then every problem is solved" (ibid., 245).

63. Oberkommando des Heeres, Gen St d H/Gen Qu, Abt. K.Verw., Nr. II/7732/41 geh., Betr. Ernährung der Zivilbevölkerung im Operationsgebiet, November 4, 1941, reproduced in Hamburger Institut für Sozialforschung, ed., *Verbrechen der Wehrmacht: Dimensionen des Vernichtungskrieges 1941–1944* (Hamburg: Hamburger Edition, 2002), 301.

64. Merkpunkte aus der Chefbesprechung in Orscha am 13.11.41, reproduced in Ueberschär and Wette, eds., *Der deutsche Überfall auf die Sowjetunion*, 308–9.

65. Besprechung O.Qu. am 1.12.1941, RH 24-50/175, BA-MA.

66. Monatserfassungbericht des Wi Kdo Görlitz, Aussenstelle Opotschka Gr. La für die Zeit vom 1.–29.11.41, RW 31/584, BA-MA.

67. Wi In Nord, Fp.Nr. 46376 Az.: Chefgr.Fü/Id, B.Nr. 1133/41 geh., December 18, 1941, Betr.: Lagebericht für die Zeit vom 1.–15.12.41, RW 31/584, BA-MA.

68. Already in August, the 87th Infantry Division as well as two field commandants were calling for the Economic Staff East to provide assistance to those starving in Minsk; see Gerlach, *Kalkulierte Morde*, 268.

69. Norbert Müller, ed., *Die faschistische Okkupationspolitik in den zeitweilig besetzten Gebieten der Sowjetunion (1941–1944)* (Berlin: Deutscher Verlag der Wissenschaften, 1991), 212, doc. 53.
70. Wi In Nord, Fp.Nr. 46376 Az.: Chefgr.Fü/Id, B.Nr. 1133/41 geh., December 18, 1941, Betr.: Lagebericht für die Zeit vom 1.–15.12.41, RW 31/584, BA-MA.
71. Wi.Kdo. Krasnogwardeisk Gruppe La, Bericht [no date; presumably end of December 1941], RW 31/948, BA-MA.
72. Wi In Nord, Fp.Nr. 46376 Az.: Chefgr.Fü/Id, B.Nr. 1133/41 geh., December 18, 1941, Betr.: Lagebericht für die Zeit vom 1.–15.12.41, RW 31/584, BA-MA. The remainder of the discussion is based on this document unless otherwise noted.
73. Wi.Kdo. Krasnogwardeisk Gruppe La, Bericht [no date; presumably end of December 1941], RW 31/948, BA-MA.
74. Wirtschaftskommando Krasnogwardeisk, Monatsbericht vom 1.–31.1.1942, February 5, 1942, RW 31/948, BA-MA.
75. For more on this issue, see Jeff Rutherford, "Soldiers into Nazis? The German Infantry's War in Northwest Russia, 1941–1944" (PhD diss, University of Texas, 2007), 196–97.
76. Wi.Kdo. Krasnogwardeisk, Gruppe La, Monatsbericht Februar 1942, February 23, 1942, RW 31/948, BA-MA.
77. Divisionsintendant 121. Inf. Division, Tätigkeitsbericht für die Zeit vom 21.9.1941 bis 30.4.1942, RH 26-121/65, BA-MA; Wirtschaftskommando Krasnogwardeisk, February 5, 1942, RW 31/948, BA-MA.
78. O.Qu. Tagesmeldung XXVIII AK für den 8.10.1941, T-312, Roll 763, NARA. Holstein reported that "the transport situation of the railroad is so bad that Army Group North has discontinued all transport to and from the *Heimat* indefinitely [*bis auf weiteres*].... Here as well there is a considerable deficit of fuel. Locomotives are frozen by the extreme cold, as there aren't enough available garages for them"; Wi In Nord Fp. Nr. 46376 Az.: Chefgr. Fü/Id, B.Nr. 1139541 geh., December 31, 1941, Betr.: Lagebericht für die Zeit vom 16.–31.12.41, RW 31/584, BA-MA.
79. Tagebuchartige Aufzeichnungen des Lt. E., Btl. Adj., August 2, 1941, RH 37/3095, BA-MA. Catherine Merridale suggests that many of these stores were in fact looted by Soviet citizens after the Red Army had pulled out of an area; see *Ivan's War: Life and Death in the Red Army, 1939–1945* (New York: Picador, 2006), 107.
80. Wi.Kdo. Görlitz, Gef.St.Krasnogwardeisk, Lagebericht (Monat Dezember 1941), RW 31/948, BA-MA.
81. Gen.Kdo.XXVIII, Erfahrungsbericht über den Umgang mit der Zivilbevölkerung, November 15, 1941, RH 24/28-110, BA-MA.
82. Chrezvychainaia Gosudarstvennaia Komissiia po Ustanobleniiu i Rassledobaniiu Zlodeianii Nemetsko-Fashistskikh Zakhvatchikov i ikh Soi-

uznikov, United States Holocaust Memorial Museum, RG 22-002M, Reel 18, Pavlovsk, 1.
83. Ibid.
84. Ibid., 6. While this is the total number of starvation deaths during the entire occupation, it is clear from the context that the overwhelming majority of these deaths occurred during the first winter of war.
85. Ibid., 4.
86. "Ereignismeldung UdSSR Nr. 169," February 16, 1942, T-175, Roll 234, NARA.
87. Wi.Kdo. Krasnogwardeisk, Gru.Fü., Monatsbericht Februar 1942, February 23, 1942, RW 31/948, BA-MA.
88. Chronik der 2. Kompanie Nachrichten-Abteilung 121, 44/381, BA-MA; "Ereignismeldung UdSSR Nr. 169," February 16, 1942, T-175, Roll 234, NARA.
89. Sicherheitspolizei u. S.D., Außenstelle Pawlowsk, April 3, 1942, RH 26-121/70, BA-MA.
90. Besprechung des Chefs mit Genst. Arzt Dr. Gunderloch, October 26, 1941, KTB 18 AOK, T-312, Roll 782, NARA.
91. For more on these efforts by individual soldiers, see Rutherford, "Soldiers into Nazis?," 215–17.
92. Tagebuchaufzeichnungen aus dem Rußandfeldzug des Kp.Chef.San Kp. 21. Dr. Werner Schneider vom 18.6.1941–27.7.1943, December 26, 1941, Msg 2/2778, BA-MA.
93. Generalkommando L AK, Abt. Qu., Besondere Anordnungen für die Versorgung Nr. 170, February 7, 1942, RH 24-50/176, BA-MA.
94. "Ereignismeldung UdSSR Nr. 130," November 7, 1941, T-175, Roll 234, NARA.
95. "Ereignismeldung UdSSR Nr. 190," April 8, 1942, T-175, Roll 234, NARA. The men of the 121st Infantry Division were not the only soldiers who attempted to alleviate the suffering of Russians in their area of responsibility. In the spring of 1942, Third Panzer Army, operating southwest of Moscow, noted in its war diary that "although no provisions may be handed over to the civilian population, for the most part the civilian population is being fed by the Wehrmacht"; quoted in Müller, "Das Scheitern der wirtschaftlichen 'Blitzkriegstrategie,'" in Boog et al., *Der Angriff auf die Sowjetunion*, 1223n335.
96. 121. Inf. Division, Winterausstattung, January 10, 1942, RH 26-121/65, BA-MA. Despite the soldiers' procuring of needed items from Russian POWs and civilians, the division had, for example, 827 fur coats, 989 felt boots, and 2,519 pairs of woolen underwear for the 12,719 men in the division. While a significant number of these men undoubtedly were replacements who came equipped for the winter, the difference between the

number of total soldiers and the number of coats, boots, and underwear is striking.

97. Besprechungspunkte!, T-312, Roll 766, NARA. One example of the results of these shortages concerns a raiding party sent out for several hours on January 24. Upon its return, "90 percent of the men suffered light to medium frostbite"; KTB, January 24, 1942, RH 26-121/16, BA-MA.

98. Tagebuchartige Aufzeichnungen des Lt. E., Btl. Adj., August 18, 1941, RH 37/3095, BA-MA; and *Leutnant* Heinz E., Feldpostbriefe, September 4, 1941, and October 14, 1941, in Jahn, *Blockade Leningrads*, 136–38.

99. "Der Todesmarsch nach Leningrad," Msg 2/2580, 63, BA-MA.

100. Abt. Ib KTB, December 7, 1941, RH 26-121/65, BA-MA; Generalkommando L AK, 18.8.42 Tätigkeitsbericht der Abt. IVa Gen. Kdo. L AK für die Zeit vom 13.8.31–7.5.42, RH 24-50/173, BA-MA.

101. Wi In Nord, Fp.Nr. 46376 Az.: Chefgr.Fü/Id, B.Nr. 1133/41 geh., December 18, 1941, Betr.: Lagebericht für die Zeit vom 1.–15.12.41, RW 31/584, BA-MA.

102. XXVIII AK, Tätigkeitsbericht Teil III, October 21–22, 1941, RH 24-28/109, BA-MA.

103. Wi.Kdo. Krasnogwardeisk, Gru.Fü., February 23, 1942, Monatsbericht Januar 1942, January 7, 1942, January 14, 1942, RW 31/948, BA-MA; Erfahrungsbericht Heeresversorgung, December 7, 1941, RH 26-121/65, BA-MA.

104. Wi.Kdo. Krasnogwardeisk, Gru.Fü., February 23, 1942, Monatsbericht Januar 1942, January 26, 1942, RW 31/948, BA-MA.

105. Wi.Kdo. Görlitz, Gef.St.Krasnogwardeisk, Lagebericht (Monat Dezember 1941), RW 31/948, BA-MA.

106. On the production of boots, see Divisionsarzt 121. Division, Tätigkeitsbericht über den Einsatz der Sanitätsdienste bei der 121. Inf.-Division im Ostfeldzug vom 1. Oktober 1941–30. April 1942, June 10, 1942, RH 26-121/65, BA-MA; and Generalkommando L AK, Tätigkeitsbericht der Abt. IVa, Gen.Kdo. L AK für die Zeit vom 13.8.41–7.5.42, RH 24-50/173, BA-MA. On the repair shop, see Wi. Kdo. Görlitz, Gef. St. Krasnogwardeisk, Lagebericht (Monat Dezember 1941), RW 31/948, BA-MA.

107. Lagebericht vom 10.1.42, RW 31-498, BA-MA.

108. Ortskommandantur I (V) 309 Abt. Ia, Pawlowsk 23.2.1942, Vorschläge der Ortskommandantur zur Bekämpfung von Flecktyphus, RH 26-121/18, BA-MA.

109. Such thinking permeates Hürter, "Die Wehrmacht vor Leningrad."

110. Wilhelm von Heesch, *Meine 13. Infanterie-Geschütz-Kompanie Grenadier-Regiment 408* (self-published, 1962), 103.

111. Geoffrey P. Megargee, *War of Annihilation: Combat and Genocide on the Eastern Front, 1941* (Lanham, MD: Rowman & Littlefield, 2007), 143.

CHAPTER 6

THE EXPLOITATION OF FOREIGN TERRITORIES AND THE DISCUSSION OF OSTLAND'S CURRENCY IN 1941

Paolo Fonzi

1941: Escalating the Exploitation of Foreign Territories

Historians have traditionally maintained that a significant amount of the resources that supported the German war economy in World War II came from outside the national territories. While this still holds true, at least two crucial issues have become a point of controversy in the last decades: the role played by foreign resources in the German war effort as a whole and the significance of this finding for an overall reassessment of the military strategy of the Third Reich.

Alan Milward's well-known thesis of a planned economic short-war strategy (*wirtschaftliche Blitzkriegstrategie*) assumed that from the very beginning the Reich had envisaged the exploitation of foreign countries in order to fill the gaps in the undermobilized German economy.[1] Rolf-Dieter Müller criticized Milward's theories by pointing out that the undermobilization of the German war economy was not part of a strategy, since Hitler had always striven for a total war, but was simply due to the administrative chaos that marked the power structure of the Third Reich.[2] This view has also been rejected by recent analyses that shed new light on the shortcomings of the statistical evidence used so far for evaluating Germany's war production. A recent analysis based on alternative and more accurate statistical sources called into question the very idea that has dominated the historiography since its very beginning, namely, that the German economy was undermobilized.[3] A third issue regards the employment of foreign resources to alleviate the hardships of war for the German population. This question had already been raised during the discussion of Tim Mason's studies on the working class during the Nazi era.[4] More recently the resumption of this discussion, originating with the publication of Götz Aly's controversial book *Hitlers Volksstaat*,[5] has loaded the problem with strong ethical implications. Indeed, Aly's account stressed the fact that everyday Germans had profited indirectly but consciously from the economic scarcity imposed on dominated countries; this allowed them to maintain prewar living conditions in Germany long after 1939.

While further research is needed in order to reach a proper understanding of these complex issues, scholars agree that the German war effort relied a great deal on imports, which were not compensated for by a comparable amount of exports.[6] Direct or indirect control of foreign economies allowed the Third Reich to feed its own war economy through the exploitation of foreign economies. This chapter will focus on how German institutions dealt with the organizational problems connected with this extraction of resources. As with other issues discussed in this book, 1941 constituted a crucial turning point. This will become clear by considering a controversy that developed between the main economic institutions during the course of that year, namely, the discussion about the foundation of a national bank in some of the territories conquered by the Reich in eastern Europe. In order to assess the significance of this episode in the general economic developments of the war, it will be first necessary to illustrate how the exploitation system was shaped and then managed up to that moment. Pointing a spotlight at the controversy of 1941 will then allow us to gain an overview of the cumulative crisis of the German exploitation system and of the war economy itself.

The victory over France in 1940, which brought the Third Reich to the peak of its power, was the most significant turning point in the history of German foreign trade during World War II. The enormous increase in German imports was due to two main factors: on the one hand, the direct grip on the economies of the occupied territories, and on the other, a political "force of attraction" on all European countries based on a political vision that put Germany at center stage in the future New Order. In this context, it is surprising that the new master of Europe renounced the possibility of directly controlling foreign resources by simply creating a joint currency area. In fact, two major Berlin institutions—the Foreign Office and the Office of the Four-Year Plan[7]—had elaborated some plans for a fast-track implementation of a currency union with several countries. This notwithstanding, Germany chose to act in continuity with the past and maintained the existing forms of foreign trade.

The flows of exploited resources from European economies went through three main channels. Let us take a closer look at each of them. The first method was the so-called *Reichskreditkassenscheine* (*RKK-Scheine*), which were notes issued by special banks, the Reich Credit Offices (*Reichskreditkassen*). These were set up in every occupied country to supply the invading troops with readily available cash. The notes were declared legal tender in the occupied countries, to be replaced—as soon as military operations were over—by credits issued by the Central Bank in local currency. It was conceived so as to avoid a double monetary circulation in occupied countries.[8] This method, a sort of German innovation in modern warfare, did not immediately produce an outflow of goods to the Reich, since the troop money was not used in international exchanges. In informal ways, however, it contributed to supplying the German population at home with goods from the subjugated countries.[9] The effective implementation of the *RKK-Scheine* varied from country to country. For example, in the Netherlands they were withdrawn after a few months, while in France they were used until the end of 1943.

The second method was the imposition of occupation costs on almost every occupied country, not only to finance the real expenses of the German army but also to guarantee imports to the Reich, thus contravening the rules of the Hague Convention. Occupation costs contributed in two ways to the German war expenses: first by feeding the German army abroad, and second as credit for normal but concealed trade.[10]

The third way was the clearing system, which contributed by and large to unpaid imports. As already mentioned, in the summer of 1940 some institutions argued that since the Reich had achieved such unprecedented victories, the time was ripe for the monetary unification of Europe. This process involved eliminating the clearing system, as well as the foreign exchange rationing introduced in Germany in 1931. Because of structural economic differences among the various European areas, this proposal had been restricted to the so-called inner circle of the *Großraumwirtschaft* (namely, Belgium, the Netherlands, Denmark, and Norway). The eventual rejection of the project was caused by technical problems and by the opposition of the Ministry of Economics and the Reichsbank, backed by the Ministry of Finance. It was decided to implement the monetary unification of Europe through a more gradual process; at the beginning of this process, the first step would have been represented by the multilateralization of clearing. This program foresaw that clearing payments had to be centralized in the German Compensation Office (*Deutsche Verrechnungskasse*) in Berlin and compensated not only bilaterally, as the system had worked hitherto, but also multilaterally. Thus the clearing system was to be maintained as a first step toward a currency and customs union to be realized in the future.[11]

In a clearing system, which is necessarily based on previous international agreements, transfers of goods do not produce a corresponding transfer of currency. If, for instance, an exporter from country A sells commodities to an importer from country B, the former will not be paid directly by the latter. The importer will pay the sum due to the Central Bank of its own country in local currency. Similarly, the exporter will be paid a corresponding sum by the Central Bank of its country. Discrepancies in the balance of payments are normally settled between the banks. The crucial point is that they do not produce any automatic consequence. This allowed the German Reich to let its clearing debt increase freely without paying the consequences of any immediate effect upon its own economy.

In a normal situation, the government of the country that has an export surplus can either stop delivering goods or suspend payments to the exporters, which will similarly produce a delay in the exports. During the first years of war, given the great military and political power of Germany, this did not actually happen. In summer 1940, German economic institutions explicitly planned that the Reich would accumulate debts in order to feed the war effort. Only five days after the beginning of the Western campaign, Reich Minister of Economics Walther Funk stated that the newly occupied countries had to prepare to export to Germany without expecting any compensation.[12] In this framework, accumulating debts was not deemed to be a problem, since after the war a "conspicuous part of the balances" was to be counted as payment for the "protection" provided by the Reich to the European countries, that is, simply cancelled.[13]

From summer 1940 at the latest, foreign resources were an integral part of the German war economy, and their exploitation held pace with the increase in German military production. The escalation in the use of unpaid imports can be easily recognized in a chart produced by the Reichsbank in 1943, which represents the development of German clearing debt during the period 1939–42. This chart was written to support the stance of the Reichsbank in the debate between the major economic institutions about how to solve the problems caused by the clearing imbalances. It shows that the debt increased steadily up to December 1940, except for a slight acceleration in June 1940. In December the curve shows the first significant discontinuity becoming much steeper and growing continuously until June 1941, when the second evident increase in the pace of growth takes place. Another important element illustrated by the chart is that while up to June 1941 the lines of debts with allied and occupied countries increased at the same pace, after this month the imbalances with occupied countries grew much more rapidly than those with the allied.

What do these discontinuities and changes stand for? In the absence of month-by-month analyses of the flow of goods from the European economies into the Reich, we can only attempt an explanation drawing on existing scholarship. Let us now analyze the discontinuities one by

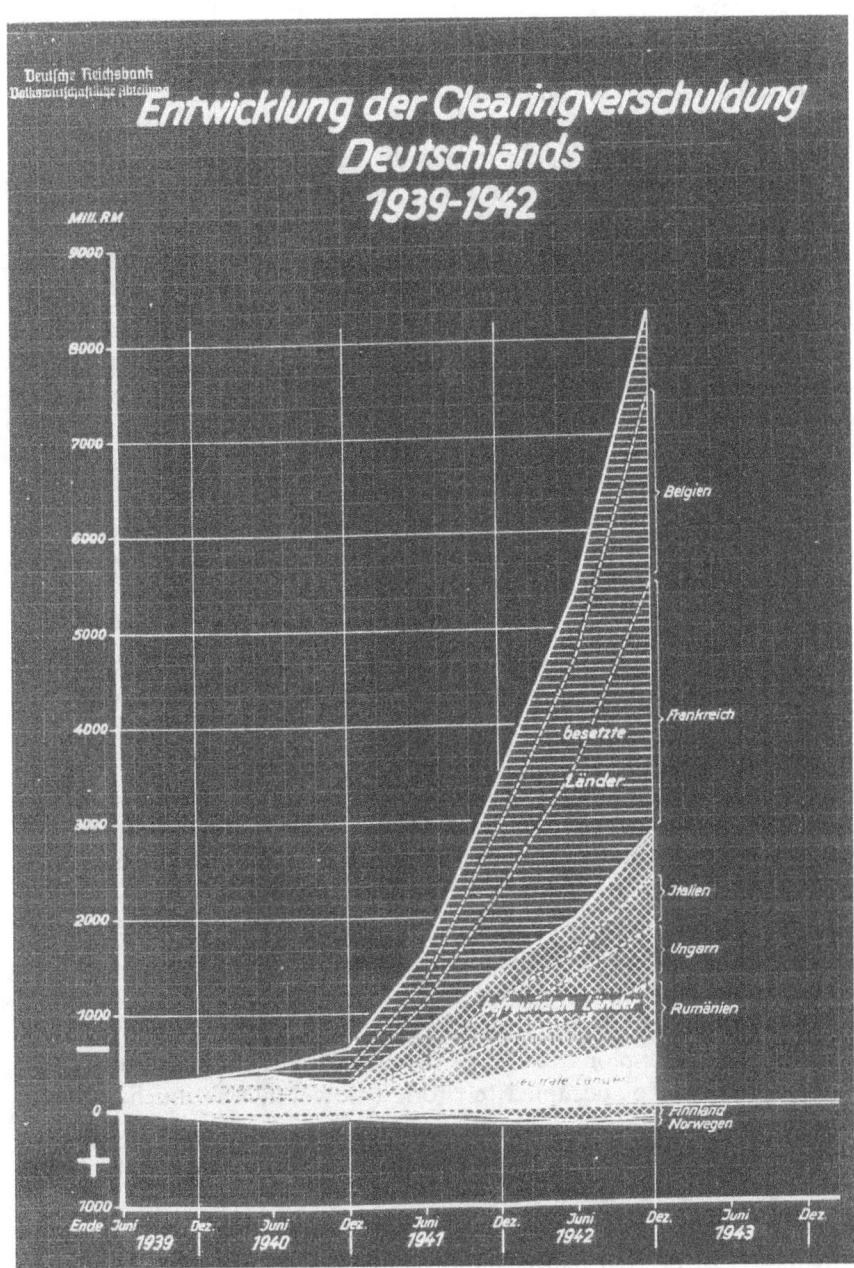

Figure 6.1. Development of Germany's Clearing Debt, 1939–42. Courtesy of Bundesarchiv Berlin-Lichterfelde (R2501-6448).

one. Shortly after the victory over France, preparations for the Eastern campaign began. The preparations for Barbarossa, because of its huge dimensions, marked a turning point in the economic history of the Third Reich. The so-called *Rüstungsprogramm B*, which was carried out from October 1940 onward, had a remarkable effect on industrial output. At the same time, there were significant increases in the long-term investments to prepare Germany for the future war after the defeat of the USSR. These productive efforts made the months between the victories in the west and the commencement of Barbarossa a period of considerable economic activity.[14]

In the same period, a program of outsourcing of production for the Wehrmacht began, the so-called *Auftragsverlagerung*.[15] This policy was promoted by Hermann Göring, at that time a sort of dictator of the German economy, who in the summer and autumn of 1940 issued a series of decrees in which he invited the economic institutions and the occupation administrations to stimulate German companies to place orders in occupied countries. Delays in setting up the necessary administrative structure hindered the full realization of the program until the end of the year; thus, the first remarkable results were visible only in the first quarter of 1941.[16] Moreover, as the graph clearly shows, the bulk of the debt increase was borne by Belgium and France. The clearing with France began only after the agreement of November 14, 1940. These elements provide an explanation for the shift in the clearing debt curve of December 1940.

In assessing the second discontinuity, there are at least two factors that need to be taken into account. First of all, the interruption of trade with the USSR, which had represented a vital source for the German economy in 1939–40, forced the Reich to raise the imports from occupied countries.[17] Moreover, soon after the start of the campaign the so-called *Göringsprogramm* was released, a program that attempted to concentrate the German war economy in order to develop the air force. Its realization, as Dietrich Eichholtz expressed it, implied an "escalating brutalization of the exploitation"[18] of the allies and of occupied territories. The exploitation of occupied territories, however, was much easier to carry out than increasing imports from formally independent countries. Imports from the southeastern European allies had to be, if only partially, balanced out by a certain amount of exports.[19] Moreover, as has been widely recognized, war and occupation did not really alter the westward orientation of the German economy, which during the war returned to the structure of trade typical of the years before the Great Depression. This accounts for the expanding area between the line of the debt toward occupied countries and that toward Germany's allies.

In order to explain the increase in clearing debt, another element needs to be accounted for. The clearing debt was induced to grow by a vicious circle of debt and import prices. In the clearing system, since importers and exporters pay and are paid by the Central Bank in local currency, any imbalance in the balance of payments necessarily turns into an imbalance between receipts and expenses of a single Central Bank. In order to preserve the "willingness to deliver" (*Lieferwilligkeit*) of foreign exporters, the Reich imposed a condition on negotiations with its trade partners. It was decided that the Central Banks of their counterparts pay the exporters to the Reich in advance, even if the export expenses were not matched by corresponding import receipts. These advances were mostly financed using the press, that is, by coining new money and therefore stimulating inflation. While German export prices, as well as the German internal price level, remained relatively stable during the war, prices of imports from other countries tended to rise as the clearing debt grew. Importing the same quantity of goods at higher prices raised the German imbalance and, in turn, the clearing debt. This simple mechanism, which in internal documents was labelled "the clearing problem," induced a self-reproduction of indebtedness.[20]

The shifts in the Reichsbank's graph lead us to the conclusion that the year 1941 witnessed a significant radicalization in the exploitation of both the occupied countries and Germany's allies. This phenomenon had significant links with the simultaneous radicalization in the political field. First, carrying out such an escalation required an increased level of violence to impose it upon the subjected populations. Furthermore, the principle on which this policy was based was part of a racist ideology. It implied, in fact, that the Germans had to be spared, as far as possible, the harshness of war at the expense of foreign populations. At the end of 1941, an official in the Reich Finance Ministry addressed the matter very frankly: "Regarding the occupied regions we have hitherto always supported the standpoint: if there must be inflation, then better there than in Germany."[21] Such a determination had heinous consequences for those living "there," as the terrible famine unleashed by the German policy in Greece clearly illustrated.[22]

The increasing exploitation, however, reached its own limits in the same period. We have already analyzed the mechanism through which the clearing debt reproduced itself and the consequences this had on the price levels of the exploited countries. It is true, though, that the consequences on the German economy of inflation in Europe were more worrying than the effect on the debt itself. Importing goods at growing prices, Germany incurred the risk of importing the inflation itself. German price levels were stabilized by the tight grip of the Reich authorities, especially the Reich commissar for price setting. Nevertheless, the possibility that the state would lose control of prices was an ever-present specter for the National Socialist leadership.

As early as the beginning of 1941, the Reichsbank had started worrying about the price increases in southeastern Europe. The exchange rate policy practiced between the end of 1940 and the first half of 1941 had pursued the goal of eliminating the reichsmark disagio in southeastern Europe through a revaluation of the mark. The aims of this policy were twofold: first, unification of the exchange rates of the reichsmark as a logical premise to the multilateralization of the clearing system; second, strengthening of the purchasing power of the reichsmark abroad, that is increasing the amount of imported goods from those countries.

In January 1941, at a meeting of the *Handelspolitischer Ausschuss*—the leading institution in matters of foreign trade—all the representatives of economic institutions unanimously expressed misgivings that the increase of export prices from the Reich could produce inflation abroad. The Reichsbank, which had been the advocate of this policy, agreed with their assessment and proposed a slowing down of the revaluation of the reichsmark.[23] The same problem was dealt with at a meeting of the *Handelspolitischer Ausschuss* in August.[24] At this meeting, two issues were discussed: the current state of the clearing debt, which was becoming a contentious point in trade negotiations, and the price increases in Europe. No general solution could be found for either problem, and it was agreed to intervene case by case. The Reich committed itself to trying to obtain better conditions in future bilateral negotiations regarding the clearing debt. As for the occupied countries, every concession for diminishing or only consolidating the clearing debt was considered an unjustified concession to a defeated country. The most obvious proposal to tackle price increases—namely, a modification of the exchange rates—was rejected, and it was decided that in the next round of negotiations the Reich would try to impose bilateral price stops.

It is therefore clear that all the economic institutions involved, although submitting different insights, recognized that the current levels of exploitation were unsustainable. A sort of "inflation community"[25] was taking shape in Europe and this raised concerns within the German leadership. A wide and systematic debate about how to solve these problems was to take place only one year later, but in the course of 1941 a deeper awareness of the necessity of a change in strategy was emerging.

The first signs of crisis within the exploitation system established in Europe were caused by two main factors: an extremely disorganized administration and a disproportion between the wealth of the *Großraumwirtschaft* and the real needs of the German war effort. The first point has been traditionally recognized in the historiography as a typical mark of the German administration of occupied Europe.[26] During the war, Germany was unable to establish a rational system of exploitation in Europe; therefore, it did not fully utilize European resources. As for the second reason, Adam Tooze suggests that the economic potential of the European *Großraumwirtschaft* was simply not sufficient to win the war for world power, as envisaged by Hitler.[27] It is difficult to properly assess the relative weight of these two factors, as any appraisal necessarily entails a judgment on the root causes of German defeat. The discussion of the problem of European inflation, however, and the following attempts at centralizing the exploitation show that the German leadership perceived the rationalization as a feasible way to maximize the benefits of occupation. In any case, since the beginning of 1941 significant shortages of important supplies—notably food, workers, and oil—became apparent.[28] The perception of supply difficulties was an important factor underlying the plans for the occupation of the Soviet Union. In fact, occupying the USSR was seen as a necessary economic completion (*Ergänzungsraum*) of the *Großraumwirtschaft*. The war against the Soviet Union was planned from the very beginning as a "war of economic plunder" (*wirtschaftlicher Raubkrieg*),[29] an undertaking that had to provide a much-needed solution for every present and future economic shortage.

The intertwining of the economic factors discussed above—actual shortages, first signs of a crisis in the exploitation system, attempt at rationalizing the extraction of resources—have been the focus of this paper thus far. I will now explore a debate that took place during the second half of 1941 in economic quarters of the Reich and that dealt with monetary reform and the foundation of the Central Bank of a newly conquered territory in the east.

Ostland's Monetary Issues

Early ideas on how to shape the monetary circulation in the soon-to-be occupied regions of the east were developed during the planning phase, which began in December 1940 and finished with the launch of the campaign. However, plans in the monetary field were far less elaborate than in other issues, such as the seizure of food or oil supplies. This was probably the case because of the relative unimportance of monetary mediations in a war of economic plunder.

In the occupation of the Soviet Union, informal methods like requisitioning and "obscure receipts"[30] issued by the army played a much greater role than in the west. In this respect, plans in the monetary field confirm a largely acknowledged fact, namely, the peculiar brutality of the occupation in the east in comparison with that of the western countries. Moreover, envisioning a certain monetary organization depended upon the final political order that the Reich would impose upon the conquered territories. Since ruthless economic exploitation had a certain priority over long-term political projects in the east, political aims had not been strictly defined before the invasion.

Nevertheless, a program for the immediate supply of troops was outlined by the Economic Staff East, the institution responsible for economic policy in the occupied Soviet Union. The Guidelines for the Management of the Economy—the so-called Green Folder, issued in June 1941—contained brief instructions on this matter. *Reichskreditkassen* were to be set up in the occupied regions and would issue *RKK-Scheine* "to keep the economy of the occupied country intact, as far as this is important for us in the interest of peace and order, as well as to satisfy and balance the money requirements of the German troops."[31] The notes of the *Reichskreditkassen* would circulate along with the existing currency.

As in all other occupied countries during the war, the Reichsbank was responsible for the elaboration of these guidelines. In the previous weeks, when they had been made known, they had met with strong opposition from Alfred Rosenberg. The future minister for the occupied eastern territories and his collaborators, in fact, rejected the issue of *RKK-Scheine* and, for the immediate supply of troops, proposed that the Reich press rubles. This would allow—they believed—the occupation authorities to introduce, as soon possible, national currencies in those regions for which the creation of a nation-state was foreseen, especially in Ukraine.

Though Rosenberg's arguments initially met with Funk's approval, his opposition failed to change the Guidelines for the Administration of the Economy.[32] It is probable, however, that his intervention unleashed a discussion about the second phase of the monetary policy in the east. Judging from a survey written by the head of the department in the Ministry of Finance, Walther Bayrhoffer, an agreement must have been reached on general guidelines to be realized after the Blitzkrieg was over.[33] After the implementation of the first phase—the issue of *RKK-Scheine* to be coined by motorized *Reichskreditkassen*—the reestablishment of the Russian Central Bank and the issue of rubles were envisaged. These measures were intended to bring the economy back to a regular monetary circulation. If this had proved impossible, a new central bank would have been established with the aim of issuing rubles. Finally, a third phase had been envisaged, namely, the creation of four new central banks corresponding to the four Reich commissariats. Indeed, plans for a civil administration had foreseen the establishment of four Reich commissariats (Ostland, Ukraine, Caucasia, and Moscovia). The foundation of four central banks was to be realized only after the definitive political reorganization of the territory.

Thus, up to the start of the campaign, plans for restructuring the monetary circulation of the new regions remained rather ambiguous. The idea of establishing four central banks was a logical consequence of the intention to dismember the Soviet Union and to create four political entities dependent on the Reich. However, a more definite plan was formulated for Ostland, which was the Reich commissariat that would encompass the three former Baltic States and parts of Belarus. It was decided quite early on that in this territory the reichsmark was to be introduced as a consequence of its anticipated incorporation into Greater Germany (*Grossdeutsches Reich*).[34] This special treatment was for the reason that, compared to the other three commissariats, Ostland held a special position in the Nazi view of the east. Because of its supposed comparative racial purity and the fact that it had not been spoiled by long-lasting Bolshevik domination, this territory was judged "capable of Germanization" (*eindeutschungsfähig*) and therefore worthy of being attached to the Reich.[35] Given this political aim, the policy of plunder here was to be restrained within certain limits in order to preserve the stability of the region in the long run. In a meeting on November 8, 1941,[36] Göring, who had been charged by Hitler with the economic administration in the eastern territories, explicated the nature of this particularity. Point one of the economic goals to be pursued in the east stated that the needs of the German war economy were to be considered the "supreme law of every economic action in the newly occupied regions of the east." In the long run (point two), these territories were to be ruled "from a colonial point of view and with colonial methods." An exception was to be made for those parts of Ostland that Hitler had decided to Germanize. Yet for the time being these territories stood under the first rule as well. To show that the difference was only a relative one, Göring provided a telling example: "Imports of consumer goods to the east are out of the question. . . . Also in the Baltic only so much food can be dispensed as is necessary to prevent people from starving."[37] A major consequence of this policy of radical exploitation was that the level of prices and wages, and in general the standard of living, was to be maintained as low as possible in order to free up the greatest amount of food and raw materials for the Reich. In this respect, concluded Göring, no exception was to be made for Ostland.[38]

On August 1, the day the army handed over Galicia, Bialystok, and a region around Vilnius to the civil administration, a meeting was held in the Ministry for the Occupied Eastern Territories—the so-called *Ostministerium*—to discuss monetary issues relating to the newly occupied area. Hinrich Lohse, who on July 17 had been appointed Reich commissar for Ostland, proposed to start immediately introducing the reichsmark in order "to put an end as soon as possible to the unbearable conditions in the price and wage sector."[39] All those present, representatives of the major institutions, opposed Lohse's view and agreed that a more cautious procedure was necessary. The eastern border, it was argued, was still not fixed and there was the risk that notes would flow eastward and would be used by the enemy to devaluate the reichsmark. The *Reichskreditkassen* would instead allow the "low-key" (*auf kaltem Wege*) implementation of the second stage—the substitution of the double circulation with the *RKK-Scheine*. This meant that the *Reichskreditkassen* would collect rubles and issue exclusively *RKK-Scheine* without announcing publicly a monetary reform.[40] In other meetings held in the same weeks, it was agreed that agricultural prices were to be set at 56 percent of the Reich's level. The price gap between agriculture and industry had to be maintained.[41]

The low-key withdrawal of rubles was seen only as a first step toward a monetary reform to be carried out in the future. Indeed, no institution deemed the *RKK-Scheine* to be a satisfying solution, except for the first supplies. Because of the structural differences between the German and Soviet monetary economies and, for the Ostland, the chaotic circumstances brought by the Soviet invasion in 1940, it had been impossible to calculate in advance an adequate exchange rate.

In a meeting on May 28, Funk had recognized that setting an exchange rate between *RKK-Scheine* and rubles was necessarily an "arbitrary act."[42] Thus, the *RKK-Scheine* underwent a rapid devaluation after the invasion. This is why the discussion was carried on in the following weeks. At the end of August, plans had focused on three possible reforms: Direct introduction of the reichsmark, to be prepared by equalization of Ostland's price and wage levels to those of the Reich. Foundation of a central bank with a separate, new currency. Foundation of a Reich credit office specific to the region, to be called Ostland Credit Office (*Ostlandkreditkasse*), which would issue special notes circulating only in Ostland. Like the normal *RKK-Scheine*, these notes would not be legal tender in the Reich, but they would be denominated as reichsmark; for this reason, the latter method was considered as a means for preparing the introduction of the reichsmark.[43]

The first solution, which Lohse had endorsed as late as the end of August, was soon rejected. At the beginning of September, it was definitively clear that conditions were not ripe for such a step. The direct introduction of the reichsmark therefore disappeared from the political agenda. From this moment until the eventual foundation of the Central Bank, the discussion crystallized around two options: the foundation of a new bank with a new currency and the creation of special notes issued by a credit office for Ostland.[44] The latter proposal was discussed on September 24 in a meeting held in the Reich Ministry for the Occupied Eastern Territories. Gustav Schlotterer, who at that point held offices in the Ministry of Economics, in the Economic Staff East, and in the *Ostministerium* itself, expounded upon Rosenberg's intentions regarding the monetary reform in Ostland. A new central bank, which would issue Ostland credit notes with an exchange rate of 1:1 with the reichsmark, was to be established. The intention was to create a sort of transitional period, which would prepare the future introduction of the reichsmark. Lohse, the vice president of the Reichsbank Emil Puhl, and Hans-Joachim Riecke of the Economic Staff East approved this project.[45]

A few days later, Göring intervened directly in the discussion. In a private talk with Walther Funk, the *Reichsmarschall* revealed his misgivings regarding the increasing devaluation of the *RKK-Scheine* toward the ruble. The stability of the exchange rate between *RKK-Scheine* and local currencies had been explicitly mentioned in the Guidelines for the Administration of the Economy as a matter of primary importance. To stop this unwelcome process, Göring ordered the foundation of a new central bank and the creation of a new currency to be called the Ostland crown (*Ostlandkrone*). The exchange rate was to be set at 2 crowns to 1 reichsmark, which meant an undervaluation of 100 percent in comparison with the rate proposed by the *Ostministerium*. The new money would replace the existing double circulation of rubles and *RKK-Scheine*.[46] Funk undertook to carry out the project outlined by Göring.

A few days later, probably due to Funk's intervention, the Reichsbank had already begun preparing two draft laws for the foundation of the National Banks of Ukraine and Ostland.[47] Shortly before, Finance Minister Count Schwerin von Krosigk had expounded the same line of thought as that developed by Göring. His stance was based on a calculation of the gains that the Reich had to draw from the Ostland. His first interest lay in producing so-called sluice profits (*Schleusegewinne*), that is, profits arising from the differential between the price at which a commodity was bought in Ostland and the price at which it was sold in the Reich. As trade with the eastern territories was to be managed by monopoly firms and would be easily controlled, a conspicuous share of this profit was to flow into the public finances. This motivated the finance minister's interest in maintaining prices in the new Reich commissariat at the lowest possible level. At the beginning of October, Schwerin von Krosigk and Göring exchanged ideas about the *Schleusegewinne*. Göring argued that Germany should appropriate all profits, while the finance minister deemed that profits should be used first to balance the budget of the Reich commissariat; only the excess amount would flow into the Reich budget.[48]

Given these premises, Schwerin von Krosigk advocated the creation of a new currency for Ostland with a new denomination. This measure would draw a sharp currency border between Germany and Ostland. Moreover, he requested that the exchange rate be set as low as possible in order to maximize the price gap between Germany and Ostland. Acquainted with the existence of different plans on the matter, the finance minister proposed that a meeting be called to discuss it.

Given the scope of disagreement between the leading institutions and Schwerin von Krosigk's request, it should come as no surprise that a meeting on this topic was summoned for October 3 in the Ministry of Economics. Remarkable, on the other hand, is the range of offices held by those convened. Six ministers, three *Staatssekretäre*, three members of the board of directors of the Reichsbank, and many heads of department (*Ministerialdirigent*) were present, which makes the meeting comparable to a Reich cabinet session. Several so-called *Chefbesprechungen* (head meetings), as this gathering was designated in the minutes, were held during the war. Since regular cabinet sessions had ceased to be summoned after the end of 1937,[49] they assumed the crucial role of coordinating government business.

The agenda to be discussed was also rather unusual: "Money, Currency, Price, and Wage Problems, in particular on the Currency of Ostland," as the title of the minutes read.[50] In the opening speech, Funk explained that he had summoned the meeting to discuss two issues: first, the currency of Ostland, regarding which Schwerin von Krosigk, Rosenberg, and Göring had very different projects; second, the "ominous developments arising in the price and money sectors, as well as in the wage sector."[51] That said, the Reich minister turned to the second issue, the internal monetary problems. Private talks with the finance minister and the Reich commissar for price setting had led him to the conclusion that the situation of the German economy was critical. The amount of money put in circulation by the war finance had largely exceeded the goods available to civilians. The competent authorities had already registered unapproved increases in both prices and wages. In this situation, it was possible that a general inflationary process would be triggered, which was politically dangerous. "The authoritarian state that allows inflation," he stated, "forgoes its authoritarian possibilities of intervention and direction, and therefore is not an authoritarian state anymore."[52]

In order to prevent this from happening—in Funk's words "to again make our money a sound money with real purchasing power"—there were two alternatives. The first was "through additional cheap raw materials from the dominated and occupied territories and through additional cheap outputs produced in these territories." The second one was through a "cut in the debt," which entailed increased austerity in civilian sectors, reduction of wages and prices, and rationalization.[53] If we are to fully understand the monetary problems referred to by Funk, we need to indulge in a short digression. Germany financed its war effort mainly through state indebtedness and only in small part through taxation. Though several attempts were made during the war to change this method by raising the fiscal burden on the German population, the higher echelons of the Reich leadership always refused to undertake such a step.[54] The reduction in civilian consumption, necessary to channel resources into war production, was not practiced at source, that is, by cutting the income, but only at the mouth, that is, by rationing civilian consumption. This freed a considerable amount of purchasing power, which the population was not able to realize. Consequently, the Reich was forced to absorb "wandering purchasing power" in some way. As the economic institutions, and Hitler himself, were rather skeptical as to the success of a "war loan," which would have constituted an undesirable opinion poll on the war, it was decided to use the so-called noiseless war financing.[55] Given the high rate of unspent income deposited in banks, chiefly in small credit institutes, and the impossibility for the banks to invest this money, it was easy for the Reich to place its treasury bills in the banks themselves. Thus the Reich did not absorb the excess of purchasing power directly, but only indirectly through the private banking system. This eventually turned the entire German population into a lender to the state, albeit unwittingly.

Though this method proved quite effective throughout the war,[56] it was judged rather dangerous from the very beginning. It threatened, indeed, to trigger an inflationary process, which raised the specter of the social collapse experienced in the 1920s. As early as October 1939, the Reichsbank economics department, in a memorandum on war financing, pointed to such dangers. Two months later, the same fears were expressed in a second memorandum, which suggested increasing taxation to tackle the problem.[57] In the same period, the finance minister launched the same proposal. The discussion was stifled by a veto from Hitler,[58] but also faded out because after the summer of 1940, seizing foreign resources seemed the solution to internal economic problems.

In September/October 1941, however, the Reichsbank economics department renewed its warnings in a series of memoranda.[59] Since April 1941, according to the diagnosis produced by the Central Bank, the economic effort for the Russian campaign had caused a considerable acceleration in the amount of money in circulation. As the big tasks facing Germany—namely, "Soviet Russia, the Mediterranean, and Britain"[60]—were not to be accomplished in a short time, war financing had to be adapted to a long-lasting war. The same fears induced Göring to arrange a series of meetings in the first days of November, when he released special instructions for the exploitation of the east.[61]

In his speech at the meeting of October 3, Funk expressed the same reasoning, drawing on the analyses of the Reichsbank economics department. His worries about the money expansion were related to expectations about the duration of the war. The first solution he had envisaged, namely, the increased import of resources "from the dominated and occupied territories," had encountered considerable difficulties. First, as already mentioned, the growing inflation in Europe made an increased drain of resources difficult to manage. Second, after the failure of the short-war strategy in the east, a seizure of Soviet resources in quick time became unlikely.[62] This is why in the following days Funk tried to convince Hitler to change the economic policy. On October 13, the minister went to see Hitler in the Wolfschanze, the Führer's headquarters in the east, and communicated to him his fears for Germany's internal economic situation. Hitler replied in the form of a monologue on "his financial theory to the minister of economics,"[63] which stands out as a confused mix of visions about a future prosperous Europe. Oil and wheat would flow into Germany from the east and the rest of Europe would receive its share of this enormous wealth. As Hitler stated after Funk was gone, the minister had been "enthusiastic" about his ideas. In this way, he had recognized, Germany would cancel its war debt in ten years "without any shock for our internal purchasing power."[64] Against economic rationality, the Führer's charisma had led the Reich minister to put aside his misgivings.

Funk's behavior gives a clear picture of the extent to which pure faith in victory in the east had been substituted for political decision making. For the time being, however, price controls and rationing had to provide for the stability of the reichsmark. This is what Hitler meant two days later, when, thinking back to the monetary policy carried out since 1933, he said: "Inflation doesn't come from the fact that more money comes into trading, but only then, if the individual demands more payment for the same performance. Here one must intervene. I also had to explain to [Hjalmar] Schacht that the cause of the consistency of our currency is the KZ [i.e., the concentration camp]." Hitler's monologues of October and November 1941 focused unusually often on monetary policy, the New Order of Europe, and foreign trade, that is, the same set of problems that, as we have seen, was under discussion by other German institutions in the autumn of 1941.

The gravity of the situation in the second half of 1941 was addressed by Goebbels in his usual direct style. After having read a letter from his longtime friend Funk about the situation in the monetary sector, the propaganda minister entrusted his fears about an imminent collapse of the regime to his diary. "It's a very serious and by no means marginal problem. The people can legitimately expect from us that we ensure that the currency remains stable. We would survive a new inflation only with great difficulty."[65]

Different Positions and Motivations

If we now return to the meeting of October 3, the link between the two subjects under discussion becomes clearer. The pace of the exploitation of Ostland, which was to fill the gaps in the internal monetary policy, depended on the exchange rate and the currency chosen by the Reich. Let us now take a closer look at the actors involved and their motivations.

The existence of conflicting strategies for the administration of the newly occupied Soviet territories has been widely acknowledged by scholars. The fundaments of the institutional conflicts, which were to emerge after the invasion, were laid down before the beginning of the campaign. Already in the planning phase, Göring had assumed a leading position in the economic administration of the east, as was already the case in the other occupied countries. This power was guaranteed him by his appointment as head of the Economic Command Staff East, the committee set up for coordinating economic policy in the east. Moreover, the majority of members of the committee were at the same time on the general council of the Four-Year Plan Organization, which was Göring's bastion of power.

Significantly, the economic administration of the eastern territories had been set up before the political one was even envisaged. Hitler entrusted Rosenberg with the preparation of a political administration only on April 2, 1941.[66] By the end of June at the latest, it became clear that

Göring's authority would not be undermined by Rosenberg's appointment. On June 29, a "Führer decree" was issued, which entrusted the *Reichsmarschall* with responsibility for the "most extensive possible exploitation of the available supplies" and "expansion of the economic forces in favour of the German war economy."[67] Finally, the decree of July 17 appointing Rosenberg Reich minister for the occupied eastern territories specified (§3) that the Reich commissars were directly subordinated to him *unless* Göring decided to issue instructions on economic matters.[68] Thus, as the decree illustrates, the relationship between the two power centers remained confined to case-by-case decisions. Moreover, what was to be understood under the expression "economy" was and remained ambiguous. Thus a wide range of problems was left open to the intervention of both institutional actors.

Traditionally, feuds between these two power centers have been seen as reflecting a contradiction between political and economic goals. I hereby suggest though that, at least in the case of the currency of Ostland, it is more appropriate to interpret the difference between their strategies as one between a long-term economic policy orientation and a short-term policy of ruthless exploitation. Göring's intention was to draw a sharp currency border between the Reich and the commissariat and to set a low exchange rate for the new currency in order to force imports at low prices. By contrast, political goals played a more important role in Rosenberg's position but were not his only motivation. The minister did not want to sacrifice the incorporation of Ostland into the Reich to the immediate exploitation. In addition, setting the exchange rate at 1:1 was aimed at restraining the exploitation in order to preserve its sustainability for a longer time. The debate on this issue, which took place at the meeting of October 3, exemplifies the nature of the conflict. What induced all these institutions to seek a quick monetary reform in Ostland was the fact that a fast reduction of the price gap was already taking place. The price increase was mainly due to the economic disorder brought about by the Soviet annexation of significant parts of Ostland in 1939–40 and by the false exchange rate between *RKK-Scheine* and roubles (1:10), which was set at the beginning of the German invasion. Schlotterer and Rosenberg feared that the introduction of a new currency at the exchange rate of 1:2 would have undermined the population's confidence in the stability of the money. This in turn would have made it impossible to keep a low price level and would have contributed to the spreading of a natural economy.

The opposing faction (Schwerin von Krosigk, Göring's representative Erich Neumann, and the Reich commissar for price setting representative Erich Flottmann) wanted to ensure the permanence of the price gap through a low exchange rate. Neumann was very explicit in his criticism of Rosenberg's proposal when he stated that choosing an exchange rate of 1:1 amounted to "forgoing all the fruits of victory."[69] Schwerin von Krosigk's position was directly linked with his strategy of the *Schleusegewinne*. Given the importance of this economic goal in the east, the finance minister was granted significant authority by Göring at the meeting of November 8. A few days later, a note specified that the finances of the occupied Soviet territories constituted "a part of the global finances of the Reich" and were therefore to be administered "following the general guidelines, which the responsible minister defines for the global Reich finances."[70] The purpose of this instruction was to influence the contemporaneous preparation by the Reichsbank of the draft laws for the foundation of the Central Banks of Ukraine and Ostland. Rosenberg, indeed, sought to ensure control over the banks by taking the appointment of the presidents upon himself.[71] As we have already seen, the *Schleusegewinne* were considered as a solution to the internal monetary instability, because they were to be partially absorbed by the Reich Treasury.

Before the start of the Soviet campaign, the finance minister had expounded his criticisms on the economic rationality of Operation Barbarossa itself,[72] which he judged would not yield the promised economic profits. Nevertheless after June 22, Schwerin von Krosigk became one of the most convinced partisans of the strategy of exploitation aimed at solving internal problems. The finance minister saw this strategy as a means to enduring a long-lasting war. This intention was openly addressed by the *Staatsskretär* of this ministry, Fritz Reinhardt, in the opening speech of a meeting with the representatives of the major institutions of the Reich, which deserves to be quoted at length:

> The war costs a lot of money. It has so far been possible to meet the financial needs of the Reich without difficulty. In the first and second years of the war more than 50 percent [of its costs] have been covered by natural revenues (taxes, revenues of the administration, war contribution of municipalities, matricular contribution [*Matrikularbetrag*], occupation tributes), the rest has been covered with borrowed funds. The financial requirements of the Reich in the third year of the war (September 1, 1941 to August 31, 1942) will probably be 11 billion more than in the second. Of this sum, 4 billion reichsmarks will be covered with an increase of tax revenues. The remaining 7 billion reichsmarks are the contribution that the occupied territories of the east should raise, if the local conditions were the same as in the other occupied territories. This is not the case.... The Reich's debt has grown out of the rearmament and the war. The interests and the amortization on this debt cannot be imposed on the German population if the hitherto existing standard of living is to be maintained.

On the contrary, it is desirable that we come to a diminution of the tax burden after the war. . . . The Führer has pointed out—the *Reichsmarschall* has stressed it at the meeting of October 8—that the interests and the amortization of the Reich debt must be covered with sufficiently high revenues from the new eastern territories. Through a corresponding wage and price policy in the new eastern territories, sufficiently high revenues in favor of the Reich must be achieved. Woe to those who endanger the corresponding wage and price policy in the eastern territories.[73]

Hitler himself, as Reinhardt noted, agreed with this plan in detail. "The prices are different," he said on August 11, 1942, referring to the eastern territories, "and they must always remain totally different so that we can exploit the price levels in favor of the Reich and in this way amortize the war debts."[74]

A similar intention lay behind the intervention of the Reich commissar for price setting, Josef Wagner. His primary interest was to keep German internal prices as stable as possible by draining resources from abroad. The importance of the institution for price setting can hardly be overestimated, as it was deemed a pivot of the loyalty of the Germans to the Third Reich.[75] As early as 1934, Hitler recognized that "he *had* given his word to the workers that he would not tolerate any price increase. The wage earner, if he would not act against price increases, would accuse him of not keeping his word. A revolutionary situation would be the further consequence."[76] Since the inflationary monetary policy practiced during the Third Reich constantly contradicted "Hitler's word," the Reich commissar for price setting became a vital pillar of his power. Thus Wagner, as well as his successor Hans Fischböck in 1942, was prone to sacrifice the stability of foreign economies on the altar of internal social peace.

Lohse's stance in the debate needs some further elaboration. The Reich commissar for Ostland, at the same time the *Oberpräsident* and *Gauleiter* of Schleswig-Holstein, fully backed Rosenberg's project. As stated in a declaration issued in mid-December to all major economic institutions, he feared that realizing Göring's proposal would make it impossible for him to keep the price level stable in Ostland.[77] The historian Alexander Dallin has described Lohse as "less the dynamic leader than the comfortable bureaucrat." As the Reich commissar recognized that not everything could be achieved by force, he sought in "his personal empire" to maintain economic life in order.[78]

This is why Lohse established an extended and complicated system of price controls, even for the most insignificant goods. His line of conduct was very different from that followed by his colleague Erich Koch, who ran the administration of the Reich Commissariat Ukraine. As on other issues,[79] conflicts between Koch and Rosenberg on the monetary organization of Ukraine were quite heated from the very beginning. Contentious points included the right to appoint the president of the National Bank and to issue the law on the foundation of the Central Bank. A conflict also arose regarding the name of the currency to be issued.[80] Koch wanted the name of the currency to reflect the colonial nature of German rule and therefore proposed to name it crown. It is difficult to know where the name eventually chosen for the new Ukrainian currency (karbowanez) stemmed from, but it is likely that it had been proposed by Rosenberg. In fact, this is what the currency of the independent Ukrainian People's Republic in 1917–18 had been called. Koch explicitly opposed every name that evoked a Ukrainian national identity.[81] In any case, from the very beginning of the discussion on the Ukrainian Central Bank, when Schlotterer went to see Koch to obtain his assent to the proposal, a point of agreement was the exchange rate. This was set at 1 ruble = 1 karbowanez = 0.10 reichsmark, and was thus 500 percent lower than the exchange rate proposed by Göring for the Ostland crown. At the final meeting, at which the decree was signed, the exchange rate was not a matter of discussion. Eugen Einsiedel, head of the Reichsbank economics department, who was to be appointed president of the new bank of Ukraine, only noted that the reform was very urgent because the price increase was leading the peasants to withdraw from the market and threatened to compromise the export of agricultural goods to the Reich.[82] The foundation of the Ukrainian Central Bank was evidently far less controversial because the majority of the participants shared a strategy of ruthless exploitation.

Setting up the National Bank of Ostland

The meeting of October 3 was not sufficient to reach an agreement. In the following days, Rosenberg sent a note to Schwerin von Krosigk in which he articulated his position. "The benefits for the war economy," stated the minister for the occupied eastern territories, "are not dependent upon the fixation of an exchange of 2:1 or on other measures of a purely technical nature, but rather presupposes that the populace of the Ostland works and accepts the currency we introduce. This requires that the present low level of agrarian prices, which also enables corresponding low prices in the secondary sector, be maintained."[83]

Göring answered on October 15 with a letter addressed to the main institutions, in which he reaffirmed his initial project.[84] In the meantime, a representative of the Reich commissar for price setting, Wilhelm Rentrop, had been sent to Ostland to give an expert's opinion on the sustainability of the exchange rates in question. His report stated that "the introduction of the crown currency, and in addition at the rate of 1:2, would destroy the remaining confidence in the credit economy and would induce a fall in the primitive natural economy that is already strongly developed."[85] It is impossible to know if Wagner changed his mind as a result of this report. He did not, however, directly intervene anymore in the discussion.

Backed by Rentrop's results, Lohse warned a week later that if Göring's requests were to be realized, he would not be able to guarantee the existing price level.[86] As an alternative, he proposed leaving the status quo unchanged, which meant abandoning the idea of founding a new bank and keeping the *RKK-Scheine* in circulation. Launching this proposal, the Reich commissar consciously put strong pressure on Schwerin von Krosigk to accept his position. In fact, the Reich was responsible for the redemption of the *RKK-Scheine*.[87] Thus it was in the Finance Ministry's interest if "the finance of Ostland were as soon as possible to be detached from the treasury"[88] and Lohse's counter-proposal deferred indefinitely. For this reason a new meeting, this time a meeting of *Staatssekretäre*, was summoned in the Ministry of Economics for January 6, 1942. The most remarkable news of the meeting was Funk's change of mind on the matter. While on October 3 the minister of economics had joined Göring's faction, expressing at the same time his understanding for Schlotterer's and Rosenberg's reasons, at the new meeting his representative supported the opposing faction. Without giving any further explanation, Vice President Emil Puhl said that this change was due to developments in the economic situation. It is likely that Rentrop's report had played an important role in this change of direction. At the meeting, Rosenberg adopted the same tactic as Lohse had done, proposing, in case of rejection of his project, that the *RKK-Scheine* remain in circulation.[89] The threat was sufficient to bring Schwerin von Krosigk to capitulation. A few days later,[90] the finance minister made it public that he accepted the Ostlandmark with an exchange rate of 1:1, because the maintenance of the *Reichskreditkasse* issuing *RKK-Scheine* would rest on the Reich Treasury.

Obtaining the finance minister's capitulation, however, did not suffice for the imposition of Rosenberg's and Lohse's projects. At the end of January, Göring still opposed the idea. While at the beginning of March 1942, when Rosenberg signed the decree, preparations for the Bank of Ukraine were finished, the foundation of the Bank of Ostland was still under discussion in July. At this point, Göring had fully accepted the line of the Reich Ministry for the Occupied Eastern Territories, but still did not give his approval to the decree.[91] On the contrary, the finance minister, whose primary interest was the foundation of the bank itself and not so much the currency, insisted that the bank be established and proposed that it issue *RKK-Scheine*. These further discussions delayed the preparation of the decree, which was signed on July 30 and published only four months later.[92] In August it had been foreseen that the new notes would be issued and that this would require seven to eight months.[93] In November, however, this measure was suspended for the time being.[94] The eastern border was still not assured, and now Lohse and Rosenberg themselves deemed the issuing of a new currency a premature act. Therefore the foundation took place in practice, but the bank worked with *RKK-Scheine*. This was evidently a compromise, as *Reichsbankdirektor* Winter explained to the representatives of the economic press. "The necessity of immediate economic attachment to the Reich (through currency adjustment) was confronted by fears about currency perturbation and worrying consequences of a not fully adequate exchange rate. As a result of different desires on the one hand and of objections on the other, a compromise has now been reached. A new bank is formed, which will later receive the competences of a currency bank, but temporarily works on the basis of *Kreditkassenscheine*."[95]

The Central Bank opened only on April 1, 1943, and never issued any other currency than *RKK-Scheine*. Considering this further delay, it can be concluded that the monetary reform in Ostland had little consequence for the development of the local economy. At its very beginning, the establishment of the bank was hindered by the mutual vetoes of the institutions involved. During the course of 1942, developments in the military situation imposed a slowdown in the decision-making process, and this left the status quo unchanged for a long time. Finally, the Red Army reconquered the territory of Ostland piecemeal, putting an end to any further implementation of the project.

Conclusions

The history of the debate about the Ostland Bank and currency provides a vivid account of the alternative strategies for exploitation confronting each other in the second half of 1941. The setting for this confrontation was the perception of a looming crisis in the German economy owing to monetary instability, and for the regime itself.

The concept of radicalization can be usefully employed to understand a dynamic, immanent to the Nazi regime, that culminated in 1941. From its very beginning, Nazi economic policy followed a dynamic of crisis and degeneration, in which the mechanisms of self-reproduction of the internal economic system were progressively removed. Foreign resources were used, before the outbreak of war, as a means for slowing down the crisis and for producing an internal stabilization, as the monetary policy clearly illustrates.[96] As the Reich reached the peak of its power in 1940, this strategy was radicalized to such an extent that in 1941 it began to be hindered by its own measures. This problem, as we have already seen, had been clearly recognized by those who were in charge of the economic administration. Nevertheless, in the second half of 1941 the complete failure of the strategy was still not generally recognized. The grip on foreign resources was still generally perceived as *the* solution to every financial problem, though it was to be reached only by means of a longer war. In October 1941, Eugen Einsiedel intervened in a congress of academic economists, which strongly criticized the expansive monetary policy practiced by the Reichsbank. Einsiedel defended the work of his institution, declaring that "in a struggle for existence one cannot abdicate prematurely the stimulating power of money supply." In any case, he continued, with the "successes in Russia, which hides enormous productive possibilities," the Reich was approaching the "turning point in the sphere of goods," which would "progressively relieve the monetary sector."[97]

While waiting for the turning point, the major economic institutions argued about how many resources could be drained from an occupied country without compromising the sustainability of the exploitation itself. Göring and Schwerin von Krosigk advocated furthering the radicalization of the strategy pursued in the past, which was doomed to be a short-term policy. Rosenberg, Lohse, and the Reichsbank called for a slight change, a restriction in the exploitation within limits, which would allow a longer extraction of resources. The pivot of the reasoning of both factions was the price level of the occupied country.

In 1942, attempts at seeking a way out of the vicious circle between exploitation and price increase became more systematic. The Ministry of Economics and the Reichsbank put forward an attempt at rationalizing the economic administration of Europe to restrain the collapse of its economies. This policy, however, did not yield any significant result.[98] The logic of the war effort and the peculiarities of the National Socialist structure of power did not allow the implementation of such reforms.

Notes

1. Alan S. Milward, "*Der Einfluss ökonomischer und nicht-ökonomischer Faktoren auf die Strategie des Blitzkrieges*," in *Wirtschaft und Rüstung am Vorabend des Zweiten Weltkrieges*, ed. Friedrich Forsteimer and Hans-Erich Volkmann (Düsseldorf: Droste, 1975), 189–201; criticism of this interpretation already in Richard J. Overy, "'Blitzkriegswirtschaft'? Finanzpolitik, Lebensstandard, und Arbeitseinsatz in Deutschland 1939–1942," *Vierteljahrshefte für Zeitgeschichte* 36, no. 3 (1988): 379–435.

2. Rolf-Dieter Müller, "Die Mobilisierung der Deutschen Wirtschaft für Hitlers Kriegsführung," in Bernhard R. Kroener, Rolf-Dieter Müller, and Hans Umbreit, *Organisation und Mobilisierung des deutschen Machtbereichs: Kriegsverwaltung, Wirtschaft, und personelle Ressourcen, 1939–1941*, vol. 5, pt. 1, of *Das Deutsche Reich und der Zweite Weltkrieg* (Stuttgart: Deutsche Verlags-Anstalt, 1988), 349–63.

3. Adam Tooze, "No Room for Miracles," *Geschichte und Gesellschaft* 31, no. 3 (2005): 439–64.

4. See Timothy W. Mason, "Innere Krise und Angriffskrieg," in Forsteimer, *Wirtschaft und Rüstung*. 158–88; Richard J. Overy, "Germany, 'Domestic Crisis' and War in 1939," *Past and Present* 116, no. 1 (1987): 138–68; D. Kaiser and T. Mason, "Germany, 'Domestic Crisis' and War in 1939," *Past and Present* 122, no. 1 (1989): 200–221; and Richard J. Overy, "Germany, 'Domestic Crisis,' and War in 1939: Reply," *Past and Present* 122, no. 1 (1989): 221–40.

5. Götz Aly, *Hitlers Volksstaat: Raub, Rassenkrieg, und nationaler Sozialismus* (Frankfurt am Main: S. Fischer, 2005). For a recent assessment of this question, see Christoph Buchheim, "Der Mythos vom 'Wohlleben': Der Lebensstandard der deutschen Zivilbevölkerung im Zweiten Weltkrieg," *Vierteljahrshefte für Zeitgeschichte* 58, no. 3 (2010): 299–328.

6. Bucheim, "Der Mythos," 301. A good evaluation of German imports during the war can be found in Jonas Scherner, "German Industrial Productivity and Exploitation of Occupied Europe during World War II: New Insights from Revised German Import Statistics," Working Paper, November 2008, http://economics.rutgers.edu/dmdocuments/Scherner_German.pdf.

7. Marc Buggeln, "Währungspläne für den Großraum: Die Diskussion der nationalsozialistischen Wirtschaftsexperten über ein zukünftiges europäisches Zahlungssystem," *Beiträge zur Geschichte des Nationalsozialismus* 18 (2002): 41–76; and Paolo Fonzi, *La moneta nel grande spazio: La pianificazione nazionalsocialista dell'integrazione monetaria europea (1939–1945)* (Milan: Unicopli, 2011).

8. Erich Neumann, *Staatssekretär* in the Office of the Four-Year Plan, proposed maintaining the *RKK-Scheine* in circulation in every country and, in this way, unifying the occupied territories; see Währungsumstellung in

Nordwesten, June 1940, R2501-7013, fols. 129–32, Bundesarchiv Berlin-Lichterfelde (hereafter BAB).

9. As described in Götz Aly, *Hitler's Beneficiaries: Plunder, Racial War, and the Nazi Welfare State* (New York: Picador, 2007), 94.

10. In an average month of 1943, imports from Belgium and France financed with occupation costs were less than half of official imports; see Scherner, "German Industrial Productivity," 20.

11. Jean Freymond, *Le IIIe reich et la réorganisation économique de l'Europe 1940–1942* (Leiden: Sijthoff, 1974); Buggeln, *Währungspläne*; and Fonzi, *La moneta nel grande spazio*.

12. Minutes of a meeting held in the Ministry of Economics. List of those present: Funk, Finance Minister Schwerin von Krosigk, *Staatssekretär* Landfried, Posse (Ministry of Economics), and Kretschmann (Reichsbank), May 15, 1940, R2-13499, fols. 297–99, BAB.

13. Statement of Wilhelm, member of the board of directors of the Reichsbank, at a meeting of the *Beirat der deutschen Reichsbank*, R8119F-P349, fol. 19, BAB.

14. Adam Tooze, *The Wages of Destruction: The Making and Breaking of the Nazi Economy* (London: Allen Lane, 2006), 432–40.

15. Hans Umbreit, "Auf dem Weg zur Kontinentalherrschaft," in Kroener et al., *Organisation und Mobilisierung des deutschen Machtbereichs*, pt. 1, 233–36. See also Werner Röhr, "Forschungsprobleme zur deutschen Okkupationspolitik im Spiegel der Reihe *Europa unterm Hakenkreuz*," in *Europa unterm Hakenkreuz: Die Okkupationspolitik des deutschen Faschismus (1938–1945)*, vol. 8, *Analysen, Quellen, Register*, ed. Bundesarchiv (Heidelberg: Hüthig, 1996), 242–343.

16. Johannes Houwink Ten Cate, "Die rüstungswirtschaftliche Ausnutzung Westeuropas während der ersten Kriegshälfte," in *Das organisierte Chaos: "Ämterdarwinismus" und "Gesinnungsethik": Determinanten nationalsozialistischer Besatzungsherrschaft*, ed. Johannes Houwink Ten Cate and Gerhard Otto (Berlin: Metropol, 1999), 188.

17. See Rolf-Dieter Müller, "Von der Wirtschaftsallianz zum kolonialen Ausbeutungskrieg," in Horst Boog, Jürgen Förster, Joachim Hoffmann, Ernst Klink, Rolf-Dieter Müller, and Gerd R. Ueberschär, *Der Angriff auf die Sowjetunion*, vol. 4 of *Das Deutsche Reich und der Zweite Weltkrieg* (Stuttgart: Deutsche Verlags-Anstalt, 1983), 89–189.

18. Dietrich Eichholtz, *Geschichte der deutschen Kriegswirtschaft, 1939–1945*, vol. 2, *1941–1943* (Berlin: Akademie, 1985), 17.

19. Albrecht Ritschl, "Nazi Economic Imperialism and the Exploitation of the Small: Evidence from Germany's Secret Foreign Exchange Balances, 1938–1940," *Economic History Review* 54, no. 2 (2001): 335–36.

20. See, for example, the Reichsbank's review of the proposed solutions, *Über die Pläne zur Lösung des Clearingproblems*, November 15, 1943, R2501-6449, BAB.

21. *Vermerk über eine Sitzung am 22.11 bei St. Neumann*, November 25, 1941, R2-60244, Doc. 3, BAB.

22. Violetta Hionidou, *Famine and Death in Occupied Greece, 1941–1944* (Cambridge: Cambridge University Press, 2006).

23. HPA Session, January 10, 1941, R901-68939, BAB; see also *Dezernat Wilhelm, Notiz nr. 9*, February 19, 1941, R2-13696, fol. 53, BAB.

24. HPA Session, August 19, 1941, R901-68939, BAB.

25. Willi A. Boelcke, "Die 'europäische Wirtschaftspolitik' des Nationalsozialismus," *Historische Mitteilungen der Ranke-Gesellschaft* 5 (1992): 226.

26. Umbreit, "Auf dem Weg zur Kontinentalherrschaft," 216–50; and Mark Mazower, *Hitler's Empire: How the Nazis Ruled Europe* (New York: Penguin, 2008), 140–57.

27. Tooze, *Wages of Destruction*, 411–20.

28. See R.-D. Müller, "Von der Wirtschaftsallianz"; Alex J. Kay, *Exploitation, Resettlement, Mass Murder: Political and Economic Planning for German Occupation Policy in the Soviet Union, 1940–1941* (New York: Berghahn, 2006), 38–42; and Dietrich Eichholtz, *Krieg um Öl: Ein Erdölimperium als deutsches Kriegsziel, 1938–1943* (Leipzig: Leipziger Universitätsverlag, 2006).

29. Rolf-Dieter Müller, "Das 'Unternehmen Barbarossa' als wirtschaftlicher Raubkrieg," in *"Unternehmen Barbarossa": Der deutsche Überfall auf die Sowjetunion, 1941; Berichte, Analysen, Dokumente*, ed. Gerd R. Ueberschär and Wolfram Wette (Paderborn: Ferdinand Schöningh, 1984), 173–96.

30. Aly, *Hitler's Beneficiaries*, 165.

31. *Nazi Conspiracy and Aggression*, vol. 4, Doc. 1743-PS: Guiding Principals for the Economic Operations in the Newly Occupied Eastern Territories, June 1941, accessible online via http://avalon.law.yale.edu/imt/1743-ps.asp.

32. The document summing up the reasons for the conflict is dated May 23, 1941, and is not signed, NI6148, Archiv des Instituts für Zeitgeschichte, Munich (hereafter IfZ-Archiv). Following Rosenberg's request, a meeting was summoned on May 28. *Besprechung bei Reichsminister Funk*, May 28, 1941, PS-1031, in International Military Tribunal, ed., *Der Prozess gegen die Hauptkriegsverbrecher vor dem Internationalen Militärgerichtshof, Nürnberg, 14. November 1945–1. Oktober 1946*, vol. 26 (Nuremberg: Sekretariat des Gerichtshofs, 1947), 580–92.

33. *Die vorgesehene Organisation für den russischen Raum (Bayrhoffer)*, R2-30921, BAB. The same ideas circulated in the Administrative Council of the *Reichskreditkasse*; see Aly, *Hitler's Beneficiaries*, 165–66.

34. This was stated already in the General Instruction for all Reich Commissars in the Occupied Eastern Territories issued by Rosenberg on May 8, 1941, *Allgemeine Instruktion für alle Reichskommissare in den besetzten Ostgebieten*, in International Military Tribunal, *Prozess*, vol. 26, PS-1030, 576–80.

35. Kay, *Exploitation*, 75.

36. Report on the meeting, November 8, 1941, is reproduced in Ueberschär and Wette, *"Unternehmen Barbarossa,"* 387–91.

37. Ibid., 386.

38. Ibid., 387.

39. R2-14586, fol. 118, BAB. List of those present: Rosenberg, Landfried (RWM), Neumann (VJP), Schlotterer, Malletke, Kretzschmann, and Winter (Reichsbank).

40. Ibid.

41. Communication of the Economic Staff East to Emil Puhl, *Maßnahmen und Erfolg des bisherigen Osteinsatzes*, R2-14586, fol. 71, BAB.

42. *Besprechung bei Reichsminister Funk*, May 28, 1941, International Military Tribunal, *Prozess*, vol. 26, PS-1031, 582.

43. Note of Riehle (Ministry of Economics), August 23, 1941, R2-14586. fols. 18–19, BAB.

44. See *Vermerk über die Besprechung im RWiM am 2.9.1941 betreffend Waren- und Zahlungsverkehr mit den neu besetzten Ostgebieten*, R2-25242, BAB; Communication of the Administrative Council of the RKK, September 19, 1941, R2-14586, fol. 141, BAB; and *Protokoll über die Besprechung im RWiM vom 8. September 1941*, R2-25242, BAB.

45. Minutes of a meeting in the Reich Ministry for the Occupied Eastern Territories on *Währungsfragen im Reichskommissariat Ostland*, September 24, 1941, RW31-277, fol.109, Bundesarchiv-Militärarchiv, Freiburg im Breisgau (hereafter BA-MA).

46. Account given by Funk in a meeting in the Ministry of Economics on January 20, 1942, RW19-1584, fols. 143–46, BA-MA.

47. See the drafts of the decrees in R2-14586, BAB.

48. R2-14586, fol.142, BAB. For the *Schleusegewinne* in general, see Rolf-Dieter Müller, ed., *Die deutsche Wirtschaftspolitik in den besetzten sowjetischen Gebieten, 1941–1943: Der Abschlußbericht des Wirtschaftsstabes Ost und Aufzeichnungen eines Angehörigen des Wirtschaftskommandos Kiew* (Boppard am Rhein: Harald Boldt, 1991), 120–24.

49. Kay, *Exploitation*, 2.

50. *"Geld-, Währungs-, Preis, und Lohnfragen insbesondere über Ostland-Währung,"* October 3, 1941, RW19-1584, fols. 116–26, BA-MA.

51. Ibid., 116.

52. Ibid., 118.

53. Ibid., 117.

54. See Willi A. Boelcke, *Die Kosten von Hitlers Krieg* (Paderborn: Ferdinand Schöningh, 1985); and Overy, "Blitzkriegswirtschaft," 381–94.

55. This explanation is provided, retrospectively, by Schwerin von Krosigk himself in his memoirs. See *Staatsbankrott: Finanzpolitik des deutschen Reiches, 1920–1945* (Göttingen: Musterschmidt, 1974), 230; slightly different is the explanation of Tooze, *Wages of Destruction*, 354.

56. Ibid., 356.

57. Manfred Oertel, "Über die Reichsbank im zweiten Weltkrieg" (PhD diss, University of Rostock, 1979), 56–65.

58. Overy, "'Blitzkriegswirtschaft,'" 390.

59. *Kriegsfinanzierung und Währung*, September 17, 1941, R2501-7007, fols. 266–69, BAB; and *Zur inneren Währungslage*, October 4, 1941, R2501-7007 fols. 294–302, BAB; see also *Protokoll über den Presseempfang im Hause der Deutschen Reichsbank am 30. Oktober 1941*, October 1, 1941, R2501-7007 fols. 412–18, BAB. For the general setting of the monetary crisis, see Tooze, *Wages of Destruction*, 493–97; and Manfred Oertel, "Die Kriegsfinanzierung," in Dietrich Eichholtz, *Geschichte der deutschen Kriegswirtschaft, 1939–1945*, vol. 3, *1943–1945* (Berlin: Akademie, 1996), 728–34.

60. *Kriegsfinanzierung und Währung*, fol. 267.

61. One of these was the meeting of November 8, already cited in note 36. See also Rolf-Dieter Müller and Gerd R. Ueberschär, eds., *Hitler's War in the East, 1941–1945: A Critical Assessment* (New York: Berghahn, 1997), 302.

62. See Müller, "Das Scheitern der wirtschaftlichen 'Blitzkriegstrategie,'" in Boog et al., *Der Angriff auf die Sowjetunion*, 949–59.

63. Werner Jochmann, ed., *Monologe im Führerhauptquartier, 1941–1944* (Hamburg: Albrecht Knaus, 1980), 80.

64. Ibid., 88.

65. Elke Fröhlich, ed., *Die Tagebücher von Joseph Goebbels: Sämtliche Fragmente*, part 2, vol. 1 (Munich: K. G. Saur, 1987), 510.

66. Kay, *Exploitation*, 75.

67. Ibid., 183.

68. Ibid.

69. "Geld-, Währungs-, Preis, und Lohnfragen," fol. 120.

70. R2-14586, fols. 222, 250, BAB.

71. Note of the Reichsbank board of directors, November 14, 1941, R2-14586, fol. 218, BAB.

72. Müller, "Von der Wirtschaftsallianz," 145.

73. Meeting on the Ostgesellschaften, R2-30675, BAB. The document reproduces a draft of the speech. Thus it contains several handwritten corrections. I quote the first version, which has the same meaning but a more vivid style.

74. Jochmann, *Monologe*, 337.

75. See Andre Steiner, "Der Reichskommissar für die Preisbildung—'eine Art wirtschaftlicher Reichskanzler'?," in *Beiträge zur Geschichte des Nationalsozialismus* 22 (2006): 93–114.

76. Friedrich Hartmannsgruber, ed., *Kabinettsitzung vom 5 November 1934*, in *Akten der Reichskanzlei: Regierung Hitler 1933–1945*, vol. 2, *1934–35*, pt. 1 (Munich: Oldenbourg, 1999), 148 (doc. 37).

77. Lohse's memorandum, December 15, 1941, RW31-277, fols. 138–40, BA-MA.

78. Alexander Dallin, *German Rule in Russia, 1941–1945* (London: Macmillan, 1957), 186.

79. Ibid., 130–33.

80. Note of the Reichsbank board of directors, January 14, 1941, R2 14586, fol. 218, BAB; and *Vermerk über eine Sitzung beim Führer*, February 15, 1942, MA 824 (99/499), IfZ-Archiv.

81. R2-14586, fols. 219–20, BAB.

82. *Aktenvermerk betr. Zentralnotenbank Ukraine*, die Einsiedel, March 5, 1942, R2-14587, fol. 71, BAB.

83. *Währungsordnung im Reichskommissariat Ostland*, October 9, 1941, R2-1486, fol. 187, BAB.

84. The note was sent to Rosenberg, the Reichsbank, and the Ministry of Economics, R6-23, BAB.

85. Communication of Schlotterer to Funk, December 8, 1941, R2-30703, BAB.

86. Memorandum on monetary issues in Ostland (Lohse), December 15, 1941, RW31-277, fols. 138–40, BA-MA.

87. This was stated in §4 of the *Verordnung über Reichskreditkassen*, May 15, 1940, Reichsgesetzblatt, pt. 1, 774.

88. Report of the General Office of the Reich Finance Ministry, December 17, 1941, R2-14586, fol. 266, BAB.

89. Rosenberg had released a memorandum on January 10, quoted by Schwerin von Krosigk in his answer *Währung im Ostland*, January 17, 1942, R2-30915, BAB.

90. Ibid.

91. Administrative Council of the RKK, June 23, 1942, R2-13502, fols. 68–70, BAB.

92. Oertel, *Über die Reichsbank*, 177–82; and *Verordnungsblatt des Reichsministers für die besetzten Ostgebiete*, no. 15 (1942): 85.

93. Administrative Council of the RKK, August 15, 1942, R2-14586, fols. 78–81, BAB.

94. Administrative Council of the RKK, November 4, 1942, in Oertel, *Über die Reichsbank*, 179.

95. *Wirtschaftspressekonferenz*, November 25, 1942, R8136-3990, BAB.

96. Ludolf Herbst, *Das nationalsozialistische Deutschland. Die Entfesselung der Gewalt: Rassismus und Krieg* (Frankfurt am Main: Suhrkamp, 1996), 9–24.

97. Einsiedel's report on the congress of the *Arbeitsgemeinschaft Geld und Kredit* of the *Akademie für Deutsches Recht*, October 17–18, 1941, R2501-7021 BAB.

98. Hans Umbreit, "Die deutsche Herrschaft in den besetzten Gebieten," in Bernhard R. Kroener, Rolf-Dieter Müller, and Hans Umbreit, *Organisation und Mobilisierung des deutschen Machtbereichs: Kriegsverwaltung, Wirtschaft, und personelle Ressourcen, 1942–1944/45*, vol. 5, pt. 2, of *Das Deutsche Reich und der Zweite Weltkrieg* (Stuttgart: Deutsche Verlags-Anstalt, 1999), 4–274, 181–211; Müller, "Mobilisierung," 591–96; and Müller and Ueberschär, *Hitler's War in the East*, 303–11.

CHAPTER 7

AXIS COLLABORATION, OPERATION BARBAROSSA, AND THE HOLOCAUST IN UKRAINE

Wendy Lower

The history of the Nazi-led genocide against the Jews is inseparable from Operation Barbarossa and the Axis occupation of the Soviet Union. Today such a statement is taken as a given in the fields of Holocaust studies and World War II. But this was not always the case. Prior to the 1990s, few military specialists followed the lead of Gerhard Weinberg and Jürgen Förster by connecting the battles on the front with the genocide behind the lines. Even the pioneering study by American Sovietologist Alexander Dallin, *German Rule in Russia, 1941–1945*, while paying much attention to the totalitarian framework of the SS terror, skimmed over the unique plight of the Jews, dealing with it marginally as a demonstration of Nazi internecine struggles over *Ostpolitik*. In the past twenty years a veritable deluge of studies on the Holocaust has shifted the focus of military history to studies of genocidal violence and its development in military planning and security measures in times of war. In Holocaust studies specifically, Operation Barbarossa has been the primary focus for reconstructing the history of decision making and the escalation of atrocities against Jews in the summer and fall of 1941.

Historians Christopher Browning, Jürgen Matthäus, and Christian Gerlach have delved into the peripheral and central events that came together in the Soviet Union and precipitated the mass murder of Jews. Besides the *Einsatzgruppen*, we have now created an expanding and more detailed picture of SS-police involvement, especially the role of the Order Police (*Ordnungspolizei*) and the Waffen-SS. As it turns out, more Jews were shot in Ukraine by regular order policemen than by special security personnel in the *Einsatzgruppen*. The criminal activities of the Wehrmacht have been diligently researched and controversially exhibited. Furthermore, a plethora of civilian agencies, foremost among them the Reich Ministry of Food and Agriculture, also have blood on their hands, by introducing plans to starve out the cities of the Soviet Union and the less fertile agricultural regions in Belarus and northcentral Russia. The unique Nazi targeting of Jewish POWs and civilians was no secret, or at least as historian Richard Breitman discovered, it remained an "official secret."[1] During the first months of the invasion, British radio intercepts of German SS-police communiqués from Ukraine and Belarus revealed in shocking numbers the pattern of anti-Jewish killings. So striking was this intelligence information that British analysts surmised in September 1941 that the Nazis were pursuing a "policy of savage intimidation if not of ultimate extermination."[2] Thus the extensive research and historiography on Nazi decision making, the origins of the Final Solution, and Allied intelligence have established without a doubt that the Nazi *Vernichtungskrieg* against the Soviet Union coincided with the physical extermination of all Soviet Jews and other so-called undesirables, and that we can no longer study the military history of the eastern campaigns and occupation policies without their genocidal components.[3] This consensus begs the question, what now? What areas have been overlooked or remain largely unexplored in the history of Operation Barbarossa and the Holocaust? There are many, but one in particular will be the focus of this essay: Axis collaboration.

The aim is to show how Axis diplomacy and participation in Operation Barbarossa and the occupation of Ukraine shaped the history of the Holocaust there. Did Axis participation decisively bring about an acceleration of anti-Jewish policy, resulting in genocide, or did it slow developments? The so-called Jewish Question as it concerned the Soviet Union was a subject of Axis diplomacy from the planning stages through the execution of Operation Barbarossa. While there was general consensus about a "Jewish problem" in Europe, there were important differences and similarities in how Axis powers treated Jews in the territories that they conquered and occupied. More than 1.5 million Jews were killed in the territory of Ukraine by Germans, Romanians, Hungarians, Slovaks, ethnic Germans, and Ukrainians. The genocide was an interethnic phenomenon on the perpetrator side. This statement is not made to somehow minimize Germany's ultimate responsibility for a genocidal Final Solution, but rather to throw new light on the history of collaboration and its multinational features. Hitler's primary role in the planning and implementation of the war against the Soviet Union is certain; however Hitler did not act alone. He relied on his Axis allies. The "war against the Jews" was a topic of German-Romanian and German-Hungarian interaction at the highest levels and in the local small town settings of Ukraine. Germans and Austrians comprised the overwhelming majority of soldiers in the invasion (more than 3 million men), but they were joined by about half a million Slovaks, Romanians, Finns, Italians, Hungarians, as well as Spanish volunteers.[4] Every sixth soldier that marched into the Soviet Union under the Nazi banner at the end of June 1941 was a non-German ally; among them was a critical mass of ideologues driven by a similar fear and hatred of bolshevism and, to a significant extent, motivated by anti-Semitism.[5] Were these Allied forces, which were mostly deployed as separate units under direct German command, involved in the promotion or suppression of the Holocaust, for instance in sparking pogroms or assisting in the mass shootings? Did they act in accordance with superior orders that originated from possible exchanges and agreements reached between Nazi leaders and the leaders of their respective countries? In short, the interethnic dimension that has been explored recently as forms of local collaboration might also be tied back to the highest levels of Axis diplomacy. We have looked at the interaction of the center and periphery within the German administration and documented the radicalizing effects of this dynamic. The question remains to what extent did German interaction with its allies on the ground and in high-level diplomatic exchanges steer the course of the Final Solution: did it have a radicalizing effect as well? This essay will explore these questions by examining specific cases in Ukraine of German-Romanian, German-Hungarian, and German-Slovak collaboration. It provides a preliminary sketch of this piece of the history because the documentation and published research on this topic of Axis diplomacy and the Holocaust is uneven and scattered, and the source material is in multiple languages that no individual scholar in the field commands (German, Hungarian, Slovak, Romanian, Italian, Ukrainian, Serbo-Croatian, Bulgarian, and Spanish).[6] To date, most of the published research on this topic has focused on German-Romanian and German-Hungarian relations; more has appeared in recent years on local forms of German-Ukrainian collaboration, which will be addressed in this essay as well.

In the months leading to the outbreak of the war on June 22, 1941, Hitler met with his European allies and determined what each country would contribute and could potentially gain from the conquest of Soviet territory.[7] According to the war diary of the High Command of the Armed Forces (OKW), Hitler outlined these roles to the military in February and March 1941. He stated that except for Romania, the other allies should not be informed until the last possible moment, especially Hungary, since, he argued, this country would press for more political guarantees vis-à-vis its neighbors and against German territorial gains. In other words, Hitler wanted a free hand; he did not want to get bogged down in diplomatic discussions or be constrained by the geopolitical interests of his allies. Only Romania, he stated, could be informed, since the country's participation in the conquest of the Soviet Union was critical to its future. As Hitler argued, Romania was similar to Germany in that the two countries were engaged in a life and death struggle with the Soviet Union; Operation Barbarossa was, as he stated, a question of survival, a *Lebensfrage*.[8] With his top military brass, Hitler planned for an encirclement of the enemy through a strong German spearhead north toward Kiev, clinched by Romanian armies in the southern regions of present-day Moldova and Ukraine. In addition there were economic targets to consider in the German command's strategic planning and negotiations with its allies, in particular the Romanian oil fields. In mid-March 1941, the Führer decided that "Hungary should in no way participate in Operation Barbarossa, Slovakia [should] only [be] exploited for the supply and deployment of troops, and the road and bridge building operations should be assigned to Hungary."[9] As it turned out, however, Army Group South's forty-one divisions were supported by a Slovak infantry division (Mobile Combat and Rear Area Security), Royal Hungarian Army units including Jewish labor battalions attached to the Seventeenth Army, the Italian Expeditionary Corps attached to the Eleventh Army, and the Romanian Third and Fourth Armies. Additionally, non-German forces were sponsored by German military intelligence, such as the Ukrainian *Nachtigal* and *Roland* units.[10]

The diplomacy of the Jewish Question among the Axis powers was an integral feature of Operation Barbarossa. As one might expect, Germany's closest ally in this regard was Romania. Under some pressure from the German military, the Romanian military purged its rank and file of Jews.[11] Then, according to historian Jean Ancel: "On January 14, 1941, Adolf Hitler revealed to the Romanian dictator Ion Antonescu the plan to invade the USSR, and on June 12, 1941, his 'Guidelines for the Treatment of the Eastern Jews.' Well before the Wannsee Conference of January 20, 1942, Antonescu launched Romania's Final Solution in response to Hitler's cue."[12] He established his own Office for Jewish Questions and at the end of March 1941 a German "Adviser for Jewish Questions" arrived in Bucharest.[13] Antonescu aimed to recover the "lost" territories of Bessarabia and Northern Bukovina, which had been occupied by the Soviets, and schemed to build his own imperial realm free of Jews along the Nazi model. To prepare for this, the Romanian military and security services worked out an arrangement similar to the German one whereby regular troops worked side-by-side with police and special security forces.[14] The Romanian version of securing Bessarabia and Northern Bukovina was known as the *Curatirea terenului*, or Cleansing of the

Land, and it included "liquidation on the spot of all Jews in rural areas; internment of Jews in ghettos in urban centres; arrest of all persons suspected of being activists in the Communist Party."[15]

Meanwhile, between January 18 and 20, 1941, Hitler met with his Italian ally, Benito Mussolini, at the Berghof. German and Italian generals discussed the most important theaters in the European war with Italy, focusing on Albania, Libya, and eastern Africa. At the closing session on January 20, Hitler expounded on Germany's geopolitical position. He stated that America was no big threat, "much more dangerous was the huge block of Russia." Although Germany enjoyed advantageous political and economic treaties with "Russia" [Soviet Union], it would be better in the long run, Hitler argued, to abandon this "means of power." Furthermore, Hitler added, "as long as Stalin lives, he is clever and careful, we face no immediate threat. However when he [Stalin] is no longer around, then the Jews, who have stepped back now, will again return to the forefront." He warned that, in this age of aerial bombing, the Russians had become a bigger threat to Germany. Hitler surmised that the Russians would turn the precious Romanian oilfields into a smoking pile of rubble, "and these oil fields are critical for the existence [*lebenswichtig*] of the Axis powers." In closing, the Führer praised Antonescu as someone who made an excellent impression on him, as a man possessing a "glowing fanaticism" and who was ready to engage in any fight for his country.[16]

In the weeks prior to the invasion Hitler spoke more explicitly about the war of annihilation and the intended atrocities. He was quite blunt in his discussions with *Generaloberst* Alfred Jodl, operations chief of the Armed Forces High Command, about possible "preventive measures" against the "Russians," reckoning the use of gas and the poisoning of food.[17] Then on June 12, 1941, Hitler met with Ion Antonescu again, this time privately in his Munich apartment, and it was during this meeting, Ancel argues, that Hitler revealed "his regime's intention to exterminate the Jews of Eastern Europe."[18] An understanding was reached, though specifics were not committed to paper. Later, during the invasion, conflicts emerged in the field as to who was authorized to deal with the Jews, in particular those refugees who had fled from the newly reoccupied Romanian territories and were in German-occupied zones of eastern Ukraine. Apparently Antonescu and his staff in the Foreign Office were under the impression that Himmler's SS and police apparatus would take care of these Jews, while in Romanian occupation zones, local authorities (military, gendarme, and special security forces) would develop their own approaches based on the guidelines issued from superiors.

Figure 7.1. Hitler and Mussolini touring Ukraine in August 1941. United States Holocaust Memorial Museum, Washington, DC, photograph 18565, courtesy of Stanley Weithorn.

Transnistria: The "Romanian Solution to the Jewish Problem"

In the days leading to the outbreak of the war, the Romanian dictator Ion Antonescu made clear to his officials in cabinet meetings Romanian intentions vis-à-vis the Jews. Antonescu spoke of the "purification of the population" as regards the Jews and all nationalities. As he put it, "we will implement a policy of total and violent expulsion of foreign elements." On June 25, 1941, Antonescu's deputy prime minister, Mihau Antonescu (no relationship to Ion) related in another cabinet meeting what their leader wanted: "General Antonescu has taken the decision—while he is in Moldavia—to remove the Jews from this very moment from all the villages of Moldavia, Bessarabia, and Bukovina."[19] They were removed across the Dniester into German and Hungarian occupied zones, and as many as 27,000 were subjected to death marches, random shootings, rape, and starvation along the banks of the river. This refugee problem caused bitter conflicts among the Axis powers in the region.[20] Ion Antonescu was not pleased when German troops in Ukraine forced

Jews on the Bessarabian border back into Romanian territory. Antonescu raised this problem with Hitler and remarked that German soldiers were not acting according to the guidelines that they had discussed during their private meeting in Munich on June 13.[21] The conflict was resolved by a territorial change. As of August 19 the primary destination of most Romanian deportees would be the newly created territory of Transnistria, a swathe of territory between the Southern Bug and Dniester rivers, a territorial gift that Antonescu received from Hitler. According to the research of Dennis Deletant, Jean Ancel, and Radu Ioanid, about 250,000 Jews and 12,000 Roma died there in makeshift camps, ghettos, and in massacres around these sites.[22]

Ion Antonescu was less guarded in his ranting against the Jews and virulent anti-Semitism than were other Axis leaders. Like Hitler, he fumed about the Jewish commissars in the Red Army during discussions with his ministers and military brass, especially in explaining Romanian casualties in the war. Then when the massacres and abuses of Jews in occupied Romanian territory became known, and the head of the Federation of the Jewish Communities in Romania, Wilhelm Filderman, tried to protest the deportations of Jews to Transnistria, Ion Antonescu published his response to Filderman in the press:

> Mr. Filderman, no one can be more sensitive than I am to the suffering of the humble and defenseless. I understand your pain, but all of you should, and especially should have, understood mine at the time, which was the pain of an entire nation. Do you think, did you think, of what we were going through last year during the evacuation of Bessarabia and what is happening today, when day by day and hour by hour, we are paying generously and in blood, in a great deal of blood, for the hatred with which your co-religionists in Bessarabia treated us during the withdrawal from Bessarabia, how they received us upon our return and how they treated us from the Dniester up to Odessa and in the area around the Sea of Azov?[23]

Here is a strong example, uncovered by historian Dennis Deletant, of Antonescu's promotion of anti-Semitism and anti-bolshevism as part of the diplomatic territorial arrangements worked out during Operation Barbarossa. Antonescu's public scapegoating of the Jews in Bessarabia incited waves of anti-Semitic violence there and across the expanding Romanian empire.

Hitler's initial reluctance to involve Hungary in the military campaign was not solely a matter of preferring Antonescu as a like-minded fascist dictator. He and his generals in the field wanted to avoid any possible conflicts on the ground, any clashes that might emerge between

Hungarian and Romanian units during the action or in the administration of the conquered territory, although as it turned out many of the Hungarian units contained high percentages of Romanians and Ruthenians.[24] The political territorial claims that Hitler referred to in the case of Hungary were based on two treaties, the Vienna Awards of 1938 and 1940, that deprived Romania of land. As the victor in these treaties, Hungary was the potential spoiler in Germany's relations with Slovakia and Romania[25] and to some degree with the Ukrainian nationalist leaders (Stepan Bandera and Andrij Melnyk), since Admiral Miklós Horthy had received or made claims to territory that these parties considered their rightful homeland, regions such as Subcarpathia and northern Transylvania.[26] Though the Hungarian military participated in the war in Yugoslavia and its units demonstrated their willingness to carry out atrocities, in particular in the Bačka (Vojvodina, Serbia), Hitler remained wary of Hungary as a military ally or strategic partner in the campaign against the Soviet Union. Even though the Nazi example accelerated anti-Semitic trends in the 1930s in Hungary, Hitler also questioned Hungary's commitment to the Final Solution.[27] He told Croatian Minister of War Slavko Kvaternik on July 21, 1941, that Hungary would be the last European country to surrender its Jews. As historian Gerhard Weinberg has observed, "This was one of the few predictions Hitler made in July 1941 that turned out to be correct."[28]

Yet some of his more pragmatic military chiefs must have realized that they would need Hungary's help after all. Halder, for example, engaged in unauthorized negotiations to both stage German troops in Hungary and gain the direct participation of Hungarian forces.[29] Thus on the eve of the invasion, the Royal Hungarian Army was called up. According to historian Krisztián Ungváry, this was all arranged in a rather last-minute fashion and so, as Hitler assumed, the Hungarian soldiers were poorly equipped and trained. Officially, Hungary joined the Axis forces against the Soviet Union on June 27, 1941. Under the direction of German Army Group South, the Hungarian Carpathy Corps moved over Seret into Borszcow in early July. In mid-July the Hungarian *Schnell* Corps was sent to Bratslav to relieve troops of the Eleventh Army. The Second Hungarian Army, later attempting to hold the front line on the Don, was decimated by the Soviets, and nearly all two hundred thousand of its men died or surrendered. Hungarian troops tried to keep up with the German advance in their own shoddy tanks, peasant carts, bicycles, and rented automobiles, which the Germans scoffed at (though the Hungarians' horse-drawn carts moved better on the muddy country roads than did the German automobiles). As it turned out, the most valuable Hungarian contribution (in cruder Nazi terms) to the campaign in the east was in the areas of antipartisan warfare and labor (Jewish battalions that they put to work repairing roads and bridges). For their part in the initial success of the campaign, the smaller Hungarian mobile corps were praised by Army Group South observers, who commented on their high quality material and general usefulness.[30]

According to the pioneering research of Randolph Braham and Krisztián Ungváry, as many as forty thousand Jewish laborers attached to the Hungarian military perished in the territory that falls roughly within Ukraine's borders today. Some were killed in the combat zones around Stalingrad, while others died in the course of their torturous work owing to illnesses related to malnutrition, exhaustion, and beatings. Many were killed at the insistence of local German officials. Near Sumy, German members of *Sonderkommando* 4a shot a group of Hungarian Jewish laborers, and on April 30, 1943, some three hundred to eight hundred Hungarian Jewish laborers were burned in the barns of a collective farm in Korosten, near Zhytomyr.[31]

Several thousand non-Jewish civilians who were branded partisans were massacred in Hungarian-led raids on villages in Komorovka, Nosovk, Karjukova, Luky Hutor, Ivangorod, Jelino, Seredina Buda, and many other places in and around the Bryansk Forest.[32] German officers complained that Hungarian methods of partisan warfare were excessive; one reported in May 1942:

> In propaganda terms, their undisciplined and completely arbitrary behavior towards the local population can only harm German interests. Looting, rape and other breaches are the order of the day. In addition to the ill feeling caused among the local population, it is apparent that the Hungarian troops are not in a position to defeat the enemy.[33]

Behind the front, during 1942 and 1943, Hungarians and Slovaks served under the Wehrmacht Commander for Occupied Ukraine; they were stationed in various spots within the *Reichskommissariat* and attached to the local German *Feldkommandantur*, but also recruited for anti-Jewish security measures including ghetto liquidations and deportations. According to plans devised by the High Command of the Army, Himmler's SS-police, and representatives of Alfred Rosenberg's Reich Ministry for the Occupied Eastern Territories:

> The security of the part of the Reich Commissary [sic] Ukraine to be set up on September 1, 1941 will be carried out in the south by a Hungarian Division (two brigades), connected in the north with a Slovakian security division

besides four battalions of militia. All units, including the Hungarian and Slovakians, are under the command of the commander of the Wehrmacht.[34]

Documentation on Hungarian involvement in the Holocaust during Operation Barbarossa in the military occupation administration and in the civilian administration (the *Reichskommissariat* and General Government) is spotty, but in the evidence that has emerged one sees certain patterns of ad hoc collaboration in antipartisan warfare and the Final Solution. According to Ungváry, most of the Hungarian records from Ukraine are not in the archives, and he relied on those bits and pieces he located and then combined them with German reports. Here are some examples. In the Chernihiv region, near Konotop, the German *Sonderkommando*, being short staffed and lacking trucks and petrol, relied on members of the Hungarian military stationed there to carry out anti-Jewish massacres in July 1942. Near Cholmy on February 10, 1942, "two partisans and a Jewish woman were shot while escaping by a Hungarian patrol in the vicinity."[35] Nazi officials in Ukraine routinely employed the stock phrase "shot while trying to escape"; it infers that the Jews were guilty fugitives, when in fact innocent men, women, and children (mostly hiding and seeking refuge in the forests) were gunned down. Some Jewish males were accepted into the Soviet partisan movement, but the elderly, women, and children were left to fend for themselves in these war zones.[36] In another report, the claim is made that ninety Jews (perhaps a small community) supported enemy partisans: "A group of Jews supplied food to the partisans. The band of Jews, numbering 90, was executed." This was communicated to the chief of staff of the 105th Infantry Division [Hungarian] on December 22, 1941.[37] One of the better documented German-Hungarian murder operations occurred in Chernihiv on February 28, 1942. Eight surviving photographs show the massacre of between forty and sixty civilians (identified as Jews on the back of the photos). The Hungarians apparently kept guard while the German military Secret Field Police (*Geheime Feldpolizei*) carried out the killing to ensure an orderly execution.

In another more detailed case, investigated by the Hungarians immediately after the war and by the West Germans in the late 1960s,[38] Hungarian troops participated in the liquidation of the Haisyn/Gajsin ghetto at the end of May 1942. A meeting was held on May 26, 1942, in the office of the local Wehrmacht *Ortskommandantur* that included the local Hungarian military commander; the German district commissioner, Becher; the Wehrmacht major, Heinrich; and the station chief of the gendarme post, Dreckmeier. Because they intended to round up the Jews from three villages, Commissioner Becher split the action into two transports. One of these was led by *Major* Heinrich and supported by Ukrainian *Schutzmänner* and Hungarian infantry. In the early morning at 3:00 a.m., Hungarian and Ukrainian auxiliaries sealed off the ghetto; they then forced the Jews onto trucks and drove them to the execution site at Teplyk where a shooting commando of SD men stood ready. About four hundred Jews were killed in these massacres. According to Ungváry's research in the Hungarian trial records, some of the Hungarian volunteers shot Jews.[39]

One of the more infamous massacres in Holocaust history that marked the escalation in the summer of 1941 from the selective killing of Jewish males to the annihilation of entire communities occurred at Kamianets-Podilskyi (Kamenets-Podolsk). An important aspect of this history that has not been researched fully is Hungary's role and the presence of Hungarians in the massacre as victims, bystanders, and perpetrators. Here the Hungarian perpetrators and accomplices were on the ground, involved in the shooting of approximately 23,600 Jews over a few days, and they were also responsible for an anti-Jewish diplomacy that drove almost half the victims, Hungarian Jewish refugees, into the mass graves of Ukraine.

On August 25, a meeting of army commanders and Rosenberg's representatives took place in Vinnytsia, Ukraine. The purpose of the meeting was to discuss how territory in the rear area of Germany's Army Group South would be transferred to the jurisdiction of the civilian administration, the Reich Commissariat Ukraine. During the meeting the following issue was raised (as it was recorded in the official meeting notes):

> Near Kamenets-Podolsk, the Hungarians have pushed about 11,000 Jews over the border. In the negotiations up to the present it has not been possible to arrive at any measures for the return of these Jews. The higher SS and police leader (*SS-Obergruppenführer* Jeckeln) hopes however to have completed the liquidation of these Jews by September 1, 1941.[40]

To the Hungarian government, these 11,000 refugees were alien Jews. They resided in territories annexed by Hungary in 1938 (Carpatho-Ukraine) or were Polish, German, Austrian, Czech, and Slovak Jews who had crossed over the border into these territories.[41] As Operation Barbarossa was getting under way, the Hungarians decided this might be an opportune moment to deport these Jews eastward into Ukraine. In the chaos of the military campaign, and indeed under the cover of war, they were shoved into freight cars, dumped across the Hungarian border, and then marched as far as Kamianets-Podilskyi.[42] The town was captured by the Germans and Hungarians in early July and fell under the regional military administration of the 183rd Field Command. As the refugee Jews began arriving in the thousands, the local German military officials began to complain that the Jews were taking up housing and food, that they would spread epidemics and represented a security problem. They wrote to superiors that an "immediate order for their [the Jews'] evacuation is urgently requested."[43] According to historian Dieter Pohl, "diplomatic efforts to convince the Hungarians to take back these Jews failed."[44] The crisis was resolved by bringing in the higher SS and police leader for Southern Russia, Friedrich Jeckeln, Himmler's right-hand man in Ukraine. Jeckeln deployed Order Police Battalion 320 and an Orpo company of *Volksdeutsche* (from the Baltic). He contacted the Hungarian authorities and, according to historian Randolph Braham, a Hungarian sappers' platoon was put at Jeckeln's disposal.[45] Local Ukrainian auxiliaries were also recruited. On August 26 the massacre commenced. Some 4,200 men, women, and children were gunned down in pits; each was forced to lie on top of layers of corpses and killed with a bullet in the back of the head. The next day another 11,000 were killed in this manner. Postwar testimony of eyewitnesses placed Jeckeln at the scene, observing from a nearby hill with a group of Wehrmacht officers.[46] Among the eyewitnesses was Gyula Spitz, a Jewish truck driver with the Hungarian army, who secretly photographed events from the front seat of his vehicle. When the *Aktion* was over, Jeckeln radioed to Himmler's Command Staff that his units had killed 23,600 Jews (14,000 from Carpatho-Ukraine). This was the largest massacre in the Barbarossa campaign thus far, only to be outdone in Kiev at Babi Yar about a month later, then at Odessa and Bogdanivka.

The crisis that prompted this large-scale massacre began with Hungary's expulsion of the Jewish refugees. Like the tensions that arose between German and Romanian regional military and SS-police leaders over refugee Jews who were becoming border problems, the Kamianets-Podilskyi massacres manifest the fact that each of the Axis powers refused to take in Jews from other countries and that their views of the Jewish problem, while broadly anti-Semitic, were also at the center of specific clashes over national borders and territorial gains. The Germans wanted the Hungarians to take back "their Jews," and in the final German SS-police report submitted by HSPFF Jeckeln, the local Jews killed there were distinguished from the refugee Jews from Hungary.

The Jewish Question or the plight of the Jews, who were viewed as the most detested or unwanted minority in Europe, was an important feature of Axis diplomacy. When conflicts arose, such as the Kamianets-Podilskyi crisis, these moments of diplomatic exchange might have opened up the possibility of bringing Jews into less life-threatening circumstances, to move them from the path of mobile killing units, or out of Jeckeln's reach, for example. But this did not happen. Instead, both the local and senior level problem solving and crisis management was almost always resolved to the detriment of the Jews and usually triggered a *radicalization* of the genocidal violence. Already in the pogroms of July 1941 and increasingly in the mass shootings in August, Axis genocidal policy targeted entire Jewish communities. This was the case in Romania during the summer and fall of 1941 (though it was reversed in 1942 when Marshal Antonescu suspended deportations), and was increasingly so in Hungary, leading ultimately to the deportations of Hungarian Jews in the summer of 1944.[47]

The horrors of the Kamianets-Podilskyi massacre were reported by survivors who made their way back to Hungary. The more liberal member of the Interior Ministry, Mr. Fischer, tried to halt these expulsions of Jews to the eastern territories. However, the deportations continued. In fact four months later, on December 22, 1941, an urgent notice was sent from the highest offices of the Reich Commissar for Ukraine informing German regional governors of Hungarian deportations of Jews:

> The Foreign Office has informed us that the Hungarian government has been attempting to expel Hungarian Jews into the occupied eastern territories. This is supposedly already happening to a large extent with those [Jews] who were sent to the General Government. I request an immediate report about whether such cases have occurred in your respective regions and, if yes, what measures have you taken against the Jews in question who have been seized in your areas.[48]

Unfortunately, the requested reports from the regional governors are not in the files. But one can assume that such reports would have revealed anti-Jewish atrocities undertaken by German regional officials and would have perhaps illuminated relations between German and Hungarian officials over the Jewish problem. It is interesting to note the timing of this communication; it coincided with German plans for the mass murder of all European Jews and deportations from the Old Reich to ghettos and killing sites in Ukraine. As German officials across Reich offices, including the Foreign Office, prepared for the meeting at Wannsee, regional officials in Ukraine were asked to provide information about their Jewish populations, local and alien, as well as to report on local railway connections to ghettos that could accommodate deported Jews.[49]

The documentation surrounding this history also reveals an important irony in German-Hungarian and German-Romanian relations over the Jewish Question and occupation policies in Ukraine. The German accounts of Hungarian treatment of local Jews tended to exaggerate

Hungarian behavior as barbaric and disorderly. As with the German critiques of marauding Romanian soldiers, the anti-Semitism as such was not questioned and no expressions of pity toward the Jews emerged; rather, the inferior nature of Germany's subordinate allies was criticized. For instance, one local German official complained that "wherever you go, occupation by Hungarians and Romanians is viewed as the worst kind of scourge. There was general agreement that Hungarian and Romanian behavior in the occupied territories was solely motivated by greed and lust."[50] In a similar vein, but occurring at a higher level, Ungváry found: "The German Foreign Office's liaison officer in the *Generalgouvernement* drafted a complaint which, among other issues, dealt with the 'murder tourism' of Germany's allies. He hoped to achieve the Hungarians' removal." The excesses of Hungarians in Galicia were carefully documented by German intelligence. The foreign/counter-intelligence department in the Lemberg *Abwehr* office compiled a list of misdemeanors, which included "activities by Hungarian officers [who are] collecting photographs relating to the treatment of Jews (trenches, camps, and evacuation points)."[51] At first glance one might view such reports as the petty criticisms of rival powers or as German arrogance vis-à-vis its subordinate allies. Upon reflection, however, it seems that these German reports can be read in yet another way. By asserting the inferior methods of Hungarians and Romanians regarding the treatment of the Jews, local Germans were attempting to legitimize their own more thorough policy of genocide. In asserting that we Germans can do it better, were these German critiques not also asserting that the German approach was correct, even more civilized?

Slovakia

Little is known about Slovak involvement or input in Operation Barbarossa. Though Hitler was in principle against having Slavs actually participate in the Eastern campaign, the High Command of the Army had already reckoned in the prewar planning that they would utilize Slovak units in the occupation of the southern sector. The formal arrangements for this were not finalized, however, until the day of the invasion. According to Dieter Pohl's research, just "two days later the units marched off" with a similar ideological motivation: to combat bolshevism, fortified by their own campaign of state-sponsored anti-Semitism with a strong religious, Catholic component.[52] Furthermore, Slovakia had Germany to thank for its newly gained autonomy; the breakup of Czechoslovakia had been orchestrated by Hitler and the Munich Pact in 1938–39. In conjunction with this, German-Slovak relations were formalized in March 1939 under the terms of a "protective treaty," which gave Germany the upper hand over Slovakia's foreign, military, and economic policies. Slovakia's precarious status was also demonstrated in Germany's upholding of the First Vienna Award, which resulted in Hungary's annexation of one-third of Slovakia's territory.

The Slovak presence in Nazi-occupied Ukraine began with expeditionary groups. To keep apace with the German units advancing eastward, the Slovaks of the 1st (Mobile) Infantry Division formed mobile units, *Schnell* divisions, consisting of about 10,000 men attached to the Seventeenth Army (e.g., The Brigade Pilfousek). At the end of August 1941, the Slovak Army Group was reorganized into two infantry divisions, the 1st (Mobile) and 2nd Infantry Divisions (about 42,000 men). The *Schnell* divisions were active in the Zhytomyr region, in the battle for Kiev around the Dnieper, near Rostov, Melitopol, and in coastal patrols in the Crimea. The 2nd Slovak (Security) Infantry Division (about 6,000 to 8,000 men, 101st and 102nd Regiments) carried out policing and combat duties against alleged saboteurs, partisans, and other security threats behind the lines, especially concentrating their activity in the northern half of the Zhytomyr region after October 1941. It is not clear if they were involved in anti-Jewish massacres, but they were involved in security raids of villages around Choiniki and Ovruch.[53] Research on this has been hampered by the loss of the war diaries of the German liaison officer attached to the Slovakian units.[54] Besides the broken chronological record, the Slovak unit histories are tricky to follow, as they underwent several transformations including assignments that combined regular combat and special security duties.[55]

Among the scant evidence on Slovakian participation in the massacres is the diary of an SS officer, Felix Landau. While leading a special *Einsatzkommando* in the summer of 1941, Landau wrote that near Drohobych on July 2, 1941, he and his comrades shot Jewish laborers and prisoners. He continued: "In this instance the Slovaks dug the graves and [afterward] immediately covered them."[56] Another incident has recently come to light from the records of the Security Services Archive in Prague. On October 13, 1941, in Miropol (about forty kilometers southwest of Zhytomyr), ninety-four Jews (forty-nine of them children) were shot in the local park. A Slovak, Škrovina Łubomir, testified in 1958 that he was in the area assigned to guard bridges for the Wehrmacht. His Slovak commander, Hruska, ordered him and two other Slovak soldiers to attend the mass shooting. Łubomir brought his camera. He testified that the two Ukrainian militia who shot the Jews were locals, because they knew the victims. The three commanders in the photo were attached to Order Police Battalion 303 (see figs. 7.2 and 7.3).[57]

Figures 7.2. German Order Police commanders and Ukrainian policemen shoot a Jewish woman and child at close range in the public park in Miropol while a member of the Slovakian Army photographs the murders, October 1941. Courtesy of Security Services Archive, Prague, Czech Republic (H-770-3.0020).

Figure 7.3. German Order Police commanders and Ukrainian policemen shoot a Jewish woman. The Slovakian photographer was questioned after the war in Prague, and the Ukrainian policemen were arrested by the KGB, tried, and convicted in 1987. The identities and fates of the German Order Policemen are unknown. Courtesy of Security Services Archive, Prague, Czech Republic (H-770-3.0020).

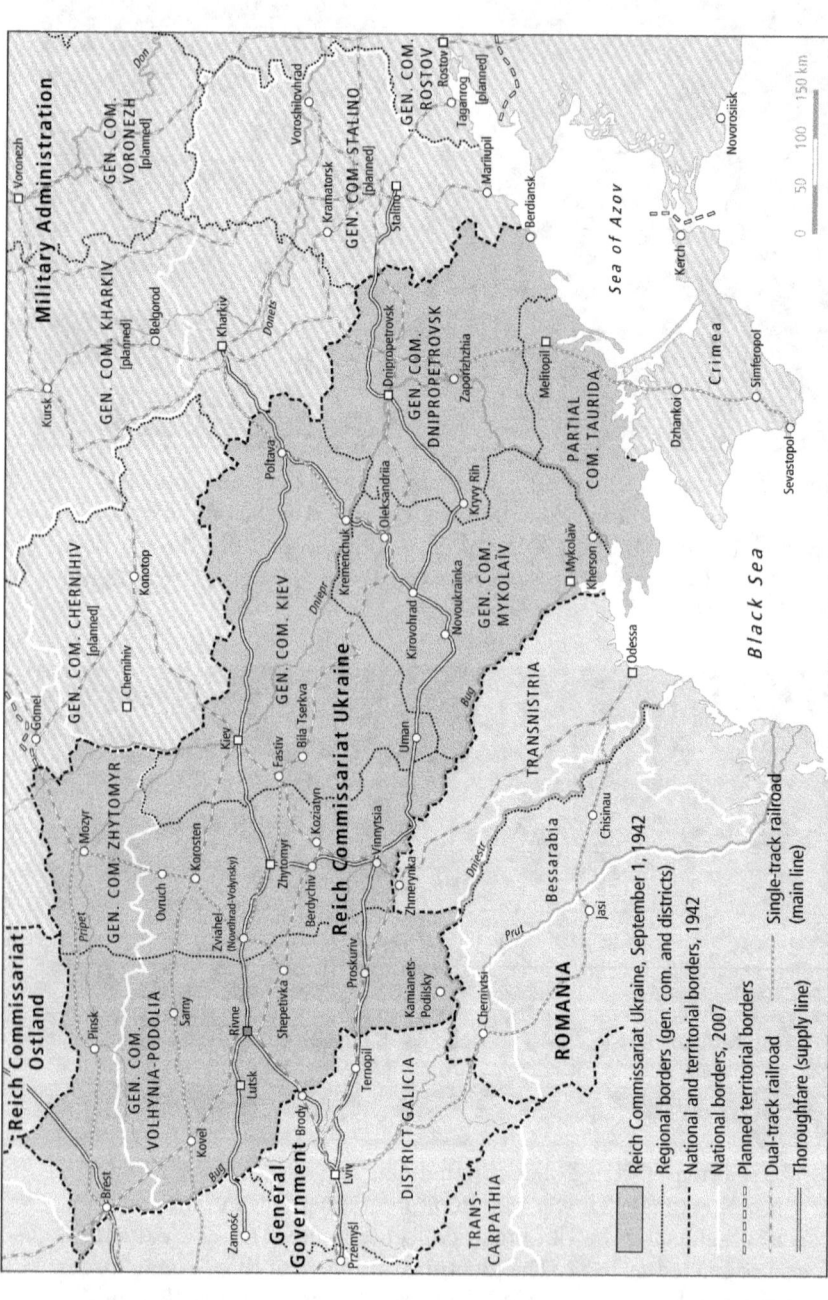

Figure 7.4. Occupied Ukraine, September 1942. Ray Brandon and Wendy Lower, eds. *The Shoah in Ukraine: History, Testimony, and Memorialization,* Bloomington: Indiana University Press, 2009, 45. Courtesy of Indiana University Press.

About this time in early November 1941, President Jozef Tiso traveled through Ukraine and stopped in Zhytomyr, which was a Slovak garrison town. According to historian James Mace, who researched Tiso's postwar testimony, during Tiso's tour in Ukraine he learned from the chief of the Slovak military, General Ferdinand Catlos, about the mass shootings of Jews and that conflicts had emerged between local Slovak and German military. As Tiso explained:

> German civilian commissars wanted to order our soldiers on what they should do in the occupied territory and how they should behave towards civilians. They wanted to use [our troops] for ... purposes that our soldiers did not consider reconcilable with the laws of war. ... I then talked about this with Ludin [the German Ambassador in Slovakia] and requested him to announce to Berlin that our soldiers will not accept such instructions from civilian commissars.[58]

Once German military and SS-police started to systematically kill all Jews in Ukraine as of August 1941, the enormous task required the acquiescence and compliance, if not direct involvement, of the local population and occupation forces. Tiso claimed that his men resisted participation because they did not want to take orders form German civilian leaders. It is not clear if the conflict was purely about jurisdictional matters, if this issue was used to spare Slovaks the dirty work of the genocide, or if regional Slovak military leaders were voicing their opposition to the Holocaust on moral grounds. In fact, according to Mace, some of the first reports of the atrocities to reach the Vatican came from Slovak field curates in October 1941.

Tiso's postwar testimony is problematic. Though it reveals his presence in Ukraine and perhaps a conflict among his forces there, it perhaps overstates the "misunderstanding" between Germans and Slovaks; Tiso sought to minimize his close collaboration with Nazi leaders regarding the Jews, a collaboration that is documented. In September 1941, Tiso's government issued a series of anti-Jewish laws along the German model. On October 20, 1941, just prior to his tour of Ukraine, Tiso had tea with Himmler and they discussed deportations of Jews to the east.[59] The first Jews deported to Auschwitz were Slovak Jewesses, in March 1942. Apparently Tiso was so anxious to rid his country of Jews that he paid Hitler five hundred reichsmarks for each deported Jew.

Axis Occupation Forces and Local Collaborators: Pogroms

Pogroms became a common feature of the first days and months of the Axis "liberation" of the Soviet Union. The role of the Germans and other

Axis forces (Hungarians, Slovaks, Romanians) in inciting the violence varied from place to place. However, western Ukraine saw some of the worst cases, not only in the region's capital of Lviv, but also across the villages and towns extending eastward and southward. What details about and explanations for this violence have emerged in recent research? Did certain situational factors or an interethnic dynamic cause or aggravate tensions that led to massacres? Once the Red Army had left, did local populations attack Jews before the Germans had arrived? What role did the Axis troops, Romanian, Hungarian, and Slovakian, play?

In eastern Galicia, historian Dieter Pohl estimates that as many as twelve thousand Jews died in about one hundred pogroms, the largest occurring in the city of Lviv, where approximately four thousand Jews were brutally murdered between June 30 and July 25, 1941. As was the case in nearby Stanyslaviv, Zolochiv, Drohobych, Buchach, and Ternopil, the Jews in Lviv were blamed for the mass murder of political prisoners and others whose mutilated remains were found in NKVD jails. The pattern of events during World War II is clear. The Soviets carried out a policy of mass murder of Ukrainian prisoners during the retreat, and the Germans and their Ukrainian allies exploited this policy to organize anti-Semitic retaliation campaigns. The fact that Jews, Russians, and Poles were also victims of NKVD atrocities in Galicia and Volhynia was conveniently suppressed. Typically, Jewish men were forced to exhume bodies of dead prisoners; in some cases they had to wash the corpses and dig the graves to prepare for a religious burial. While the Jews carried out these gruesome tasks, the local population was allowed to vent their rage against them; they beat the Jews at random with clubs, rods, and other blunt instruments.[60]

Ukrainian nationalists from the Organization of Ukrainian Nationalists (OUN), both those supporting Stepan Bandera (OUN-B) and those supporting Andrij Melnyk (OUN-M), were useful, expedient local collaborators for securing the territory in these first chaotic months. German military intelligence and field offices relied on Ukrainian nationalist activists (*pokhidny hrupy*) who had joined them in the invasion, as well as local Ukrainians who stepped forward to join the local administration as militia forces, leaders in self-help, and other local governing committees. These Ukrainian officials and militia members became involved in anti-Bolshevik, anti-Jewish security measures. Their work was incited by the collaboration of senior Ukrainian and German officials in the Wehrmacht, Abwehr, and SD who supported the secret training and deployment of Ukrainian legions, *Nachtigal*, and *Roland*. In fact, among the first units to arrive in Lviv on June 30, 1941, was the German Brandenburg Division led by the *Nachtigal* Battalion. Their arrival was followed by a Ukrainian (OUN) proclamation of statehood, which was abruptly suppressed by the Germans, and the first in a series of pogroms in Lviv, among the most well known in the history of the Holocaust.[61]

Further east in the Podolian towns of Bar and Shpykiv, the Ukrainian militiamen attached to OUN-B, who wore the nationalist symbol of the trident on their sleeves, issued the first security directive to the locals, Order No. 1: all Jews over seven years of age must wear the white star.[62] The *Polissian Sich*, supporting the nationalist faction under Taras Bulba-Borovets, was active until November 1941 in the cleansing of the Pripet marshlands. According to Karel Berkhoff's research, one fifteen-year-old member of the Sich recalled that "we did everything they [the Germans] asked. I went everywhere, rode everywhere, fought and shot Jews who had treated me badly." The Sich had its own newspaper, in which it announced at the end of 1941 that "now the parasitical Jewish nation had been destroyed."[63] Jared McBride also documented Sich pogroms north of Zhytomyr at Olev'sk. In this case, the robbing, torture, and killing of Jews was done with no German involvement.[64] Historian Franziska Bruder uncovered a diary of an OUN-B member of the *Nachtigal* Battalion. The diarist described the battalion's actions during its march in mid-July 1941 from Lviv to Vinnytsia: "During our march, we saw with our own eyes the victims of the Jewish-Bolshevik terror, which strengthened our hatred of the Jews, and so after that we shot all the Jews we encountered in two villages."[65] In these cases, Ukrainian paramilitary and militia forces shot Jews independently of the Germans because they wanted to and apparently because they could.

In terms of the links between local collaborators and official Axis policy toward Jews, events in Odessa were more revealing than those in Kiev. In October 1941 an estimated thirty-four to thirty-five thousand Jews were shot or burned alive in Odessa. Such a high death toll clearly shows the result of a highly organized series of massacres. In fact the killings were ordered by Marshal Ion Antonescu himself, who demanded (in Order No. 302.26) "immediate retaliatory action, including the liquidation of eighteen thousand Jews in the ghettos and the hanging in the town squares of at least one hundred Jews for every regimental sector."[66] This order was issued after an explosion in Romanian military headquarters that killed dozens of occupation officials including the commanding officer. Romanian methods of murder included throwing grenades at and shooting Jews who had been crammed by the thousands into wooden buildings. In an act reminiscent of the burning of Strasbourg's Jews in the fifteenth century, Romanians forced Jews into the harbor square and set them on fire. Except that in this twentieth-century version, the Romanians did not allow Jews to save themselves through conversion (baptism). Thus the barbarism of the religious wars was outdone by these modern campaigns of colonization and national purification. Still they shared demotic elements that rippled across the borderlands and reappeared throughout the war. Anti-Jewish massacres in places such as Bogdanivka and Domanivka continued into 1942 and were caused in part by expulsions of Jews over the Bug River. This time the Germans were forcing Jews from their occupation area into the Romanian zone. Many Jewish refugees hoped that conditions on the Romanian side might be better and fled across the German-Romanian border, but in 1941 those refugees did not fare much better.[67]

German officials in Ukraine rationalized that they were more civilized than the Romanians in their approach to the Final Solution.[68] For example, in the activity report of the Sipo and SD in the USSR (covering the period July 29 to August 14, 1941), *Einsatzgruppe* C described the situation in Romanian territory, in Bessarabia, as "catastrophic," mainly owing to the rampant plundering by Romanian troops along with gunfights and mass raping. A German member of the Security Police intervened in Borowka, where "marauding" Romanian soldiers had settled in with the Jews and from there operated their "plundering business." The German official apprehended the Romanian soldiers and handed them over to officers in the Romanian headquarters.[69] The atrocities at Bogdanivka during Christmas 1941 were among the bloodiest in the history of the Holocaust; at least forty-eight thousand died in mass shootings, an orgy of violence perpetrated by Romanian soldiers and Ukrainian and ethnic German militia, among others. These were not spontaneous acts; they were ordered by Marshal Antonescu.[70] On the other hand, as Vladimir Solonari discerned in his research, there was an important difference between the Romanian occupation administration and the German: "Returning Romanian officials [to Bukovina and Bessarabia] knew local realities incomparably better than newly arrived Germans [in Poland or Ukraine] did, and they could and did rely on a much broader societal support than Nazis ever enjoyed."[71]

Both the Germans and Romanians had to rely on the local population because manpower was lacking to carry out all the tasks needed to fully exploit the Jewish population and commit the genocide. One of the challenges, as historians, is to determine on the ground where official orders ended and locally initiated violence started, with or without direct Nazi oversight. Yet Frank Golczewski finds that

> even non-Ukrainian scholars have sometimes gone too far in minimizing the depth of anti-Jewish, anti-Communist, and anti-Russian sentiment in these regions. Raul Hilberg, for example, argues that "truly spontaneous pogroms, free from

Einsatzgruppen influence, did not take place," and that "all pogroms were implemented within a short time after the arrival of the [German] killing units." This, however, does not explain the pogroms that broke out in places such as Stanyslaviv (today, Ivano-Frankivs'k), Kolomyia, Horodenka, and Obertyn, towns that were in the Hungarian zone of operations and occupation in Galicia.[72]

Actually, the interethnic dynamic in the history of the pogroms is far from clear. There are conflicting reports about the Hungarian role in Kolomyia, Horodenka, and Stanyslaviv. Historian Andrzej Zbikowski found that Ukrainians there expressed their "delight at their sudden rescue from Soviet oppression" by carrying out a two-day pogrom in the town as soon as the Soviets had left. In his assessment, only the firm attitude of the commander of the Hungarian troops that seized the town brought events under control. In his essay, "Local Anti-Jewish Pogroms in the Occupied Territories of Eastern Poland, June–July 1941," Zbikowski quotes testimonies to support his argument of Hungarian moderation, but does not footnote them. Most likely his conclusions are drawn from survivor testimonies held at the Jewish Historical Institute at Warsaw, which is referenced as a source elsewhere in this essay.[73] And in the case of Zhytomyr, Hilberg cites another incident documented in an *Ereignismeldung* from *Einsatzgruppe* C, in which the Hungarian military headquarters stopped the local auxiliary policy from launching a pogrom. Historian Yitzhak Arad also concludes (based on Jewish survivor testimony) that Hungarian forces stopped pogroms in Kolomyia, Kosov, Obertyn, and Bolekhov because they feared Ukrainian reprisals against Hungarians in Transcarpathia, and sought "conditions of relative calm."[74] Yet *Einsatzgruppe* C also reported on another incident in western Ukraine: apparently, rumor had it that Hungarian soldiers encouraged Ukrainians to plunder, then filmed them as marauders so that the Hungarians could cover up their own crimes. In a deliberate act meant to foment local interethnic tensions, Hungarians employed Polish officers to carry out anti-Ukrainian measures.[75] The lines here between reality and rumor are blurry, but at the very least one can see from the mixed reports that interethnic rivalries and tensions were a key feature of the escalating measures against the Jews.

Conclusion

This essay set out to establish the role of Axis collaboration in Operation Barbarossa as a contributing factor to the Holocaust in Ukraine. The historiography on the crimes of German Wehrmacht soldiers has recently shown that the military was heavily involved in the anti-Jewish violence leading to genocide. The myth of the clean Wehrmacht has been debunked. At the same time the role of Germany's allies in the war of extermination has not been fully elucidated. In fact, Antonescu did not begrudgingly go along with or follow Hitler's radical course in 1941 out of pressure. He seems to have been included in the prewar conspiracy, and once the war was underway he implemented his own purification programs, deportations from northern Bukovina and Bessarabia, established ghettos in Transnistria, ordered death marches from Odessa, and sponsored large massacres in the area of Bogdanivka. Hitler did correctly predict that Hungary would be the last to give up its Jews. However, the country was more than willing to deport its alien Jews in the summer of 1941; as one leading Hungarian official put it, "the largest number possible and as fast as possible."[76] Hungarian military units participated in mass murder in Kamianets-Podilskyi and in smaller massacres in eastern Galicia. Hungarian formations were also active in antipartisan warfare and routinely killed Jewish civilians; indeed many German officials reported that the Hungarians were excessively cruel. The use of Jewish labor battalions by the Hungarian army is also well documented; tens of thousands perished in these units across Ukraine (and Yugoslavia). Though the paper trail for the Slovak Security Division operating north of Zhytomyr is thin, the history of antipartisan warfare in this area is similar to the catalog of atrocities and ethnic cleansing that occurred around Bryansk. The likelihood that Slovak units participated in anti-Jewish massacres is rather high.

Why did these Axis forces perpetrate crimes against Jews and other so-called enemies or inferiors? In fact, according to Ungváry's calculations, the Hungarian rate of murdering civilians condemned as partisans was comparable to that of the more notorious Waffen-SS Brigades. Ungváry explains that from the start of the campaign, Hungarians on the Eastern Front felt they were taking part in a war that was not their war. The Hungarian occupation forces were a diplomatic maneuver, used to placate German demands for armed assistance. They did not have a big stake in the eastern territory; at least Hitler did not offer it. Thus, as an outsider or guest in the wild east of Ukraine, there was no need to fuss about the consequences of their criminal actions against the local population. With the claim of fighting partisans, like any other good soldier facing an enemy, Jewish civilians were killed with a sense of impunity.

What about the cases in which Hungarian intervention saved lives, such as in the halting of pogroms in some Galician villages or in Zhytomyr? This reveals just how much leeway there was in the field; local commanders could intervene, slow the course of the genocide, and without any recourse from above. In these specific cases, the Hungarian commanders could not fully control events over time in the localities. Their stations were temporary, as the front moved, and eventually their independent action was limited by German field commanders, to whom they reported. But the documented variation in Hungarian collaboration in Ukraine, from full participation (for example in Haisyn/Gajsin) to obstructionism, may also reflect back on Ungváry's observation about not being fully invested in the region, but rather just acting as mercenaries in the fight against bolshevism intended to secure Hungary's own border to the west. Horthy and his military leaders apparently neither pressured their units nor incited them to commit genocide in a manner that has turned up in the German and Romanian documentation.

Does the radicalization thesis commonly applied to the history of the Nazi origins of a genocidal Final Solution apply to the Axis powers as a whole? In the constellation of forces that conquered and occupied Ukraine in the summer and fall of 1941, can one identify a coordinated effort to annihilate Jewry, or an escalating process whereby the most extreme ideas and practices of anti-Semitism were uniformly pursued to advance some political, territorial, or social aim? By the time of the invasion in June 1941, each Axis country had introduced its own anti-Jewish laws, following the German model. But as far as we know, these countries did not have the history of anti-Jewish violence comparable to that in Nazi Germany between 1938 and 1941. A further radicalization of anti-Jewish practices was more than likely in the Nazi case, but not so predictable among Germany's allies. The post-1941 history of Romanian, Hungarian, and Slovak treatment of Jews reveals an important unevenness and vacillation. Over time, German leaders had to place increasing pressure on their allies to turn over all of their Jews, and in the cases of Hungary and Slovakia, German occupation of the countries was necessary. Yet when it concerned foreign, "bolshevized" Jews in conquered areas such as Ukraine, such pressure was not necessary in 1941 and 1942.

In the history of genocide perpetration it is important to distinguish between the most radical idea of mass murder and the realization of this intent across time and space. Axis powers found common ground in the notions that Europe had to be liberated from Judeo-bolshevism and that the spread of communism was a dire threat to Western civilization and Christianity. Nazi Germany was the primary aggressor; it took on the role of the chief crusader, conqueror, and "liberator." Central to this mission was the removal of Jewish influence in Europe; thus Hitler and his cohorts conceived of their anti-Semitic measures as a European solution to the Jewish Question not limited to the German Reich. The implementation of anti-Jewish measures was a matter of diplomacy, intergovernmental policy making, and decisions that involved myriad agencies and collaborators. This history did not occur in a straight line of radicalization and mutual, unconditional support. The Jews became a pawn in traditional Realpolitik terms, but within an ideological context of extremes, as a factor in negotiations over territory, population exchanges, war matériel, troops, and property, all subject to the dynamic, cataclysmic Nazi-Soviet struggle that engulfed eastern Europe. As the war dragged on, and the victory of fascism seemed less certain, diplomacy and collaboration regarding anti-Jewish measures entered another phase. Hitler's allies were more concerned about securing their place in a postwar world dominated by the victors—Stalin, Churchill, and Roosevelt. In the case of Hungary, Slovakia, and Romania there is evidence of de-escalation occurring at the diplomatic level, and escalation or a spiralling of mass violence at a popular level. But, as this essay stresses, at a critical time of imperial conquest, Hitler's allies contributed to the onset of the genocide in the summer of 1941 by folding their own anti-Semitic agenda into the Nazi one and by initiating their own violent measures. In the Romanian case, Antonescu and his colleagues organized their own anti-Jewish deportations and massacres in southern Ukraine and its borderlands. In the Slovak case, Tiso's military forces carried out security measures that included the organization of mass shootings in the rear areas of west-central Ukraine. In the Hungarian case, government leaders deliberately pushed Jewish refugees and forced laborers into the massacre zones, Hungarian military units participated directly in the mass shooting sprees at Kamianets-Podilskyi, and in some parts of western Ukraine they initiated pogroms.

The diplomacy of the Jewish Question among Axis powers was an integral feature of Operation Barbarossa that extended to events in the field. By and large, the anti-Semitic actions of local Ukrainian and *Volksdeutsche* pogromists and nationalists were not contained or supported by the occupying powers and authorities, be they Hungarian, German, Romanian, or Slovak. German and Romanian fantasies of imperial realms cleared of Jews were nearly realized. As this became apparent during the military invasion in the summer of 1941, Hitler and Antonescu were increasingly emboldened, opting for ever more radical measures and becoming more explicit about their aims in the autumn of 1941. Such cataclysmic events forever changed the life of one Polish-Jewish lawyer, Raphael Lemkin, who was fleeing the advance of Axis military forces in the summer of 1941. Witnessing the devastation in Nazi-occupied Europe, having lost his own family in the Holocaust, and barely escaping the *Vernichtungskrieg* via Sweden to the United States, he wrote an important study that contributed to the drafting of the United Nations

Convention on Genocide. In *Axis Rule in Occupied Europe*, he argued for a new concept of war and occupation:

> In this respect genocide is a new technique of occupation aimed at winning the peace even though the war itself is lost. For this purpose the occupant has elaborated a system designed to destroy nations according to a previously prepared plan. Even before the war Hitler envisaged genocide as a means of changing the biological interrelations in Europe in favor of Germany. Hitler's conception of genocide is based not upon cultural but [upon] biological patterns.[77]

Lemkin realized in 1944 that the Holocaust was more than a war crime or atrocities committed under the cover of war. He argued that genocide was a form of war behind the lines, in the conquered, occupied areas. It was a continuation of the war by other means, and though the military campaign of imperial conquest made it possible, the two could lead to different outcomes. The battle for Moscow was a major defeat for the Axis military, yet in the rear areas of occupation another genocidal war against the "nations" or peoples, above all against the Jews, was advancing with success. This was the peace that Hitler and his non-German allies hoped to achieve in their war against the Soviet Union.

Notes

1. Richard Breitman, *Official Secrets: What the Nazis Planned, What the British and Americans Knew* (New York: Hill and Wang, 1988).

2. Report covering German SS-police actions of August 15–31, Records of the Code and Cypher School, HW 16, Piece 6, September 12, 1941, 1941, British National Archives, Kew, England. Thanks to Eric Steinhart for supplying me with a copy of this document.

3. Establishing the causal links between the Nazi-Soviet war and the Holocaust has not been without controversy, and has been a major subject of research, much of which was ignited by the *Historikerstreit*, and a controversial book by Arno Mayer. Mayer argued that Hitler's defeatist attitude in December 1941 incited his decision for a final solution and that Nazi anti-bolshevism was a more significant ideological force than anti-Semitism. Some of his points have been elaborated on by others, but Mayer's overall thesis has not held up against the evidence of an earlier decision to annihilate Jews in the Soviet Union and Europe. See Peter Baldwin's critique in *Reworking the Past: Hitler, the Holocaust, and the Historians' Debate* (Boston: Beacon Press, 1990); and Arno Mayer, *Why Did the Heavens Not Darken?* (New York: Pantheon, 1988). More recently, Christopher Browning has argued that "euphoria of victory," not frustration or fear of defeat, accounts for the origins of the

genocide. See Christopher Browning, with contributions by Jürgen Matthäus, *The Origins of the Final Solution: The Evolution of Nazi Jewish Policy, September 1939–March 1942* (Lincoln: University of Nebraska Press, 2004).

4. Gerhard Weinberg, *A World at Arms: A Global History of World War Two* (Cambridge: Cambridge University Press, 1994), 264.

5. Dieter Pohl, *Die Herrschaft der Wehrmacht: Deutsche Militärbesatzung und einheimische Bevölkerung in der Sowjetunion, 1941–1944* (Munich: Oldenbourg, 2008), 80.

6. I am aware of only a few scholars who can deal with most of these languages at once. See the work of Holly Case, *Between States: The Transylvanian Question and the European Idea During World War II* (Stanford: Stanford University Press, 2009).

7. Horst Boog, Jürgen Förster, Joachim Hoffmann, Ernst Klink, Rolf-Dieter Müller, and Gerd R. Ueberschär, *Der Angriff auf die Sowjetunion*, vol. 4 of *Das Deutsche Reich und der Zweite Weltkrieg* (Stuttgart: Deutsche Verlags-Anstalt, 1983). See the war diary of the high command of the armed forces, entry of March 3, 1941, for example. In Hitler's reworked version of the initial draft of the Barbarossa Directive, and its circulated guidelines, Hitler clarified that "dieser kommende Feldzug ist mehr als nur ein Kampf der Waffen; er führt auch zur Auseinandersetzung zweier Weltanschauungen. Um diesen Krieg zu beenden, genügt es bei der Weite des Raumes nicht, die feindliche Wehrmacht zu schlagen." Hitler stressed the need to crush a Judeo-Bolshevik intelligentsia, condemned as oppressors of the people, and to eliminate the formerly bourgeois aristocratic classes; he expressed the importance of the occupation regimes behind the battlefront, and that the political aims of the campaign in the rear areas were very difficult undertakings, which the army could not be expected to implement. According to Hitler's guidelines, specific directives were revised concerning the role of the *Reichsführer-SS* and the nonapplication of military courts when it came to rendering harmless Bolshevik big wigs and commissars. March 3, 1941, entry in Percy Ernst Schramm, ed., *Kriegstagebuch des Oberkommandos der Wehrmacht (Wehrmachtführungsstab) 1940–1945*, vol. 1, *1. August 1940–31. Dezember 1941*, ed. Hans-Adolf Jacobsen (Bonn 1965; repr., Munich: Bernard & Graefe, 1982), 341 (hereafter OKW war diary). A few weeks later, on March 30, 1941, Hitler would speak more explicitly with his generals about Operation Barbarossa as a "war of extermination." See Geoffrey P. Megargee, *War of Annihilation: Combat and Genocide on the Eastern Front, 1941* (Lanham, MD: Rowman & Littlefield, 2006), 33–41. In addition to military and security operations, genocidal hunger plans were also part of pre-Barbarossa discussions and guidelines. See Alex J. Kay, *Exploitation, Resettlement, Mass Murder: Political and Economic Planning for German Occupation Policy in the Soviet Union, 1940–1941* (New York: Berghahn, 2006).

8. OKW war diary, 1:299 (February 3, 1941). On the prominence of Romania as Hitler's ally in the Soviet Union in the southern sector, see Jürgen Förster, "Die Gewinnung von Verbündeten in Südosteuropa," in Boog et al., *Der Angriff auf die Sowjetunion*, 327–64.

9. OKW war diary, 1:361 (March 18, 1941).

10. Army Group South consisted of the Sixth, Seventeenth, and Eleventh Armies as well as Panzer Group 1. See Boog et al., *Der Angriff auf die Sowjetunion*.

11. Pohl, *Herrschaft*, 81. Förster, "Gewinnung," 341.

12. Jean Ancel, "The German-Romanian Relationship and the Final Solution," *Holocaust and Genocide Studies* 19, no. 2 (2005): 252. Hitler was also candid with the Croatian minister of war, Slavko Kvaternick, telling him on July 21, 1941, that no Jews would be allowed to remain in Europe. See Gerhard Weinberg, "Germany's War for World Conquest and the Extermination of the Jews," Meyerhoff Lecture, June 11, 1995 (Washington, DC: US Holocaust Memorial Museum, 1995). Besides Kvaternick, Hitler spoke about the fate of the Jews with the Grand Mufti of Jerusalem. Weinberg elaborated on this recently in his speech "Another Look at Hitler and the Beginning of the Holocaust," at the conference Lessons and Legacies, Northwestern University, November 3, 2009.

13. Pohl, *Herrschaft*, 81.

14. Ibid.

15. Ancel, "The German-Romanian Relationship," 257. Romanian and German intellectuals shared research and ideas about the science of population transfers. This scientific form of ethnic cleansing (with and without massacres) was a common approach to stabilizing national boundaries (or expanding imperial ones) in the interwar and immediate postwar period across Europe. On the Romanian approach during World War II, see Viorel Achim, "Romanian-German Collaboration in Ethnopolitics: The Case of Sabin Manuilă," in *German Scholars and Ethnic Cleansing, 1919–1945*, ed. Ingo Haar and Michael Fahlbusch (New York: Berghahn, 2005), 139–54.

16. OKW war diary, 1:276 (January 22, 1941).

17. OKW war diary, 1:402 (June 9, 1941).

18. Ancel, "The German-Romanian Relationship," 253; Ian Kershaw, *Hitler, 1936–1945: Nemesis* (New York: W. W. Norton, 2000), 383–84. It is possible that mass deportation and not extermination of Jews was discussed. See Peter Longerich, *Politik der Vernichtung: Eine Gesamtdarstellung der nationalsozialistischen Judenverfolgung* (Munich: Piper, 1998), 292. Alternative structuralist interpretations stress that there was no preinvasion decision to kill all Soviet Jews. See Ralf Ogorreck, *Die Einsatzgruppen und die "Genesis der Endlösung"* (Berlin: Metropol, 1996).

19. Dennis Deletant, "Transnistria and the Romanian Solution to the 'Jewish Problem,'" in *The Shoah in Ukraine: History, Testimony, Memorialization*, ed. Ray Brandon and Wendy Lower (Bloomington: Indiana University Press, 2008), 159.

20. The areas around Yampil' (Yampol) and Mohyliv Podilsky (Mogilev Podolsk) were most effected. See Andrej Angrick, "The Escalation of German-Rumanian Anti-Jewish Policy after the Attack on the Soviet Union, June 22, 1941," *Yad Vashem Studies* 16 (1996): 203–38.

21. Peter Longerich, *Holocaust: The Nazi Persecution and Murder of Jews* (Oxford: Oxford University Press, 2010), 176.

22. Some of the worst documented massacres committed by Romanian forces (with assistance from Ukrainian and ethnic German helpers), which rank among the largest in the entire history of the Holocaust, occurred at the end of December in Bogdanivka, where some 48,000 Jews were killed. The recent commission concluded that "between 280,000 and 380,000 Romanian and Ukrainian Jews were murdered or died during the Holocaust in Romania and the territories under its control.... Between 45,000 and 60,000 Jews were killed in Bessarabia and Bukovina by Romanian and German troops in 1941. Between 105,000 and 120,000 deported Romanian Jews died as a result of the expulsions to Transnistria. In Transnistria between 115,000 and 180,000 indigenous Jews were killed, especially in Odessa and the counties of Golta and Berezovka. At least 15,000 Jews from the Regat (Old Kingdom) were murdered in the Iasi pogrom and as a result of other anti-Jewish measures. Approximately 132,000 Jews were deported to Auschwitz in May–June 1944 from Hungarian-ruled Northern Transylvania." See the "Final Report of the International Commission on the Holocaust in Romania: Presented to Romanian President Ion Iliescu," November 11, 2004, Bucharest, Romania. Executive Summary in English available on line at: http://www.ushmm.org/research/center/presentations/features/details/2005-03-10/pdf/english/executive_summary.pdf.

23. Deletant, "Transnistria," 160.

24. OKW war diary, 2:421 (June 27, 1941). Additional notation on the wish to separate the Romanian and Hungarian troops during combat on the Ostrog-Rowno line, July 5, 1941. In Bukovina, the German commanders of Army Group South drew the lines of administrative rule between the Romanian and Hungarian forces according to old Romanian borders (July 15, 1941, 432).

25. Croatia will not be dealt with here as a major player in the Nazi-led conquest and occupation of Ukraine, since the contingent of Croatian forces in Operation Barbarossa was small; only one regiment of volunteers was active on the Eastern Front as of the end of August 1941.

26. Holly Case, "Between Hungary and Romania: The Diplomacy of Revision and the Jews of Cluj-Kolozsvar, 1940–1944," paper presented at Lessons and Legacies Conference, Brown University, November 4–7, 2004. See also Holly Case, "Navigating Identities: The Jews of Kolozsvár (Cluj) and the Hungarian Administration, 1940–1944," in *Osteuropa vom Weltkrieg zur Wende*, ed. Wolfgang Mueller and Michael Portmann (Vienna: Verlag der österreichischen Akademie der Wissenschaften, 2007), 39–53.

27. Joseph Rothschild, *East Central Europe Between the Two World Wars* (Seattle: University of Washington Press, 1974), 197. In addition to the more common *numerus clausus*, Hungary introduced anti-Semitic legislation in 1938 with Law 15, and the restrictive Act 4 in 1939. Hungarian government spokesmen argued that the legislation, the first of its kind in East Central Europe, set an example of a just and fair approach in contrast to the terror violence of Nazi Germany and therefore should be reassuring to Jews. Exra Mendelsohn, *The Jews of East Central Europe Between the World Wars* (Bloomington: Indiana University Press, 1987), 116. Margit Szöllösi-Janze, *Die Pfeilkreuzlerbewegung in Ungarn: Historischer Kontext, Entwicklung, und Herrschaft* (Munich: Oldenbourg, 1989).

28. Weinberg, "Another Look at Hitler," 3.

29. See Ernst Klink, "Die militärische Konzeption des Krieges gegen die Sowjetunion," in Boog et al., *Der Angriff auf die Sowjetunion*, 237, 243. See also Förster, "Gewinnung," 355–56. I am grateful to David Stahel for sharing these references with me.

30. Jürgen Förster, "Der Krieg gegen die Sowjetunion bis zur Jahreswende, 1941/42: Die Entscheidungen der 'Dreierpaktstaaten,'" in Boog et al., *Der Angriff auf die Sowjetunion*, 891. Thanks to the editors for this distinction and source.

31. On the burning of Hungarian Jewish laborers in the barn at Kupyshche, see RKU Rivne to Omi Berlin, May 21, 1943, 3676-4-480, Central State Archive, Kiev; microfilm at United States Holocaust Memorial Museum, Washington, DC (hereafter USHMM), RG 31.002M, reel 13. The German report states 300 Jews, but the Hungarian account by Minister of Defense Nagy states 800 Jews. See Randolph Braham, *The Hungarian Labor Service System, 1939–1945* (New York: Columbia University Press, 1997), 39; and Randolph Braham, *The Politics of Genocide: The Holocaust in Hungary* (New York: Colombia University Press, 1981), 45. For an extremely interesting case of one Jewish laborer in the Hungarian units (in Yugoslavia), see Zsuzsanna Ozsváth, *In the Footsteps of Orpheus: The Life and Times of Miklós Radnóti* (Bloomington: Indiana University Press, 2000).

32. Braham, *Hungarian Labor System*; and Krisztián Ungváry, "Ungarische Besatzungskräfte in der Ukraine, 1941–1942," *Ungarn-Jahrbuch* 26 (2003): 125–63. See also Istvan Deak, "Endgame in Budapest," *Hungarian Quarterly* 46, no. 179 (2005), http://www.hungarianquarterly.com/no179/2.shtml, a lengthy review of Krisztián Ungváry's work, *The Siege of Budapest: 100 Days in World War II*, trans. Ladislaus Löb (New Haven, CT, Yale University Press, 2005); and Ungváry, "Hungarian Occupation Forces in the Ukraine, 1941–1942: The Historiographical Context," *Journal of Slavic Military Studies* 20, no. 1 (March 2007): 81–120; on the partisan raids, 86. See also Truman O. Anderson, "A Hungarian Vernichtungskrieg? Hungarian Troops and the Soviet Partisan War in Ukraine, 1942," *Militärgeschichtliche Mitteilungen* 58, no. 2

(1999): 353; and a Ukrainian source: M. V. Stetiukha, ed., *Vinok Bezsmertia* (Kiev: Vyd-vo politychnoi lit-ry Ukraïny, 1988), 57–61.

33. In Ungváry, "Hungarian Occupation Forces in the Ukraine," 96. Ungváry's source is: Report by Lt. Col. Cruwell on his experiences, dated May 29, 1942, RH 23/176, Bundesarchiv-Militärarchiv, Freiburg im Breisgau (hereafter BA-MA). For a similar evaluation of Hungarian brutality in the rear areas, albeit from the following year, see Ben Shepherd, *War in the Wild East: The German Army and Soviet Partisans* (Cambridge: Harvard University Press, 2004), 173–74.

34. "Notes concerning the conference that has taken place at the OKH concerning the transfer of a part of the Ukraine to the civil administration," August 27, 1941, International Military Tribunal at Nuremberg, Exhibit, RG 238, PS-197, National Archives and Records Administration, Washington, DC (hereafter NARA).

35. Cited from Ungváry, "Hungarian Occupation Forces in the Ukraine," 109. Ungváry's source for this report is the BA-MA, file N 22/173.

36. Yitzhak Arad, *The Partisan: From the Valley of Death to Mount Zion* (New York: Holocaust Library, 1979), 115–72.

37. Cited in Ungváry, "Hungarian Occupation Forces in the Ukraine," 109.

38. "Abschlussbericht," Koziatyn case, 204a AR-Z 137/67, vol. 2, 225, Bundesarchiv Ludwigsburg, Ludwigsburg, Germany (hereafter BAL).

39. Magyar Köztársaság Belügyminisztériumának Irattára, Magyar Államrendőrség Budapesti Főkapitányának Politikai Rendészeti Osztálya. Kocsis Lajos ügye. Rendezés alatt. Former Archives of the Ministry of Home Affairs of the Hungarian Republic, now the recently [1996] established Historical Archives of Hungarian State Security Agencies (Állambiztonsági Szolgálatok Történeti Levéltára, ÁBTL). Records of the Hungarian state police, political administration department, Lajos Kocsis case. Ungváry offers no archive number, but gives a date of June 1946. This investigation was based on a series of ghetto liquidation photos taken at Gajsin (sixteen photos of three massacres). The current whereabouts of the photos is unknown. See Ungváry, "Hungarian Occupation Forces in the Ukraine," 110. The West German account of events is summarized in Wendy Lower, *Nazi Empire-Building and the Holocaust in Ukraine* (Chapel Hill: University of North Carolina Press, 2005), 142.

40. "Notes concerning the conference that has taken place at the OKH concerning the transfer of a part of the Ukraine to the civil administration." August 27, 1941, Nuremberg Exhibit, RG 238, 197-PS, NARA. See also the related memo, including the High Command and the Foreign Office, stating that Jeckeln would deal with the problem: Kriegstagebuch von Roques, August 24–25, 1941, RG 242, T-501/R5/000773, NARA.

41. Randolph Braham, "Roundup and Massacre of Alien Jews," in Braham, *Politics of Genocide*, 32–35.

42. Breitman, *Official Secrets*, 64.
43. Dieter Pohl, "The Murder of Ukraine's Jews," in Brandon, *Shoah in Ukraine*, 29.
44. Ibid.
45. Randolph Braham, "The Kamianets-Podilskyi and Delvidek Massacres: Prelude to the Holocaust in Hungary," *Yad Vashem Studies* 9 (1973): 141.
46. Pohl, "Murder of Ukraine's Jews," 31.
47. On a comparable Romanian example of diplomatic tensions surrounding the Jews, see Deletant, "Transnistria," 161–67.
48. Office of Reich Commisar Koch to General Commissars, December 22, 1941, fond 1151- opis 1- delo 37, Zhytomyr State Archives, Ukraine (hereafter ZSA).
49. The scant but important documentation on this survived in the Zhytomyr regional archives. See the report from von Wedelstaedt on the "Abschiebung von ungarischen Juden," December 22, 1941, and the report on "Einrichtung von Ghettos" and Jews from the *Altreich*, sent by the RKU Koch and HSSPF Prützmann, January 12, 1942, P1151-1-137, ZSA.
50. Ungváry, "Hungarian Occupation Forces in the Ukraine," 103.
51. Ibid., 111–12, which cites a memo by Erich Kloetzel from November 23, 1943, in 78PA-AA, R101884, Foreign/counter-intelligence office, Lemberg *Abwehr* office, February 24, 1944, Political Archives of the German Foreign Office.
52. Pohl, *Herrschaft*, 82.
53. The Slovak Security Division completed a sweep in the area near Zhytomyr where German Security Division 213 was operating and supporting the First Armored Division. The Slovak Division was then assigned to the areas of Szepetowka, Polonne, and Starokonstantinow. In this same report there is mention of the building up and assignment of the Slovak Schnelle Brigade Pilfousek. Records of the Commander of the Rear Occupied Area South, August 20, 1941, RG 242, T501- roll 5, frame 000970-971, NARA. See also *Czechoslovakia in a Nationalist and Fascist Europe, 1918–1948*, ed. Mark Cornwall and R. J. W. Evans (Oxford: British Academy, 2007); and Tatjana Tönsmeyer, "Kollaboration als handlungsleitendes Motiv? Die slowakische Elite und das NS-Regime," in Christoph Dieckmann, Babette Quinkert, and Tatjana Tönsmeyer, *Kooperation und Verbrechen: Formen der "Kollaboration" im östlichen Europa, 1939–1945*, vol. 19 of *Beiträge zur Geschichte des Nationalsozialismus* (Göttingen: Wallstein, 2003).
54. I am grateful to Ray Brandon for this information. (See Guide to the Captured German Records, Guide no. 76, issued by the NARA).
55. Mark Axworthy, *Axis Slovakia: Hitler's Slavic Wedge, 1938–1945* (New York: Europa, 2002).
56. Felix Landau was convicted in 1962. See the trial records: 162/3380, vol. 1, Sta Stuttgart, II 208 AR-Z 60a/1959, BAL.

57. I am grateful to Mr. Peter Rendek for sharing these photos with me and assisting with the translation of the Slovak testimony. Thanks to Alexandr Kruglov for sharing documentation with me about the 1987 murder conviction and execution of Ukrainian policemen who shot Jews in Miropol in October 1941.

58. James Mace, "No Saint: Josef Tizo, 1887–1947" (PhD diss, Stanford University, June 2008), 430.

59. Peter Witte, Michael Wildt, Martina Voigt, Dieter Pohl, Peter Klein, Christian Gerlach, Christoph Dieckmann, and Andrej Angrick, eds., *Der Dienstkalender Heinrich Himmlers, 1941/42* (Hamburg: Christians, 1999), 241.

60. Material in this section is reprinted with the permission of the *Journal of Genocide Research*. See Wendy Lower, "Pogroms, Mob Violence and Genocide in Western Ukraine, summer 1941: Varied Histories, Explanations and Comparisons," *Journal of Genocide Research* 13 (2011): 217–46.

61. Frank Golczewski, "Shades of Grey," in Brandon, *Shoah in Ukraine*, 114–55.

62. Lower, *Nazi Empire-Building*, 91.

63. Karel Berkhoff, *Harvest of Despair: Life and Death in Ukraine Under Nazi Rule* (Cambridge: Harvard University Press, 2004), 64.

64. Franziska Bruder, *"Den ukrainischen Staat erkämpfen oder sterben!" Die Organisation Ukrainischer Nationalisten (OUN), 1929–1948* (Berlin: Metropol, 2007). The Bulba-Borovets faction looked to the legacy of the nationalist movement in eastern Ukraine, specifically the Ukrainian People's Republic formed in November 1917, but defeated by the Bolsheviks. In the summer and fall of 1941 Borovets and his recruits (in the Polis'ka Sich) operated independently of the OUN, and were based mainly in the border region of Ukraine and Belarus. On Olevs'k, see the paper presented by Jared McBride, "Eyewitness to an Occupation: The Holocaust in Olevs'k, Zhytomyr, Ukraine," at "The Holocaust in Ukraine: New Resources and Perspectives," Mémorial de la SHOAH, Paris, October 1–2, 2007.

65. Bruder, *"Den ukrainischen Staat erkämpfen oder sterben!,"* 150.

66. "Final Report of the International Commission on the Holocaust in Romania," chap. 5, p 54, http://www.ushmm.org/research/center/presentations/features/details/2005-03-10/pdf/english/chapter_05.pdf.

67. On the connection between expulsions and typhus, see Mark Levene, "The Experience of Armenian and Romanian Genocide, 1915–1916 and 1941–1942," in *Der Völkermord an den Armeniern und die Shoah*, ed. Hans-Lukas Kieser and Dominik Schaller (Zurich: Chronos, 2002), 452–54.

68. The modern versus premodern aspects of the Holocaust and their comparability to other cases of mass violence have been explored by Mark Mazower in his comparative analysis "Violence and the State in the Twentieth Century," *American Historical Review* 107, no. 4 (2002): 1158–78.

69. Similar scenarios occurred in Sokol and Jelenowka, according to this report. Tatigkeits- und Lagebericht Nr. 2 der Einsatzgruppen der Sicherheitspolizei und des SD in der UdSSR, Berichtszeit v 29.7.–14.8.1941, reprinted in *Die Einsatzgruppen in der besetzten Sowjetunion 1941/42: Die Tätigkeits- und Lageberichte des Chefs der Sicherheitspolizei und des SD*, ed. Peter Klein (Berlin: Edition Hentrich, 1997), 174–75.

70. These events are recounted in Radu Ioanid, *The Holocaust in Romania: The Destruction of Jews and Gypsies under the Antonescu Regime, 1940–1944* (Chicago: Ivan R. Dee, 2000); and Dalia Ofer, "Life in the Ghettos of Transnistria," *Yad Vashem Studies* 25 (1996): 228–74. Also see the "Final Report of the International Commission on the Holocaust in Romania," http://www.ushmm.org/research/center/presentations/features/details/2005-03-10/.

71. On the local mass violence in Bukovina, see Vladimir Solonari's research on the Romanian, Ukrainian, Jewish, and German dynamic, and the importance of the local power hierarchies, in "Patterns of Violence: The Local Population and the Mass Murder of Jews in Bessarabia and Northern Bukovina, July–August 1941," *Kritika* 8, no. 4 (2007): 749–87; and *Purifying the Nation: Population Exchange and Ethnic Cleansing in Nazi-Allied Romania* (Baltimore: Johns Hopkins University Press, 2009). See also Levene, "Experience of Armenian and Romanian Genocide," 423–62.

72. Frank Golczewski's critique of Ukrainian historians is presented in "Shades of Grey," in Brandon, *Shoah in Ukraine*, 132. Raul Hilberg's statement is from *The Destruction of the European Jews* (New York: Holmes & Meier, 1985), 1:312.

73. Andrzej Zbikowski, "Local Anti-Jewish Pogroms in the Occupied Territories of Eastern Poland, June–July 1941," in *The Holocaust in the Soviet Union: Studies and Sources on the Destruction of the Jews in the Nazi-Occupied Territories of the USSR, 1941–1945*, ed. Lucjan Dobroszycki and Jeffrey S. Gurock (New York: M. E. Sharpe, 1993), 173–81.

74. Hilberg, *Destruction of the European Jews*, 1:304; Yitzhak Arad, *The Holocaust in the Soviet Union* (Lincoln: University of Nebraska Press, 2009), 91.

75. See "Ereignismeldung UdSSR Nr. 30," July 22, 1941, R 58/214, Bundesarchiv Berlin-Lichterfelde.

76. Apparently the words of Sándor Simènvalfy, the Hungarian chief of the KEOKH office that managed aliens, as quoted in Braham, *Politics of Genocide*, 33.

77. Raphael Lemkin, *Axis Rule in Occupied Europe: Laws of Occupation, Analysis of Government, Proposals for Redress* (Washington DC: Carnegie Endowment for International Peace, 1944), 81.

CHAPTER 8

The Radicalization of Anti-Jewish Policies in Nazi-Occupied Belarus

Leonid Rein

Introduction

At dawn on June 22, 1941, after a heavy artillery barrage and aerial bombings, the forces of Nazi Germany crossed the border into the Soviet Union. The German invasion of the Soviet Union brought with it a qualitative change in the war. From the very beginning, the war was perceived by Hitler and the leadership of Nazi Germany not merely as a struggle between two armies, but rather as a struggle between two ideologies, a struggle in which all the norms of conventional warfare were supposed a priori to be set aside. The Germans intended from the very beginning to not only defeat the enemy's armed forces, but also to suppress and annihilate the real or imaginary bearers of the hostile Bolshevik ideology. For the Nazis, the main bearers of the Communist ideology were Jews. The millions of Jews living in the invaded territory were seen as the very embodiment of the proverbial Jewish bolshevism dominating the Soviet state, the image of which had been propagated by Hitler and other Nazi leaders long before their ascendance to power in Germany. Thus the extermination of Soviet Jewry was perceived not merely as the annihilation of a racial enemy, but also as a precondition to achieving Nazi geopolitical goals in the east.

Around a million Jews were living in Belarus, which was situated along the German route to Moscow, at the time of the Nazi invasion.[1] This chapter examines the extermination process of this large Jewish community, a process that underwent an escalation and radicalization in the course of the second half of 1941, starting with the persecution, humiliation, and killing of individual Jews and ending in the total annihilation of entire Jewish communities. Since the invasion of the Soviet Union in June 1941 signalled a new level of Nazi anti-Jewish policies, which had been developing since Hitler's rise to power in Germany, it is worth providing a very brief overview of these policies before June 22, 1941.

Nazi Anti-Jewish Policies before June 1941

The eight and a half years that elapsed between the National Socialist rise to power in Germany and the attack on the Soviet Union witnessed a progressive radicalization of anti-Jewish policies first in Germany proper and then also in the German-occupied countries of Europe. In Germany itself from 1933 on, Jews were subjected to a mix of legalistic and physical violence. Beginning in April 1933, a whole array of laws was introduced that isolated the Jews living in Germany from the rest of society, robbed the Jews of their means of existence, and made their life unbearable.[2] The legal discrimination was accompanied by sporadic physical violence against Jews, though Nazi leaders largely strove to restrain this brutality, realizing that the majority of Germans were against wild, illegal actions. The anti-Jewish violence reached its peak on November 9/10, 1938, in what became known as the Night of Broken Glass (*Reichskristallnacht*), a Germany-wide pogrom following the assassination of a German diplomat by a young Jew.[3] After 1938 the Nazis stepped up their efforts to get the Jews out of both Germany proper and the so-called Greater German Reich, turning the emigration process into a kind of conveyor belt, at the end of which a Jew, robbed of all of his belongings, had no other choice but to leave the German Reich.

The Nazi invasion of Poland in September 1939 marked a further evolution of Nazi anti-Semitic policies. More than three million Jews lived in Poland. Thousands of those living in Polish territories annexed to the Reich were expelled to the General Government, part of occupied Poland under German civilian administration, while those Jews living in the General Government itself were concentrated in several large towns and confined to closed ghettos, which were initially seen by the Nazis as a kind of transit station for future deportations of the Jews farther to the east.[4] It was also planned to create a Jewish reservation in the Nisko area near Lublin, where Jews were to be dumped in the most inhumane conditions with the option of deportation farther eastward. The whole plan was ultimately abandoned primarily because of the protests of the Nazi General Governor Hans Frank, who wanted to clear his own territory of Jews and not take more in.[5]

The outbreak of World War II also brought with it the escalation of the discriminatory policies directed against the Jews still living inside Germany. They were subjected to new discriminatory measures and to new limitations,[6] as well as to harassment by the SS, which increased its power with the outbreak of the war.[7] The conquest of Poland was followed by the German conquests in northern, western, and southeastern

Europe in 1940–41. In almost every country that came under Nazi rule, the arrival of Germans marked the introduction of measures aimed at robbing Jews of their civil and human rights, isolating their communities, and making preparations for future expulsions.[8]

Already after the conquest of Poland, the murder of Jews carried out, inter alia, by the infamous *Einsatzgruppen* of the Security Police and the SD began. During the period 1939–41, however, the Final Solution of the Jewish Question still meant expulsion, not murder. While the Nisko project had been abandoned, the idea of creating a Jewish reservation within or outside of Europe's borders had not. Thus, after the conquest of France in the summer of 1940 the idea of deporting all the Jews from the European continent to the island of Madagascar (the so-called Madagascar plan) became quite popular in Nazi circles.[9] But ultimately this project too was abandoned because of logistical considerations relating to the failure of Nazi Germany to defeat Great Britain.[10]

Preparations for the Genocide

The preparations for the war against the Soviet Union also included provisions for radical measures against the Soviet Jews. On March 3, 1941, Hitler himself demanded the "removal" of "the Jewish-Bolshevik intelligentsia."[11] Among the documents worked out on the eve of the invasion of the USSR, arguably the most fateful for the Soviet Jews was the agreement reached on March 26, 1941, between the chief quartermaster of the German army, *Generalmajor* Eduard Wagner, and the head of the Reich Security Main Office (RSHA), Reinhard Heydrich, which gave the *Einsatzgruppen* carte blanche to proceed against the civilian population, with special emphasis on the Jewish-Bolshevik intelligentsia and Communist functionaries.[12] In anticipation of its murderous tasks and the scope of the murders it was to carry out, the *Einsatzgruppen* increased the numbers of its personnel as compared with the Polish campaign. All four groups combined now numbered over three thousand members.[13]

Apart from the *Einsatzgruppen*, other units were concentrated in Poland on the eve of the invasion of the Soviet Union that were to participate in the "war of extermination." These included more than twenty-five battalions of the Order Police.[14] Already before Operation Barbarossa all these units had undergone an extensive radicalization. Thus, for example, even before the start of the invasion, the commander of the 309th Order Police Battalion,[15] Major Weiss, explained to the battalion's officers that the coming war would also be a war against Jews and that "the Jews regardless of age, were to be destroyed."[16] The question whether the order to exterminate all Soviet Jews existed before June 22, 1941, still plays a role in the historiography of the Holocaust.[17] The existence of such an order received by the *Einsatzgruppen* shortly before the invasion of the Soviet Union is mentioned in numerous postwar proceedings against the leaders of these units.[18] The order itself, however, has never been found. It may be assumed with a great deal of probability that references to this order in postwar trials were nothing more than a defence strategy and therefore a fabrication. The earliest order of which we know are the instructions of the chief of the RSHA, Reinhard Heydrich, to the higher SS and police leaders dated July 2, 1941, demanding the execution of only "Jews in party and state" positions.[19] The words of Major Weiss must thus be taken as an expression of his own genocidal views and not as a reflection of the state of orders at this time. It is possible to say with a high degree of certainty that there was no written order about the total annihilation of Soviet Jews with which German troops and the security troops following them came into the Soviet Union. There was, however, a mindset that was formed already during the Polish campaign of 1939 and that certainly facilitated the extermination process. It must be remembered that already in Poland the traditional German "obsession with a guerrilla movement" (*Freischärlerwahn*, as defined by German historian Jochen Böhler)[20] was coupled with the notion that Jews were the main driving force behind the anti-German resistance. German soldiers and officers fighting in Poland believed sincerely that Jews "exhort[ed] the Poles into a fanatical, anti-German frenzy."[21] This belief was coupled with a traditional German aversion to the so-called Eastern Jews (*Ostjuden*), which existed in Germany long before the Nazi ascendance to power,[22] and which led in turn to multiple assaults and even killings of Jews, characterized by Arno Lustiger as *Blitzpogroms*.[23] Generally, German soldiers in Poland absorbed the thought that Jews were fair game that could be abused, looted, maimed, and murdered without fear of serious punishment.[24]

At the same time, after 1917 the negative images of Jews generally and of Eastern Jews in particular became overlaid with images of Jewish Bolshevists."[25] It was this combination of the old and the new stereotypes radicalized by Nazi anti-Semitic propaganda that produced genocide on an unprecedented scale following the German invasion of the Soviet Union.[26]

Early Stages of the Persecution

June 22, 1941, marked a watershed for Nazi anti-Jewish policies. It opened up the final chapter in the Nazi persecution of European Jews and signalled the abandonment of expulsion plans and the gradual shift to the systematic murder of entire Jewish populations. The invasion caught the Soviet authorities unprepared. Almost a week passed before the general decision about evacuation measures was reached by the highest echelons of the Soviet regime. Priority was given to the evacuation of militarily important plants and their personnel. Regarding the population not working in war-related industries, the decision about their evacuation was left to local initiative and often to the people themselves. The policies regarding the evacuation of Jews did not differ in any way from the general evacuation policies. Many of them were evacuated to the east as employees of militarily important industries or as personnel of the local administrative apparatus, while many others fled on their own, though due to the rapid advance of the German armies not all of them managed to reach the safety of the Soviet rear.[27] There were also Jews, mostly of the older generation, who drew upon their experiences of the German occupation during World War I, when relations between German soldiers and the local population, including Jews, were mostly correct, and they viewed Germans as "cultured, industrious, wonderful people"[28] whom they had no reason to fear and from whom they had no reason to flee.

The German advance into Belarus was lightning fast indeed: Brest (except for the fortress, which managed to hold out well into July) and Grodno in western Belarus were conquered on June 22–23, 1941; the capital of Soviet Belarus, Minsk, in the center of the country, fell on June 28; while in the southeast, Gomel managed to hold out until August 10, 1941. Thus, in merely a month and a half, the whole of Belarus was in German hands. The persecution of Jews occurred practically simultaneously with the German advance.

The German invasion of the Soviet Union was accompanied from the first day by physical assaults on and murder of Jews. Both regular Wehrmacht troops and the SS and police units that followed them were eager to nip in the bud any sign of real or imaginary resistance and took it for granted that Jews formed the backbone of anti-German resistance.[29] Already on June 28, 1941, the first Jewish massacre on Belarusian territory occurred. The 309th Police Battalion, which entered the city of Bialystok[30] together with the 221st Security Division, began a genuine hunt for the Jews of the city in the course of which at least 250 Jews were killed. The persecution in Bialystok culminated when some 800

Jews of both sexes and all ages were driven by the members of the 1st and 3rd Companies of the 309th Police Battalion into a local Orthodox synagogue. The perpetrators brought a canister of petrol into the synagogue, locked the doors, and threw a bundle of hand grenades through the window. All those in the synagogue were burnt alive. The fire that spread as a result of this burning claimed the lives of more than 1,000 additional Jews.[31]

As opposed to practices in occupied Western Europe, various steps in the persecution of Jews in the Soviet territories followed one another with lightning speed and often even overlapped. Already in the first days of the invasion, throughout Belarus orders signed by the commander in chief of the German army were posted that prescribed such measures as marking Jews with white armbands featuring the Star of David, confining Jews to their homes, and conscripting all the male Jews aged sixteen to fifty to forced labor.[32] As soon as a particular locality was occupied by German forces, Jews living in it were showered with an array of discriminatory orders. Within days following the arrival of the Wehrmacht, all Jews were ordered to register themselves and were marked first by the armbands and then by the yellow patches. The marking of Jews was supposed to preclude their hiding among the local population.[33] Next, the so-called Jewish councils (*Judenräte*) were created. From the German point of view, the chief purpose of the Jewish councils was to transfer German orders to the Jewish population, to collect from Jews the so-called contributions in cash and valuables, and to provide the occupying authorities with forced workers. Whereas in occupied Poland Jewish councils consisted in many cases of the Jewish prewar leadership, in the Soviet territories, where no organized Jewish communities existed, better looking and better clothed people or those who knew German were often appointed as members of the *Judenräte*.[34] The next step was the confining of Belarusian Jews to ghettos, mostly (but not necessarily) closed, generally in the poorest neighborhoods of the cities and towns. The ghettoization orders were issued primarily by the German military administration or by local collaborationist bodies (this was the case in Mogilev, in eastern Belarus)[35] or jointly by both authorities (this was, for example, the case in Minsk).[36]

Whereas in occupied Poland ghettos usually existed for several years, in the occupied Soviet territories many of the ghettos existed only for a short period of time. According to Jürgen Matthäus, the rationale behind the establishment of the ghettos in the occupied Soviet territories was "the systematic extraction of economic value from Jews by forced labor and the smooth execution of mass murder."[37] In the Soviet territories, including Belarus, the process of isolating Jews from the rest of society overlapped with their outright murder. German soldiers proceeding into the depths of the Soviet Union were supplied with orders such as those of the commander of the Sixth Army, *Generalfeldmarschall* Walter von Reichenau, which spoke of the "necessity of the harsh but just retaliation against the Jewish subhumans."[38] German army units were followed closely by the *Einsatzgruppen* of the Security Police and SD, who were supplied with orders, as mentioned earlier, to execute the "Jews in party and state positions." In practice, already in July 1941 the murders were extended first to the so-called members of the Jewish intelligentsia,[39] and then in August 1941 to the entire Jewish male population of various localities. The murders were carried out not only by the *Einsatzgruppen* of the Security Police and SD, but by other German units as well. One of the best examples of the steady radicalization of extermination policies in Belarus and of the extension of the circle of victims were the activities of the Order Police's 322nd Battalion. This battalion arrived in Bialystok at the beginning of July 1941 and began its murderous activities by shooting small groups of Jewish civilian prisoners held at the transitory detention camp (Dulag) no. 185 in the vicinity of Bialystok under the pretext of escape attempts.[40] Only a few days later, the battalion's members took part in the shooting of "Jewish male plunderers aged seventeen to forty-five,"[41] also in Bialystok, and then during the first half of August 1941 the unit's 3rd Company carried out mass shootings of Jewish men in Bialowieza[42] and Narewka-Mala,[43] in today's border area between Belarus and Poland. The executions proceeded in a similar way: the victims were led outside the locality, compelled to lay face down in the grave dug in advance, and shot in the back of their heads. Jews murdered during the first months of the German invasion were often listed in German reports as saboteurs or partisans' accomplices.

Already the initial massacres in Belarus illustrated that German agencies of genocide did not need explicit orders from above to proceed in the most radical manner against Jews. Often the extermination orders issued by commanders of individual German units followed the less formal wishes or caprices of the senior and highest authorities. Thus, the order issued on July 11, 1941, by the commander of the police regiment Center (the 322nd Order Police Battalion was part of this regiment), Max Montua, and demanding the shooting of "all male Jews aged seventeen to forty-five detained as plunderers"[44] followed the complaints of Himmler during his visit to Bialystok in early July 1941 that the "police had rounded [up] too few Jews" and his wish "that the police members would become more actively engaged to this end."[45] In other cases, the extermination orders were issued directly by the occupying authorities at the local level on their own initiative. Thus, the arrest and murder of between four thousand and six thousand Jewish men in Brest on July 6–7, 1941, was ordered by the field commandant's office (*Feldkommandantur*) 184 without any orders from above.[46]

Beginnings of Total Annihilation

In late summer 1941 German armies were rapidly advancing through Soviet territory. The euphoria and expectation of the imminent victory reigned in Nazi ruling circles.[47] For Hitler and his entourage the time seemed to have come for implementing their visions regarding the *Ostraum*. These visions included a ruthless purging of all undesirable elements as a necessary precondition for redesigning the "Eastern space." Thus, at the meeting between Hitler and senior officials of the Third Reich on July 16, 1941, the Führer spoke of "shooting [and] resettlement" as measures to be adopted in the occupied eastern territories.[48] Christopher Browning ascribes to this meeting an utmost importance in the radicalization of the extermination process. Even though the views expressed at this meeting were little more than Hitler's visions, the Führer's cronies, including, most importantly, the SS chief Heinrich Himmler,[49] saw them as a guide to action. Already in the second half of July 1941, Himmler ordered several measures, including the expansion of local auxiliary forces in the Baltic area, Belarus, and Ukraine, as well as the reassignment of the SS Cavalry Brigade from Himmler's Command Staff to the command of Erich von dem Bach-Zelewski, the higher SS and police leader in Central Russia, for the cleansing of the Pripet Marshes area (today's border area between Belarus and Ukraine). The activities of this brigade, commanded by *SS-Gruppenführer* Hermann Fegelein, marked the transition to the systematic extermination of the entire Jewish population in the late summer and early autumn of 1941 in Belarus.[50]

The brigade received orders to comb the Pripet Marshes area and to cleanse it of "undesirable" and "German-hostile elements." One of the most notorious of these orders reached the brigade on August 1, 1941, and read as follows: "Explicit order by R[eichs]F[ührer]-SS. All Jews must be shot. Drive the female Jews into the swamps."[51] The members of the cavalry brigade tried to follow this order literally, but as reported by the commander of the horse detachment of the brigade's 2nd regiment, Franz Magill, the "driving of women and children into the swamps did not have the success it was supposed to have, since the swamps were not deep enough for sinking to occur."⁵² As can be seen here, while the initial orders received by the brigade were quite vague with regard to women, let alone children, the members of the brigade's regiments in the field pursued from the outset the politics of total annihilation, or de-Judaization (*Entjudung*), of the area of operations.⁵³ What this meant in practice was shown already in the first August days of 1941 in the little towns of Chomsk and Motol, to the east of Brest, in which a total of five thousand Jews lived.⁵⁴ In Chomsk, the members of the staff of the horse detachment and of the 2nd Squadron of the 1st SS Cavalry Regiment had driven all the Jews, including women and children, to the local church and the next morning shot all of them with machine guns at the pits outside the locality. In Motol too, all male Jews were gathered at the marketplace, while women and children were locked in the local synagogue and in a school. In the course of a few days, all of the Motol Jews were exterminated outside the locality by members of the same staff of the horse detachment and of the 1st Squadron of the 1st SS Cavalry Regiment.⁵⁵ During the next few weeks, these massacres repeated themselves in other places in the Pripet area, as a result of which centuries-old Jewish communities ceased to exist.⁵⁶ Only the so-called specialists, that is, persons who might be of some use to the murderers, were spared. According to the German historian Martin Cüppers, the horse detachments of both the 1st and 2nd SS Cavalry Regiments alone murdered about twenty-five thousand Jewish men, women, and children in the period between August 2 and 13, 1941.⁵⁷

In other parts of Belarus too, August and September 1941 marked the transition to the extermination of Jewish women and later also children, in addition to Jewish men. The process of total extermination of Jewish communities began in central Belarus and spread by the end of the year to other parts of Belarus.⁵⁸ Thus, from August 31 to September 1, 1941, the 7th and 9th companies of the 322nd Police Battalion in cooperation with *Einsatzkommando* 8 of *Einsatzgruppe* B and the National Socialist Motor Corps (NSKK) carried out an *Aktion* in Minsk, in the course of which over one thousand Jews, including sixty-four women, were shot outside the city.⁵⁹

Over the course of September 1941, hundreds of smaller localities in central and eastern Belarus were declared by the Germans to be free of Jews (*judenfrei*).⁶⁰ In Staro-Bykhov, to the south of Mogilev, for example, about five thousand Jews and "Communists," including children, were murdered by members of Ukrainian auxiliary police battalions.⁶¹ Then, in October 1941, it was the turn of large Jewish communities in eastern Belarus. On October 2–3, a large-scale massacre of Mogilev Jews took place. Members of *Einsatzkommando* 8, the staff of the higher SS and police leader of Central Russia, Erich von dem Bach-Zelewski, the 7th[62] and 9th (3rd) companies of the 322nd Police Battalion, and Ukrainian auxiliary policemen carried out the executions. The course of this mass murder was similar to previous massacres. On the first day, October 2, two thousand Jews were gathered at an abandoned factory building, where they spent a night without food or water. The next day, October 3, they were carried by lorries to antitank ditches outside of Mogilev and shot. The Germans and their accomplices murdered men, women, and children, including babies.[63]

The Mogilev massacre was followed by mass murders in Vitebsk (October 8–10, between 4,000 and 8,000 victims),[64] Borisov (October 20–21, 7,000 to 8,000 victims),[65] and Gomel (November 4, 2,365 victims).[66] In these massacres, women and children were also included among the executed. At the time of these massacres, the majority of Belarusian territory was divided into military (the rear area of Army Group Center) and civil (the General Commissariat of White Ruthenia) administrative areas. The mass murders in the last months of 1941 encompassed both these areas, even though in eastern Belarus these massacres were much more thorough. Thus, according to Christian Gerlach, whereas at the end of 1941 merely 30,000 Jews still lived in the area under military administration, the number of Jews who survived the wave of murders of 1941 in the area under civil administration was approximately 145,000.[67] There are several explanations for this difference. First of all, it must be remembered that in eastern Belarus the Jews had more time to flee and thus, upon the arrival of the Germans, there were fewer Jews; this fact facilitated the work of the Nazi killing machine.[68] However, it should also be noted that there may have been an added motivation for extermination in eastern Belarus, since the Jews living in these areas, that is, in the areas that were already part of the Soviet Union before 1939, were precisely those whom the Nazis considered to be the embodiment of Jewish bolshevism, as described so often in their propaganda. Finally, the economic factor should not be ignored. The economy in the so-called old Soviet part of Belarus was completely Sovietized and based on large industries, making it easier to dispense with the Jews, whereas in western Belarus, which had been annexed only two years before the German invasion, the Sovietization of industry was only in its early stages and there were still small businesses in which Jews played an important role.[69] At first many of them could be exploited for the German military effort, although the Nazis strove constantly to replace the Jews with non-Jews, even if in many cases this constituted an impairment of economic efficiency.

Even though the prominent role in expanding the extermination program in most of Belarus in the second part of 1941 was played by the units belonging to Himmler's SS and police apparatus, the role of other bodies active in occupied Belarus was of paramount importance too. An especially notorious role was played by the military administration, which was responsible for a large part of Belarus. Senior military commanders in both eastern and western Belarus fully shared the vision of Jews as "anti-German elements" and openly demanded the most radical measures against them, regarding them as the primary supporters of the (at this time still nascent) guerrilla movement. Thus, during the training course for antiguerrilla warfare that took place in Mogilev at the end of September 1941, the commander of the rear area of Army Group Center, which encompassed eastern Belarus, *General der Infanterie* Max von Schenckendorff, complained that "proceeding against the population is not energetic and ruthless enough" and demanded explicitly "in the event that a unit is stationed in a locality for a longer time, the Jewish quarters or ghettos are to be set up directly, if it is impossible to annihilate them [the Jews] immediately."[70] The commander of the 707th Infantry Division, *Generalmajor* Gustav Freiherr von Bechtolsheim, responsible for the General Commissariat White Ruthenia (the western part of Belarus under civil administration), issued explicit extermination orders; he defined Jews as "mortal enemies of Germandom" and demanded their "disappearance from the countryside."[71] These orders were then put into practice by the units of Bechtolsheim's division, which up to December 1941 massacred nineteen thousand people, mostly Jews, in the rural areas of General Commissariat White Ruthenia.[72] The lower levels of the German military administration shared the genocidal views of their superiors and were eager to put them into practice. In the central and eastern parts of Belarus the troops subordinated to the 221st and 286th Security Divisions (units that shared both military and administrative tasks) murdered on their own or in cooperation with the SD hundreds of Jews in the autumn and winter of 1941 under the guise of "pacifying operations."[73]

The widening of the scope of the annihilation policies also led to the search for new, more effective and impersonal killing methods. The murder of women and children became a problem for those perpetrators who had families back in Germany; their wives and children looked not all that different from the women and children they were about to murder. The commanders of the killing units were aware of this problem and thus, for example, the murder of children during the Mogilev massacre was entrusted not to members of the 322nd Police Battalion, but rather to SS men, members of *Einsaztkommando* 8, and to the Ukrainian auxiliaries.

The top echelons of the German SS and police apparatus were also aware of this problem. After attending a shooting of Jews in the vicinity of Minsk and visiting Minsk's mental asylum, Himmler ordered the commander of *Einsatzgruppe* B, Arthur Nebe, on August 15, 1941, to produce "less cruel" execution methods.[74] Gas had already been used during the euthanasia program in 1939–40 and it was utilized again in Poland to murder the inmates of mental asylums.[75] In mid-September 1941, the experiments with killings through gas installations—at this point still a stationary improvised gas chamber in a hermetically sealed room—were carried out in Minsk and Mogilev, whereby the patients of the mental asylums were used as guinea pigs. Among the patients of the Mogilev mental asylum gassed around September 17, 1941, there were some sixty Jews.[76] Even though the leading role in these first gassings was played by members of *Einsatzgruppe* B, other bodies, including the Order Police, participated as well. According to the postwar testimonies of the commander of the 322nd Police Battalion, Gottlieb Nagel, members of the battalion took part in gassings of the inmates of an orphanage in Minsk and of a mental asylum in Mogilev between November 1941 and January 1942.[77] It is unclear when the first gas vans were used for the murder of Belarusian Jews. It can be proven without doubt that two gas vans of the Diamond model and one of the Saurer model were stationed in Minsk in the spring of 1942. By the summer there were already eight gas vans operating in Belarus.[78] It is unclear, however, whether the gas vans were used at the end of 1941. One idea behind the use of the gas vans, which were employed widely in Jewish massacres in Belarus from 1942, was to make the murder impersonal and to diminish the negative effect that the shooting of Jews had upon the perpetrators' psyche.[79] The use of gas vans rather than stationary gas chambers was, moreover, designed to keep pace with the mobility of the *Einsatzgruppen* and their subordinated units.[80]

If we are to compare the course of the annihilation process in Belarus with the neighboring Baltic area and Ukraine, we can identify both differences and similarities. In the Baltic area, the annihilation of Jews was both very rapid and all-encompassing because of the large-scale collaboration of local nationalist forces. At the time when the first wave of extermination was at its height in Belarus, most of the Jews in the three Baltic countries had already been murdered: at the end of 1941 merely 40,000 Lithuanian Jews (out of 220,000 Jews who had lived there on June 22, 1941) remained alive; in Latvia close to 50 percent of the Jews were already dead by October 1941; and in Estonia, where many Jews successfully fled the Nazis, German authorities declared it free of Jews toward the end of 1941.[81]

The course of the annihilation process in Ukraine, especially in its eastern part, was similar to that in Belarus. Here too the total and systematic annihilation of the Jews of all ages and both sexes began in autumn 1941. The only difference between the neighboring countries was quantitative, as the Ukrainian Jewish population was larger than the Belarusian population. Thus, in Ukraine the massacres in large cities claimed the lives of tens of thousands of Jews.[82] It should also be kept in mind that the genocide of the Jewish population in Ukraine was related closely to German colonization and exploitation plans pursued in this country.[83]

Summary

The German invasion of the Soviet Union brought with it a radicalization of many aspects of National Socialist policies. One area in which this radicalization was most evident was anti-Jewish policy. The extermination of the Soviet Jews, which started practically from the day German troops invaded the Soviet Union and which in the late summer and early autumn of 1941 assumed a total character, was but the logical culmination of a process that started soon after the Nazi rise to power in Germany; there, robbing Jews of their civil and human rights ended with robbing them of their lives. In Belarus, we can see in the course of merely a couple of months an evolution from the extermination of certain categories of the Jewish population (Jews in state and party positions, the intelligentsia, Jewish men) to the total annihilation of the entire Jewish population regardless of sex or age.

Even if the German troops who crossed the Soviet border on June 22, 1941, did not have explicit orders to murder all the Jews, both German frontline troops and the forces following the advancing German armies carried with them a mindset that facilitated the unleashing of the genocide. The racial indoctrination to which German units were subjected; the negative attitudes toward the so-called Eastern Jews, widespread in Germany long before Hitler's ascendance to power; and the perception of Jews as, on the one hand, free game to which German soldiers became accustomed in the Polish campaign, and on the other hand, as the main supporters of the Bolshevist system and therefore the leaders of anti-German resistance, produced anti-Jewish violence practically from the first day of the German invasion of the Soviet Union. The German advance into Belarus was accompanied by a mixture of anti-Jewish measures and outright murder. The transfer to the total extermination of the entire Jewish population was a result of euphoria[84] reigning in Nazi ruling circles in the summer of 1941, when the impression was created that the victory over the Soviet Union was imminent and that the time had come for the Germans to begin the implementation of the racial rebuilding of the Eastern space.

The radicalization of the extermination policy in Belarus expressed itself in both a qualitative and a quantitative increase in the murder scope. It was to a very high degree a result of close cooperation between various occupying bodies: the SS and SD, the Order Police, local military authorities, and native collaborationist institutions. Proceedings against Jews in Belarus were based upon a mixture of racial-ideological premises that viewed all Jews as the enemies of Germandom, and of security or rather pseudosecurity considerations that saw Jews as the main instigators of anti-German resistance.

The radicalization of anti-Jewish policies in the late summer and early autumn of 1941 is probably most evident in the growing numbers of victims. If these numbers were mostly two- or three-figured in June 1941, they became four- or even five-figured toward the end of 1941. The widening of the scope of murder forced the murderers to search for new murder techniques; thus, toward the end of 1941, experimentation in the killing process began with the use of gas.

In 1941 a radical change in the very term "Final Solution of the Jewish Question" occurred as it shifted from the forceful emigration of Jews from Europe to mass murder. Belarus was a country in which this change expressed itself to the fullest extent.

Notes

1. See the data in Israel Gutman, ed., *Encyclopedia of the Holocaust* (Jerusalem: Yad Vashem, 1990), 1:170–72.

2. On the development of Nazi anti-Jewish policies see Yehuda Bauer, *A History of the Holocaust*, rev. ed. (New York: Franklin Watts, 2001).

3. See Saul Friedländer, *Nazi Germany and the Jews*, vol. 1, *The Years of Persecution, 1933–1939* (New York: HarperCollins, 1997), 267–68. See also the entry "Kristallnacht," in Gutman, *Encyclopedia of the Holocaust*, 2:836–40.

4. See Friedländer, *Nazi Germany and the Jews*, 1:160–71.

5. Bauer, *A History of the Holocaust*, 159.

6. Christopher R. Browning, with contributions by Jürgen Matthäus, *The Origins of the Final Solution: The Evolution of Nazi Jewish Policy, September 1939–March 1942* (Jerusalem: Yad Vashem, 2004), 169–78.

7. See Robert Gellately, *Backing Hitler: Consent and Coercion in Nazi Germany* (New York: Oxford University Press, 2001), 73.

8. See Browning, *Origins of the Final Solution*, 193–212.

9. The idea was actually neither a Nazi nor even a German one. It was first proposed by Paul de Lagarde as early as 1885 and taken up in the 1920s by two British anti-Semites, Henry Hamilton Beamish and Arnold Leese. See Ian Kershaw, *Hitler, 1936–1945: Nemesis* (London: Allen Lane, 2000), 320; and Browning, *Origins of the Final Solution*, who writes that the idea was raised repeatedly in the late 1930s by the Polish, French, and British governments and even by the Joint Distribution Committee (81–82).

10. Browning, *Origins of the Final Solution*, 88.

11. Ibid., 216.

12. Ibid., 216–17.

13. Ibid., 225. See also Yitzhak Arad and Shmuel Spector, eds., *The Einsatzgruppen Reports: Selections from the Dispatches of the Nazi Death Squads' Campaign against the Jews, July 1941–January 1943* (New York: Holocaust Library, 1989), vi.

14. Wolfgang Curilla, *Die deutsche Ordnungspolizei und der Holocaust im Baltikum und in Weißrußland, 1941–1944* (Paderborn: Ferdinand Schöningh, 2006), 59.

15. This battalion staged a massacre of the Bialystok Jews in the first days of the invasion (discussed below).

16. Browning, *Origins of the Final Solution*, 232–33.

17. Some historians have answered this question in the affirmative; see, for example, Helmut Krausnick, "Hitler und die Befehle an die Einsatzgruppen im Sommer 1941," in *Der Mord an den Juden im Zweiten Weltkrieg. Entschlußbildung und Verwirklichung*, ed. Eberhard Jäckel and Jürgen Rohwer (Stuttgart: Deutsche Verlags-Anstalt, 1985); others deny the existence of a general annihilation order prior to June 22, 1941. Christian Gerlach maintains that the intention to starve most of the Soviet Jews to death existed, but there were no explicit orders to this effect. Christian Gerlach, *Kalkulierte Morde: Die deutsche Wirtschafts- und Vernichtungspolitik in Weißrußland, 1941 bis 1944* (Hamburg: Hamburger Edition, 1999), 628–37.

18. See Curilla, *Deutsche Ordnungspolizei*, 86.

19. "Heydrichs nachträgliche schriftliche Einweisung der vier Höheren SS-und Polizeiführer im Osten vom 2.7.1941," reproduced in Peter Klein, ed., *Die Einsatzgruppen in der besetzten Sowjetunion 1941/1942: Die Tätigkeits- und Lageberichte des Chefs der Sicherheitspolizei und des SD* (Berlin: Edition Hentrich, 1997), 323–28.

20. Jochen Böhler, *Auftakt zum Vernichtungskrieg: Die Wehrmacht in Polen, 1939* (Frankfurt am Main: S. Fischer, 2006), 54.

21. Alexander B. Rossino, *Hitler Strikes Poland: Blitzkrieg, Ideology, and Atrocity* (Lawrence: University Press of Kansas, 2003), 27.

22. Trude Maurer, *Ostjuden in Deutschland, 1918–1933* (Hamburg: Christians, 1986), 104–53.

23. Arno Lustiger, ed., *The Black Book of Polish Jewry: An Account of the Martyrdom of Polish Jewry Under the Nazi Occupation* (Bodenheim: Syndikat Buchgesellschaft, 1995), 5.

24. Actually in Poland quite a number of German soldiers and SS men were brought before the disciplinary courts for assaults and murders of Jews. They all, however, were ultimately pardoned by the highest officials of the Third Reich. Thus, for example, *Leutnant* Bruno Kleinmischel, whose shots initiated the massacre in the locality of Końskie in the course of which twenty-two Jews were killed, was sentenced to one year imprisonment for illegal use of his weapon and manslaughter, but ultimately enjoyed the general amnesty granted by Hitler after the end of the Polish campaign. Rossino, *Hitler Strikes Poland*, 186.

25. See, for example, Wolfram Wette, *The Wehrmacht: History, Myth, Reality*, trans. D. Lucas Schneider (Cambridge: Harvard University Press, 2006), 42–43.

26. Thus *Gefreiter* G. from the 111th mountain artillery regiment wrote home: "In Bircza we have recognized the necessity of the radical solution of the Jewish question. Here one can see these humanoid beasts at home. They made a vile impression on us with their beards and caftans, with their devilish mugs. Everybody who still was not a radical opponent of Jewry was to become one here." Cited in Böhler, *Auftakt*, 48.

27. See: Ben.-Cion. Pinchuk, *Yehudej Brit-aMoatsot mul Pnej aShoa* [Soviet Jewry in the Face of the Holocaust] (Tel-Aviv: Organization for the Study of Jewish History at the Diaspora Research Institute, 1979), 73–106.

28. See the memoirs of Frida Skorokhod from Minsk, "Rimonim bli Napatsim" [Grenades without detonators], in *Minsk: Ir ve-Em* [Minsk: Mother-city], ed. Shlomo Even-Shoshan (Tel-Aviv: Organization of the Former Minsk Inhabitants in Israel, 1988), 2: 387.

29. Characteristic of this type of behavior were events in the Ukrainian city of Brusilov in July 1941. Soldiers of the 3rd Motorized Corps occupied the locality. After a German soldier was found dead, the Germans arrested three local Jews, who claimed to have nothing to do with the alleged murder. Even though the investigation was unable to prove their guilt, the three were shot all the same, because in the words of the chief of staff of the 3rd Motorized Corps, *Oberst* Ernst Felix Faeckenstedt, "Considering the well-known hostile attitude of the Jews... toward the Germans, the initiative or the complicity of the Jews in the murder of *Gefreiter* Valenkamp can be seen as proven." See Report of the Chief of Staff of the 3rd Motorized Corps, *Oberst* Ernst Felix Faeckenstedt, July 19, 1941, JM 5224, Yad Vashem Archives, Jerusalem (hereafter YVA) (original in T 314/187, cadre 000213, National Archives and Records Administration, Washington, DC [hereafter NARA]).

30. Bialystok, the largest city in western Belarus with a predominantly Polish population, was annexed by the Soviet Union in the aftermath of the German-Soviet Nonaggression Pact of August 1939. After the war Bialystok was returned to Poland.

31. Curilla, *Deutsche Ordnungspolizei*, 512–18; Ben Shepherd, *War in the Wild East: The German Army and the Soviet Partisans* (Cambridge: Harvard University Press, 2004), 66–68; and Klaus-Michael Mallmann, Volker Rieß, and Wolfgang Pyta, eds., *Deutscher Osten, 1939–1945: Der Weltanschauungskrieg in Fotos und Texten* (Darmstadt: Wissenschaftliche Buchgesellschaft, 2003), 70–74.

32. See Gerlach, *Kalkulierte Morde*, 514–15.

33. Ibid., 518.

34. In Minsk, for example, according to one version, Germans stopped ten Jewish men in the street, brought them to the former Government House and announced to them that from now on they were the *Judenrat*. According to another version, Germans stopped a group of Jews in the street and ordered those who had knowledge of the German language to step forward. An engineer, the former Communist and deputy director of the Belarusian Soviet Ministry of Industry and Trade Ilya Mushkin, stepped forward and was appointed on the spot the chief of the *Judenrat*. See *Chjornaja Kniga* [The black book], ed. Vasilij Grossman and Ilya Erenburg (Jerusalem: Tarbut, 1980), 136; and Hersh Smolar, *The Minsk Ghetto: Soviet-Jewish Partisans against the Nazis* (New York: Holocaust Library, 1989), 19–20.

35. The order establishing the Mogilev ghetto was signed by the local city administration. See "Order no. 51 of the Mogilev's city administration, September 25, 1941," M-41/274, 4–5, YVA (original in 260-1-15, State Archives of Mogilev Province, Mogilev, Belarus).

36. See "Order regarding the creation of Jewish living quarters in Minsk, July 20, 1941" (in Belarusian), in Even-Shoshan, *Minsk: Ir ve-Em*, 279.

37. Browning, *Origins of the Final Solution*, 296.

38. "Armeebefehl des Oberbefehlshabers der 6. Armee, Generalfeldmarschall von Reichenau, vom 10.10.1941," reproduced in Gerd R. Ueberschär and Wolfram Wette, eds., *Der deutsche Überfall auf die Sowjetunion: "Unternehmen Barbarossa," 1941*, new ed. (Frankfurt am Main: S. Fischer, 1991), 285–86.

39. Thus the head of *Einsatzgruppe* B, Arthur Nebe, whose activities covered most of Belarusian territory, reported on July 5, 1941, about the activities of *Einsatzkommando* 9 in Bielsk-Podliaski (then western Belarus, today Poland): "Leaders of Jewish intelligentsia (in particular teachers, lawyers, Soviet officials) liquidated." See "Operational Situation Report USSR, no. 13, July 5, 1941," reproduced in Arad, *Einsatzgruppen Reports*, 8–9.

40. See the war diary of the battalion's 3rd company: "*Auswärtiges Einsatz der PolizeiBataillon 322 in der Zeit, vom 9.6.1941 bis . . . ,*" O.53/86,

YVA (original in T.1, Central Office of the State Judicial Administration, Ludwigsburg, Germany), list 22.

41. See "Secret order of the *Oberstleutnant* of the uniformed police (*Schutzpolizei*) and commander of the police regiment 'Center' Montua, July 11, 1941," O.53/128, YVA (original in Central Office of the State Judicial Administration, Ludwigsburg, Germany), list 2. Actually the date of the massacre is not clear. Thus, according to the German historians Andrej Angrick, Martina Voigt, Silke Ammerschubert, and Peter Klein the massacre directly followed Himmler's visit to Bialystok on July 8, 1941. Christopher Browning maintains that the massacre followed Montua's order, which was issued only on July 11. See Andrej Angrick, Martina Voigt, Silke Ammerschubert, Peter Klein, Christa Alheit, and Michael Tycher, "'Da hätte man schon ein Tagebuch führen müssen': Das Polizeibataillon 322 und die Judenmorde im Bereich der Heeresgruppe Mitte während des Sommers und Herbstes 1941," in *Die Normalität des Verbrechens: Bilanz und Perspektiven der Forschung zu den nationalsozialistischen Gewaltverbrechen*, ed. Helge Grabitz, Klaus Bästlein, and Johannes Tuchel (Berlin: Edition Hentrich, 1994), 334–35; and Christopher R. Browning, *Ordinary Men: Reserve Police Battalion 101 and the Final Solution in Poland*, 2nd rev. ed. (New York: Harper, 1998), 13–14.

42. *Auswärtiger Einsatz des Polizeibataillons 322*, lists 54–55.

43. Ibid., list 57.

44. See "Secret order of the *Oberstleutnant*," list 2.

45. Quoted in Angrick, "'Da hätte man schon ein Tagebuch führen müssen,'" 334.

46. Gerlach, *Kalkulierte Morde*, 547.

47. Browning, *Origins of the Final Solution*, 309.

48. See the minutes of this meeting in International Military Tribunal, ed., *Der Prozess gegen die Hauptkriegsverbrecher vor dem Internationalen Militärgerichtshof, Nürnberg, 14. November 1945–1. Oktober 1946*, vol. 38 (Nuremberg: Sekretariat des Gerichtshofs, 1949), doc. 221-L, 86–94, here 87.

49. Himmler did not actually attend the July 16 meeting, but was informed about the course of it by Alfred Rosenberg and the chief of the Reich Chancellery, Hans-Heinrich Lammers, the next day.

50. The murderous activities of the SS cavalry brigade have been analyzed in detail by German scholar Martin Cüppers. See *Wegbereiter der Shoah: Die Waffen SS, der Kommandostab Reichsführer-SS, und die Judenvernichtung 1939–1945* (Darmstadt: Wissenschaftliche Buchgesellschaft, 2005).

51. Quoted in Gerlach, *Kalkulierte Morde*, 560. English translation in Browning, *Origins of the Final Solution*, 281.

52. "Bericht der Reitenden Abteilungs des SS Kavalerie-Regiments 2 über den Verlauf der Pripjet-Aktion vom 27.7–11.8.1941, 12.8.1941," in *Unsere Ehre heisst Treue: Kriegstagebuch des Kommandostabes Reichsführer SS,*

Tätigkeitsberichte der 1. und 2. SS-Inf.-Brigade, der 1. SS-Kav.-Brigade und von Sonderkommandos der SS, ed. Fritz Baade, Richard F. Behrendt, and Peter Blachstein (Vienna: Europa, 1965), 220.

53. According to Martin Cüppers, the term *Entjudung* as an operative goal, which meant the total annihilation of Jews irrespective of sex or age was first used by the commander of the horse detachment of the 1st Regiment of the SS Cavalry Brigade, Gustav Lombard, in his orders dated August 9 and 11, 1941. Cüppers, *Wegbereiter der Shoah*, 143–44.

54. Some two thousand Jews lived in Chomsk, and some three thousand in Motol. Motol, among other things, was the birthplace of the first Israeli president, Chaim Weizman (ibid., 144–45).

55. Ibid., 144–47.

56. Ibid., 147–65.

57. Ibid., 151, 165.

58. Gerlach, *Kalkulierte Morde*, 569.

59. The number of victims of this massacre varies between various sources. Thus the diary of the 9th (3rd) company of the 322nd Police Battalion speaks of 1,000 Jews shot, whereas a daily report of *Einsatzgruppe* B speaks of 214 persons shot. See "*Auswärtiger Einsatz des Polizeibataillons 322*," lists 65–66; and "Operational Situation Report USSR No. 73 of *Einsatzgruppe* B, September 4, 1941," reproduced in Arad, *Einsatzgruppen Reports*, 123.

60. Gerlach, *Kalkulierte Morde*, 585–87.

61. Ibid., 586.

62. It was numbered 1st before the battalion's restructuring, which took place in August 1941, and was then renamed as the 3rd battalion of Police Regiment Center.

63. *Kriegstagebuch Nr. 1 des PolizeiBataillons 322*, O.53/127 (Ludwigsburg Files), lists 109, 111, YVA.

64. Gerlach, *Kalkulierte Morde*, 596–97.

65. A peculiarity of the massacre in Borisov was that it was carried out exclusively by local policemen. This massacre has been depicted in various sources. See John Loftus, *The Belarus Secret* (New York: Alfred A. Knopf, 1982), 25–28. See also materials from the KGB interrogation of Borisov police chief David Egoff, M 41/119, YVA (original: "Interrogation Protocol of David Egoff by Soviet Security Organs," KGB Archives, Minsk, Belarus).

66. See "Tätigkeits- und Lagebericht Nr. 8 der Einsatzgruppen der Sicherheitspolizei und des SD in der UdSSR (Berichtszeit v. 1.12.–31.12.1941)," reproduced in Klein, ed., *Einsatzgruppen*, 268; and Gerlach, *Kalkulierte Morde*, 599.

67. Gerlach, *Kalkulierte Morde*, 606, 609.

68. Thus, according to the data quoted by Shalom Cholawski in Bobruysk, 25 to 30 percent of the thirty thousand city Jews managed to evacuate

themselves. In Gomel too, according to the same source, eighty thousand people left the city, many of them Jews. See Cholawski, *Be-Sufat Ha-Kilajon: Yahadut Belorussia ha-mizrakhit be-Milkhemet ha-Olam ha-Shniyya* (Tel Aviv: Yiśro'el-bukh, 1988), 48. See also "Tätigkeits- und Lagebericht Nr. 2 der Einsatzgruppen der Sicherheitspolizei und des SD in der UdSSR (Berichtszeit v. 29.7.–14.8.41)," reproduced in Klein, ed., *Einsatzgruppen*, 136.

69. See Gerlach, *Kalkulierte Morde*, 645.

70. Ibid., 644.

71. "Order No. 24 of the Commandant in White Ruthenia and Wehrmacht's Commander in Ostland, von Bechtolsheim, November 24, 1941," M 41/104, YVA.

72. Gerlach, *Kalkulierte Morde*, 615–19.

73. For example, the 350th Infantry Regiment, 45th Reserve Regiment, and 230th Reserve Battalion (all of them part of the 221st Security Division) shot or hanged at least 63 Jews in the period between October 7 and November 26, 1941, in the eastern part of Belarus and the eastern part of Russia. They also transferred at least 1 Jew to the SD. All of the murdered were portrayed in the troop reports as commissars, partisan supporters, or suspected of partisan activities. Several were executed "while attempting to escape." Reports of various units of the 221st Security Division, M.29. FR/216, YVA (original in Bundesarchiv-Militärarchiv, Freiburg im Breisgau, RH 26-221/226 and RH 26-221/22a).

74. Peter Witte, Michael Wildt, Martina Voigt, Dieter Pohl, Peter Klein, Christian Gerlach, Christoph Dieckmann, and Andrej Angrick, eds., *Der Dienstkalender Heinrich Himmlers, 1941/42* (Hamburg: Christians, 1999), 195.

75. Mathias Beer, "Die Entwicklung der Gaswagen beim Mord an den Juden," *Vierteljahrshefte für Zeitgeschichte* 35, no. 3 (1987): 404–6.

76. Gerlach, *Kalkulierte Morde*, 1069–70.

77. Ibid., 764.

78. Ibid., 765–66.

79. See Beer, "Entwicklung," 402–17.

80. Ibid., 409.

81. See the entries "Estonia," "Latvia," and "Lithuania," in Gutman, *Encyclopedia of the Holocaust*, 2:449, and 3:852, 898–99.

82. See the entry "Ukraine," in ibid., 4:1528–30.

83. On German plans regarding Ukraine and their connection to the Holocaust see Wendy Lower, *Nazi Empire-Building and the Holocaust in Ukraine* (Chapel Hill: University of North Carolina Press, 2005).

84. Browning, *Origins of the Final Solution*, 308–9.

CHAPTER 9

The Minsk Experience

German Occupiers and Everyday Life in the Capital of Belarus

Stephan Lehnstaedt

The Belarusian Soviet Socialist Republic was one of the first territories of the Soviet Union to be invaded by the German Wehrmacht in the summer of 1941. With at least 1.6 million dead from a total prewar population of 9 million, nearly one-fifth of its inhabitants died during the war.[1] In parts of Belarusian SSR and eastern prewar Poland, Nazi Germany erected the *Generalkommissariat Weißruthenien* (General Commissariat White Ruthenia), governed by *Generalkommissar* Wilhelm Kube, and based in the Belarusian capital of Minsk; it encompassed some 60,000 square kilometers, had 2.5 million inhabitants, and was divided into eleven *Gebietskommissariate*. Minsk, conquered on June 28, 1941, and liberated by the Red Army on July 3, 1944, numbered about 240,000 inhabitants before the German invasion—more than half of them died during the three years of occupation.[2] The Nazi racial war of extermination not only led to the death of a large part of the country's population, but also to the destruction of Minsk, which suffered near complete destruction in 1944.[3]

Although long neglected by historians, the German crimes and the occupation regime in Belarus are both now fairly well researched. The opening of the Communist archives during the 1990s led to the availability of previously inaccessible sources. Primarily younger German historians made use of these possibilities and produced monographs of great depth and content; unfortunately, only rarely have these research results been translated into English or made accessible via scholarly articles. Thus, when studying the fate of Belarus during World War II, not only the historical documents[4] but also the secondary literature demands knowledge of German—although Russian sources are also important.

Christian Gerlach's magisterial doctoral thesis, *Kalkulierte Morde: Die deutsche Wirtschafts- und Vernichtungspolitik in Weißrußland, 1941 bis 1944*, unfortunately remains accessible only in the original German version. Comprehensively researched and critically engaging with a multitude of sources, Gerlach's groundbreaking study delineates German plans for the occupation; the tasks of the civil administration; the exploitation of agriculture, the economy, and the labor force; as well as the murder of Jews, prisoners of war, and partisans. A second key study on this subject that fundamentally differs from Gerlach's in its emphasis was authored by Bernhard Chiari. Spreading its focus quite wide, *Alltag hinter der Front: Besatzung, Kollaboration, und Widerstand in Weißrußland, 1941–1944* looks at German administrative personnel and policemen as well as Belarusian collaborators, children, Jews, and Poles in the *Generalkommissariat Weißruthenien*. Chiari's work also pioneers the study of the local population, incorporating perspectives and experiences gleaned from Russian material.[5]

Several monographs and articles on related topics have appeared in the last few years; they investigate the other major groups and institutions involved in the occupation: the civil administration, the Wehrmacht, and the SS and police units. The latter proved crucial in implementing the mass murder of more than half a million Jews in Belarusia.[6] After *Einsatzgruppe* B worked its way through the region,[7] its men were deployed to establish a stationary police administration. Institutions such as the *SS- und Polizeiführer* (SSPF)[8] and its staff, the *Kommandeur der Sicherheitspolizei und der SS* (KdS), and various battalions of *Schutz-* and *Ordnungspolizei* were located in Minsk.[9] Commanders such as Georg Heuser and Eduard Strauch,[10] two notorious murderers convicted after the war for their crimes during German rule in *Weißruthenien*, led such units. After peaking in 1941, the number of SS and police forces stationed in Belarus stabilized at a level of about three thousand men;[11] some ten thousand local policemen provided assistance.[12] The most important figures were the *Höhere SS- und Polizeiführer* Erich von dem Bach-Zelewski,[13] and Curt von Gottberg,[14] the SSPF promoted to *Generalkommissar* as a reward for murdering the local population after the assassination of Kube in 1943 by a partisan girl.

The *Generalkommissar Weißruthenien*, Wilhelm Kube, has not been the subject of a biography.[15] Kube's office, formally subordinate to the *Reichskommissariat Ostland* of Hinrich Lohse in Riga and Alfred Rosenberg's Reich Ministry for the Occupied Eastern Territories, led the economic exploitation of the country. But it was primarily Kube who organized the deportation of workers to Germany,[16] the transportation of foodstuffs and goods to the Reich that led to impoverishment and famine, and the systematic depopulation and deindustrialization of the country.[17] The ferocious results were achieved by roughly 200 employees who worked in the large Soviet *Hochhaus* (literally: high rise) in the city center.[18] Additional Nazi institutions worked alongside Kube's civil administration, including the postal service and the railways, the latter responsible for the deportation of Jews to the Minsk ghetto.[19] It also maintained 5,700 kilometers of rail tracks, 379 stations, and 1,050 locomotives, and employed 21,000 Germans in Belarus, of which 406 were women.[20] Just like the SS and policemen, all of these German organizations could not function without help from local personnel, who greatly outnumbered their German overseers; collaboration in its many forms was ubiquitous and has been fairly well investigated.[21]

In terms of sheer numbers, most Germans in Belarus belonged to the Wehrmacht, but army practices at the lower level have yet to be sufficiently investigated; only the eastern parts of the former Soviet republic, which were under military administration, have been thoroughly examined.[22] This approach at the upper levels of the army's occupation is somewhat unjustified, as it neglects the fact that some 5,000 Wehrmacht men were stationed in Minsk alone.[23] In addition to its primary task of fighting the Soviets, the army also waged a war against partisans—some 345,000 civilians lost their lives during antipartisan sweeps carried out by the Wehrmacht as well as SS and police forces.[24] Furthermore, the Wehrmacht was responsible for the annihilation of prisoners of war; some 700,000 soldiers of the Red Army died in German custody on the territory of Belarus during the war.[25]

The Wehrmacht, SS, and civil administration could not have accomplished all this without the German civilians who worked for private companies, in restaurants and hotels, as secretaries, in healthcare, or for various Nazi Party organizations. At the beginning of 1942 in Minsk alone there were some 1,800 German women, of which 850 worked outside the home; the others were married housewives.[26] In addition, some 5,000 ethnic Germans (*Volksdeutsche*) lived in the *Generalkommissariat Weißruthenien*, most of them in Minsk and its immediate surroundings.[27] But these people were too heterogeneous as a group to attract greater attention.

While the German occupation of Belarus is rather well researched, the same cannot be said about the fate of those under occupation. The victims of the Nazis remain quite passive in almost all studies. They are more or less objects in German hands, and, with the notable exception of antipartisan warfare, their agency and scope for action have not been taken into account. The fate of the Jews has at least found some interest,[28] and the Minsk ghetto, one of the biggest in Europe with well over one hundred thousand inmates, has garnered a certain degree of attention, even if there is no monograph available.[29] It is also quite remarkable that the extermination camp of Maly Trostenez, situated just outside of Minsk, where a six-figure number of Jews was murdered, is still almost unknown, and that only one larger work examines it.[30]

These works primarily describe the concrete crimes of the occupation. Specific surveys examining the occupiers' everyday life,[31] however, and the characteristics of their actions in Belarus, as well as the concrete motivations for such behavior, are lacking. This chapter attempts to fill this gap in the record. It examines the perception of everyday life[32]—and everyday violence—held by Germans in Minsk. As such it seeks to answer the questions, to what extent did the Minsk experience differ from that of other occupied cities in eastern Europe—mainly from Warsaw—in 1941 and how did the self-perception of the Germans contribute to the radicalization of the war of annihilation? First, I will outline the violence in the initial year of the occupation and also examine the degree to which it was noticed by the occupiers. Second, I will consider the Germans' perception of the local Belarusian and Jewish population as well as their self-perception as occupiers. Finally, I will analyze virtually private crimes such as individual cases of looting, rape, and murder, and how they were integrated into everyday life. Such an inquiry will show that force and oppression were quite natural for the Germans in Minsk.

Witnessing Violence

When the Germans occupied Minsk on June 28, 1941, they brought with them not only the military power of the Wehrmacht but also the brutality inherent in a *Vernichtungskrieg*. The campaign against the Soviet Union was planned as a war of annihilation and was conducted as such. Until September 1, Minsk belonged to the zone of military administration, and the first measures against the local population started immediately after conquest. Approximately three weeks later, on July 19, the *Feldkommandantur* ordered the formation of a ghetto that soon incarcerated some 106,000 Jews.[33] It encompassed two square kilometers, lacking both electricity and a supply of drinking water.[34] And while it was not nearly as much of a showcase as its Warsaw counterpart, almost every German living in Minsk for more than just a few days would have visited it.[35]

The Jews from Germany were of special interest: some sixteen thousand arrived in Minsk in November 1941.[36] In order to provide them with accommodation, the Germans murdered more than ten thousand local Jews beforehand, so that their quarters would be available for the deportees from the Reich.[37] Separated from the local Jews, the occupiers easily identified their Jewish countrymen, and Wehrmacht physician Wolfgang Lieschke reported already on November 13, two days after the first train from Hamburg had reached Minsk, that rumors about the arrival of German Jews were spreading.[38] This group of deportees was so well known among the Nazi occupiers that a secretary even managed to talk to a Jewish woman from Frankfurt—the hometown of both. This deportee told the secretary that the Nazis had already murdered some of her relatives in Minsk, who were also from Frankfurt.[39] On November 22, Lieschke wrote in a letter to his wife that one could hear dialects from Hamburg, Frankfurt, and Cologne among these Jews, thus clearly indicating that he had already spoken to them.[40] He appreciated the deportations, for now rooms in Germany had been freed up for those affected by air raids.[41]

The Wehrmacht also operated a camp for prisoners of war, Stalag 352, which soon held roughly one hundred thousand soldiers[42] and thirty thousand male civilian inhabitants of Minsk between the ages of eighteen and forty-five.[43] The latter were preventatively arrested immediately after the conquest of the city and released only some time later. The camp itself was known for its high mortality rate owing to malnutrition.[44] The officer Carl von Andrian, stationed in Minsk, reported that prisoners more than once ate the corpses of fallen comrades.[45] The occupiers witnessed on a daily basis endless columns of ragged prisoners walking all the way to the Reich on the downtown roadway. The Germans could not help but see and hear how the defeated enemy soldiers beseeched their fellow countrymen for a piece of bread—sometimes dropping unconscious on the spot and dying owing to malnourishment.[46]

But it was not just the soldiers of the Red Army who were starving. The field doctor Wolfgang Lieschke correctly observed that the supply of the city's inhabitants depended on the mercy of the Wehrmacht.[47] Even two months after the invasion the situation was strained, although no longer catastrophic—nevertheless nine thousand people had already starved to death.[48]

It was also in the Minsk POW camp that soldiers of the German 354th Infantry Regiment together with only eight to ten members of the *Einsatzkommando* 8 of *Einsatzgruppe* B shot several thousand Jews in July 1941.[49] In October, the 12th *Schutzmannschaftsbataillon* with 250 Lithuanians was deployed in Minsk and murdered other Jews.[50] Additionally, the gruesome so-called antipartisan warfare already had begun in 1941. During this year, sections of the notorious 707th Infantry Division under its commander *Generalmajor* Gustav von Mauchenheim genannt von Bechtolsheim, together with subordinated units, killed roughly 20,000 people, half of them Jewish, in the vicinity of Minsk.[51] According to Bechtolsheim, commander in chief in *Weißruthenien*, "the Jews have to disappear from the countryside, and the gypsies are to be annihilated, too"—and although it should not be the Wehrmacht's duty to "resettle" the Jews, where smaller groups were found they were to be "handled by oneself," that is, executed.[52]

Both the local population as well as the German occupiers noticed these crimes and even approved of some of them. The murder of the Jewish rural population was especially welcomed, for often the Jews were thought to be the heads of partisan units; killing them thus meant ending the partisan threat. These executions were placed in the context of *Bandenkampf* (literally: battle against gangs); with this word the Nazi leaders tried to avoid the term "antipartisan warfare," for this might have legitimized the resistance movement.[53] Thus an asymmetrical antonym was created for the term "soldier," a wording used only for the Wehrmacht. This procedure increased the delegitimization of resistance[54] while simultaneously legitimating murder. A typical *Bandenkampf* report by the 707th Infantry Division dating from October 1941 spoke of 10,940 prisoners, of whom 10,431 were shot—their own losses were 7 men; ninety rifles were found with the partisans.[55]

Later in the occupation, it was primarily the SS who conducted these operations and the accompanying executions; during their time in Minsk, everyone serving at the KdS took part in at least one of these mass murder operations.[56] Neither the SS men nor the other Germans ever questioned the legitimacy of these measures. Already in 1941 many occupiers nourished the hope that a "big mass mortality" might start among the partisans.[57] If skepticism existed at all, it was directed against the manner in which the *Bandenkampf* was conducted,[58] although its cruelties were rarely considered more than "aggravating occurrences."[59] More than once Carl von Andrian noted mass murder committed by SS and police units, often with Wehrmacht troops, in his diary. He complained about the soldiers' lack of discipline as they sometimes looted the corpses after the crime.[60] And although Andrian occasionally had fundamental concerns about these deeds, his concerns—in keeping with a form of "compassion" that was widespread among the occupiers—typically related to the circumstances in which the murders were conducted, not the murders themselves.

Even Germans who did not have much contact with the resistance movement—such as railway men—appreciated the violence against the population.[61] Such thinking can be seen in an article from the local occupation paper *Minsker Zeitung*,[62] which celebrated the execution of 150 "members of sniper gangs" with the words: "A hard, but fair judgment."[63] Thus it became an everyday phenomenon in *Weißruthenien* to see hanged men and women by the roadside with labels denoting them as gang members.[64]

At first violence and even executions generated a certain interest, and some occupiers actually found it fascinating to watch them. The most prominent Nazi voyeur was *Reichsführer-SS* Heinrich Himmler, who on August 15 accompanied a mass murder expedition of Police Battalion 322 in the vicinity of Minsk.[65] In contrast to this spectacular event, gradual death in the ghetto and on the streets, the exploitation and starvation of the local population, or the misery of the Red Army prisoners all soon became ordinary aspects of everyday life. When curiosity was stilled, the Germans reacted with callousness toward and approval of the surrounding violence. Criticism was neither typical nor frequent.

German Life in Minsk

Nothing like the immense and brutal occupation of Minsk that developed in 1941 had occurred in eastern Europe up to this time. Warsaw, the biggest occupied city east of Berlin, had a ghetto with some five hundred thousand Jewish inmates, and although it was much more a tourist attraction than its Minsk counterpart, and although starvation and mass death were visible there too, the excessive violence of open mass murder had not yet reached the former Polish capital. The annihilation of the Jews of Warsaw in the Treblinka death camp did not start until July 1942, the Warsaw ghetto uprising occurred in 1943, and the Polish Warsaw uprising in the whole city took place in 1944. In Minsk in 1941, Nazi occupation reached a new level of radicalization, whereas in Warsaw criticism of German policies or at least compassion for the ghetto inmates was not as rare.[66] Further to the east, however, most of the Germans in towns approved of this kind of regime.

In their eyes, the local population of Belarusians and Jews consisted only of subhuman beings (*Untermenschen*) not worth caring about. At first they were just defeated enemies whose country was to be conquered. But even before the occupation, Nazi propaganda created a certain image of these people, one that was spread by word of mouth and amplified by Nazi scholarship. In official announcements, the Belarusians were declared to be a mixture of eastern Baltic and eastern European races, and they were viewed with disdain, though on the Nazi racial scale—because of some Nordic "additives"—they were above Poles,[67] notwithstanding their alleged lesser intellectual abilities compared with other Slavs.[68] And despite the establishment of a minor collaborating regime, most of the occupiers saw Belarusians as subhuman beings.[69]

These racial categories proved highly relevant in determining the nature of contact between the occupiers and the locals. In general, Minsk seemed strange and different to the Germans. The overwhelming first impression was that of a heavily destroyed, rather primitive city, whose poor inhabitants lived in desperate and dirty circumstances. The physician Wolfgang Lieschke wrote to his wife that he had seen riffraff, unsavory elements, and barely dressed people with beastlike faces.[70] This widespread impression corresponded very closely to the propaganda picture,[71] and Carl von Andrian summarized his observations in this regard by assessing that agitation against the Jews had been so successful that no one any longer felt that Jews were human.[72] These perceptions of the local inhabitants did not differ much in Warsaw and Minsk.[73] Nevertheless, as Belarus was a much poorer country than Poland, better living conditions existed in the more prosperous city of Warsaw. Racist attributes, based on the linkage of external factors—such as living conditions—and internal characteristics, were thus far more unfavorable in the former Soviet Union.

To increase the efforts of collaboration, orders instructed soldiers to win over the locals through kindness and good nature.[74] Yet orders demanding consideration were generally issued because actual German behavior proved far different—and this was also the case in Minsk.[75] Rarely did even Belarusians working for the occupiers reach a higher status than that of useful servants, and as long as the supply of forced laborers did not run dry there was no necessity to care about individual fates. A foreman at Organization Todt, when asked by interrogators in 1971 about his assignment in Minsk, reported quite airily about 150 Jewish workers who were regularly replaced after two weeks because of exhaustion. The foreman did not care that these men were murdered after being exchanged, as they were in his view not really hardworking.[76]

Other locals were seen as a threat, and fear accompanied the Germans wherever they travelled in the region.[77] After sunset they were only allowed to go outside in groups of at least two,[78] and they always needed to be wary of assassination attempts. In October 1941, a *Reichsbahn* employee wrote that one was not safe even hundreds of kilometers behind the front or in a city like Minsk.[79] Already in 1941 a climate of distrust, suspicion, and fear developed among the occupiers—they viewed the local inhabitants as untrustworthy.[80] Fear among the Germans in Warsaw only emerged early in 1943, whereas it was manifest in Minsk right from the beginning of the occupation. Based on a subjective and partially irrational notion,[81] the community of the occupiers believed they were constantly threatened from outside their tight group: all locals became malicious, ignoble enemies.

In stark contrast to these abject images stood the perception of the occupiers' own existence as Germans in Minsk. Nazi ideology provided a clear default for German self-perception. *Generalkommissar* Wilhelm Kube later expressed it with the pathetic words that anyone going eastward had to be the best guy possible, someone who stood fast for the German people and the Reich.[82] In fact, even the most convinced Nazi could not avoid recognizing that this was more or less wishful thinking with no grounding in reality. The more that these ideas failed to correspond to reality, however, the more the leaders tried to convince their subordinates of the *Herrenmenschen* concept.

Of even greater relevance for self-perception was everyday life, because here all the advantages of an occupier's existence—especially in contrast to the locals' standard of living—became quite obvious. The occupier not only heard why he was superior to those conquered, but he also saw, felt, and tasted it as well. This was quite evident when looking at the accommodation of the Germans. They lived in the city center built in the Soviet style, close to the administrative buildings. In the *Hochhaus*, a multistorey house with the offices of the *Generalkommissariat* and the *Stadtkommissariat*, there were also several flats for employees. As many parts of Minsk consisted of wooden dwellings—which led to the widespread impression of a poor town[83]—only some newer stone houses from the Stalinist period seemed acceptable to the occupiers; in contrast to Warsaw, an actual German quarter, separated and barricaded, was not established. Living in the town center also proved beneficial to the Germans for short distance travel. This became especially important because, owing to power shortages, public transportation did not resume before May 1943, and only from October 1942 onward could the Germans rely on a bus operated by the *Ostbahn*, which commuted between the city's major institutions every two hours.[84]

Only a few occupiers had their own apartment; most of them shared quarters or lived in barracks or residential homes. Here they were stacked together with their colleagues. The authorities rarely allowed mixed homes; males and females did not live together. Since communal meals were the norm in these accommodations, individuals spent the majority of their time with their colleagues. The head of the quarters generally organized leisure activities, as this guaranteed a supervised occupation. Since they had not been built as hostels, houses rarely met the demands of the Germans, making modifications indispensable. Thus, for instance, the Wehrmacht initiated a competition for the three most beautiful rooms. Soldiers acted as painters, carpenters, or decorators; here the talent to organize—that is, buying, commandeering, and stealing rare goods—was essential. From the German perspective, theft was no longer a crime, because they only utilized things that were allegedly unused or useless for their original purpose.[85] Moreover, these items were just gathered from ruins, where only defeated enemies lived.[86]

Yet it was not like home. For example, the 127 postmen in Minsk all lived with their colleagues in rooms that held two or more occupants; this had nothing in common with an apartment in the Reich, especially with a custodian constantly checking on cleanliness and order. In every respect, reality differed from the propagated ideal of German *Gemütlichkeit*.[87] Small, messy, and inadequately heated quarters remained the norm, not the exception.[88] Strictly separated from the men, 130 female employees of the Reichsbahn lived in rooms containing four to six persons. While the possibility of washing and ironing clothes existed, with only one common room there was not much space for relaxation.[89]

At least relaxation was not a problem for male soldiers; the Wehrmacht's central casino advertised seventy "fresh, young" Belarusian waitresses.[90] These girls, however, were an exception when it came to contact with the locals. Already separated from the occupiers by spatial barriers, an additional language barrier existed. Only a few inhabitants of Minsk spoke German, and even fewer Germans spoke Russian or Belarusian. But this speechlessness was fostered by the Nazi leaders because fraternization needed to be avoided at all costs. Only in March 1944, for instance, almost three years after the invasion of the Soviet Union, did railway men have the possibility to acquire a textbook of "one thousand Russian words" for private study.[91] The language barrier proved to be a serious obstacle for the occupiers, for even as late as 1943 the *Generalkommissariat* had only one German employee capable of speaking Belarusian—and he was to be transferred to Poland.[92] The occupiers relied almost completely on interpreters, but even large institutions like the Organization Todt had only a few and mostly unreliable translators.[93]

The locals certainly did not welcome contact with the Germans, and because of the linguistic and spatial barriers it was hardly possible in any event. However, the occupying authorities only rarely desired such contact anyway. The Nazi regime organized a vast array of leisure-time amusements exclusively for Germans. Many of these activities were quite popular, and of course it was much easier to participate in them than to seek one's own personal experiences in such unfamiliar surroundings. Entertainment in the evening aimed to create social activities for both men and women while stifling individual initiative. Whether Minsk's policemen played the accordion or acted as comedians and singers,[94] or whether Belarusian entertainers appeared in front of Wehrmacht soldiers,[95] it was not merely a form of amusement; the men were required to attend. Absence was seen as antisocial and above all as separation. Consequences could range from informal exclusion by one's companions to formal exhortations by superiors. On the one hand, most men happily joined these diversions; on the other hand, they rarely had any alternative.

In Belarus, very few periods of unorganized free time existed for the occupiers. Apart from the fact that contacts outside of the office or unit were rare, there simply were no possibilities for such events to occur. Cinema screenings were booked by the authorities, as were theaters; the few bars and cafés open to Germans were overcrowded, whereas all others were off limits to them. As the city almost completely lacked movie theaters, the occupiers had to build cinemas to ensure an adequate supply of entertainment for themselves. They did so by erecting a standardized wooden house with enough space for 450 persons; all material was delivered from the Reich.[96] This cinema and another Soviet-built cinema were the sole possibilities to see a movie individually—all other screenings were organized.[97]

Radio provided another type of entertainment, though this was also experienced mainly in the common rooms and therefore became yet another joint activity for the occupiers. The Nazis established channels that broadcast both distracting, light fare as well as more educational material all across Europe. A central program was designed to prevent homesickness; it therefore mainly consisted of folk music and popular local texts from across the Reich.[98] Blatant Nazi propaganda was rare. The Wehrmacht opened the first broadcast station in August 1941; this was later transformed into *Landessender* Minsk (State Broadcasting Minsk) and was governed by the civil administration.[99] One can hardly overestimate the importance of radio broadcasts—but in fact it is hard to establish it exactly, for no audience rates were measured. The high demand is illustrated by the fact that the Wehrmacht failed to supply enough radio sets; even a senior officer like Carl von Andrian constantly noted either listening to the broadcast or voicing his anger that his reception failed.[100] Particularly popular were programs like *Klingende*

Feldpost (literally: vocalized army postal service), which read letters to and from home and arranged contacts with female pen pals.[101]

Other forms of organized leisure activities included theater, concerts, and opera. Here Minsk differed only partially from Warsaw, mainly because fewer activities were available owing to its smaller size. Because of the severe damage done to the city in 1941, it was primarily office buildings that offered space where performances could be staged. Besides movies, the railway directorate offered several concerts and variétés on Saturdays and Sundays.[102] In 1941, the less prohibitive racial barriers erected by the Nazis allowed occupiers to visit shows at the Belarusian theater, where in one instance *Eugene Onegin* was performed.[103] But apart from this occasion, most of the performances were to be watched by exclusively German audiences.

In general, entertainment and not ideological indoctrination dominated the Germans' spare time. This fact was widely appreciated for three reasons. First, this distracted the men from duties that were tough and violent. Second, in a new und strange environment, it served as a bridge to their homeland and offered some common activities. Third, it offered the opportunity to spend time with comrades and thus helped establish a community of friends in a foreign and inimical environment. Of course, the setting of these leisure activities was quite strict, and separating oneself from the group was not encouraged. Other leisure-time activities were rare; choices were generally limited to various organized events. Even books, a popular form of escape for those uninterested in company, were only rarely available and only in the later years of the war.[104] The Nazi claim to control all aspects of life became especially visible among the occupiers. Civil and military institutions intended to dissolve the border between public and private space, and their totalitarian grasp did not stop at the limits of the private sphere; instead it was invasive.[105]

The type and nature of leisure-time pursuits also contributed to the radicalization of the occupation in Minsk, even if this was not so obvious to contemporaries. They isolated the Germans from the locals, which meant that prejudices could not be corrected and were even reinforced. The occupiers were welded together because their colleagues were the only individuals they had contact with. These people shared the same experiences, impressions, and feelings in the same environment around the clock. This newly established community of occupiers was perceived as a great political, social, and cultural achievement, especially when contrasted with Belarusian life. It was seen as a value in itself and as a reward for their battles and efforts. Therefore it was to be conserved and defended by any means.

The Community of Occupiers

Of course, Germans did negatively perceive various aspects of the occupation in Belarus. As previously mentioned, many of these complaints resulted from the strange new environment and the absence of family and friends. Only rarely were those arriving from the Reich happy about serving in Minsk, and apart from some idealistic letters written home, most commented skeptically or critically on the living conditions.[106] Compared to France or Warsaw, occupation duty in Belarus was indeed full of privations.[107] The climate was harsh, heating installations were often inadequate, and the buildings lacked adequate insulation, so that winter was hard even in the cantonment.[108] Tap water was not available, and even in Minsk water had to be boiled before drinking.[109] Because of a lack of proper quarters, soldiers frequently slept in tents, which was an especially aggravating circumstance.[110] In Minsk, several men became ill and had to be sent home because they were not fit for "a job in the east."[111] Frequently, official documents declared that the mood among the occupiers was rather negative owing to the unpleasant general circumstances in which they lived and worked. After having gathered some experience on the job, *Generalkommissar* Kube wrote that he required only strong Germans accustomed to austerity.[112]

It is hardly surprising that the organized spare time and the resulting community quickly became an appreciated perk for the occupiers. Even if the first impressions were negative, the vast majority of the Germans soon became accustomed to the conditions in Minsk.[113] This was not only because of the commodities and care offered by the occupation authorities, but also the potential material gains. Therefore the perception of violence played a vital part, for soon it was natural not only to witness it or carry it out when ordered, but also to use it on one's own initiative for personal advantage. This aspect of the war against the Soviet Union was unique; although occupiers of all eras and areas have always tried to profit from their victories, the implicitness with which violence was applied reached a new dimension in Minsk. Such practices only emerged in Warsaw in 1942.[114]

Already in 1941, privately committed crimes were frequent in Minsk. It was rather common to rob locals, to beat, rape, or even murder them. As long as discipline and obedience existed, the authorities did not mind. Violence was so natural that even the use of service weapons within the city limits caused no alarm. Shooting in the air was an ordinary display of joy while drinking and partying.[115] Guns were used so frequently that even the number of German victims multiplied; the reckless handling of weapons caused casualties more than once. If such actions turned out to be accidents, punishment was comparatively light. This is especially true if locals were the victims; a slap on the wrist did little to prohibit the use of guns and even led to a greater tolerance of violence. The Minsk *Sondergericht* in 1942 sentenced a railway employee to a fine of 450 reichsmarks for accidently killing a female Belarusian. In cases of manslaughter of Germans, punishment was more severe; another railway employee was sentenced to one year in prison.[116]

Rank and file occupiers profited from the Nazi racial state, especially by expropriating the property or possessions of Jews.[117] When the authorities drove Jews out of their homes and into the ghetto, they also organized the looting of private possessions,[118] including the theft of furniture, valuables, money, and also clothing such as fur coats.[119] In Minsk, even foodstuffs were taken from Jews arriving in deportation trains from Germany, and they were then handed out to the staff in the kitchen of the security police as "Jew sausage" (*Judenwurst*).[120] Furthermore, the occupiers could buy confiscated property stored at the opera after acquiring vouchers that cost considerably less than the actual value of the stolen items.[121] Particularly disgusting is a story related by a Minsk police secretary after the war. After visiting a dentist for a toothache, she was told that it required a filling. The dentist wrote a medical certificate enabling the woman to receive three gold wedding rings from her superior to be melted down for the filling. These three rings were quite obviously looted from Jews,[122] and such events graphically highlight the connection between the murder of locals and the well-being of the occupiers. And although certainly not all Germans in Minsk became murderers themselves, they could not avoid noticing that their actions and their greed made them direct profiteers of the Holocaust.

As the Jewish population in particular lacked all rights, the Germans had almost nothing to fear when plundering them. Organizing goods—which actually meant stealing—was so widespread among the occupiers that even the local newspaper *Minsker Zeitung* devoted an approving article to the topic.[123] Further profit was possible by bringing food from the countryside to town or by selling stolen items on the black market—which, although not as large as in Warsaw, reached a considerable size in Minsk owing to the constant movement of troops through the city on their way to the front.[124] All these material gains led to a certain satisfaction among the occupiers.

As individuals increasingly accepted their own place and situation in the occupied east, the acceptance of crimes against the local population also grew. In this respect, one further point has to be mentioned when considering the normalcy or approval of violence: alcohol. One can hardly overestimate the influence of hard and constant drinking in the east, and there was a clear relationship between murders the Germans committed and their degree of alcohol consumption. This attitude was common at all levels of the occupation hierarchy, not only during leisure time but also on the job.[125]

The official distribution of spirits was supposed to relieve the occupiers from their onerous duties. Binge drinking among SS and police units after executions and antipartisan warfare was notorious at the time.[126] At the Minsk *Sicherheitspolizei* (SiPo) too, when colleagues went on a bender, it was an indicator to those not directly involved that another murder operation had concluded.[127] Here alcohol had a numbing effect and was utilized to forget one's own terrible deeds.[128] On the other hand, it ensured comradeship after the crime and helped ease the task of performing further massacres, because they were connected with the subsequent somewhat joyful event of collective binge drinking.

Several witnesses testify that within the Minsk police force, drinking took place not only during and after duty, but also deep into the night. More than once employees were awakened and pulled out of their beds to carouse with their colleagues. Of course female secretaries were particularly popular; they would be called for note taking or stenograph service, but were actually seduced into sexual intercourse.[129] Anyone refusing a bottle or isolating themselves from the collective flush was soon subjected to peer pressure[130] and was suspected of being weak or effeminate; comradeship as understood here staged a cult of masculinity that enforced drinking,[131] as nonparticipation was punished with exclusion from the community of occupiers. Thus binge drinking among the comrades served to consolidate cohesion.[132] When liquor was unavailable, there could be no real relaxation and recreation. Wolfgang Lieschke wrote to his wife that with only small amounts of alcohol the atmosphere among his comrades did not reach "the usual high."[133]

Even the highest ranks were not immune to alcohol abuse. *Generalkommissar* Kube and his immediate subordinates were rumored to be drinking too much spirits.[134] Eduard Strauch, the head of Minsk's security police, was given a disastrous evaluation by his superior. He wrote that Strauch was actually unsuited to commanding subordinates; he was described as animalistic, impulsive, explosive, and rarely logical. His character seemed to be imbalanced, and in the review one can read: "Most influential is this side of his personality when having drunk alcohol. The personal behavior of the leader is—especially because of binge drinking—not without influence on his subordinates."[135]

The many letters reporting alcohol abuse usually resulted only in reminders to remain abstinent. Only in the case of Strauch was a relocation seen as absolutely necessary—in 1943—and he continued his career as SS-commander in Wallonia. His drinking problem was only seen as a result of the conditions in Minsk, and a general understanding of the hard living and working conditions led to a lenience that applied to all occupiers. Because of the nature of duty in the east, it seemed somehow natural that higher amounts of alcohol were consumed there than elsewhere. As it was so common among the Germans in Minsk to drink spirits every day, even the *Minsker Zeitung* celebrated—contrary to a policy that tolerated but officially condemned alcohol abuse—the restoration of a vodka distillery. The Wehrmacht operated this model plant that produced half-liter bottles thought to "strengthen" soldiers.[136]

A Nazi Society in the East

Before German troops arrived in Minsk, the Wehrmacht, SS, and civilian agencies had already committed numerous crimes during their two years of occupation in eastern Europe. But the extensive massacres and the everyday violence the Germans planned and carried out in the Soviet Union possessed a hitherto unknown dimension. The occupiers quickly adapted to daily life in Minsk, which became even more extreme than in occupied Warsaw. They rapidly caught up with and then surpassed the radical nature of life on the Vistula: when the occupation of Poland and Warsaw is compared to the Soviet Union and Minsk, it is clear that a drastic radicalization occurred in 1941.

Violence played a vital part in the occupier's everyday life in Minsk. On the one hand, Germans viewed it as a somewhat external phenomenon not concerning them, because its victims were Jews and Belarusians. On the other hand, the occupiers carried out such practices. In any case, it needed to be integrated into everyday life, as it took place both in the vicinity of and even directly in Minsk itself. The Germans did so not only by accepting such violence, but soon also by approving it. Legitimization was easy to find, and indeed several reasons made murder a seemingly normal, logical consequence of one's presence in the east. Violence became so common that it was soon accepted for private use, too.

Homicide or at least force seemed the only way to secure the occupier's status, to guarantee well-being and material status and to protect comradeship. Furthermore, it was the necessary measure to express a perceived natural superiority over local Jews and Belarusians and to defend

German culture against primitive, uncivilized savages. The mix of utilizing, experiencing, and finally appreciating violence led to an ever-increasing circle of brutality and murder. A normal life in Minsk with all its inherent massacres meant that murder was no longer a taboo and thus could be committed again and again.

This is somewhat surprising, for in many ways the perception of the inhabitants and the self-perception of the occupiers only differed minimally between Minsk and Warsaw in 1941.[137] Alas, these small discrepancies made a tremendous difference. Thus, for instance, the Jews of Warsaw were at least viewed with compassion by a smaller section of the German population, whereas in Minsk the correspondence of the area with propaganda images—and the foreignness of the new arrivals—was greater. Here one's perceived superiority was also viewed as a given and absolute because everyday life was enclosed around a tight-knit community and the locals were excluded from nearly all social events. Furthermore, after its conquest Minsk did not present itself as a wealthy city with an impressive heritage and culture, but rather as a ruined and poor Soviet town. Another important aspect was the perceived threat posed by the locals to the Germans. In contrast, Germans only began to feel under siege in Warsaw at the end of 1942.

In Minsk, everyone could envisage a newly constituted community of occupiers, although it by no means accorded with the Nazis' racial image.[138] The Germans only very generally fit into the propagated ideal of a master race; their actions and their self-perception were driven by other criteria. What really mattered for the everyday suppression of the locals were not only racial conceptions, but also very strict definitions of "us" and "them,"[139] the latter word encompassing all those who were not occupiers. This classification made Germans the only humans in town; all others were classified as subhumans or even nonhumans. Such thinking proved extremely relevant to the atmosphere of violence and murder, for there was no need to consider the others.

Sociology teaches us that even marginal and seemingly incidental changes in a society can have serious consequences for the self-perception of individuals. Every change in the position of others implies a change in one's own position.[140] In the east, a completely new society was constructed around the two poles of the occupiers and the occupied, and for both sides their former lives and roles underwent a kind of landslide change. While the locals were totally degraded, the Germans were ennobled and now possessed a sole and undisputed mastery. The subjectively perceived value of belonging to the community of occupiers was rewarding and prestigious, thus increasing cohesion among the comrades and the legitimacy of German rule and indirectly also of violence, for it was the consequential and logical next step to permit the application of violence for the defense of the community.

Notes

1. Christian Gerlach, *Kalkulierte Morde: Die deutsche Wirtschafts- und Vernichtungspolitik in Weißrußland, 1941 bis 1944* (Hamburg: Hamburger Edition, 1999), 1158.

2. Masha Cerovic, "De la paix à la guerre: Les habitants de Minsk face aux violences d'occupation allemandes (juni 1941–février 1942)," *Relations Internationales* 126 (2006): 78–79.

3. Paul Kohl, "Verbrannte Erde—verbrannte Menschen, 2. Juli 1944: Die 'Beschleunigte Räumung' von Minsk," in *Schlüsseljahr 1944*, ed. Peter März (Munich: Bayerische Landeszentrale für politische Bildungsarbeit, 2007), 163–72.

4. A valuable source edition is Wolfgang Benz, Konrad Kwiet, and Jürgen Matthäus, eds., *Einsatz im "Reichskommissariat Ostland": Dokumente zum Völkermord im Baltikum und in Weißrußland, 1941–1944* (Berlin: Metropol, 1998).

5. For Belarusian research on the occupation, see Dieter Pohl, "Die einheimische Forschung und der Mord an den Juden in den besetzten sowjetischen Gebieten," in *Täter im Vernichtungskrieg: Der Überfall auf die Sowjetunion und der Völkermord an den Juden*, ed. Wolf Kaiser (Berlin: Propyläen, 2002), 204–16. Historical research in the context of Belarusian history in the twentieth century is described by Bernhard Chiari, "Deutsche Herrschaft in Weißrußland: Überlegungen zum lokalen und historischen Umfeld," in Kaiser, *Täter im Vernichtungskrieg*, 137–59.

6. Wolfgang Curilla, *Die deutsche Ordnungspolizei und der Holocaust im Baltikum und in Weißrußland, 1941–1944* (Paderborn: Ferdinand Schöningh, 2006); and Stefan Klemp, *"Nicht ermittelt": Polizeibataillone und die Nachkriegsjustiz. Ein Handbuch* (Essen: Klartext, 2005). For an overview in English, see Erich E. Haberer, "The German Police and Genocide in Belorussia, 1941–1944," *Journal of Genocide Research* 3, no. 2 (2001): 13–29, 207–18, 391–403. For a general history, see Edward B. Westermann, *Hitler's Police Battalions: Enforcing Racial War in the East* (Lawrence: University Press of Kansas, 2005). For the overall number of casualties, see Gerlach, *Morde*, 1158.

7. Christian Gerlach, "Kontextualisierung der Aktionen eines Mordkommandos: Die Einsatzgruppe B," in Kaiser, *Täter im Vernichtungskrieg*, 85–95. A selection of Einsatzgruppen reports are published in Yitzhak Arad,

Shmuel Krakowski, Shmuel Spector, eds., *The Einsatzgruppen Reports: Selections from the Dispatches of the Nazi Death Squads' Campaign against the Jews, July 1941—January 1943* (New York: Holocaust Library, 1989). See also Peter Klein, ed., *Die Einsatzgruppen in der besetzten Sowjetunion, 1941/42: Die Tätigkeits- und Lageberichte der Chefs der Sicherheitspolizei und des SD* (Berlin: Edition Hentrich, 1997).

8. In 1941 and again from February 1943 the *Höhere SS- und Polizeiführer (HSSPF) Russland-Mitte* was stationed in Minsk, Tagesbefehl No. 1 of the Bevollmächtigter des Reichsführers-SS für Bandenbekämpfung, March 17, 1943, R 70 SU / 21, fol. 87, Bundesarchiv Berlin-Lichterfelde (hereafter BAB). See also Ruth-Bettina Birn, *Die Höheren SS- und Polizeiführer: Himmlers Vertreter im Reich und in den besetzten Gebieten* (Düsseldorf: Droste, 1986); and Bernd Gottberg, "Die Höheren SS- und Polizeiführer im Okkupationsregime des faschistischen deutschen Imperialismus in den zeitweilig besetzten Gebieten der Sowjetunion, 1941 bis 1944," PhD thesis, [East] Berlin, 1984.

9. Andrej Angrick, Martina Voigt, Silke Ammerschubert, Peter Klein, Christa Alheit, and Michael Tycher, "'Da hätte man schon ein Tagebuch führen müssen': Das Polizeibataillon 322 und die Judenmorde im Bereich der Heeresgruppe Mitte während des Sommers und Herbstes 1941: Mit einer Auseinandersetzung über die rechtlichen Konsequenzen," in *Die Normalität des Verbrechens: Bilanz und Perspektiven der Forschung zu den nationalsozialistischen Gewaltverbrechen. Festschrift für Wolfgang Scheffler zum 65. Geburtstag*, ed. Helge Grabitz, Klaus Bästlein, and Johannes Tuchel (Berlin: Edition Hentrich, 1994), 325–85; and Jürgen Matthäus, "What about the 'Ordinary Men'? The German Order Police and the Holocaust in the Occupied Soviet Union," *Holocaust and Genocide Studies* 11 (1996): 134–50.

10. Jürgen Matthäus, "Georg Heuser: Routinier des sicherheitspolizeilichen Osteinsatzes," in *Karrieren der Gewalt. Nationalsozialistische Täterbiographien*, ed. Klaus-Michael Mallmann and Gerhard Paul (Darmstadt: Primus, 2004), 115–25. For Strauch, see Polizeipräsidien, Sammlung Primavesi / 208, Staatsarchiv Münster, Münster (hereafter StAM).

11. Forces of Höherer SS- und Polizeiführer Rußland-Mitte, July 20, 1943, MA 1790 / 4; 359-1-6, Archiv des Instituts für Zeitgeschichte, Munich (hereafter IfZ-Archiv).

12. Curilla, *Deutsche Ordnungspolizei*, 398. The numbers are from a report dated September 11, 1942. For more details see Martin Dean, *Collaboration in the Holocaust: Crimes of the Local Police in Belorussia and Ukraine, 1941–1944* (London: Palgrave Macmillan, 2000). See also Richard Breitman, "Himmler's Police Auxiliaries in the Occupied Soviet Territories," *Simon Wiesenthal Center Annual* 7 (1990): 23–39.

13. Władysław Bartoszewski, *Erich von dem Bach* (Warsaw: Wydawnictwo Zachodnie, 1961).

14. Peter Klein, "Curt von Gottberg: Siedlungsfunktionär und Massenmörder," in Mallmann, *Karrieren der Gewalt*, 95–103.

15. Some documents concerning Kube's crimes in Minsk can be found in Helmut Heiber, "Aus den Akten des Gauleiters Kube," *Vierteljahrshefte für Zeitgeschichte* 4, no. 1 (1956): 65–92. For the recruitment of the administrative personnel, see Stephan Lehnstaedt, "'Ostnieten' oder Vernichtungsexperten? Die Auswahl deutscher Staatsdiener für den Einsatz im Generalgouvernement Polen, 1939–1944," *Zeitschrift für Geschichtswissenschaft* 53 (2007): 701–21, esp. 718–19. For the tasks and responsibilities of the civil administration, see Robert J. Gibbons, "Allgemeine Richtlinien für die politische und wirtschaftliche Verwaltung der besetzten Ostgebiete," *Vierteljahrshefte für Zeitgeschichte* 25, no. 2 (1977): 252–61. For a general overview in English, see Jonathan Steinberg, "The Third Reich Reflected: German Civil Administration in the Occupied Soviet Union 1941–1944," *English Historical Review* 40 (1995): 620–51.

16. Babette Quinkert, "Terror und Propaganda: Die 'Ostarbeiteranwerbung' im Generalkommissariat Weißruthenien," *Zeitschrift für Geschichtswissenschaft* 47 (1999): 700–721.

17. For the civil administration itself, see Gerlach, *Kalkulierte Morde*, 156–80. Its crimes are the subject of the whole book. The expropriation is described in Anja Heuss, *Kunst- und Kulturgutraub: Eine vergleichende Studie zur Besatzungspolitik der Nationalsozialisten in Frankreich und der Sowjetunion* (Heidelberg: Universitätsverlag Winter, 2000); and Martin Dean, *Robbing the Jews: The Confiscation of Jewish Property in the Holocaust, 1933–1945* (London: Cambridge University Press, 2008).

18. Report No. 4 of the Beauftragter des Reichsleiters Bormann im Oberkommando der Wehrmacht, Albert Hoffmann, concerning Weißruthenien Minsk, May 26, 1942, Fa 91 / 4, p. 866ff, IfZ-Archiv.

19. Alfred Gottwald and Diana Schulle, *Die "Judendeportationen" aus dem Deutschen Reich, 1941–1945: Eine kommentierte Chronologie* (Wiesbaden: Marixverlag, 2005), esp. 230–47.

20. Organization and personnel of Reichsverkehrsdirektion Minsk, dating from 1943, R 5 Anh. I / 144, p. 1391ff., BAB.

21. Antonio J. Munoz and Oleg. V. Romanko, *Hitler's White Russians: Collaboration, Extermination, and Anti-Partisan Warfare in Byelorussia, 1941–1944* (New York: Europa, 2003); and Leonid Rein, "Local Collaboration in the Execution of the 'Final Solution' in Nazi-Occupied Belorussia," *Holocaust and Genocide Studies* 20 (2006): 381–409.

22. Dieter Pohl, *Die Herrschaft der Wehrmacht: Deutsche Militärbesatzung und einheimische Bevölkerung in der Sowjetunion, 1941–1944* (Munich: Oldenbourg, 2008). See also Manfred Oldenburg, *Ideologie und militärisches Kalkül: Die Besatzungspolitik der Wehrmacht in der Sowjetunion* (Cologne: Böhlau, 2004); and Theo Schulte, *The German Army and*

Nazi Politics in occupied Russia (Oxford: Oxford University Press, 1989). A rather general overview is in Hannes Heer, "Killing Fields: The Wehrmacht and the Holocaust in Belorussia, 1941–1942," *Holocaust and Genocide Studies* 11 (1997): 79–101; and Peter Lieb, "Täter aus Überzeugung? Oberst Carl von Andrian und die Judenmorde der 707. Infanteriedivision, 1941/42," *Vierteljahrshefte für Zeitgeschichte* 50, no. 4 (2002): 523–58.

23. Uwe Gartenschläger, *Die Stadt Minsk während der deutschen Besetzung (1941–1944)* (Dortmund: Internationales Bildungs- und Begegnungswerk, 2001), 65.

24. Gerlach, *Kalkulierte Morde*, 1158.

25. Ibid., 855–59.

26. Gartenschläger, *Stadt Minsk*, 65, and Bernhard Chiari, *Alltag hinter der Front: Besatzung, Kollaboration, und Widerstand in Weißrußland, 1941–1944* (Düsseldorf: Droste, 1998), 61.

27. "Holz—Kartoffeln—Federbetten. Über 500 Volksdeutsche Familien werden von der NSV für den Winter versorgt," *Minsker Zeitung*, October 23, 1942. See also Gerlach, *Kalkulierte Morde*, 124–25.

28. Belarussians and Jews as victims are presented in Paul Kohl, *"Ich wundere mich, daß ich noch lebe": Sowjetische Überlebende Berichten* (Gütersloh: Gütersloher Verlagshaus, 1990).

29. Shalom Cholawsky, *The Jews of Bielorussia During World War II* (Amsterdam: Harwood, 1998); Shalom Cholawsky, "The Judenrat in Minsk," in *Patterns of Jewish Leadership in Nazi Europe, 1933–1945: Proceedings of the Third Yad Vashem International Historical Conference*, ed. Israel Gutman and C. J. Haft (Jerusalem: Yad Vashem, 1979), 113–32; and Raisa A. Chernoglasova, *Judenfrei! Svobodno ot evreev!: Istoriia minskogo getto v dokumentkh [The History of the Minsk Ghetto in Documents]* (Minsk: Asobny Dakh, 1999). Other research is focused mainly on resistance; see Barbara Epstein, *The Minsk Ghetto, 1941–1943: Jewish Resistance and Soviet Internationalism* (Berkeley: University of California Press, 2008). For an account by a survivor, see Hersh Smolar, *The Minsk Ghetto: Soviet-Jewish Partisans against the Nazis* (New York: Holocaust Library, 1989). Specifically on the history of German Jews in the Minsk Ghetto, see Karl Loewenstein, *Minsk: Im Lager der deutschen Juden* (Bonn: Bundeszentrale für Heimatdienst, 1961), which is also a survivor's account; and Shalom Cholawsky, "The German Jews in the Minsk Ghetto," *Yad Vashem Studies* 17 (1986): 219–45.

30. Paul Kohl, *Das Vernichtungslager Trostenez: Augenzeugenberichte und Dokumente* (Dortmund: Internationales Bildungs- und Begegnungswerk, 2003).

31. Stephan Lehnstaedt, *Okkupation im Osten: Besatzeralltag in Warschau und Minsk, 1939–1944* (Munich: Oldenbourg, 2010).

32. For the most recent treatment of this historical concept, and an outline of the mainly German methodological discussion, see Paul Steege, Andrew Bergerson, Maureen Healy, and Pamela E. Swett, "The History of Everyday Life: A Second Chapter," *Journal of Modern History* 80 (June 2008): 358–78.

33. The order is printed in Kohl, *Ich wundere mich*, 218.

34. Clara Hecker, "Deutsche Juden im Minsker Ghetto," *Zeitschrift für Geschichtswissenschaft* 56 (2008): 826.

35. Smolar, *Minsk Ghetto*, 22. Curiosity as a reason for visiting the ghetto is reported, for example, in Interrogation of Erna L., December 14, 1960, B 162 / 1682, pp. 1778–82., Bundesarchiv Ludwigsburg (hereafter BAL).

36. Gottwald and Schulle, *Judendeportationen*, 230–47. The relevant letters of the Reichsbahn can be found in Fb 85-II, IfZ-Archiv.

37. Hecker, "Deutsche Juden," 826–27.

38. Letter from Wolfgang Lieschke to his wife, November 13, 1941, private collection of Gerhard Lieschke.

39. Interrogation of Erna L., December 14, 1960, pp. 1778–82.

40. Letter from Wolfgang Lieschke to his wife, November 22, 1941.

41. Letter from Wolfgang Lieschke to his wife, November 13, 1941.

42. Kommandanturbefehl Minsk No. 51, November 14, 1942. MA 1790 / 3; 379-2-45, IfZ-Archiv. Gerlach, "Kontextualisierung," 85.

43. Gartenschläger, *Stadt Minsk*, 21.

44. Pohl, *Herrschaft*, 211.

45. Diary of Carl von Andrian, October 5, 1941 (unpublished transcript by Peter Lieb, pp. 48f; the original is held by the Bayerische Kriegsarchiv, Munich).

46. Karl E. Hahn, *Eisenbahner in Krieg und Frieden: Ein Lebensschicksal* (Frankfurt am Main: Lanzenreiter, 1954), 50.

47. Letter from Wolfgang Lieschke to his wife, August 8, 1941, private collection of Gerhard Lieschke.

48. Pohl, *Herrschaft*, 229.

49. Gerlach, *Kalkulierte Morde*, 506–10; and Gerlach, "Kontextualisierung," 89.

50. Dean, *Collaboration*, 43–46, 60–63.

51. Lieb, "Täter," and Gerlach, *Kalkulierte Morde*, 617–20.

52. Order No. 24 of Wehrmachtkommandant in Weißruthenien, November 24, 1941, MA 1790 / 2; 378-1-698, IfZ-Archiv.

53. Concept of a letter by *Reichsführer-SS* to *Major* Suchanek [end of 1941], MfS - HA XX / 3817, Bundesbeauftragte für die Unterlagen des Staatssicherheitsdienstes der ehemaligen Deutschen Demokratischen Republik, Berlin.

54. Reinhart Koselleck, "Zur historisch-politischen Semantik asymmetrischer Gegenbegriffe," in *Vergangene Zukunft: Zur Semantik geschichtlicher Zeiten*, ed. Reinhart Koselleck (Frankfurt am Main: Suhrkamp, 1979), 257–58.

55. Annex no. 4 of the monthly report by 707. ID, November 10, 1941, RH 26-707 / 2, Bundesarchiv-Militärarchiv, Freiburg (hereafter BA-MA). For this unit see Lieb, "Täter."

56. Matthäus, "Georg Heuser," 117.

57. Letter from *Unteroffizier* Georg Heidenreich, October 24, 1941: "das große Massensterben eintrifft," Sammlung Sterz, Bibliothek für Zeitgeschichte, Stuttgart (hereafter BfZg).

58. Diary of Carl von Andrian, October 26, 1941, 61–62.

59. Letter from *Unteroffizier* Georg Heidenreich, October 24, 1941, Sammlung Sterz, BfZg.

60. Diary of Carl von Andrian, examples, partly with numbers, on October 4, 16, 19, 24, 1941.

61. Letter from Reichsbahn-Inspekteur Kurt Schmid, October 8, 1941, Sammlung Sterz, BfZg.

62. This newspaper was established in 1942 and had a circulation of some 22,000 copies in 1944. It was edited by fifteen German journalists. More than two-thirds of the circulation was sold to the Wehrmacht, which circulated it free of charge. See *Minsker Zeitung*, February 12–13, 1944: "Bitte— eine Minsker Zeitung"; and April 17, 1943: "Die 'Minsker Zeitung' feierte Jubiläum."

63. *Minsker Zeitung* May 3, 1942: "Ein hartes, aber gerechtes Urteil."

64. Hahn, *Eisenbahner*, 50.

65. Angrick, "'Da hätte man schon ein Tagebuch,'" 340, and Klemp, "Nicht Ermittelt," 289–94.

66. Stephan Lehnstaedt, "Alltägliche Gewalt: Die deutschen Besatzer in Warschau und die Ermordung der jüdischen Bevölkerung," in *Besatzung, Kollaboration, Holocaust: Neue Studien zur Ermordung der europäischen Juden*, ed. Johannes Hürter and Jürgen Zarusky (Munich: Oldenbourg, 2008), 88–89.

67. Gerlach, *Kalkulierte Morde*, 100.

68. Alex J. Kay, *Exploitation, Resettlement, Mass Murder: Political and Economic Planning for German Occupation Policy in the Soviet Union, 1940–1941* (New York: Berghahn, 2006), 166.

69. Lehnstaedt, *Okkupation im Osten*, 210–23.

70. Letter from Wolfgang Lieschke to his wife, August 8, 1941.

71. Klaus Latzel, "Feldpostbriefe: Überlegungen zur Aussagekraft einer Quelle," in *Verbrechen der Wehrmacht: Bilanz einer Debatte*, ed. Christian Hartmann, Johannes Hürter, and Ulrike Jureit (Munich: C. H. Beck, 2005), 178.

72. Diary of Carl von Andrian, October 24, 1941, p. 60.

73. Lehnstaedt, "Alltägliche Gewalt," 89–90.

74. Lagebericht by 707th ID, February 20, 1942, RH 26-707 / 15. BA-MA.

75. Gerlach, *Kalkulierte Morde*, 104–5.

76. Interrogation of Alois H., July 28, 1971, B 162 / AR 1495/69, fols. 165ff, BAL.
77. Chiari, *Alltag*, 74–80.
78. Order issued by Wehrmachtkommandant in Weißruthenien, October 27, 1941, MA 1790 / 2; 378-1-698, IfZ-Archiv.
79. Letter from Reichsbahn-Inspektor Kurt Schmid, October 8, 1941, Sammlung Sterz, BfZg.
80. Diary of Carl von Andrian, September 23, 1941, p. 39.
81. Harald Welzer, *Täter: Wie aus ganz normalen Menschen Massenmörder werden* (Frankfurt am Main: S. Fischer, 2005), 245.
82. Minutes of the conference of the Gebietskommissare, Hauptabteilungsleiter, and Abteilungsleiter of Generalkommissariat Minsk, April 8–10, 1943, Fb 85-I /, fols. 22–44, IfZ-Archiv.
83. See, for instance, letter from *Hauptmann* Hermann Göbel, August 13, 1941, Sammlung Sterz, BfZg. Thanks to an agreement between the Bundesarchiv and Wikipedia, photos from Minsk during the war can bee seen at http://commons.wikimedia.org/w/index.php?title=Special:Search&ns0=1&ns6=1&ns12=1&ns14=1&redirs=1&search=minsk+bundesarchiv&limit=20&offset=60.
84. "Straßenbahn der Minsker Stadtverwaltung in Betrieb," *Minsker Zeitung*, May 19, 1943.
85. "Quartier in Weißruthenien," *Minsker Zeitung*, August 8, 1942.
86. "Das Heim der Gendarmerie," *Minsker Zeitung*, September 6–7, 1942.
87. "Ein deutsches Richtfest: Neues Unterkunftsgebäude für Eisenbahner entsteht," *Minsker Zeitung*, September 15, 1942.
88. Diary of Carl von Andrian, August 23, 1941, 19–20.
89. Letter from Generalkommissariat Weißruthenien (Morsbach) to Reichskommissariat Ostland, August 10, 1942, R 90 / 229, BAB.
90. "'Haus der Roten Armee'—Soldatenheim," *Minsker Zeitung*, August 11, 1942.
91. *Amtsblatt der Reichsverkehrsdirektion Minsk*, no. 15, March 20, 1944.
92. Letter from Generalkommissariat Minsk to personnel department of the Regierung des Generalgouvernements, April 13, 1943, R 93 / 1, p. 62, BAB.
93. Karl I. Albrecht, *Sie aber werden die Welt zerstören* (Munich: Neuner, 1954), 220–24.
94. "Fröhlichkeit nach hartem Dienst," *Minsker Zeitung*, May 23, 1942.
95. Letter from Wolfgang Lieschke to his wife, August 18, 1941.
96. "Standard-Holzbau-Kino in Minsk," *Minsker Zeitung*, May 26, 1944.
97. Decree of Generalkommissariat Weißruthenien, June 23, 1942, MA 1790 / 11; 370-1-468, IfZ-Archiv.
98. "Hier ist der Landessender Minsk," *Minsker Zeitung*, June 21, 1944.

99. "Wechsel in der Leitung des Landessenders Minsk," *Minsker Zeitung*, January 13, 1944; and "Großer Betriebsappell beim Landessender Minsk," *Minsker Zeitung*, January 16–17, 1944.

100. Diary of Carl von Andrian.

101. "Vom Soldatenfunk zu Landessender," *Minsker Zeitung*, January 8, 1943.

102. Internal letter from Reichsverkehrsdirektion Minsk, October 14, 1943, MA 1790 / 2; 378-1-388, IfZ-Archiv.

103. Letter from Wolfgang Lieschke to his wife, November 13, 1941.

104. "Eine Tür zum Reich," *Minsker Zeitung*, May 3–4, 1942; and "Oase inmitten der Wüste," *Deutsche Zeitung im Ostland*, November 25, 1941.

105. Peter Reichel, *Der schöne Schein des Dritten Reiches: Faszination und Gewalt des Faschismus*, 3rd ed. (Munich: Hanser, 1996), 170.

106. Chiari, *Alltag*, 72–73.

107. Klaus Latzel, *Deutsche Soldaten—Nationalsozialistischer Krieg?: Kriegserlebnis, Kriegserfahrung, 1939–1945* (Paderborn: Ferdinand Schöningh, 1998), 135–42.

108. Diary of Carl von Andrian, January 29, 1942. A similar anticipating assessment is in: letter from Wolfgang Lieschke to his wife, August 8, 1941. See also Kommandanturbefehl Minsk No. 32, September 2, 1942, MA 1790 / 3; 379-2-45, IfZ-Archiv.

109. Kommandanturbefehl Minsk No. 12, November 4, 1941, MA 1790 / 3; 379-2-45, IfZ-Archiv.

110. Letter from Wolfgang Lieschke to his wife, July 6, 1941, private collection of Gerhard Lieschke.

111. Report by Generalkommissariat Weißruthenien, August 9, 1942, MA 1790 / 11; 370-1-53, IfZ-Archiv.

112. Ibid., December 12, 1942.

113. Lehnstaedt, *Okkupation*, 165.

114. Lehnstaedt, "Alltägliche Gewalt," 92–95.

115. Letter from SS- und Polizeiführer to Generalkommissariat Weißruthenien, May 12, 1942, MA 1790 / 22; 370-6-4, IfZ-Archiv.

116. Amtsblatt der Haupteisenbahndirektion Mitte (Minsk), No. 43, October 19, 1942.

117. Report concerning procurement by Generalkommissariat Weißruthenien, October 15, 1942, R 93 / 3, p. 6, BAB; see also *Mitteilungsblatt des Reichskommissars für das Ostland* 1 (September 30, 1941): 1–4. Process instructions concerning the order of September 17, 1941.

118. For a comparative overview on eastern Europe, see Dieter Pohl, "Der Raub an den Juden im besetzten Osteuropa, 1939–1942," in *Raub und Restitution: "Arisierung" und Rückerstattung des jüdischen Eigentums in Europa*, ed. Constantin Goschler and Philipp Ther (Frankfurt am Main: S. Fischer, 2003), 62–65; see also Dean, *Robbing*, esp. 383–84, 395–96.

119. Dean, *Robbing*, 191–213.
120. Interrogation of Sabine H., April 27–29, 1960, B 162 / 1673, fols. 347–50, BAL.
121. Interrogation of Karl-Heinz G., May 24, 1961, B 162 / 1681, fols. 1548ff, BAL; and Interrogation of Wilhelm C., May 16, 1961, B 162 / 1681, fols. 1517ff, BAL.
122. Interrogation of Sabine H., April, 27–29, 1960, B 162 / 1673, fols. 347–50, BAL.
123. "'Papyrossi' aus Leerwagenzetteln," *Minsker Zeitung*, January 10–11, 1943.
124. Gerlach, *Kalkulierte Morde*, 210–11.
125. Interrogation of Friedrich G., November 9, 1960, B 162 / 1672, fols. 21–24, BAL.
126. Interrogation of Herbert K., May 24, 1961, B 162 / 1681, fols. 1597–1602, BAL.
127. Interrogation of Theodor O., March 3, 1961, and May 23, 1960, B 162 / 1689, fols. 3378ff, BAL.
128. Christopher R. Browning, *Ordinary Men: Reserve Police Battalion 101 and the Final Solution in Poland*, 2nd rev. ed. (New York: Harper, 1998), 81–82.
129. Interrogation of Erna L., December 14, 1960, B 162 / 1682, fols. 1778–82, BAL.
130. Interrogation of Karl G., October 18, 1960, B 162 / 1672, fols. 92–97, BAL.
131. Thomas Kühne, *Kameradschaft: Die Soldaten des nationalsozialistischen Krieges und das 20. Jahrhundert* (Göttingen: Vandenhoeck & Ruprecht, 2006), 132–33.
132. Karin Gundel, "Vergleich der Soziogenese des weiblichen und männlichen Alkoholismus anhand einer Sekundäranalyse klinischer Daten" (PhD diss., Ludwig Maximilians University Munich, 1972), 44–45.
133. Letter from Wolfgang Lieschke to his wife, November 13, 1941.
134. Ernst Klee, Willi Dreßen, and Volker Rieß, eds., *"Schöne Zeiten"; Judenmord aus der Sicht der Täter und Gaffer* (Frankfurt am Main: S. Fischer, 1988), 171–77.
135. Assessment of *SS-Obersturmbannführer* Eduard Strauch by Befehlshaber der Sicherheitspolizei und des SD Ostland, April 1, 1943, Polizeipräsidien, Sammlung Primavesi / 208, StAM.
136. "Wo der Wodka gebraut wird," *Minsker Zeitung*, September 9, 1942.
137. Lehnstaedt, *Okkupation*, esp. 210–23, 244–53.
138. Tobias Jersak, "Entscheidungen zu Mord und Lüge: Die deutsche Kriegsgesellschaft und der Holocaust," in *Die deutsche Kriegsgesellschaft, 1939 bis 1945: Erster Halbband: Politisierung, Vernichtung, Überleben*, ed. Jörg Echternkamp (Munich: Deutsche Verlags-Anstalt, 2004), 321, spotting

a racially "ideal society" in the east. For differences in comparison to the "Volksgemeinschaft," see Michael Wildt, "Die politische Ordnung der Volksgemeinschaft: Ernst Fraenkels 'Doppelstaat' neu betrachtet," *Mittelweg 36*, no. 12 (2003): 45–61, esp. 58–59.

139. Welzer, *Täter*, 245.

140. Ibid., 251.

CHAPTER 10

EXTENDING THE GENOCIDAL PROGRAM

Did Otto Ohlendorf Initiate the Systematic Extermination of Soviet "Gypsies"?

Martin Holler

As far as the historiography on the Nazi genocide of Roma[1] is concerned, the situation in the German occupied territories of the Soviet Union during World War II belongs to the most neglected topics. At the same time, this very region plays a key role for the evaluation of Nazi genocidal policy. The German assault on the Soviet Union marked the transition toward a systematic physical extermination of Jews, "Gypsies," and other so-called undesirable elements. Furthermore, the Soviet Roma doubtlessly represent a substantial share of the total number of people that were killed by the Nazis as "Gypsies."[2]

The same can be said, however, about Yugoslavia, which in regard to Jews and Roma foreshadowed to a certain degree the development of Operation Barbarossa. As early as the end of May 1941, the Wehrmacht in occupied Serbia united the status of "Gypsies" with that of Jews and shot "Gypsy" and Jewish hostages in combined retaliatory actions for partisan attacks on army units. On July 25, 1941, the status of Roma who were "integrated" and "sedentary since 1850 [sic]" was softened—an idea that seemed to be copied a few months later in some regions of the occupied Soviet territories.[3] Furthermore, the *Ustasha* transformed Croatia into one of the largest killing grounds of Roma outside of the Soviet Union.[4]

Until today, the state of research on the Soviet case—although often used as evidence in the discussion about the comparability or incomparability of the Nazi genocide of Roma and the Holocaust—has been rather insufficient. After the pioneering work of Donald Kenrick and Grattan Puxon, it was Wolfgang Wippermann who first surmised that there was an intended and systematic extermination of Soviet Roma, pointing in a more general way to the Nazis' racist ideology as historical background.[5] He presumed that the mobile killing units of the SS killed every "Gypsy" they could locate. A major difference between the murder of "Gypsies" and Jews, according to Wippermann, was that the *Einsatzgruppen* (Task Forces) had problems recognizing "Gypsies," who successfully hid their ethnic identity.[6]

Michael Zimmermann also recognized an intended Nazi genocide of Soviet "Gypsies" as alleged racial inferiors, but he assumed a lesser systematic intensity for the reason that the *Einsatzgruppen* targeted primarily itinerant "Gypsies," who were supposed to be vagabonds, antisocials, and potential partisan spies. Sedentary and socially assimilated Roma, who did not fit into the cliché of continually travelling nomads, could become victims of mass shootings, too, but the perpetrators would not especially search for them, particularly as the killing of Jews had absolute priority for the Nazi occupiers. One of Zimmermann's main arguments was that the *Einsatzgruppen* never thought of employing the same measures against the "Gypsies" as they did against the Jews, such as special registration, isolation, or calls for a fake resettlement. In his eyes, this was also linked to the—incorrectly, as I will show—supposed circumstance that Roma did not live in compact settlements.[7]

Most historians have accepted Zimmermann's point of view. The main problem with his research is its exclusive reliance on materials from German archives, such as *Einsatzgruppen* reports and postwar trials. In relation to Soviet Roma, such sources offer only a fragmentary and very contradictory insight into the actual events. More promising are contributions with a combined research of German and Soviet materials. In this respect, it is a very fortunate development that in recent years historians from the post-Soviet states have also been discovering the topic step by step.[8] Although a general academic monograph on the Nazi genocide of Soviet Roma is still lacking, some articles with a special geographical focus have already helped to complete the picture from a new point of view.[9] Hence, the most promising possibility to prove how systematic the Nazi persecution of Soviet Roma was is to examine files from the former Soviet Union, which have been completely ignored by the aforementioned Western scholars. A variety of helpful materials on the topic can be found in archives in the former Soviet Union, such as the remaining files of the occupation administration at the local level, the partisan reports to Moscow, political reports, the investigations carried out by the Red Army,[10] the voluminous files of the Extraordinary State Commission for the investigation of German-Fascist crimes,[11] open and closed Soviet tribunals against war criminals and traitors, that is, collaborators, and, last but not least, memoirs of eyewitnesses and survivors.

The files of the Extraordinary State Commission are of central importance. Beginning in November 1942, the commission started its work in the first territories liberated by the Red Army, investigating with the help of interrogations of eyewitnesses, exhumations of mass graves, and comparisons of prewar statistical records with the actual situation in the liberated towns and villages. Some of the results were used in the Nuremberg trials and also published in newspapers.

The key question in order to evaluate the systematic character of the Nazi persecution is, as we can see, what degree of differentiation was made between itinerant and sedentary Roma. Were Roma killed as a supposed danger to security, as antisocial elements, or for racial reasons, that is, for the pure fact that they were born as "Gypsies"? In this respect, *Einsatzgruppe* D plays an important role in the interpretation of German policy. Most historians agree that the persecution and extermination of "Gypsies" in the Crimea had a systematic and total character.[12] Thanks to the Nuremberg *Einsatzgruppen* trial in 1947–48 and the remaining archival sources of *Einsatzgruppe* D, the peninsula belongs to the best-analyzed Soviet regions under Nazi control. *SS-Oberführer* (from June 1942, *SS-Brigadeführer*) Otto Ohlendorf, the former leader of *Einsatzgruppe* D, justified before the court his responsibility for the murder of more than ninety thousand people, most of them Jewish civilians, with alleged security concerns and the compulsion to obey orders.[13] In his words, "Gypsies" had to be treated "like Jews," because "as itinerant people" they had a traditional "inner willingness" to engage in espionage.[14] Were the Roma therefore killed as itinerants? The confrontation of well-known materials from German archives with newly discovered sources of Soviet origin helps us to refute this. The majority of Roma in the Crimea were town dwellers and had assimilated into Tatar society. Nevertheless, Ohlendorf tried to liquidate all Roma he was able to find. In doing so, he was the spearhead of a development that can be observed in other parts of the German-occupied territories of the Soviet Union during later stages of the war. In comparing the anti-"Gypsy" activities of *Einsatzgruppen* A, B, C, D and the Wehrmacht, I shall evaluate what role Otto Ohlendorf played in this question during the early stages of the German-Soviet war.

The geographical focus of my article is on the permanently militarily administered territories, where we find the greatest gap of knowledge. Geographically speaking, all occupied parts of Soviet Russia (including the Crimea) and eastern Ukraine (the territories of Chernihiv, Sumy, Kharkiv, and Stalino, now Donetsk) and parts of eastern Belarus (the territories of Mogilev and Vitebsk) belonged to these territories.

Figure 10.1. Otto Ohlendorf as defendant at the *Einsatzgruppen* trial, October 9, 1947. United States Holocaust Memorial Museum, Washington, DC, photograph 43038, courtesy of National Archives and Records Administration, College Park, Md.

In my research, I have employed a twofold methodological approach. First, I compared and contrasted the existing German reports and statements on mass shootings of "Gypsies" with the Soviet investigation of the same events. The second approach was to examine in particular the territories of compact Romani settlement, in order to learn more about the actual treatment of sedentary and socially assimilated Roma—the most controversial question in the historiography.

The Early Murders of *Einsatzgruppe* D

The earliest known mass shootings of Soviet Roma were committed by *Einsatzgruppe* D in the area around Nikolayev. It is important to note that from the very beginning no differentiation was made between sedentary and nonsedentary Roma. As early as September 1941, between 100 and 150 Roma—men, women, and children—were killed in front of their homes after they had refused to climb into the vans that would have brought them to the prepared place of execution.[15] Around the same time, another "Gypsy" group was shot in the Nogai steppe near Nikolayev. The alleged reason for this murder was that they had carried a Russian machine gun into one of their vehicles.[16]

The intensity of the persecution reached a new level when *Einsatzgruppe* D entered the Crimea, where large numbers of Roma had lived in towns for centuries and had almost completely assimilated among their Tatar neighbors—a fact that made the identification of "Gypsies" very difficult for the German perpetrators. In the town of Simferopol, which had a special "Gypsy" quarter, the extermination of Roma started in the first days of the occupation and proceeded almost parallel to the extermination of the Jewish community. The method of persecution likewise included registration and the call for resettlement. On December 9, 1941, more than eight hundred Roma were driven out of the town by trucks and shot in pits, after they had handed over their valuables and clothes to members of *Sonderkommando* 10a. According to eyewitnesses, some of the victims were only wounded by the bullets and then buried alive.[17]

At the same time, *Sonderkommando* 11b established a camp for Jews and "Gypsies" in Alushta; a few weeks later, all prisoners were murdered.[18] In spring 1942, too, "Gypsies" were regularly listed in the shooting reports of *Einsatzgruppe* D.[19] *Ereignismeldung* (Incident Report) 190 from April 8, 1942, concluded concerning the Crimea that—with a few exceptions in the north—"Jews, Krimchaks, and Gypsies no longer exist."[20]

The files of the Extraordinary State Commission offer much additional information that confirms the systematic character of the extermination of Roma in the Crimea. Similar to the example of Simferopol, mass shootings of comparable scale took place in two other Crimean towns. At the end of December 1941, "all Gypsy families" of Kerch were arrested and imprisoned. During the next day, twelve trucks drove them to a place outside the town where they were shot in pits.[21] Detailed information also exists about Yevpatoria, where the murder of the Roma followed shortly after the extermination of the Jews and Krimchaks of the town. The Rom Jakub Kurtuliarov, who survived the massacre with a bullet in his shoulder, described for the ChGK the course of the events:

> At the beginning of 1942, I cannot recall the exact month, the German authorities called all Gypsies to register for special bread rations. The Gypsies understood, however, that this lure was motivated by the wish to catch the Gypsies for extermination. Therefore, nobody appeared for the registration, [and] they

began to hide themselves. After that, the Germans organized raids and hunted for Gypsies. More than a thousand people were arrested in Yevpatoria, myself among them, after our Gypsy quarter (*nasha tsyganskaia slobodka*) was sealed off by army units.... After that, the Gypsies were brought to Krasnaia Gorka and shot in antitank pits with machine guns and submachine guns.[22]

Apart from the big mass shootings in Simferopol, Kerch, and Yevpatoria, ten inhabitants of Feodosia and a seven-strong family in Biiuk-Onlarskii were murdered in the same period "for belonging to the Gypsy nationality (*za natsional'nuiu prinadlezhnost' kak tsygane*)."[23]

After a winter break, which *Einsatzgruppe* D had used for the recruitment of Tatar volunteers, the extermination continued in the spring of 1942 in the rural areas of the peninsula. In March 1942, a large part of the Romani population of the Dzhankoi district, about two to three hundred persons, were suffocated in gas lorries—six weeks after the Jews of the region had been shot.[24] In the same month, Roma in Staryi Krym and the surrounding area were murdered too.[25] Finally, several separate shootings that totalled eighty victims were carried out in the Kolaiskii district.[26]

Both the German sources and the Soviet investigations give the impression that the Nazi persecution of Crimean Roma led to a complete extermination. Soviet postwar sources reveal, however, that at least 1,109 "Gypsies" survived the German occupation; a number of Roma were subject to the Soviet deportations of the whole Crimean Tatar population in May 1944 and subsequently lived among "special settlers" of the Gulag system.[27] It seems likely that all remaining "Gypsies" were concerned about deportation, since a statistical overview, written for the NKVD in February 1945, remarked that "no Gypsies" live in the Crimea.[28] This allows the conclusion that approximately 30 percent of the Crimean Roma survived the German occupation.[29]

How was this possible? Was the commander of *Einsatzgruppe* D poorly informed when he reported the complete annihilation of Crimean "Jews, Krimchaks, and Gypsies" to the Reich Security Main Office (*Reichssicherheitshauptamt*, or RSHA)? The aforementioned problems confronting the German occupiers when identifying Roma could serve as a possible explanation. The Germans forced Tatar representatives to point out ethnic "Gypsies" they could not identify themselves.[30] However, the Tatar population did not want to support the anti-"Gypsy" policy of the Nazis at all. With the help of Tatar memoirs and protocols on interrogations of "traitors" from the Archive of the Ukrainian Secret Service (Arkhiv Golovnogo Upravleniia Sluzhbi Bezpeki Ukraini—Arkhiv GU SBU) and its branches, the Ukrainian historian Mikhail Tiaglyi gives some idea about the extraordinary solidarity of the Tatar population with the persecuted Moslem Roma. The Muslim Committee and other Tatar organizations tried to defend their brothers in faith with newspaper articles, petitions to the German authorities, open protest, and other measures.[31] As early as December 1941, the clergy of Simferopol made the (futile) attempt to rescue those "Gypsies" who had gathered for resettlement, as the eyewitness Lashkevich noted in his diary: "For some reason, they [the "Gypsies"] put up a green flag, the symbol of Moslem belief (*magometanstva*), and the procession was led by a mullah. The Gypsies tried to convince the Germans that they are no Gypsies, some of them called themselves Tatars, others Turkmen. But their protests were not recognized. . . ."[32] According to the collective memory of Crimean Tatars, the protests became more and more successful at the beginning of 1942, to the extent that the Germans even stopped the persecution of "Gypsies" in the urban areas.[33] However, the actual influence of such protests against the extermination of Roma should not be overestimated, because *Einsatzgruppe* D usually did not consider Tatar interests while enacting security police matters.[34] Actually, even in Simferopol, with its central Muslim Committee, the murder went on: on January 11, 1942, about 1,250 people were arrested as "unreliable elements" and brought to Dulag 241. In the camp, "Jews, Communists, and Gypsies" were selected for execution, while the other civilians were deployed for forced labor.[35] Military units also engaged in the persecution of "Gypsies." In the spring of 1942, the *Geheime Feldpolizei Gruppe* 647 (Secret Field Police Group 647) handed over fifty-one "Gypsies" to the SD in Simferopol.[36]

For the town administrations and local Tatar auxiliary police forces, which had the exclusive power of definition owing to their local knowledge, the most promising way to rescue Roma was to have them maintain their ethnic disguise and register them as Tatars. In the rural areas, the village elders played a similar role.[37] In most cases, the common belief was enough to evoke solidarity, but it also happened that the elders and organizations demanded various favors in return. This led in some cases to the grotesque situation that "Gypsies" had to fill up the ranks of Tatar volunteer units or even to serve in the German SD. The statements of the "Gypsy collaborators" during NKVD interrogations show that the loss of their Tatar camouflage would have meant their certain death.[38]

"Security Measures"—Ohlendorf's Defense in Nuremberg

As mentioned above, during his testimony at the Nuremberg *Einsatzgruppen* trial in 1947–48, Ohlendorf justified the mass extermination of Roma with alleged security concerns and the compulsion to obey orders.[39] He tried to convince the court that every "Gypsy" was a kind of "itinerating spy" and potential danger for German military, and that therefore the Roma had to be exterminated "like Jews."[40] At the same time, Ohlendorf tried to play down the real extent of the extermination, asserting that the mass shooting of "Gypsies" in Simferopol was the only case known to him.[41] None of Ohlendorf's statements were sincere. Orders to eradicate the *whole* Jewish and "Gypsy" population had definitely not (yet) been given in June 1941, as Ohlendorf asserted.[42] Furthermore, "Gypsies" were not mentioned at all in the main written orders in the summer of 1941, such as the Heydrich letter to the higher SS and police leaders (*höhere SS- und Polizeiführer*, or HSSPF) of July 2, 1941, or the guidelines for the filtration of prisoner of war camps of July 17, 1941.[43] It might nevertheless be possible that Ohlendorf himself issued verbal orders to eradicate "Gypsies" in his operational zone. *SS-Obersturmführer* (from July 1942, *Hauptsturmführer*) Felix Rühl stated in 1968 that *SS-Obersturmbannführer* Alois Persterer, leader of *Sonderkommando* 10b, informed his men in Chernovtsy about instructions to liquidate Jews in leading positions (*führende Juden*), Communists, Commissars, and "Gypsies" as potential enemies.[44] If this is true, it would mean that the order for a total extermination of "Gypsies" was given even earlier than the one for Jews, who were still only partially targeted. However, the early date of the supposed instruction—*Sonderkommando* 10b reached Chernovitz on July 6, 1941—makes such a far-reaching decision against Roma very unlikely. Two months later, when the killings of Roma by *Einsatzgruppe* D commenced, such a verbal order from Ohlendorf or one of his *Kommandoführer* is more likely. In any case, with regard to Roma, *Einsatzgruppe* D was in fact the pioneer of the systematic genocide, as a comparison with the other *Einsatzgruppen* will show.

The "Gypsy image" created by Ohlendorf before the court was a peculiar mixture of traditional anti-"Gypsy" clichés and absurd historical parallels with the Thirty Years' War, "as described by Ricarda Huch and Schiller."[45] Only after the presiding judge, Musmanno, demanded concrete examples of partisan support or espionage in the German-Soviet war did Ohlendorf add that "several cases" were known to him from the Yayla Mountains.[46] The barely accessible Yayla Mountains in the south of the Crimean peninsula gave, indeed, perfect shelter to partisans and remained a permanent threat. The German Security Police did not have enough forces to counter this menace and the Wehrmacht was still committed to the ongoing siege of Sevastopol, which did not fall until July 1942.[47] If "Gypsy spies" had been involved in the Yayla conflict, it would certainly have been mentioned in the *Einsatzgruppen* reports, which frequently dealt with this topic between November 1941 and the summer of 1942. However, "Gypsies" were never mentioned in this context.[48]

Since Ohlendorf's comments could not convince the court, he added some further, more general remarks on "Gypsies as such." His point of view in no way corresponded to the reality on the ground, as statistics confirm. In December 1941, even the German civil administration was aware that 75 percent of the Crimean "Gypsies" were town dwellers and worked as traders, blacksmiths, jewellers, and musicians, but this fact obviously did not influence the decision of the Security Police and the military commanders.[49]

Militarily Administered Areas in Comparison

As early as July 17, 1941, Lithuania, Latvia, Estonia, and parts of Belarus were officially united to form the *Reichskommissariat Ostland*, with a civil administration under the control of the newly founded *Reichsministerium für die besetzten Ostgebiete* (Reich Ministry for the Occupied Eastern Territories). In practice, however, the actual civil administration could only be established one step at a time, as military operations lasted several weeks.[50] Northwest Russia, which was near the front and consisted of (parts of) the territories of Leningrad, Novgorod, Pskov, and northern Velikie Luki, remained under military administration until the end of the German occupation.

The terrain between Lakes Peipus and Ilmen had a dispersed Romani population.[51] At the same time, the operations area of Army Group North was a militarily administered territory where we find concrete written orders about the treatment of local "Gypsies." The order of the *Berück* (general in command of Army Group North's rear area), Franz von Roques, from November 21, 1941, differentiated between "itinerant Gypsies," who were to be "handed over to the next *Einsatzkommando* of the SD" [for shooting], while "sedentary Gypsies, who have lived for two years in their place of residence" and were "politically and criminally unsuspicious," should be left where they lived.[52] Of course the assessment of political reliability allowed the Security Police and military units great latitude; the idea of "itinerants" is, in times of war and its masses of refugees, a relative term too. Obviously the vague definition was officially retained until the end of the occupation, because instructions of the 281st Security Division in Army Group North's rear area from 1942 and 1943 still refer to the order from November 1941.[53]

German files do not allow a clear judgment about the practical implementation of the official "Gypsy" orders, as only four reports on shootings of Roma in the year 1942 are preserved. The files of the Extraordinary State Commission help to complete the picture about the actual course of events: concerning the year 1941, no large-scale mass shootings of Roma were registered in this military area.[54] The ChGK files do not allow an exact conclusion as to how Roma were treated in this period. It is very likely, however, that they were put under strengthened Security Police control and used for forced labor, as happened in Estonia.[55] At least one example confirms this assumption: in 1941, several Romani families, altogether twenty-six persons, were deported from Luga to the village of Filippovshchina in the region of Gdov, where they were quartered with Russian farmers and forced to serve in agriculture. Thus, the deportation was also economically motivated. At the end of February 1942, however, an *Einsatzkommando* consisting of Germans, Finns, and Estonians came to Filippovshchina and shot the Roma. The murder of the Roma of Filippovshchina was the beginning of a whole series of massacres beginning in spring 1942. According to the—far from complete—data of the Extraordinary State Commission and MVD materials, between thirteen hundred and fifteen hundred Roma were killed in the area. Geographically, the mass murders were spread all over the territory and were committed by different groups of perpetrators. The mass killings of Roma began in February and March 1942 and were initially perpetrated by mobile killing units of *Einsatzgruppe* A,[56] while in April 1942 stationary Security Police and SD units contributed to the persecution. In the same month, stationary local military units (*Ortskommandanturen*, Secret Field Police), started to engage in the persecution of Roma too, and it culminated in a frenzy of killing.[57]

The eastern parts of Belarus (the territories Vitebsk, Mogilev, Bobruysk, and Gomel) as well as the Soviet-Russian territories Smolensk, Velikie Luki (central and southern part), Bryansk, Orel, Kursk, and Belgorod belonged to the militarily administered territories under Army Group Center—in accordance with Soviet administrative practice.[58] The Wehrmacht troops were followed by *Einsatzgruppe* B, which consisted of 650 men and was divided into two *Einsatzkommandos* (8 and 9), two *Sonderkommandos* (7a and 7b), as well as a so-called *Vorkommando Moskau* (Advance Commando Moscow), which was dissolved after the German defeat in front of Moscow.[59] According to reports of *Einsatzgruppe* B, the mobile killing units had liquidated 142,359 persons up to the end of March 1943.[60] Among the victims were numerous Roma. The earliest reports about mass executions of "Gypsies" came from eastern Belarus. In September 1941, *Einsatzkommando* 9 killed 23 Roma near Lepel, who had been handed over to the mobile unit by the *Feldkommandantur* (Field Headquarters) 181.[61] In October and November, the military commanders issued some very harsh orders concerning *all* Roma. On October 10, 1941, the Wehrmacht Commander in Belarus, *General* Gustav Freiherr von Bechtolsheim, ordered that "Gypsies be immediately shot at their place of capture." Six weeks later, he explicitly linked the fate of "Gypsies" and Jews by ordering that "the Jews must disappear from the countryside and the Gypsies, too, must be annihilated."[62] On the other hand, we have no proof, neither in German nor in Soviet sources, that this radical command was put into practice, at least not immediately. Only beginning in 1942 did the area of Mogilev turn into the main killing field of Roma, when *Einsatzkommando* 8 undertook several "Gypsy actions." Christian Gerlach estimates the number of murdered Roma in Belarus at no fewer than 3,000.[63]

Concerning the occupied parts of Soviet Russia, the territory of Smolensk plays a key role for the general evaluation of the Nazi's systematic persecution of "Gypsies." Smolensk was one of a few Soviet regions with a relatively compact sedentary Romani population. The local Bolsheviks celebrated this fact as the supposed result of Soviet nationalities policy, which helped the "miserable itinerants" to become sedentary, although most of the members of the newly founded "national Gypsy kolkhozes" had been farmers long before the October Revolution.[64] Furthermore, some national kolkhozes were ethnically mixed, as more and more Russian families joined them during the 1930s. It could be for this reason that the Smolensk "Gypsy kolkhozes" survived the turning point of Soviet nationalities policy in 1938, when smaller ethnic minorities lost their cultural rights and institutions.[65]

Before the German occupation, the ethnically mixed village of Aleksandrovka[66] belonged to a "national Gypsy kolkhoz" named Stalin's Constitution (*Stalinskaia konstitutsiia*), which was founded in 1937. In the early evening of April 23, 1942, two German officers came to the village of Aleksandrovka and ordered the bookkeeper to write a list of the villagers. She was supposed to divide it into family groups and nationalities.[67] At around five o'clock in the morning, an armed SS unit[68] intruded into the villagers' houses and drove them by force to a nearby lake. A short time after, several "Gypsy" families of the neighboring village Devkino were led to the same place. Right after their arrival, a German officer, "who knew the Russian language well," read the list of names out loud, separating the "Gypsies" from the others. After the selection had finished, the Russian villagers were sent home, whereas the remaining

"Gypsies" were put under a strengthened guard. The physically strongest men were chosen for digging two pits with shovels. At around 2 p.m., the Germans "drove" the women, children, and old men "like cattle" to the pits, "beating them with sticks and whips," whereby "a lot [of them] were beaten to unconsciousness." In the rising panic and disorder some persons managed to escape.[69] Others implored for mercy and claimed to be Russians. As a result, the Germans undressed them and carried out a kind of "racial examination." According to the witnesses' statements, the colors of hair and skin played the decisive role for the decision.[70] Later on, the male "Gypsies" went through the same procedure. Andrei Semchenkov recalled: "The officers began to examine the Gypsies, they lifted their clothes and looked at the naked bodies of the women and men.... The officers inspected my body, touched my breast and hands, seized my nose and ears, and let me go home after all."[71] One woman was even allowed to return to her house under an escort to get her passport to prove that she was Russian by nationality.[72] The other "Gypsies" had to undress in a barn and to hand over their valuables. The eyewitness Lidiia Krylova described to the commission the terrible details of the subsequent shooting:

> Each family was led separately to the pit, and if someone did not move to it, they lugged him. The shooting was carried out by a soldier with a pistol. First the ten- to twelve-year-old children were shot in front of their mothers' eyes, then the babies were torn out of the mothers' arms and thrown alive into the pit. Only after all this was the mother shot. Some of the mothers could not stand the torture and jumped alive after their babies.... But not only children were thrown alive into the pit. With my own eyes I saw how they threw the old woman Leonovich [in], who could not move and was put into a blanket by her daughters and carried by hand.[73]

After the shooting, the male "Gypsies" had to fill the mass grave with earth, before they were shot in the second pit. Returning to the town of Smolensk, the Germans took with them the valuables and some clothes of the murdered victims.[74]

The exhumation of the dead bodies revealed that 176 persons were shot on April 24, 1942. One hundred forty-three of them—62 women, 29 men, 52 children—were identified, whereas 33 persons could not be identified because of missing documents and family books.[75] Among the adult victims were kolkhoz workers, educators, and three teachers. The degree of social adaptation and the extent to which they were settled, however, did not play any role for the mass shooting in Aleksandrovka. Furthermore, the Germans did not investigate possible partisan activity.

The Roma were killed as Roma. The twofold selection with the help of a list of names and a physical examination demonstrates without any doubt the racist-ideological motivation of the perpetrators.

Further mass murders were perpetrated by the mobile killing units in other Romani settlements of the Smolensk territory. Hence the persecution of Roma in the Smolensk territory was—beginning in the spring of 1942—systematic and aimed at complete extermination. The chairman of the local Extraordinary State Commission of Smolensk, Popov, came to the same conclusion in his final report to Moscow: "Special racial atrocities (*rasovye izuverstva*) were committed [by the Germans] against the Jewish and Gypsy population. Jews and Gypsies were completely (*pogolovno*) and everywhere exterminated."[76]

The same can be said about the Bryansk region. From the spring of 1942 on, the "Gypsies" of the Bryansk territory were not only treated like Jews, but in some cases were also even killed and buried together with them.[77] The fact that the complete extermination of the Soviet Romani population started only in the spring of 1942 does not call into question the intentional and total nature of this genocide. Although the files of the Extraordinary State Commission do not permit an estimation of the total number of Romani victims, it is nevertheless possible to observe that in regard to intensity and quantity, the western parts of Soviet Russia were a center of the Nazi extermination of "Gypsies" during World War II.

Conclusion

Otto Ohlendorf, the leader of *Einsatzgruppe* D, played without any doubt an important role in the radicalization of the Nazi persecution of Soviet Roma. Although some military leaders like von Bechtolsheim in Belarus issued radical anti-"Gypsy" orders in the autumn of 1941, Ohlendorf's units in the south of the Soviet Union were the only ones that actually murdered Roma on a large scale, and in doing so initiated a practical genocide. Already in the autumn of 1941, the *Sonderkommandos* of *Einsatzgruppe* D committed the first mass shootings of sedentary Roma in the region of Nikolayev. The persecution in the Crimea, where the extermination of "Gypsies" proceeded more or less parallel to the extermination of Jews and Krimchaks, took a particularly systematic course. In December 1941 the bigger cities of the peninsula, which had separate "Gypsy quarters," were "cleansed." As in the Jewish case, the perpetrators used calls for registration and alleged resettlement in order to trick the Romani victims. By January 1942 the towns of Simferopol, Kerch, and Yevpatoria were considered to be *zigeunerfrei* (free of Gypsies). In the following months, the rural areas of the Crimea were combed too. In April 1942, Ohlendorf reported to the RSHA that with a few exceptions, "Jews, Krimchaks, and Gypsies" "no longer existed" in the Crimea. In regard to Roma, he was wrong. Almost one-third of the Roma survived the occupation thanks to the solidarity of the Tatar population—a local peculiarity of the Crimean example.

At the Nuremberg *Einsatzgruppen* trial of 1947–48, Ohlendorf justified the extermination of Roma with an (allegedly) approved general suspicion of espionage by "these nomadic people"—although the huge majority of the Crimean Roma consisted of sedentary town dwellers—and with a verbal order to place "Jews and Gypsies" on the same level in terms of treatment, which was purportedly given a few days before the assault on the Soviet Union on June 22, 1941. Some of the other defendants supported Ohlendorf's statement, but it is clear that such an order could not have been given at that early stage.

It is striking that from the outset, Ohlendorf's *Einsatzgruppe* D did not differentiate between sedentary and so-called itinerant "Gypsies." This is the most important difference to the other German-occupied Soviet territories, where the systematic obliteration of entire Romani communities did not start until the beginning of 1942. Before that time, German anti-"Gypsy" orders concentrated almost exclusively on alleged itinerants; records on the mass shootings of sedentary Roma are scarce, with some exceptions in Belarus and central Ukraine.

It becomes clear that Ohlendorf acted on his own authority when he decided to unite the fate of *all* Roma with that of the Jews. In doing so, the commander of *Einsatzgruppe* D became to a certain degree the trailblazer for the complete "solution of the Gypsy question" on Soviet soil. His murderous activity certainly influenced the decision-making process of the other *Einsatzgruppen* leaders, insofar as Ohlendorf's formal transgressions were obviously in no way restricted, neither by the *Reichssicherheitshauptamt* nor by the relevant military commander. Furthermore, Ohlendorf must have attained some position of authority among the Security Police and SD leaders, to the extent that he was the longest serving of the four original *Einsatzgruppen* commanders.[78] The continuity of his anti-"Gypsy" measures, as reflected in the *Ereignismeldungen*, obviously served as a guideline for the newcomers among the commanders of *Einsatzgruppen* A, B, and C. As a consequence, from the spring of 1942 on, in all militarily administered areas of occupation, the German Security Police treated Soviet Roma de facto like Jews and tried to eradicate them completely.

Notes

I would like to extend my gratitude for valuable critical comments on my article to the three editors of the volume—Alex J. Kay, Jeff Rutherford, and David Stahel—as well as to Andrej Angrick and Mikhail Tiaglyi.

1. In my text, I will use the ethnic and cultural expression "Roma" (fem. sing., "Romni"; masc. sing., "Rom") with respect to the Romani people. The word "Gypsy" comes from an extraneous point of view, and I will mark its constructional character by the use of quotation marks. Furthermore, I will omit fashionable political expressions such as *porraimos* or "Gypsy holocaust," which are inexact and confusing. *Porraimos* (from *porrovav*—to devour) evokes at least in some Romani dialects associations of sexuality, while "Gypsy holocaust" uses the Hebrew word polemically in order to underline parallels between the Nazi persecution of Jews and "Gypsies." See Nikolai Bessonov, "Ob ispol'zovanii terminov 'Poraimos' i 'Kholokost' v znachenii 'genotsid tsygan,'" in *Golokost i Suchasnist'* 2, no. 1 (2007): 71–82.

2. So far we have only estimates about the actual extent of the crime in the German-occupied Soviet Union. The most widespread approximate number of Romani victims is thirty thousand, which Donald Kenrick and Grattan Puxon derived from pre- and postwar censuses of the USSR. See Donald Kenrick and Grattan Puxon, *Sinti und Roma: Die Vernichtung eines Volkes im NS-Staat* (Göttingen: Gesellschaft für bedrohte Volker, 1981), 105.

3. Walter Manoschek, *"Serbien ist judenfrei!" Militärische Besatzungspolitik und Judenvernichtung in Serbien, 1941/42* (Munich: Oldenbourg, 1993), 39, 96–102; on the persecution of Roma in Serbia, see also Karola Fings, Cordula Lissner, and Frank Sparing, *". . . einziges Land, in dem Judenfrage, und Zigeunerfrage gelöst": Die Verfolgung der Roma im faschistisch besetzten Jugoslawien 1941–1945* (Cologne: Rom e.V. Köln, 1992).

4. See Tomislav Dulić, *Utopias of Nation: Local Killing in Bosnia and Herzegovina, 1941–1942* (Uppsala: Uppsala Universitet, 2005).

5. Wolfgang Wippermann, "Nur eine Fußnote? Die Verfolgung der sowjetischen Roma: Historiographie, Motive, Verlauf," in *Gegen das Vergessen: Der Vernichtungskrieg gegen die Sowjetunion, 1941–1945*, ed. Klaus Meyer and Wolfgang Wippermann (Frankfurt am Main: Haag u. Herchen, 1992), 75–90.

6. Wolfgang Wippermann, *"Auserwählte Opfer?" Shoah und Porrajmos im Vergleich: Eine Kontroverse* (Berlin: Frank & Timme, 2005), 121.

7. Michael Zimmermann, *Rassenutopie und Genozid: Die nationalsozialistische "Lösung der Zigeunerfrage"* (Hamburg: Christians, 1996), 263; and Michael Zimmermann, "The Soviet Union and the Baltic States, 1941–1944: The Massacre of the Gypsies," in *In the Shadow of the Swastika: The Gypsies*

During the Second World War, ed. Donald Kenrick (Hertfordshire: University of Hertfordshire Press, 1999), 131–48.

8. In Soviet historiography, the topic was restricted to the mention of single mass shootings, without contextualization. In the 1960s, the Russian writer and journalist Lev Ginzburg extensively collected materials for a general monograph about the Nazi genocide of Roma, but for unknown reasons he never published on this topic. On Ginzburg, see Meeting of the writer L. V. Ginzburg with the ensemble of the theatre "Romen," May 11, 1967, f. 2928, op. 1, d. 74, ll. 1–31, Rossiiskii Gosudarstvennyi Arkhiv Literatury i Iskusstva.

9. Mikhail Tiaglyi, "Chingene—Zhertvy kholokosta? Natsistskaia politika v Krymu v otnoshenii tsygan i evreev, 1941–1944," in *Odessa i evreiskaia tsivilizatsiia, sbornik materialov 4-oi mezhdunarodnoi nauchnoi konferentsii: Katastrofa, soprotivlenie, pobeda (31 oktiabria–2 noiabria 2005g., Odessa)*, ed. *Evreiskii obshchinyi tsentr "Migdal"* (Odessa: Studiia "Negotsiant," 2006), 140–75. On Ukraine, see Aleksandr Kruglov, "Genotsid tsygan v Ukraine v 1941–1944 gg.: Statistiko-regional'nyi aspekt," *Golokost i Suchasnist'* 2, no. 6 (2009): 83–113. Some details can also be found in Ilya Al'tman, *Zhertvy nenavisti: Kholokost v SSSR, 1941–1945 gg.* (Moscow: Kovcheg, 2002). The Russian author and expert on the Roma, Nikolai Bessonov, has a book in progress titled *Tragediia tsygan* (*The Tragedy of the Gypsies*).

10. These files are located in the Central Archive of the Ministry of Defense of the Russian Federation (Tsentral'nyi Arkhiv Ministerstva Oborony Rossiiskoi Federatsii). See also F. D. Sverdlov, ed., *Dokumenty obviniaiut: Kholokost: svidetel'stva Krasnoi Armii* (Moscow: Sbornik, 1996).

11. The complete name is CHREZVYCHAINAIA GOSUDARSTVENNAIA KOMISSIIA po ustanovleniiu i rassledovaniiu zlodeianii nemetsko-fashistskikh zakhvatchikov i ikh soobshchnikov i prichinennogo imi ushcherba grazhdanam, kollektivnym khoziaistvam (kolkhozam), obshchestvennym organizatsiiam, gosudarstvennym predpriiatiiam, i uchrezhdeniiam SSSR. Hereafter, "Extraordinary State Commission" or "ChGK."

12. See Zimmermann, *Rassenutopie und Genozid*; Wippermann, "Nur eine Fußnote?"; Wippermann, *"Auserwählte Opfer?"*; Guenter Lewy, *The Nazi Persecution of the Gypsies* (New York: Oxford University Press, 2000); Yehuda Bauer, *Rethinking the Holocaust* (New Haven: Yale University Press, 2001); and Helmut Krausnick, *Hitlers Einsatzgruppen: Die Truppe des Weltanschauungskrieges, 1938–1942* (Frankfurt am Main: Fischer Taschenbuch, 1985).

13. See *Trials of War Criminals before the Nurenberg Military Tribunals under Control Council Law No. 10*, vol. 4, *The Einsatzgruppen Case* (Washington, DC: US Government Printing Office, n.d.), 244 (hereafter TWC).

14. TWC, 287; and Zimmermann, *Rassenutopie und Genozid*, 261.

15. Andrej Angrick, *Besatzungspolitik und Massenmord: Die Einsatzgruppe D in der südlichen Sowjetunion, 1941–1943* (Hamburg: Hamburger Edition, 2003), 252.

16. Ibid.

17. For a detailed description of the massacre see Zimmermann, *Rassenutopie und Genozid*, 264–65.

18. In "Ereignismeldung UdSSR Nr. 150" (hereafter EM), January 2, 1942, it is mentioned that Alushta was now "free of Jews (*judenfrei*)," R 58/219, fol. 378, Bundesarchiv Berlin-Lichterfelde (hereafter BAB). That Alushta was also free of "Gypsies" was not mentioned in the report, but it was stated by Willi Hasbach, Hans Stamm, and Johann Welsch (all former members of *Sonderkommando* 11b) during the Munich trial. See Angrick, *Besatzungspolitik und Massenmord*, 346.

19. See EM 178, March 9, 1942, R 58/221, fol. 64, BAB; EM 184, March 23, 1942, R 58/221, fol. 130, BAB; and EM 190, April 8, 1942, R 58/221, fol. 268, BAB.

20. EM 190, April 8, 1942, R 58/221, fol. 267, BAB.

21. See Protokol doprosa svidetelia: Kemilev, Nejsha, June 8, 1944, f. 7021, op. 9 (Krymskaia ASSR), d. 38, ll. 212–213, Gosudarstvennyi Arkhiv Rossiiskoi Federatsii (hereafter GARF). The course of the action was confirmed by a surviving Rom, who worked before the occupation in the village Kamysh-Burun as a smith.

22. Protokol doprosa svidetelia: Kurtuliarov, Iakub, tsygan po natsional'nosti, May 22, 1944, f. 7021, op. 9, d. 57, ll. 34-34ob, GARF.

23. On Feodosiya, see f. R-1458, op. 1, d. 4, l. 122, Gosudarstvennyi Arkhiv Avtonomnoi Respubliki Krym (hereafter GAARK); and Tiaglyi, "Chingene," 161–62. On Biiuk-Onlarskii, see f. 7021, op. 9 (Krymskaia, ASSR), d. 34, l. 96, GARF.

24. See the report of the Dzhankoi ChGK commission, October 8, 1944, as well as the corresponding witness testimonies, f. 7021, op. 9 (Krymskaia, ASSR), d. 193, ll. 12, 17ob, 19ob, GARF.

25. See Tiaglyi, "Chingene," 162, 167.

26. In the village Terepli-Abash, 32 "Gypsies" were killed in total; in Arlin-Barin, 6; in Nem-Barin, 8; in Shirin, 2; in Mikhailovka, 2; in the kolkhoz "Bol'shevik," 25; in the village Avlach, 2; and in the kolkhoz "Eighth of March (8 marta)," 3. See Tiaglyi, "Chingene," 167.

27. Nachal'nik 2 Otdeleniia OSP MVD SSSR kapitan V. P. Trofimov, Spravka o kolichestve lits drugikh natsional'nostei, nakhodiashchikhsia na spetsposelenii, vyselennykh s nemtsami, s vyselentsami Kavkaza, Kryma, no ne vkhodiashchikh v sostav semei etikh kontingentov, 31 dekabria 1949, f. R-9479, op. 1, d. 436, l. 26, GARF. Printed in N. F. Bugai, ed., *Deportatsiia narodov Kryma* (Moscow: Insan, 2002), 114.

28. Sovershenno sekretno. OPERUPOLNOMOCHENNYI 1 OTD 5 OTDELA GUBB NKVD SSSR, Leitenant gosbezopasnosti SAVINOV, Spravka po tsyganskim kochevym taboram za 1944 god, February 9, 1945, f.9478 (Glavnoe upravlenie po bor'be s banditizmom MVD SSSR), op. 1, d. 459 (1945), l. 18, GARF. The actual purpose of the statistics was to find out the number of itinerant "Gypsies," but the Crimean report concluded that "no Gypsies at all" were present on the peninsula.

29. Unfortunately, the number of Roma in the Crimea can only be estimated. In Soviet censuses, the total number fluctuated greatly because numerous Roma had Tatar passports. According to the census of 1939, about 2,064 "Gypsies" lived in the Crimea, 998 of them in towns and 1,066 in the countryside. Yet at the beginning of the occupation in November 1941, around 1,700 Roma were registered in Simferopol alone. In view of the latter numbers, a total Crimean Romani population of 3,500 to 4,000 persons seems to be realistic.

30. See Zimmermann, *Rassenutopie und Genozid*, 264.

31. Tiaglyi, "Chingene," 163–65. A further indication for the unlimited solidarity with Roma in the Crimea is the fact that no denunciations against them can be found in the archives, as happened in the case of Jews on a massive scale (172).

32. From the diary of Kh. G. Lashkevich, *Peredaite detiam nashim o nashei sud'be* (Simferopol': BETs "Khesed Shimon," 2002), 63. For detailed quotations, see Tiaglyi, "Chingene," 162.

33. R. Adil'sha ogly, "Kuda podevalis' krymskie tsygane," in *Krym*, no. 48 (1994): 2; and Tiaglyi, "Chingene," 163.

34. Tatars, convicted as Soviet agents, for example, were liquidated with no consideration for their ethnic origins or religious beliefs, although the Muslim Committee tried everything to save them. See Angrick, *Besatzungspolitik und Massenmord*, 473. Against this backdrop, the way the rescue in Bakhchisarai allegedly took place seems to be unrealistic: according to Memish Reshid, the "Gypsies" were already collected for transport when the Moslem mayor Fenerov convinced the Germans that the deportees were Moslems. Fenerov warned the Germans that he "cannot be the head of a town in which Moslems are shot. After that, the repressions ended." See Memish Reshid, "Zabytoe plemia," *Golos Kryma*, September 4, 1998, 5; and Tiaglyi, "Chingene," 165. Hence, the fact that the Romani community of Bakhchisarai actually survived the occupation (at least neither German nor Soviet files speak of a mass shooting) is transformed into an exaggerated heroic rescue legend in the area's collective memory.

35. See Film WF-03/14321, O.K. I/853, B. Tgb.Nr. 1259/42, an Kommandant rückw. Armeegebiet 553 vom 31.1.1942, Betr.: Tätigkeitsbericht für die Zeit vom 16.–31.1.1942, Bundesarchiv-Militärarchiv, Freiburg im

Breisgau (hereafter BA-MA); and Angrick, *Besatzungspolitik und Massenmord*, 496–97.

36. See Angrick, *Besatzungspolitik und Massenmord*, 504.

37. The situation in the rural parts of the Crimea after the mobile killing units of *Einsatzgruppe* D had left the peninsula in early summer 1942 is rather contradictory. On the one hand, the military administration obviously knew about the existence of remaining "Gypsies"—405 of them were listed in statistics of Crimean nationalities in July 1942. See Kdt. rückw. A.Geb. 553 an A.O.K. 11, O.Qu./Qu.2—betr. Zahlenmäßige Gliederung der Volkstumsgruppen auf der Krim. 15. Juli 1942, RH 23/94, fol. 217, BA-MA. In the following statistics, the "Gypsies" had been reduced to 345 persons. See Norbert Kunz, *Die Krim unter deutscher Herrschaft, 1941–1944: Germanisierungsutopie und Besatzungsrealität* (Darmstadt: Wissenschaftliche Buchgesellschaft, 2005), 194. On the other hand, the *Feldgendarmerie* of OK I/742 continued to search intensively for hidden Roma in the district of Fraidorf near Yevpatoria. In the reports of this unit there existed a special category "Discovery (*Feststellung*) of Jews and Gypsies." See Feldgendarmerie der OK I/742 (Freidorf), TB 26.4.-10.5.1942, RH 23/100, BA-MA.

38. See the examples in Tiaglyi, "Chingene," 173.

39. See TWC, 244.

40. ND, Fall IX, Nr. IX, Nr. A 6–8, fols. 669–73, STA Nürnberg; TWC, 287; and Zimmermann, *Rassenutopie und Genozid*, 261.

41. TWC, 287.

42. See, among others, Ralf Ogorreck and Volker Rieß, "Fall 9: Der Einsatzgruppenprozeß (gegen Otto Ohlendorf und andere)," in *Der Nationalsozialismus vor Gericht: Die alliierten Prozesse gegen Kriegsverbrecher und Soldaten, 1943–1952*, ed. Gerd R. Ueberschär (Frankfurt am Main: Fischer Taschenbuch, 1999), 164–65, 167–68; and Angrick, *Besatzungspolitik und Massenmord*, 74–113.

43. Chef der Sipo und des SD, B. Nr. IV-1100/geh.RS vom 2.7.1941 an die HSSPF, R 58/241, fols. 314–19, BAB; and Alfred Streim, *Die Behandlung sowjetischer Kriegsgefangener im "Fall Barbarossa"* (Heidelberg: Juristischer Verlag, 1981), 319–21.

44. See Ralf Ogorreck, *Die Einsatzgruppen und die "Genesis der Endlösung"* (Berlin: Metropol, 1996), 89; and Angrick, *Besatzungspolitik und Massenmord*, 149. Strangely enough, both Ogorreck and Angrick mention the statement by Rühl with an exclusive focus on the Jewish question, while the listed "Gypsies" remain uncommented. In the historiography on World War II, this attitude toward the topic of the Roma can be observed very often.

45. Ironically enough, even here Ohlendorf was wrong, as Wilhelm Solms has shown. Neither Huch nor Schiller mentions "Gypsy spies" in their works on the Thirty Years' War. See Wilhelm Solms, *Zigeunerbilder: Ein dunkles*

Kapitel der deutschen Literaturgeschichte: Von der frühen Neuzeit bis zur Romantik (Würzburg: Königshausen & Neumann, 2008), 10–11.

46. TWC, 287.

47. See Angrick, *Besatzungspolitik und Massenmord*, 529–30. On the military aspects of the siege of Sevastopol, see Bernd Wegner: "Der Krieg gegen die Sowjetunion," in Boog Horst, Werner Rahn, Reinhard Stumpf, and Bernd Wegner, *Der globale Krieg: Die Ausweitung zum Weltkrieg und der Wechsel der Initiative, 1941–1943*, vol. 6 of *Das Deutsche Reich und der Zweite Weltkrieg* (Stuttgart: Deutsche Verlags-Anstalt, 1990), 845–49.

48. See EM 139, November 28, 194, and EM 143, December 8, 1941, R 58/219, fols. 213–16 and 256–59, BAB; EM 152, February 7, 1942, R 58/220, fols. 35–46, BAB; and R 58/221, fols. 8–22, BAB.

49. See Tiaglyi, "Chingene," 159; and Kunz, *Krim unter deutscher Herrschaft*, 192.

50. See Andreas Zellhuber, *"Unsere Verwaltung treibt einer Katastrophe zu. . . .": Das Reichsministerium für die besetzten Ostgebiete und die deutsche Besatzungsherrschaft in der Sowjetunion, 1941–1945* (Munich: Ernst Vögel, 2006), 130–36. In December 1941, Estonia was integrated into the *Reichskommissariat* too, but at the same time it remained part of the military administration. See Anton Weiss-Wendt, "Extermination of the Gypsies in Estonia during World War II: Popular Images and Official Policies," *Holocaust and Genocide Studies* 17, no. 1 (2003): 31–61.

51. The center of Romani life in this area was the city of Leningrad, which did not fall under German occupation. For the same reason, numerous Roma starved to death during the German blockade.

52. The complete order is not preserved, but later orders and reports often paraphrase or refer to it. Compare, for example, ND, NOKW 2072, 281. Sich.Div., Abt., Ia/Ic/VII—297/42. 23.6.42, STA Nürnberg; and ND, NOKW 2022, 281. Sdv., Abt.VII/Ia, Tgb. Nr. 457/43 geh., March 24, 1943, an Feld.-Kdtr. 822, STA Nürnberg.

53. ND, NOKW 2072, 281. Sich.Div., Abt., Ia/Ic/VII—297/42. 23.6.42, STA Nürnberg; and NOKW 2022, 281. Sdv., Abt.VII/Ia, Tgb. Nr. 457/43 geh., March 24, 1943, an Feld.-Kdtr. 822, STA Nürnberg.

54. In November 1941, two "Gypsies" from the village Botanok (Dno region) were shot together with a Russian, but this isolated case probably took place in the course of a Security Police campaign against Communists, "Soviet intelligence," and Jews, which took place in October and November 1941. See Hans-Heinrich Wilhelm, "Die Einsatzgruppe A der Sicherheitspolizei und des SD 1941/42" (PhD diss, Munich, University of Munich, 1975), 242–44. The Soviet side also registered the extraordinary intensity of German persecution measures in this period. Compare AKT o zlodeianiiach nemetsko-fashistskikh zakhvatchikov i ikh soobshchnikov v Oredezhskom

raione Leningradskoi oblasti, f. 7021, op. 30 (Leningradskaia oblast'), d. 245, ll. 3-9; 3-4, GARF.

55. See Weiss-Wendt, "Extermination of the Gypsies," 40–44.

56. The special "Gypsy operation," for which a *Sonderkommando* was sent from Tallinn to the Pskov area, as a witness remembered at an Estonian postwar trial against war criminals, probably also took place during this very period. See the testimony of Kurivskii at the "Mere-Gerrets-Viik" trial in Tallinn, 1960/61, mentioned in Weiss-Wendt, "Extermination of the Gypsies," 54.

57. See Martin Holler, *Der nationalsozialistische Völkermord an den Roma in der besetzten Sowjetunion (1941–1944): Gutachten für das Dokumentations- und Kulturzentrum Deutscher Sinti und Roma* (Heidelberg: Dokumentations- und Kulturzentrum Deutscher Sinti und Roma, 2009), 30–52.

58. During the German advance on Moscow in the autumn of 1941, parts of the territories Kalinin (today Tver) and Kaluga also belonged to the occupied zone, but this situation lasted only several weeks because of the partial withdrawal of the Wehrmacht.

59. See Krausnick, *Hitlers Einsatzgruppen*, 156–62.

60. See Christian Gerlach, "Die Einsatzgruppe B," in *Die Einsatzgruppen in der besetzten Sowjetunion, 1941/42: Die Tätigkeits- und Lageberichte des Chefs der Sicherheitspolizei und des SD*, ed. Peter Klein (Berlin: Edition Hentrich, 1997), 62.

61. Christian Gerlach, *Kalkulierte Morde: Die deutsche Wirtschafts- und Vernichtungspolitik in Weißrußland, 1941 bis 1944* (Hamburg: Hamburger Edition, 1999), 1062–63.

62. See Eric Haberer, "The German Police and the Genocide in Belorussia, 1941–1944, Part 2, The 'Second Sweep': Gendarmerie Killings of Jews and Gypsies on January 29, 1942," *Journal of Genocide Research* 3, no. 2 (2001): 207–18; and Gerlach, *Kalkulierte Morde*, 1065.

63. See Gerlach, *Kalkulierte Morde*, 1066–67.

64. Writing of Gerasimov to the Constitution Commission, October 12, 1936, f. 3316 (TsIK SSSR), op. 28, d. 794, ll. 144–144ob., GARF; and Vypolneniia postanovleniia Kollegii NKZema RSFSR ot 15 marta 1933 g. po obsledovaniiu tsyganskikh kolkhozov, April 28, 1933, f. 1235 (VTsIK), op. 123, d. 28, ll. 70–70ob, GARF.

65. Tatiana F. Kiseleva, "Tsygany Evropeiskoi chasti Soiuza SSR i ikh perekhod ot kochevaniia k osedlosti" (PhD diss., Moscow State University, 1952), 168. Only schools such as the "Gypsy" middle school in the town of Smolensk were closed in August 1938. See Protokol zasedaniia prezidiuma Smolenskogo oblastnogo ispolnitel'nogo komiteta, August 31, 1938, f. 2361, op. 1, d. 37 (Prezidium Smoloblispolkoma), ll. 499–500, Gosudarstvennyi

Arkhiv Smolenskoi Oblasti (hereafter GASO). On Soviet nationalities policy in general, see Terry Martin, *The Affirmative Action Empire: Nations and Nationalism in the Soviet Union, 1923–1939* (Ithaca: Cornell University Press, 2001).

66. The official name is Aleksandrovskoe, but it is very rarely used.

67. See the testimony protocol of the bookkeeper Fekla Riabkova, October 11, 1943, f. 7021, op. 44, d. 1091, ll. 37ob. 38, GARF.

68. In the commission reports, the perpetrators are called a "retaliation unit" (*karatel'nyi otriad*), consisting of SS forces (ibid., ll. 1–3). The witnesses also call them Gestapo, German soldiers, or simply Germans.

69. Testimony protocol of Mariia Lazareva [Romni], October 10, 1943, f. 7021, op. 44, d. 1091, l. 9ob., GARF.

70. Proskovia Timchenkova described her unexpected rescue the following way: "The German officer dragged my dress apart and examined my breast and hands, he took off my headscarf and looked at my hair, and after that he acknowledged me as Russian-like and took me to the side." The parents of Timchenkova and one of her brothers were freed too, while the rest of the family was shot. See the testimony protocol of Proskovia Timchenkova [Romni], October 10, 1943, f. 7021, op. 44, d. 1091, l. 25, GARF.

71. Testimony protocol of Andrei Semchenkov [Russian, mother Romni], October 11, 1943 (ibid., ll. 28–28ob).

72. See the testimony protocol of Lidiia Krylova [Romni], October 10, 1943, f. 7021, op. 44, d. 1091, l. 13, GARF.

73. Krylova herself was also led to the pit, but at the very last moment she was acknowledged to be Russian and sent home (ibid., ll. 13ob.–14).

74. Ibid., ll. 1–2.

75. Ibid., ll. 4–4ob., 42–44. Among the victims were two Roma from Korenevshchina and five from another village who happened to be in Aleksandrovka on that very day.

76. DOKLADNAIA ZAPISKA ob itogakh ucheta ushcherba i zlodeianii nemetsko-fashistskikh zakhvatchikov v Smolenskoi oblasti. Predsedatel' Smolenskoi oblastnoi komissii D. Popov—CHREZVYCHAINOI GOSUDARSTVENNOI KOMISSII SSSR, f. 7021, op. 44 (Smolenskaia oblast'), d. 1091, l. 19, GARF. Printed in *Vse sud'by v edinuiu slity: Po rassekrechennym arkhivnym dokumentam. K 60-letiiu osvobozhdeniia Smolenshchiny ot nemetsko-fashistskikh zakhvatchikov*, ed. Administratsiia Smolenskoi oblasti and Departament Smolenskoi oblasti po delam arkhivov (Smolensk: 2003). 136. Also to be found in f. 1630, op. 2, d. 29, ll. 182–213, GASO.

77. See Holler, *Der nationalsozialistische Völkermord*, 61–63.

78. I am grateful to Alex J. Kay, who called my attention to the importance of Ohlendorf's continuity in service in the *Einsatzgruppen*.

CHAPTER 11

THE DEVELOPMENT OF GERMAN POLICY IN OCCUPIED FRANCE, 1941, AGAINST THE BACKDROP OF THE WAR IN THE EAST

Thomas J. Laub

As they planned to invade the Soviet Union, Nazi leaders developed new policies that required soldiers to pillage conquered territory and liquidate racial enemies. In contrast to the regulations that governed the 1940 invasion of Western Europe, directives issued before the invasion of the Soviet Union ordered German soldiers to disregard the Hague and Geneva conventions and injected an unprecedented level of violence into military occupation policy. Enduring Soviet resistance elicited further changes in German military policy in the latter half of 1941. The Armed Forces High Command (*Oberkommando der Wehrmacht*, or OKW) and the Army High Command (*Oberkommando des Heeres*, or OKH) reduced the number of administrative and security personnel in Western Europe, sent all available reserves to the Eastern Front, and ordered the men in charge of all rear areas and occupied territories to suppress resistance activity with the troops who remained at their disposal. Obeying directives from Berlin as well as acting on their own initiative, field commanders employed exemplary violence against civilians, shot hostages in response to any act of resistance, and mounted a deadly campaign against alleged Jewish partisans. As the German offensive ground to a halt in December, Nazi leaders revamped German policy to offset manpower and material losses incurred during the course of Operation Barbarossa. Army quartermasters requisitioned additional supplies from conquered farms and factories while Fritz Sauckel, the plenipotentiary for labor deployment, began to collect millions of foreign workers for service in the German war economy. At every stage of Operation Barbarossa, from planning through execution, Hitler exhorted subordinates to employ ever more violent methods in an increasingly desperate bid to achieve the economic, military, and racial goals of the Nazi regime.

Situated on the western edge of Hitler's empire, France provides a vantage point from which to view the radicalization of Nazi policy and practices during 1941. Policy directives and operational orders for *Fall Gelb* (Case Yellow), the German plan for the invasion of France, directed soldiers to obey the laws of war. After Germany conquered France in the spring of 1940, Hitler installed a military government in occupied France and ordered his military commander to exploit French industrial resources. Practices applied in France between July 1940 and June 1941 usually corresponded with the terms of the Hague Convention. Departing from standards established in 1939 and 1940, policies developed for Operation Barbarossa, Hitler's plan for the conquest of the Soviet Union, violated the laws of war and gradually spread to France as Germany's strategic position deteriorated in the fall of 1941. Citing precedents established on the Eastern Front, SS leaders and some German officers pressed for disproportionate, collective reprisals as French resistance emerged in August 1941. Reluctant to alienate the cooperative Vichy regime, the military commander in France (*Militärbefehlshaber in Frankreich*, or MBF) condemned first the confiscation of Jewish property and later mass executions, but to no avail. Working through the OKW and OKH, Hitler engineered the MBF's resignation in early 1942. The Führer placed an allegedly timid general in charge of the German military administration, installed a higher SS and police leader (*Höherer SS- und Polizeiführer* or HSSPF) in France, and allowed the plenipotentiary for labor deployment to dragoon French workers. Inspired by disagreements that flared during the latter half of 1941, changes instituted in the spring of 1942 broke the army's monopoly of power in France, installed dedicated Nazis in leadership positions, and promised to harmonize German policy in occupied France with practices established in the Soviet Union.

Policies and Practices in France, October 1939–June 1941

Hitler treated France with a degree of caution at the start of World War II. During the 1939 Polish campaign, he directed ground, air, and naval units stationed on the Western Front to assume a purely defensive posture, and many of these restrictions remained in force after British Prime Minister Neville Chamberlain rejected Hitler's peace offer on October 12.[1] Convinced that time was not working in his favor, Hitler ordered military subordinates to prepare an immediate offensive against the Netherlands, Belgium, and Northern France. Designed to secure bases for subsequent operations against the British Isles, October and November 1939 versions of *Fall Gelb* admonished soldiers to respect private property, forbade attacks on large cities "without compelling military reasons," and directed

The Development of German Policy in Occupied France 291

troops to obey the provisions of the Hague Convention.² Furthermore, the Führer placed the army in charge of occupied territory and barred nonmilitary personnel from the combat zone without explicit permission from the OKH. Excluded from the German order of battle, *SS Einsatzgruppen* could not murder civilians or Jews as they had done in Poland.³ In stark contrast to orders issued shortly before Operation Barbarossa, both Hitler and senior military leaders expected a protracted battle on the Western Front and took steps to limit atrocities that might fortify resistance or discredit the Nazi regime in 1939 and early 1940.

Initial schemes for the invasion of the Low Countries and a fragment of Northern France evolved into a daring new strategy during the winter of 1939–40. Shifting the main point of attack from Army Group B opposite the Netherlands and Northern Belgium to Army Group A concentrated in the Ardennes forest, the OKH launched a revised version of *Fall Gelb* on the morning of May 10, 1940.⁴ After two weeks of combat, German armored divisions isolated the British Expeditionary Force and a substantial portion of the French army around Dunkirk and won a decisive victory. A follow-up strike launched on June 5 began with a significant numerical advantage and captured huge swathes of territory in central France and along the Atlantic coast. Viewing the military situation as hopeless, Marshal Philippe Pétain formed his own cabinet, supplanted Paul Reynaud as prime minister, and requested an armistice on June 17.

Aside from notable exceptions like the massacre of British soldiers at Le Paradis, German soldiers treated Caucasian opponents in accordance with the rules of war during the 1940 campaign, though this sense of restraint did not extend to French colonial troops. Justified by the alleged shame of being occupied by black soldiers after World War I and the rumored barbarity of African troops, some German soldiers murdered between 1,500 and 3,000 Senegalese infantrymen in 1940.⁵ During the campaign, the army captured approximately 1.5 million French prisoners of war. Half of these spent the remainder of World War II in prison camps under the protection of the Hague and Geneva conventions, and the remainder were either liberated outright or granted a furlough in France before returning to Germany as civilian workers.⁶ As in the Polish campaign, some German troops committed war crimes on their own accord, but the OKH did not organize and German soldiers did not mount a genocidal campaign in 1940. Instead, the German army treated 93,000 French civilians in military hospitals, distributed scarce gasoline to stranded travelers, and fed millions of refugees caught in the exodus of defeat. Anticipating a prolonged fight, the OKH and field commanders tried to buy French goodwill with gasoline, food, and medicine in 1940, but they adopted a very different strategy in the Soviet Union. Expecting a quick victory, German military leaders endorsed a rapacious policy of ruthless exploitation that liquidated ideological opponents and intimidated the remaining population during Operation Barbarossa.[7]

Signed on June 22, 1940, the Franco-German Armistice vested Germany with "all the rights of an occupying power," but an unsigned note appended to the agreement stated that Germany "did not intend to burden itself with the civil administration and with caring for the population." While Britain continued to defy Hitler, French cooperation had some value. Hitler sanctioned a relatively moderate policy of economic exploitation to maintain relations with the Vichy regime and discourage the defection of French colonies to the Allied cause.[8] Lenient terms of the Franco-German Armistice may have dismayed Hitler's entourage, but they did not reflect the Führer's ultimate goals.[9] Viewing France as an inveterate enemy, Hitler promised to undo four hundred years of alleged robbery by incorporating Flanders, Alsace, Lorraine, the Ardennes, and the Argonne into the Reich in accordance with *Staatssekretär* Wilhelm Stuckart's plan, but only *after* the war.[10] While hostilities with Great Britain continued, Hitler pursued modest goals set forth in obsolescent 1939 directives and ordered subordinates in Western Europe to suppress talk of future annexations, saying little about his long-term plans for France.

With vague instructions from superiors in Berlin, *General der Infanterie* Alfred Streccius assumed command of the German military government in France on June 30, 1940. Congruent with the aforementioned unsigned note attached to the armistice agreement, the MBF organized a regime that supervised the French government and ruled indirectly. Officers assigned to the military administration did not collect taxes, regulate the economy, or dispense justice on their own. With only 1,200 men at his disposal, the MBF may not have had any other choice. Acting through the Vichy regime, the military government concentrated on mundane issues like repatriating refugees and incarcerating prisoners of war in a bid to restore order and, more importantly, French industry.[11]

Although vested with substantial authority, the MBF did not have complete control over France. Abetted by Hitler, branches of the Nazi Party, various state agencies, and sections of the army obstructed Streccius's plans. Citing security concerns, field commanders preparing for the invasion of England expelled enemy (e.g., British, Dutch, and Norwegian) citizens, stateless (Polish, Czech, and Austrian) refugees, and select racial groups (Jews and Roma) from nine French *départements* along the Atlantic coast. With Hitler's permission, *Gauleiter* Robert Wagner and

Joseph Bürckel began to expel French nationalists from their respective domains in Alsace and Lorraine on August 2. Deportations stirred fears of German annexations, added another one hundred thousand refugees to the exodus created by military defeat, and aggravated relations with the French government.[12] Further complicating matters, Hitler appointed Otto Abetz to serve as the German ambassador in Paris on August 3, 1940. Responsible for "advising the military authorities on political questions," Abetz also received instructions to seize "Jewish artistic properties in accordance with special directives issued on that subject."[13] Without the MBF's knowledge, German diplomats gathered thousands of valuable objets d'art in a house adjacent to the German embassy. Opposition by the MBF and French protests convinced Abetz to stop the pillage in late August 1940, but Alfred Rosenberg's special action staff, the *Einsatzstab Reichsleiter Rosenberg*, stepped into the void and, with Hitler's approval, shipped thousands of boxcars full of cultural artefacts (*Külturgüter*) and household goods back to Germany by the end of the war.[14] At Hitler's behest, Abetz, Rosenberg, and two Nazi district leaders pursued strident Nazi agendas in France during 1940, but without executive authority or support from the MBF they struggled to fulfill their Nazi agendas until the SS took charge of German security policy on June 1, 1942.

When not fending off rivals, Streccius worried about the security of German occupation forces. Many French people acknowledged the correct behavior of German soldiers and blamed most of their problems on the Third Republic or, in an increasing number of cases, on the Jews. French police helped the MBF confiscate weapons, arrest German dissidents, and enforce price controls. Acts of resistance amounted to little more than cutting telephone and telegraph wires, and the MBF understood that such activity, although irritating, did not endanger his troops. During the month of August, German military courts sentenced three Frenchmen to death for the crimes of assault, unauthorized possession of firearms, and guerrilla activity, but the MBF and superiors in Berlin reduced two death sentences to prison terms. Statistics collected by the military administration suggest a sharp increase in the number of alleged transgressions in the final months of 1940 as police established control of the occupied zone, but most crimes amounted to little more than traffic infractions, blackout violations, and price control offenses. Thousands of petty misdeeds and some bone fide acts of resistance did not provoke harsh reprisals before the invasion of the Soviet Union.[15]

Although he did not have to contend with widespread resistance activity, *General* Streccius prepared for the worst. On September 12, 1940, he issued a directive entitled Measures to Prevent Sabotage that outlined four ways to combat resistance. Military administration officials could collect a security deposit that would be confiscated in the event of continued resistance, enroll residents in a local militia and force them to guard valuable infrastructure, and close restaurants, impose curfews, or ban the sale of alcohol. With "the greatest reserve," *General* Streccius also allowed his four regional commanders (*Bezirkchefs*) and the commandant of greater Paris to arrest hostages "who will pay with their lives if the public does not behave flawlessly." Understanding the risks associated with collective punishments, Streccius ordered subordinates to seize hostages only in response to serious atrocities, after careful consideration of all circumstances, and when other appropriate responses were unavailable. The MBF exercised direct control over all capital cases and he alone could authorize hostage executions.[16] Eight months later, the OKW and OKH broke longstanding precedents and encouraged junior officers to execute Jews, partisans, and political commissars on their own authority during Operation Barbarossa.

General der Flieger Otto von Stülpnagel replaced Streccius as MBF on October 25, 1940, but the latter's hostage policy remained in force with little alteration. Echoing cautions in Streccius's original directive, Stülpnagel argued that "the efficacy of taking hostages ... is questionable if an especially close bond does not exist between the perpetrator and the hostages. Hostages are to be arrested only if serious crimes have been committed and there are no other suitable means [of punishment] available." He warned subordinates to consider all circumstances and quash "unjust" or "unrealistic" reprisals that might discredit the military government.[17] Concurring with the MBF, military administration lawyers added that hostages could only be liable for acts that had been committed after their arrest and after the MBF had announced his hostage policy to the general public. Two months later, the military administration considered proscribing hostage seizures altogether. Distinguishing itself from civil administrations in charge of the Netherlands and Poland, the military administration in occupied France eschewed collective reprisals before the invasion of the Soviet Union.[18]

The MBF expressed a similar reluctance to apply anti-Semitic measures in his domain. Perceiving Jews as a potential security threat, the MBF's chief of staff barred Jews from reentering occupied France on September 20, 1940, and, one week later, directed Jews in the occupied zone to register with the French police. The military administration ordered Jewish businesses to display a bilingual sign reading *Jüdisches Geschäft/ Entreprise Juive*, but some German soldiers continued to patronize Jewish establishments.[19] On November 12, 1940, the OKH instructed the

MBF to confiscate abandoned Jewish businesses and use the proceeds to support the German war effort. In conjunction with the French government, a subsection of the military administration's economic division "Aryanized" 18,227 Jewish businesses during the occupation.[20] As the author of a book that detailed Allied transgressions during World War I, Stülpnagel understood the terms of the Hague Convention, condemned the confiscation of Jewish businesses and Jewish art, and let the French government manage the so-called Jewish Question under German supervision. Elmar Michel, the MBF's chief economic advisor, explained that the latter strategy would place the French administrative apparatus at the disposal of the numerically small military administration and dilute Germany's ultimate responsibility for dubious measures that, in the MBF's opinion, both dishonored the German army and violated the terms of the Hague Convention.[21]

Generals Streccius and Stülpnagel established a military government that restored order, supervised the Vichy regime, maintained security, and exploited French resources. During the first twelve months of the occupation, both MBFs championed a strategy that reflected Germany's historical experiences. Worried about a reprise of the 1870 Paris Commune but determined to avoid another debacle equivalent to the destruction of Louvain, Streccius and Stülpnagel discouraged hasty reprisals and retained firm control over the reprisal process. Although both MBFs viewed Jews as a potential security threat, neither expressed much enthusiasm for anti-Semitic measures that extended beyond the registration of people and property. The French government mounted an indigenous campaign of discrimination, despoliation, and deportation on its own accord. Vichy's willingness to implement an anti-Semitic agenda postponed direct German intervention, but the delay proved temporary. Operation Barbarossa aroused Communist resistance throughout Europe that, in turn, encouraged Hitler to expand his murderous agenda beyond Jews in party and state positions and Bolshevik commissars targeted by initial Barbarossa regulations. Determined to liquidate both real and imagined opponents who supposedly fuelled resistance activity, Hitler increased the number of people eligible for special treatment during the second half of 1941.

Eastern Policies in Western Europe

The invasion of the Soviet Union transformed both the German military government in charge of occupied France and the policies of the military administration. Orders issued for the invasion of the Soviet Union stand apart from comparable directives in France. In 1939, Hitler anticipated a protracted struggle against the Allied powers and prohibited tactics such as the sinking of large passenger liners that might stimulate British or French resistance. Flushed with confidence after the defeat of France, Hitler expected the Red Army to collapse in short order and pursued far more ambitious goals at the very start of Operation Barbarossa. Before German troops crossed the Soviet border, he called for the destruction of the Soviet state and planned to annihilate a substantial proportion of the Soviet people. To fulfill Hitler's wishes and secure *Lebensraum* or living space in the east, the OKW and OKH prepared a series of Criminal Orders that would begin to lay the foundations for Hitler's New Order during Operation Barbarossa.[22]

Working with the OKW and the OKH, Hitler issued orders that liberated German soldiers from conservative generals who had limited the Nazi racial agenda during the 1939 Polish campaign. Issued on March 13, 1941, the Guidelines in Special Fields Concerning Directive No. 21 allowed SS forces to carry out "the final struggle between two opposing political systems" on their own authority and beyond the reach of military courts-martial, and thus beyond military control. The May 13 Decree on the Exercise of Martial Jurisdiction in the Area Barbarossa and Special Measures of the Troops allowed troops to shoot civilians who had allegedly committed war crimes and fulfilled another war aim established by Hitler in the July 31 and December 5, 1940, planning conferences: "the annihilation of Russia's manpower."[23] Going one step further, the May 19, 1941, Guidelines for the Conduct of Troops in Russia required a "ruthless and energetic clampdown" against Jews and other targeted groups. While the March 13 and May 13 regulations removed impediments to mass murder, the so-called Commissar Order represented another significant radicalization in German policy. Issued on June 6, the Guidelines for the Treatment of Political Commissars described the execution of "cruel" and "inhuman" Soviet commissars who advocated "Asiatic-barbaric methods of fighting" as a necessity. It explicitly ordered regular German soldiers to ignore the terms of the Hague Convention and execute lawful combatants. Viewed as a group, regulations issued in the spring of 1941 established a radical new standard of conduct for German troops.[24]

Germany's invasion of the Soviet Union upset the political balance of power inside France. After Hitler and Stalin had signed the German-Soviet Nonaggression Pact, the French Communist Party (*Parti communist français*, or PCF) abandoned the Popular Front and condemned corrupt Allied plutocracies. In response, the Daladier government proscribed the PCF on September 27, 1939, and incarcerated party activists throughout the Phoney War.[25] Expecting succor from their newfound allies, Communist leaders made contact with German diplomats and soldiers after the conquest of Paris, but French police arrested the head of the underground PCF before talks could bear fruit. Claiming that he could not intervene in French domestic affairs, the MBF adopted a neutral stance toward the PCF and allowed the Vichy regime to persecute French Communists during the first year of the occupation.[26] After Germany invaded the Soviet Union, the clandestine PCF abandoned its neutral stance in accordance with Stalin's July 3, 1941, radio address and began to distribute anti-German leaflets throughout Parisian markets. Increased propaganda coincided with a decrease in the incidence of murder, manslaughter, assault, and espionage, and the MBF concluded that resistance activity did not undermine the security of German troops in his bailiwick.[27]

Although Hitler and the military leadership focused on the Eastern Front, *Generalfeldmarschall* Keitel did not ignore France. Eight days after the start of Operation Barbarossa, Hitler's chief military advisor reminded Stülpnagel that security should remain the MBF's top priority. He directed the MBF to report all serious incidents and subsequent reprisals to Berlin so that Hitler, the OKW, and the Foreign Office could adjust punishments as necessary. His directive neither encouraged nor discouraged deadly reprisals and endorsed the status quo. Military administration officials urged the Vichy regime to redouble French efforts against the PCF and directed SS agencies in Paris to collaborate with their French counterparts. In keeping with terms of Keitel's memorandum, the MBF let the French police do his dirty work and maintained a low profile.[28]

Pro-Allied graffiti and anti-German leaflets gave way to anti-German demonstrations as July turned to August. On the night of August 13, 1941, German policemen arrested Henri Gautherot and Samuel Tyszelman at a Communist demonstration in the Parisian suburb of St-Denis. In response, the MBF banned the PCF on August 14 and announced that all who participated in subsequent Communist demonstrations would be prosecuted for aiding the enemy (*Feindbegünstigung*). Convicted by a German military court, Gautherot and Tyszelman were shot by firing squad on August 19. Responding in kind, Communist militants gunned down a German naval cadet and a German corporal in two Paris metro stations on August 21. With Stülpnagel on leave in Germany, the task of formulating the German response to the two murders fell to *Generalleutnant* Ernst Schaumburg, the commandant of greater Paris. Following established guidelines, Schaumburg informed the public that people arrested by the German army could be executed in the event of subsequent terrorist attacks.[29] Eager to avoid German reprisals, Fernand de Brinon, Vichy's ambassador in Paris, and Jean Ingrand, the delegate for the Ministry of the Interior in the occupied territories, promised to try and execute six leading Communists within the next seven days. Despite protests from the head of Naval Group Command West that referred with approval to lethal precedents set in the Soviet Union, the MBF allowed the French government to serve as his proxy.[30]

Determined to provoke bloody German reprisals and drive a wedge between the MBF and the French public, Communist militants continued their attacks. On September 3, partisans shot *Unteroffizier* Ernst Hoffman near the *Gare de l'est* in Paris. Acting on advice from his staff, the MBF ordered the execution of three Jewish Communists who had already been convicted of noncapital offences by German military courts. Hitler focused on the Eastern Front throughout August 1941 and may not have learned about the August 21 assaults in a timely fashion.[31] During the relative calm of early September, the Führer heard about the Hoffman attack and condemned Stülpnagel's response as "much too mild," because "a German soldier is worth more than three Communists." Speaking through *General der Artillerie* Eduard Wagner, Hitler told Stülpnagel to execute fifty more hostages if police did not detain the perpetrator right away and to shoot another one hundred hostages after the next assassination.[32] After the Hoffman attack, Hitler began to pay some attention to events in France and demanded an immediate report on the entire affair.

Before Stülpnagel could reply to Wagner's telegram, however, resistance groups launched another series of attacks. On September 6, unidentified partisans mugged a German corporal. Four days later, guerrillas shot a German sailor in the leg. Finally, on September 12, someone hit a German paymaster over the head with a blackjack. Even though none of the assaults proved fatal, the MBF departed from his longstanding policy of restraint and responded to all three attacks by executing ten hostages who had been convicted by a German court-martial for illegal possession of a gun and Communist activity.[33] With Hitler now watching over his shoulder, the MBF could not afford to be lenient, but his response fell well short of the fifty executions that Hitler suggested and the reprisals focused on convicted French criminals who lived on the fringe of French society.

On June 30, 1941, Keitel authorized the MBF to shoot hostages after sensitive cases had been reviewed by Berlin.[34] During a July 16 conference, Hitler revealed the crux of his antipartisan policy to *Reichsmarschall* Hermann Göring, *Reichsleiter* Martin Bormann, chief of the Reich Chancellery Hans-Heinrich Lammers, designated Reich Minister for the Occupied Eastern Territories Alfred Rosenberg, and Keitel. He explained that "this partisan war again has some advantages for us; it enables us to exterminate everyone who opposes us."[35] As resistance activity mounted in September, Hitler explicitly denounced Stülpnagel's moderate policy and demanded deadly, disproportionate reprisals in a conversation with *General* Wagner. Synchronizing his policy with comments made by Hitler on July 16 and September 7, Keitel belatedly released a new security directive on September 16, 1941.

> In order to nip the agitation in the bud the harshest methods must be employed immediately *on the first occasion*, so as to make the authority of the occupying power prevail and prevent any further spread (of resistance).... A deterrent effect can be attained only through unusual severity.... The death penalty for fifty to one hundred Communists must be considered an appropriate atonement for the life of a German soldier.... Acts of espionage, sabotage, and attempts to enter foreign armed forces must be punished with death as a matter of principle.[36]

Using Keitel as a mouthpiece, Hitler repudiated nonlethal measures outlined in the MBF's September 1940 hostage regulations. Four weeks later, Stülpnagel denounced Berlin's antipartisan policy in a telegram to the OKH. The MBF explained that mass executions would encourage passive resistance and alienate the Vichy regime, but not deter fanatical enemies. If forced to obey the letter of Keitel's September 16 directive, Stülpnagel offered to resign.[37]

Assassinations in Nantes and Bordeaux intensified the disagreement between Paris and Berlin. On the morning of October 20, 1941, insurgents shot *Oberstleutnant* Carl Friedrich Hotz, the local commander (*Feldkommandant*) of Nantes.[38] Three hours later, Hitler discussed the incident with *Generalfeldmarschall* Keitel, and the latter passed along the Führer's reaction to *General* von Stülpnagel. According to Keitel, Hitler saw the shooting as "momentous proof" of English activity and advised the MBF to execute 100 to 150 hostages. In Hitler's opinion, moderate reprisals would not paralyze opponents with fear and were thus "inexpedient."[39] Early in the afternoon, Stülpnagel asked for a delay so police could gather evidence, identify suspects, and capture perpetrators. The Führer told the MBF to assume that Communists, perhaps influenced by Gaullists, had carried out the attack. He ordered Stülpnagel to impose a curfew, arrest suspects, and offer a reward. Furthermore, Hitler ruled that 50 hostages should be executed right away and another 50 shot on October 23 unless the perpetrators were brought to justice.[40]

The next evening, insurgents killed another German officer in Bordeaux. Stülpnagel treated both attacks as a single campaign and convinced his superiors to execute a total of 200 hostages. He imposed a curfew in Nantes and Bordeaux, fined each city, and split reprisal executions into two contingents per city. Without time to investigate either attack, Stülpnagel could not identify suspects or focus reprisals on criminal associates. To fulfill orders from Hitler, the military administration selected 100 prisoners who were somehow associated with the French Communist Party from local jails. The first Nantes contingent of 48 hostages stood before a German firing squad on October 22. Two days later, 50 more hostages perished in Bordeaux. Public opinion in both locales turned against violent resistance groups, but the Communist immigrants who had carried out both attacks eluded capture for the time being.[41]

Stülpnagel condemned Hitler's policy through official channels. He told superiors that

> the attacks were carried out by small terror groups and English soldiers or spies who move from place to place . . . the majority of Frenchmen do not support them. I clearly believe that shooting hostages only embitters the people and makes future rapprochement more difficult. . . . I personally have warned against Polish methods in France.

If the policy continued, Stülpnagel argued that he would have to arrest every male Frenchman between sixteen and sixty years of age. Stülpnagel's words and a timely retreat by Charles de Gaulle had an impact. In a speech transmitted by the BBC, the leader of the Free French directed his followers inside France to "not kill Germans . . . because it is too easy for the enemy to retaliate by the massacre of temporarily disarmed combatants." On October 28, Hitler allowed Stülpnagel to suspend the second round of executions in Nantes and Bordeaux.[42]

Given time, the MBF might have been able to restore the status quo of early 1941, but resistance groups did not relent. After unknown partisans shot a Luftwaffe major on December 5, Hermann Göring demanded harsh reprisals.[43] The request coincided with another innovation in Hitler's antipartisan policy—the so-called *Nacht und Nebel Erlass* or Night and Fog Decree. Keitel explained the new directive as follows:

> It is the long considered will of the Führer that, in the occupied zone, attacks against the Reich or occupying power should be met with other measures (*anderen Maßnahmen*). The Führer is of the opinion that punishing crimes with prison sentences, even lifelong prison sentences (*lebenslange Zuchthausstrafen*), is a sign of weakness. An effective and enduring deterrent can only be had through death sentences and equally far-reaching measures that leave relatives and the public uncertain over the fate of the perpetrator. Deportation to Germany also serves this purpose.[44]

Applied mostly in Belgium and France, the Night and Fog Decree established a conduit to concentration camps and functioned as a covert death sentence. On December 12, 1941, OKW demonstrated the proper use of the Night and Fog Decree by ordering the deportation of one thousand Jews and five hundred Communists. From Hitler's perspective, deportations deterred resistance activity, liquidated racial opponents, and enmeshed the military administration in his war against the alleged Judeo-Bolshevik conspiracy.[45]

Stülpnagel made a final attempt to assert control over German reprisal policy. On January 15, 1942, he informed Keitel that

> I only intend to carry out future executions when a member of the armed forces has been assassinated, after a series of nonfatal assassination attempts, or after cases of sabotage that have especially dangerous effects. However, I consider it essential to wait for an appropriate period of time so that a criminal investigation can uncover the perpetrators.... I intend to only order a <u>limited</u> number of executions and will adjust the number to suit the circumstances. At least under present conditions, I can no longer arrange <u>mass shootings</u> and answer to history with a clear conscience.[46]

Stülpnagel's ultimatum contradicted antipartisan guidelines developed for Operation Barbarossa and subsequent regulations issued by Keitel. While the MBF demanded time to investigate, OKW demanded immediate reprisals that focused on Jews and Communists. While the MBF wanted to tailor reprisals to suit the gravity of an attack, Hitler demanded at least fifty hostage executions because he believed that an Aryan was worth much more than a Jew or Communist. While the MBF was willing to consider nonlethal reprisals, the Führer described the death penalty "or equally far-reaching measures" as the only appropriate responses to cases of espionage, assassination, and sabotage.[47] After consulting Keitel, Wagner informed the MBF that he could control the entire hostage process as long as he followed guidelines from Berlin. Recognizing defeat, the MBF sent a bitter letter of resignation to *Generalfeldmarschall* Keitel and retired to his home in Berlin.[48]

Otto von Stülpnagel's resignation cleared the way for sweeping changes in the MBF's responsibility and authority. First, Hitler assigned Carl-Heinrich von Stülpnagel, Otto's cousin, to serve as the new MBF on February 16, 1942. As the deputy chief of the Army General Staff for operations (*Oberquartiermeister I*), Carl-Heinrich had conspired against the Nazi regime during the fall of 1939 in conjunction with Franz Halder and other senior army leaders in the OKH. After a brief tour as head of the Franco-German Armistice Commission, he assumed command of the Seventeenth Army and earned praise from an SS execution squad (*Sonderkommando*) for his attitude toward Jews during Operation Barbarossa, but later reported sick and resigned his post after Hitler maligned his performance. Reputedly a timid leader with a genial personality, Carl-Heinrich appeared to be a man who would follow orders and not cause trouble.[49] Second, Hitler diluted the authority of the MBF by appointing Carl Oberg to serve as higher SS and police leader in France on March 9, 1942. A member of the Nazi Party since 1931 and the SS since 1932, Oberg earned Himmler's trust as an SS and police leader in Poland. With control over all SS personnel in France and indirect control of French police forces, Oberg had the authority to punish resistance and persecute Jews in accordance with Hitler's wishes.[50] The installation of Carl-Heinrich von Stülpnagel and Carl Oberg in the spring of 1942 promised to align security practices in France with the policies prepared for and implemented during Operation Barbarossa.

Total War? Labor and Racial Deportations

Anti-Semitic measures developed by the Vichy regime obviated the need for direct German intervention in 1940. Without substantial German prompting, the French government enacted a comprehensive campaign of defamation, discrimination, and despoliation on its own accord. Defamation began with the August 27, 1940, repeal of the 1881 Marchandeau law, which banned press attacks on a particular race or religion. Extending an August 16, 1940, law that banned foreign Jews from practicing medicine, the October 3, 1940, *Statut des Juifs* defined a Jew and barred all Jews from government service and a host of professions including banking, journalism, and law.[51] In a bid to improve Franco-German relations after the December 13, 1940, dismissal of Pierre Laval, Prime Minister (and Admiral) Jean François Darlan created the General Commissariat for Jewish Questions (*Commissariat-général aux questions juives*, or CGQJ) on March 29, 1941. Designed to coordinate French economic, legal, and political anti-Semitic measures, the CGQJ preempted German measures that might undermine French sovereignty and persecuted Jews throughout France.[52]

Playing upon ingrained fears of Communists and Jews, German officials persuaded their French counterparts to arrest foreign Jews and thus secured invaluable administrative support for Germany's expanding racial agenda. Acting on requests from Ambassador Abetz and the military administration, Xavier Vallat, the head of the CGQJ, ordered

French police to arrest Austrian, Czech, and Polish Jews who lived in Paris. The May 14, 1941, raids sent 3,747 Jews to French internment camps in Loiret.[53] Capitalizing on fear of popular unrest in the wake of Operation Barbarossa, junior French police authorities, diplomats attached to the German embassy in Paris, and junior SS officers arranged a second roundup of Jews on August 20, 1941. Under German supervision, 2,400 French policemen sealed off the 11th arrondissement of Paris and arrested 4,232 French and foreign Jews over a three-day period.[54] In response to a wave of resistance activity in late November and early December, French and German policemen arrested 743 mostly French Jews in Paris on December 12, 1941. The SS official responsible for Jewish affairs, *SS-Obersturmführer* Theodor Dannecker, attributed the limited results of all three raids to narrow views held by German military authorities in Paris, but he added that his office had developed the ability to accomplish much more in the new year.[55]

The three roundups carried out in 1941 captured 8,722 Jews and filled French prisons beyond capacity. In order to move the "Final Solution" forward, Dannecker needed to secure transportation from Drancy, the primary concentration camp in occupied France, to Auschwitz and empty French prisons before he could arrest more Jews. Seizing the initiative, he spoke with *Generalleutnant* Otto Kohl, the officer in charge of the French railroad network, and secured transportation for 100,000 Jews from Western Europe. The deportations from Drancy to Auschwitz began on March 27, 1942. Two months later, HSSPF Oberg arrived in Paris with "executive authority" or the ability to make arrests on his own authority. After a series of meetings with Dannecker and senior SS officials, Vichy's secretary-general of police, René Bousquet, agreed to order the arrest of Austrian, Czech, German, Polish, and Russian Jews. Under German supervision, French police incarcerated 32,130 mostly foreign Jews throughout France by September 15.[56] With help from French policemen and *Generalleutnant* Otto Kohl, Theodor Dannecker sent forty-three trains filled with 41,951 mostly foreign Jews from Drancy to Auschwitz by November 1942.[57] The tempo of arrests and deportation increased dramatically after Oberg arrived in Paris and took charge of German security policy on June 1, 1942.

Roundups that began on July 16, 1942, provoked some dissent among the French clergy and dampened Laval's enthusiasm for further arrests. As he only had 3,000 German policemen at his disposal, Oberg needed French support to fulfil his mission, but his brief did not extend beyond the realm of security. The HSSPF could not trade political or economic concessions for French police assistance on his own authority. French enthusiasm for racial deportations evaporated and the number of Jews sent from France to Auschwitz dropped to 17,069 in 1943 and 14,833 in 1944. Short-lived French cooperation and a dearth of SS troops and policemen owing to so many being tied up on the Eastern Front helped approximately 75 percent of the Jews who lived in France to survive World War II.[58] High-handed SS tactics pioneered on the Eastern Front produced meager results in occupied France.

German labor policy also began slowly, but increased in ferocity as the Wehrmacht bogged down in the Soviet Union. At first the German military administration ignored French legislation that barred French men and women from working in foreign countries, and casually recruited 15,000 French workers for service in German factories during the last three months of 1940. The following year, promises of high wages and generous benefits convinced 77,501 French people to accept work in the Reich, and another 260,000 French workers manufactured products or built fortifications for the OKW in France.[59] The military administration's voluntary labor program supplied Germany with approximately 145,000 skilled and unskilled laborers between October 1940 and May 1942, but it did not satiate Germany's need for additional workers as the failure of Barbarossa became inescapable.

Hitler appointed Fritz Sauckel to serve as the plenipotentiary for labor deployment throughout territory controlled by Germany on March 21, 1942. Ordered to recruit, dragoon, or otherwise secure the services of 1.6 million workers, Sauckel assumed control of the military administration's recruiting program and opened negotiations with the French government on May 15, 1942. After contentious talks, the plenipotentiary for labor deployment agreed to repatriate one French prisoner of war for every three skilled French workers sent to Germany.[60] Announced one year after the invasion of the Soviet Union, the *Relève* program added 68,000 French workers to the German labor force between June and September 1942. Viewing *Relève* as a failure, German diplomats and military administration officials advised the Vichy regime to supply more workers or risk direct labor requisitions. Complying with German demands, Prime Minister Pierre Laval passed regulations that created a system of forced labor in September 1942, but initial regulations exempted farmers, policemen, and workers employed in strategic industries such as mining and metallurgy. By cooperating with the military administration and negotiating with the Vichy regime, Sauckel managed to increase labor deportations from just under 300,000 French workers in 1942 to 441,000 in 1943. Even though his program may have been less popular than SS racial deportations, he secured French cooperation through negotiation, supplied German industry with a steady supply of workers, and thus made a major contribution to the German war effort.[61]

Operation Barbarossa dramatically increased Germany's need for labor, and France eventually contributed approximately 850,000 workers to the German war effort, but Germany's success came at a heavy price. The coercive labor laws enacted by Laval thoroughly discredited the Vichy regime. Desperate to avoid work in Germany, thousands of young men fled to the countryside and provided resistance groups with an ample supply of potential recruits. By the end of 1943, French and German authorities had no choice but to mount brutal antipartisan sweeps across sections of southern France. Mandated by Hitler, Sauckel's recruiting methods fuelled resistance activity and accelerated the cycle of repression, resistance, and reprisals. Using humor to prove the same point, Pierre Laval joked that the AS or *armée Secrète* had become the *armée Sauckel*.[62]

Conclusion

Designed before a German victory over Britain and France seemed likely, the military administration that governed occupied France pursued modest goals between 1940 and 1941. Educated in the traditions of the Imperial German Army, neither Streccius nor Otto von Stülpnagel favored Nazi ideas and instead championed a policy of economic exploitation. They established a regime that exploited France to the limit allowed by international law and condemned anti-Semitic measures that did not enhance the German war effort. But Hitler and the Nazi regime viewed World War II as a struggle between allegedly superior Aryans concentrated in Germany and supposedly inferior Jews and Slavs spread for the most part across eastern Europe and the Soviet Union. Determined Soviet resistance—allegedly inspired by the Jews, who purportedly controlled the Soviet state—and the resulting prolongation of the war helped to persuade Hitler to implement the European-wide "Final Solution" during the war itself. From the Nazi perspective, the "Final Solution" was a potentially war-winning strategy. While Hitler viewed the liquidation of the Jews to be an essential part of the German war effort, men like Otto von Stülpnagel condemned anti-Semitic measures as unwelcome distractions that disrupted French industrial production and denounced massive reprisals that turned French men and women against Germany. Otto von Stülpnagel's resignation and the arrival of HSSPF Oberg promised to inaugurate a new chapter in the history of occupied France.

Radical policies implanted by Hitler in France ultimately failed to take root. Mirroring shifts throughout Hitler's empire, the SS gained authority at the expense of the military administration in France, but this development yielded few results. In addition to traditional law enforcement responsibilities that included counterinsurgency operations, the HSSPF had to supervise the French police, help Sauckel round up French workers, and arrest Jews with only three thousand agents who did not all speak French. With inadequate German resources at his disposal, Oberg had to rely on French assistance that evaporated as the fortunes of war turned against Germany. The number of Jews deported to Poland peaked in August 1942 and labor deportations followed suit in March 1943. German intelligence unearthed semiofficial French contingency plans for an Allied invasion that called for the arrest or execution of fanatical collaborators, but they could not come up with a practical response to widespread *attentisme* (wait and see attitude) or growing resistance. As the liberation drew near, SS personnel fled Paris before Allied forces entered the City of Light, and the soldiers who remained made no serious attempt to destroy the French capital.[63]

Ultimately, Hitler failed to initiate a war of destruction in France between 1940 and 1944, but he did not fail for lack of trying. Throughout 1941, the Führer exhorted Otto von Stülpnagel to employ ever more violent tactics against real and imagined opponents of the Nazi regime. Based on Nazi ideology, the Führer's tactics made no sense in the relatively quiet environs of occupied France. A steady decline in the incidence of murder, sabotage, and espionage between August 1940 and May 1942 belied the utility of harsh reprisals that alienated neutral and potentially friendly French men and women.[64] From the MBF's vantage point in Paris, Hitler's ruthless tactics seemed to inflame anti-German sentiments and fuel resistance activity.

Determined to have his way, Hitler placed a dedicated SS officer in charge of German security policy, but the change made little difference. Dependent on the support of French policemen, just like the MBF, Oberg had to collaborate with the Vichy government and the French police in order to achieve a degree of success. Like Otto and Carl-Heinrich von Stülpnagel, Oberg showed little enthusiasm for draconian reprisals, but as an SS officer he did not attract Hitler's attention and enjoyed Himmler's support. Ingrained prejudices, Nazi propaganda, and the primitive accommodations on the Eastern Front may have driven many German soldiers to embrace Nazi ideology during or after Operation Barbarossa, but equivalent circumstances did not materialize in France. From their billets in luxurious Parisian hotels along the *avenue Georges V* and canteens in the Ritz-Carleton, German soldiers did not identify French men and women as foreign or subhuman. Relatively pleasant first-hand experiences in Paris undercut draconian orders from Berlin. Insulated from the barbarization of warfare, officers who were educated during the *Kaiserreich* refused to embrace Hitler's *Weltanschauung*, resisted Hitler's agenda, and in some cases turned against the entire Nazi regime.

Notes

1. *Documents on German Foreign Policy 1918–1945* (London: Her Majesty's Stationery Office, 1956), ser. D, vol. 7, 477–79, 548–49 (hereafter DGFP); DGFP, ser. D, vol. 8, 135–36, 316–17; and Gerhard Weinberg, *A World at Arms: A Global History of World War II* (New York: Cambridge University Press, 1994), 89–95.

2. DGFP, ser. D, vol. 8, 248–50, 430–32; and International Military Tribunal, ed., *Trial of the Major War Criminals Before the International Military Tribunal, Nuremberg, 14 November 1945–1 October 1946* (hereafter IMT) (Nuremberg: Secretariat of the Tribunal, 1948), 30:200–36.

3. Der Führer und Oberste Befehlshaber der Wehrmacht, Erlass über die Verwaltung der besetzten Gebiete Frankreichs, Luxemburgs, Belgiens, und Hollands, 11.39, Record Group 242 (Captured German Records), Microfilm Series T-77 (Records of the German Armed Forces High Command [OKW]), Roll 1430, frames 296–97, National Archives and Records Administration, Washington, DC (hereafter NARA). (Hereafter, abbreviations for the record group number, microfilm series, or entry number [if applicable], folder number [if applicable], or microfilm reel, and page or frame number will be, for example, RG 242/T-77/1430/291–97). For German atrocities in Poland, see Alexander B. Rossino, *Hitler Strikes Poland: Blitzkrieg, Ideology, and Atrocity* (Lawrence: University Press of Kansas, 2003), 227–35.

4. Ernest R. May, *Strange Victory: Hitler's Conquest of France* (New York: Hill & Wang, 2000), 227–239; and Hans Umbreit, "The Battle for Hegemony in Western Europe," in Klaus A. Maier, Horst Rohde, Bernd Stegemann, and Hans Umbreit, *Germany's Initial Conquests in Europe*, vol. 2 of *Germany and the Second World War*, ed. Militärgeschichtliches Forschungsamt (hereafter MGFA), trans. Dean S. McMurry, Ewald Osers, trans. ed. P. S. Falla (Oxford: Oxford University Press, 1991), 280–303.

5. Charles W. Sydnor, *Soldiers of Destruction* (Princeton: Princeton University Press, 1990), 106–8; Raffael Scheck, *Hitler's African Victims: The German Army Massacres of Black French Soldiers in 1940* (Cambridge: Cambridge University Press, 2006), 98–101, 19–41, 156, 165; and Peter Lieb, *Konventioneller Krieg oder NS-Weltanschauungskrieg? Kriegsführung*

und Partisanenbekämpfung in Frankreich, 1943/44 (Munich: Oldenbourg, 2007), 15–20.

6. Julian Jackson, *The Fall of France: The Nazi Invasion of 1940* (Oxford: Oxford University Press, 2003), 180; and Richard Vinen, *The Unfree French: Life Under the Occupation* (New Haven: Yale University Press, 2006), 183–213, 281, 291–94, 307.

7. Lagebericht des Chefs der Militärvewaltung in Frankreich, Verwaltungsstab fuer den Monat, August 1940, RG 242/T-501/143/362, NARA; Allan Mitchell, *Nazi Paris: The History of an Occupation, 1940–1944* (New York: Berghahn, 2008), 4–7; and Thomas Laub, *After the Fall: German Policy in Occupied France, 1940–1944* (Oxford: Oxford University Press, 2010), 41–48. For the Soviet Union, see Christian Streit, *Keine Kameraden: Die Wehrmacht und die sowjetischen Kriegsgefangenen, 1941–1945*, 4th rev. ed. (1978; Bonn: Dietz, 1997); and Alex J. Kay, *Exploitation, Resettlement, Mass Murder: Political and Economic Planning for German Occupation Policy in the Soviet Union, 1940–1941* (New York: Berghahn, 2006).

8. DGFP, ser. D, vol. 9, 671–79; Eberhad Jäckel, *France dans l'Europe de Hitler*, trans. Alfred Grosser (Paris: Fayard, 1968), 51–69; and Alan Milward, *The New Order and the French Economy* (Oxford: Oxford University Press, 1970).

9. Walter Warlimont, *Inside Hitler's Headquarters*, trans. R. H. Barry (New York: Praeger, 1964), 102–3.

10. Adolf Hitler, *Mein Kampf* (Mumbai: Embassy, 2008), 551, 557; Hans Umbreit, "Battle for Hegemony in Western Europe," 320–24; and IMT, 6:427–30.

11. Ahlrich Meyer, *L'Occupation allemmande en France*, trans. Pascale Hervieux, Florence Lecanu, and Nicole Taubes (Toulouse: Privat, 2002), 24–28; and Laub, *After the Fall*, 44–45.

12. MBF, Kommandostab Abt. Ia/Org 2/Ic, dated July 11, 1940, Betr. Massnahmen zur Sicherung des Küstengebietes, Bestandssignatur RW 35 (Militärbefehlshaber in Frankreich und nachgeordnete Dienststellen), Archivsignatur 353, no frame numbers, Bundesarchiv-Militärarchiv, Freiburg im Breisgau (hereafter BA-MA); DGFP, ser. D, vol. 10, 498–99; and DGFP, ser. D, vol. 11, 448–49, 456, 570–71, 578–81.

13. DGFP, ser. D, vol. 10, 407–8; and Barbara Lambauer, *Otto Abetz et les français ou l'envers de la collaboration* (Paris: Fayard, 2001), 132–37.

14. Lynn H. Nicholas, *The Rape of Europa: The Fate of Europe's Treasures in the Third Reich and the Second World War* (New York: Vintage, 1995), 123–24; Der MBF, Verw Abt Verw, September 13, 1940, Betr. Zusammenarbeit des Chefs der MVW mit den obersten Reichsbehörden und Parteistellen auf dem Gebiete des Kunstschutzes, RW 35/698/13-19, BA-MA.

15. Lagebericht des Chefs der Militärverwaltung in Frankreich - Kommandostab - für den Monat, August 1940, RG 242/T-501/143/339–50, esp. 344–46, 349, NARA; Laub, *After the Fall*, 106–9.

16. Der Ob d H, Der Chef der Militärverwaltung in Frankreich, Verwaltungsstab, Abteilung Verwaltung, September 12, 1940, Betr. Vorbeugungsmaßnahmen gegen Sabotageakte, RW 35/45/no frame numbers, BA-MA; and Mitchell, *Nazi Paris*, 8–9.

17. Der MBF Verwaltungsstab, March 26, 1941, Betr. Vorbeugungs- und Sühnemassnahmen bei Sabotageakten, RG 242/T-501/166/71-82, NARA.

18. Min Rat Bälz, Vju 299.42 geh., "Geisel-Frage," RW 35/308/12, BA-MA; Walter Bargatzky, *Hotel Majestic: Ein Deutscher im besetzten Frankreich* (Freiburg: Herder, 1987), 47–49; Ulrich Herbert, "The German Military Command in Paris," in *National Socialist Extermination Policies: Contemporary German Perspectives and Controversies*, ed. Ulrich Herbert (New York: Berghahn, 2000), 138; and Martin Gilbert, *The Second World War: A Complete History*, rev. ed. (New York: Holt, 1991), 161–62.

19. DGFP, ser. D, vol.10, 513; DGFP, ser. D, vol. 11, 275–76; Serge Klarsfeld, *La Shoah en France*, vol. 2, *Le calendrier de la persécution des juifs de France, juillet 1940–août 1942* (Paris: Fayard, 2001), 25–28; and Kommandostab Abteilung Ia, Lagebericht für den Monate Dezember 1940 und Januar 1941, January 31, 1941, RG 242/T-501/143/573, NARA.

20. Stülpnagel to Oberbefehlshaber des Heeres, November 12, 1940, RW 35/255/48-49, BA-MA; Stülpnagel to Brauchitsch, April 31, 1941, RG 242/T-77/1624/folder 3/3-5, NARA; and Die Entjudung der französischen Wirtschaft, p. 33, RW 35/2/no frame numbers, BA-MA.

21. Otto von Stülpnagel, *Die Wahrheit über die deutschen Kriegsverbrechen* (Berlin: Staatspolitischer Verlag, 1921); and Joseph Billig, *Le Commissariat général aux questions juifs*, vol. 3 (Paris: Éditions du. CDJC, 1960), 75.

22. DGFP, ser. D, vol. 10, 370–74; DGFP, ser. D, vol. 11, 1056–60; Jürgen Förster, "Hitler's Decision in Favor of War Against the Soviet Union," in Horst Boog, Jürgen Förster, Joachim Hoffmann, Ernst Klink, Rolf-Dieter Müller, and Gerd R. Ueberschär, *The Attack on the Soviet Union*, vol. 4 of *Germany and the Second World War*, ed. MGFA (Oxford: Oxford University Press, 1998), 47–48; and Jürgen Förster, "Operation Barbarossa as a War of Conquest and Annihilation," in Boog et al., *Attack on the Soviet Union*, 482–88.

23. Förster, "Hitler's Decision in Favor of War," 47; and Förster, "Operation Barbarossa," 482–86.

24. Directives for the Treatment of Political Commissars [Commissar Order] issued June 6, 1941, RG 238M (Nuremberg Trial), Entry 175, Box 27, NOKW 1076, NARA.

25. Jackson, *Fall of France*, 108–10, 120–23; and *Journal officiel*, no. 11770, September 27, 1939.

26. Lambauer, *Otto Abetz*, 142–44; and OFK 671, Chef der MVW, July 24, 1943, Übersicht über die kommunistische Sabotagetätigkeit in Nordfrankreich und ihre Bekämpfung in der Zeit von 6/40–5/42), RW 36/97/1–3, BA-MA.

27. J. V. Stalin, Radio Broadcast, July 3, 1941, http://www.marxists.org/reference/archive/stalin/works/1941/07/03.htm (last accessed June 13, 2011); MBF, Lagerbericht für die Monate Juni/Juli 1941, RG 242/T-501/143/973, NARA.

28. Abschrift OKW Nr. 505/41 geh, dated June 30, 1941, Betr. Aussetzung der Vollstreckung von Todesurteilen gegen franz. Staatsangehörige, RG 242/T-501/165/353, NARA; and Polizeidienststellen in Frankreich, Bestandssignatur R 70 Frankreich, Archivsignatur 16, pp. 18–20, Bundesarchiv, Abteilung Reich und DDR, Berlin-Lichterfelde (hereafter BAB).

29. Regina M. Delacor, *Attentate und Repressionen: Ausgewählte Dokumente zu zyklischen Eskalation des NS-Terrors im besetzten Frankreich 1941/42* (Stuttgart: Thorbecke, 2000), 20–21; Mitchell, *Nazi Paris*, 48.

30. Der MBF, Kdo. Stab Abt. VOVF, August 22, 1941, Betr. Attentat gegen einen deutschen Marineoffizier, Bezug: Mündliche Besprechung am 22/8 zwischen Brinon, Ingrand, Handelsrat Wilhelm, Beumelburg, und Lt. Dr Roesch), RG 242/T-77/1624/nfn, NARA; and Laub, *After the Fall*, 114–18.

31. Das Geiselverfahren im Bereich des MBF von August 1941 bis Mai 1942, RW 35/542/11–18, 42–46, 120, BA-MA; David M. Glantz and Jonathan M. House, *When Titans Clashed: How the Red Army Stopped Hitler* (Lawrence: University Press of Kansas, 1995), 74–78; and Ian Kershaw, *Hitler, 1936–45: Nemesis* (New York: W. W. Norton, 2000), 411–19.

32. Wagner to MBF, September 7, 1941, Nr.II/1406/41g.K, RW 35/542/11–18, 42–46, 120, BA-MA.

33. Das Geiselverfahren im Bereich des MBF von August 1941 bis Mai 1942), RW 35/542/43–45, BA-MA.

34. Abschrift OKW Nr. 505/41 geh, dated June 30, 1941, Betr. Aussetzung der Vollstreckung von Todesurteilen gegen franz. Staatsangehörige, RG 242/T-501/165/353, NARA.

35. DGFP, ser. D, vol. 13, 149–56.

36. DGFP, ser. D, vol. 12, 541–43.

37. Der MBF to OKH Gen St d H Gen Qu; Nr 430/41 gKdos, October 11, 1941, Bezug zu Fernschreiben Nr II/1406/41 gKdos, RW 35/543/23–25, BA-MA.

38. Henri Noguères, in collaboration with Jean-Louis Vigier, L'armée de l'ombre, juillet 1941–octobre 1942, vol. 2 of *Histoire de la résistance en France, de 1940 à 1945* (Paris: Robert Laffont, 1969), 149; MVW Bezirk B, Abt Ic Nr. 1002/41, Lagebericht der Abt Ic für die Zeit vom 16.9 bis 15.11.41, RG 242/T-77/1588/01/nfn, NARA.

39. Das Geiselverfahren im Bereich des MBF von August 1941 bis Mai 1942, RW 35/542/48–52, BA-MA.

40. Eduard Wagner, *Der Generalquartiermeister: Briefe und Tagebuchaufzeichnungen des Generalquartiermeisters des Heeres*, ed. Elisabeth Wagner (Munich: Olzog, 1963), 208–11; Das Geiselverfahren im Bereich des MBF von August 1941 bis Mai 1942, RW 35/542/48–51, BA-MA; and Robert Gildea, *Marianne in Chains: In Search of the German Occupation, 1940–1945* (New York: Macmillan, 2001), 246–47.

41. Timeline assembled by Militärverwaltungschef Bordeaux, starting June 13, 1941, RG 242/T-77/1585/folder 6/10–11, NARA; IMT, 37:199–205; and Gildea, *Marianne in Chains*, 247–49.

42. October 23, 1941, conversation between MBF Stülpnagel and Gen St d H/Gen Qu Wagner at 22:10 hours, RG 242/T-501/122/711–12, NARA; Charles de Gaulle, *Discours et messages*, vol. 1, *Pendant la guerre, juin 1940–janvier 1946* (Paris: Plon, 1970), 122–23; Das Geiselverfahren im Bereich des MBF von August 1941 bis Mai 1942, RW 35/542/63–72, BA-MA.

43. Das Geiselverfahren im Bereich des MBF von August 1941 bis Mai 1942, RW 35/542/74–82, BA-MA; Der MBF to Keitel, dated February 15, 1942, RG 242/T-501/165/438, NARA.

44. Der Chef des Oberkommandos der Wehrmacht, 14 n 16 WR (I 3/4), Nr. 165/41 g, Betr. Verfolgung von Straftaten gegen das Reich oder die Besatzungsmacht in den besetzten Gebieten, and Der Führer und Oberste Befehlshaber der Wehrmacht, Richtlinien für die Verfolgung von Straftaten gegen das Reich oder die Besatzungsmacht in den besetzten Gebieten, dated December 7, 1941, RG 242/T-501/97/409, 410, NARA.

45. Das Geiselverfahren im Bereich des MBF von August 1941 bis Mai 1942, RW 35/542/78–80, BA-MA; and I. C. B. Dear and M. R. D. Foot, eds, *The Oxford Companion to World War II* (Oxford: Oxford University Press, 1995), 802.

46. Der MBF an OKW Gen St d H Gen Qu, Nr. 25/42 g.Kdos, dated January 15, 1942, and Bezug MBF Kdo.Stab Ic Nr 5084/41 geh. vom 25/10/41 (emphasis in the original), RG 242/T-501/196/1138–45, NARA.

47. Der MBF Kommandostab Abt. III, Tgb Nr. 164/41 geh., Paris 28.9.41, Zu allen Gerichten im Bereich des MBF, RG 242/T-77/1626/folder 01/nfn, NARA.

48. Fernschreiben von OKH Gen Qu zu MBF Stülpnagel, RW 35/543/58, BA-MA; MBF to Chef des Oberkommandos der Wehrmacht Herrn Generalfeldmarschal Keitel, Nr. 11/42 geh. Kdos., dated February 25, 1942, RG 242/T-501/165/441–43, NARA; and Laub, *After the Fall*, 160–65.

49. Peter Hoffmann, *The History of the German Resistance, 1933–1945*, trans. Richard Barry (Cambridge: Harvard University Press, 1977), 120–44; Streit, *Keine Kameraden*, 114–15, 117–19; Heinrich Bücheler, *Carl-Heinrich*

von Stülpnagel: Soldat - Philosoph - Verschwörer (Berlin: Ullstein, 1989), 220–28; and Bargatzky, *Hotel Majestic*, 52–55.

50. Ruth Bettina Birn, *Die Höheren SS- und Polizeifuhrer: Himmlers Vetreter im Reich und in den besetzten Gebieten* (Düsseldorf: Droste, 1986), 341; Der Führer und Oberste Befehlshaber der Wehrmacht, and OKW/WFSt/ Qu (Verw) Nr. 383/42, Führerhauptquartier 9 März 1942, RG 242/T-77/1634/folder 12/nfn, NARA.

51. Michael R. Marrus and Robert O. Paxton, *Vichy France and the Jews* (Stanford: Stanford University Press, 1995), 3; Klarsfeld, *La Shoah en France*, 2:29–33; and Richard H. Weisberg, *Vichy Law and the Holocaust in France* (New York: Routledge, 1996), 37–40.

52. Klarsfeld, *La Shoah en France*, 2:80, 82; Die Entjudung der französischen Wirtschaft, RW 35/2/7, BA-MA; Laub, *After the Fall*, 204–6.

53. Besprechung mit Dr. Best, April 5, 1941, R 70 Frankreich/23/3–5, BAB; Der MBF Verw Abt Verw, Az V ju 166, Betr. Besprechung mit Xavier Vallat, April 4, 1941, R 70 Frankreich/32/9–13, BAB; and André Kaspi, *Les Juifs pendant l'occupation* (Paris: Seuil, 1997), 212–14.

54. Maurice Rajsfus, *La Police de Vichy: les forces de l'ordre françaises au service de la Gestapo, 1940/1944* (Paris: Le Cherche-Midi, 1995), 71–72; Kaspi, *Les Juifs pendant l'occupation*, 214–15; and Klarsfeld, *La Shoah en France*, 2:183–88, 199.

55. Renée Poznanski, *Jews in France during World War II*, trans. Nathan Bracher (Hanover: University Press of New England, 1997), 209–210; and Klarsfeld, *La Shoah en France*, 2:329–32. See also Claudia Steuer, *Theodor Dannecker: Ein Funktionär der "Endlösung"* (Essen: Klartext, 1997).

56. Klarsfeld, *La Shoah en France*, 2: 215–16, 373–75, 422–24, 445–51; Kaspi, *Les Juifs pendant l'occupation*, 218–41; and Laub, *After the Fall*, 228–37.

57. Serge Klarsfeld, *La Shoah en France*, vol. 3, *Le calendrier de la persécution des juifs de France, septembre 1941–août 1944* (Paris: Fayard, 2001), 1916–17.

58. Bericht des Chefs der Ordnungspolizei, February 1, 1943, RG 242/T-175 (Reichsführer SS und Chef der Deutschen Polizei)/3/381-397, NARA. This comes from the US National Archives in College Park, MD; Klarsfeld, *La Shoah en France*, 2:863–64, 3:1918; Kaspi, *Les Juifs pendant l'occupation*, 241–44; Asher Cohen, *Persécutions et sauvetages: Juifs et français sous l'occupation et sous vichy* (Paris: Cerf, 1993), 300–16.

59. "Monographie D. P. 1: Exploitation de la main d'œuvre française par l'Allemagne," in Commission Consultative des Dommages et des Réparations, *Dommages subis par la France et l'union française du fait de la guerre et de l'occupation ennemie, 1939–1945*, vol. 9 (Paris: Imprimerie Nationale, 1950), 63–66 (hereafter "Monographie D.P.1," in CCDR, *Dommages subis*

par la France"). Philippe Burrin, *France Under the Germans: Collaboration and Compromise*, trans. Janet Lloyd (New York: The New Press, 1996), 283.

60. Edward L. Homze, *Foreign Labor in Nazi Germany* (Princeton: Princeton University Press, 1967), 177–82; and IMT, 15:49–50.

61. "Monographie D.P.1," in CCDR, *Dommages subis par la France*, vol. 9, 68, 85, 101, 126, 144, 157; *Akten zur deutschen auswärtigen Politik, 1918–1945* (hereafter, ADAP) (Göttingen: Vandenhoeck, 1969–1975), ser. E, vol. 2, 393–94; ADAP, ser. E, vol. 3, 3–6; Laub, *After the Fall*, 252–64.

62. H. R. Kedward, *In Search of the Maquis: Rural Resistance in Southern France, 1942–1944* (Oxford: Oxford University Press, 1993), 22–34; Lieb, *Konventioneller Krieg*, 233–416; and Renaud de Rochebrune and Jean-Claude Hazera, *Les Patrons sous l'occupation* (Paris: Odile Jacob, 1995), 85.

63. ADAP, ser. E, vol. 6, 308–25; Der BdS/SD im Bereich des MBF, Telex Nr 48518, July 28, 1943, R 70 Frankreich/17/1–11, BAB; and "Les services speciaux allemands en France pendant l'occupation," dated March 12, 1946, R 70 Frankreich/33/8, BAB.

64. Laub, *After the Fall*, 106–10.

Conclusion

Total War, Genocide, and Radicalization

Alex J. Kay, Jeff Rutherford, and David Stahel

During the pivotal year of 1941, Nazi Germany's war irrevocably turned against the German aggressor, the issue and implementation of Criminal Orders became accepted practice within the German army, anti-Jewish policy in the east developed into genocide, and plans for the exploitation of the eastern territories detailed millions of additional deaths. If in the first instance German policy was radicalized by the decision to invade the Soviet Union and the subsequent planning for both the military campaign and the occupation, the experience of warfare in the east ensured further cycles of radicalization, which influenced all areas of Nazi policy. Thus, the process was cumulative as action determined reaction in a region where legal norms counted for little or nothing and Nazi concepts for the east were given space to unfold, leading to ever bolder initiatives and a general escalation of violence.

Nazi propaganda, which spoke of an "Asian peril" and cast the whole war in the east as a preventative strike against "Bolshevik hordes," established a convenient enemy image (*Feindbild*) that justified almost any measure in the defense of "cultured Europe."[1] By the same token, the supposed backwardness of the Soviet state as well as the perceived inferiority of the Slavic peoples further justified the brutality of these measures and persuaded the German invaders that the eastern lands were indeed ripe for settlement as part of Hitler's long-envisaged *Lebensraum*. Thus, the new war in the east was not only accepted as a legitimate struggle for survival, which had been forced on a supposedly overpopulated Germany that was simultaneously under threat from enemies beyond its borders, but it was also intended to lead to the establishment of a great German racial empire centered upon eastern Europe.

In the various perspectives illuminated by this collection of essays one sees that Nazi policy in 1941 and its evolution resulted from many diverse sources and influences, but with a number of concurrent themes. The notion of a "total war" is commonly used within military history to describe a totality of effort, meaning the full mobilization of the civil, economic, and military sectors for war. While Clausewitz proposed "absolute war" as "the kind of war that is completely governed and saturated by the urge for a decision" on the battlefield,[2] Hitler's understanding of war exceeded any military rationale. Victory over the Soviet Union was not considered in doubt when Hitler advocated the issuing of Criminal Orders by the army or when he gave free rein to Himmler's SS and police forces. It was the targeting of perceived racial and political enemies, who were simultaneously defenseless noncombatants, that transformed the Soviet campaign and gave rise to new definitions of what constituted a total war. In this respect the centrality of the Eastern Front is inescapable and deserves far greater scholarly attention than has been the case to date.

Indeed, given that Nazi ideology relied so much on the idea of eternal struggle and conflict, one can say without reservation that there was a natural predisposition within Hitler's state for violence. The militarism of German society soon bred a culture celebrating the application of force, which provided a unifying bond internally and a distrustful enmity externally. When the war began with an unbroken string of victories, the Nazis were keen to play up their supposedly intrinsic superiority in warfare. The demand for maximum violence, which already existed before June 22, was then intensified in mid-July with the belief that a quick victory was within reach and that such violence was both necessary and justified in order to ensure it.[3] Yet Operation Barbarossa's failure to rapidly defeat the Red Army completely changed Germany's strategic position. With the war in the east suddenly proving so demanding and the chances of victory seemingly diminishing, German orders calling for "the harshest possible measures" and the employment of "all necessary means" to quell enemies both real and imagined took on a new significance and the Wehrmacht developed corresponding initiatives. In many ways it was the natural reaction of the Nazi state to further tighten the screws. Hitler's state dealt with challenges by attempting to crush them, and the more resistance it encountered the greater the response had to be. Radicalization was therefore built into German policy from the beginning until it reached its highest form in the summer of 1941 in Ludendorff's definition of total war and the complete blurring of any distinction between combatants and noncombatants.

Germany's total war against the Soviet Union may be considered to have been fought on two fronts. On the one hand, there was a conventional form of war in which armies engaged each other over strategic possessions, but Nazi Germany also pursued a parallel war against the Soviet people. Beyond the wholesale killing of specific groups such as

Jews and Roma, Nazi plans for the postwar administration of the Soviet territories anticipated killing on an even greater scale. Whole regions of the Soviet Union were designated as "deficit territories" in which tens of millions of Soviet people would be starved to death to allow the Wehrmacht to feed itself from the occupied territories and to ensure that the German home front did not go short. Yet just as in the Holocaust, the total approach to Germany's war in the east was not simply a top-down process. Radicalization from below also played a major role, and the conception and implementation of the so-called *Hungerpolitik* involved the regular military authorities at many levels. The death of hundreds, possibly even thousands, of Soviet civilians in Pavlovsk in 1941 reflects the consequences of the Wehrmacht's ruthless requisitions in the early stages of the war against the Soviet Union. While the starvation of Soviet citizens resulted from the deliberate practices of the army, it did not constitute an end in itself in the same way that the systematic targeting of Jews and Roma did. Yet the army was not exempt from a direct and selective policy of mass murder in the east. The Wehrmacht's own war of annihilation in 1941 took many forms, none more infamous than the so-called Criminal Orders, which—as the most comprehensive examination of military files has confirmed—were both unswervingly accepted and routinely carried out.

Within the emerging Nazi eastern empire, the separation between the rulers and the ruled was more pronounced than anywhere else in German-occupied Europe. In Minsk one sees how the everyday violence of German rule soon established itself around a daily routine—a normalization—in which almost nothing was questioned, even as Nazi policy descended into open genocide. Such a tolerance of violence was evident throughout Belarus, especially in relation to anti-Jewish policy. With the demands of the war and the size of the occupied areas placing huge demands on German security forces, acts of resistance became increasingly common, providing a convenient scapegoat for a further escalation of anti-Jewish policy. Nevertheless, the annihilation of the Belarusian Jews was not a security issue, but rather the final phase in Hitler's plan to render the eastern parts of the Nazi empire *judenfrei* (free of Jews). The processes at work in the detailing and organization of these early stages of the Holocaust's implementation have long been debated and the absence of unequivocal documentation has complicated the issue.[4] Today, the murder of Soviet Jews is understood to have resulted from many factors, including radicalizing tendencies from below as well as above. Yet here there are still many gray areas and much work remains to be done. The genocide in Ukraine includes a number of previously overlooked aspects of the killing process. The murder of the Soviet Roma and the principal role played by Otto Ohlendorf offers not only the first concrete indication as to how this killing process came about, but also suggests much about the special empowerment and scope for interpretation that was afforded to the *Einsatzgruppen* commanders. At the same time, the role played by the Axis allies suggests that the murder of Ukrainian Jews, while emanating from within the German hierarchy, received additional radicalizing tendencies from both Romania and Hungary. Such ruthlessness in the east contrasted starkly with those policies initially adopted in Western Europe, yet during the course of 1941 so-called eastern methods of occupation as well as the demands of a total war set a new precedent and soon radicalized German policy in France and many other regions of Western Europe.

While the criminal legacy of Germany's war in the east has understandably dominated recent research in the field, it is important to understand the progression of the military campaign as a framework for the Wehrmacht's central role in the war of annihilation and as an enabler for these atrocities. With Holocaust historians still drawing parallels between the killing of the Jews and the progress of Hitler's war in the east,[5] military history is hardly extraneous to questions surrounding the killing process. Yet studies concentrating on the Wehrmacht's campaigns also retain an intrinsic importance. The battles on the Eastern Front in 1941 were on a scale unknown at the time in the west, and Germany's summer campaign was to play a defining role in ending Hitler's hopes for conquest in the east and thus in his loss of the initiative in the war as a whole. Operational problems abounded during the campaign, which soon compromised the vital mobility and firepower of the panzer groups that were so essential to the Blitzkrieg. As operations slowed and losses increased, the war shifted from a lightning campaign to a war of attrition. In order to ensure that the German advance maintained its Blitzkrieg pace, the Germans needed to secure numerous Soviet cities that sat astride the relatively primitive road network; for this task, the Wehrmacht was ill equipped and poorly trained. Costly battles and ruined infrastructure were the result, which continued to affect German operations long after the battles were over. The impact of these protracted operations was also felt outside the military sphere as the management of the eastern territories was supposed to provide an economic dividend for Germany's struggling war economy. The massive increases in expenditure necessary to sustain the war as well as to establish the framework for the exploitation process led to fears of a looming financial crisis. This became a central point of discussion among high-level economic bureaucrats and led to radically divergent views over how the eastern territories should be managed. It was a debate that reflected the wider interministerial disputes over how Germany could maximize the exploitation of the east at the lowest possible cost.[6]

Clearly, Ludendorff's conception of total war, nurtured and developed by important elements of the German leadership and given a new injection of racist nihilism by Nazi ideological tenets, was transformed into reality in the east during 1941.[7] Even before the invasion it was clear that the scale and brutality of Germany's war against the Soviet Union would eclipse any other fought by the Wehrmacht. Yet what is significant about 1941 is not simply the fact that Nazi policy radicalized, but also the speed and extent of that radicalization. At the onset of Operation Barbarossa there was still much room for an intensification of the war of annihilation, though the preinvasion orders had doubtlessly laid the groundwork for this. The *Einsatzgruppen* operated under a more limited mandate and were initially "only" charged with the murder of selected party and state functionaries, while the Wehrmacht for the most part limited its murderous activities to captured Soviet commissars. Yet in the bitter struggle that ensued, German policy changed rapidly. The military successes of the first weeks as well as the "extremely satisfying and smooth"[8] cooperation between the SS-police apparatus and regular German troops led to an expansion of the remit of the former's killing operations. At the same time, the fanatical resistance of the Red Army and the difficulty of controlling the huge occupied territories evoked ever harsher responses, which for the Nazis meant ever deadlier methods. As Nazi policy radicalized across the board, spurred by Nationalist Socialist ideology, orders from Berlin, conditions at the front, and reports of Soviet battlefield atrocities, the killing process transformed from mass executions of Communist functionaries and, soon thereafter, male Jews of military service age, to an overt policy of all-out genocide against entire Jewish communities. Although Soviet Jews and Roma were the main targets, even non-Jewish villages could be destroyed to the last woman and child if anti-German elements were merely suspected, while the ruthless requisitioning of foodstuffs and other goods claimed millions of victims. As Ludendorff stipulated, once the fighting shifted to include the nation, as opposed to just the nation's armed forces, the war had indeed become total. The desire to avoid a repetition of the defeat in World War I—a defeat many German military thinkers believed was due to an ineffective and insufficient mobilization of the home front—logically led to the conclusion that victory could be achieved if the enemy home front was directly targeted and destroyed. This military consideration, working in tandem with a Nazi *Weltanschauung* that viewed the Soviet Union as a hive of "Judeo-Bolshevik" intrigue, seamlessly led to a war and occupation of unprecedented violence, brutality, and finally death.

Certainly in the subsequent years of the war, Nazi policy would continue to refine and expand its killing program, but the defining steps toward genocide were both rooted in the east and directly tied to the war there. Indeed, the war against the Soviet Union was commonly depicted in Nazi propaganda as a war against "Jewish bolshevism," deliberating blurring the lines between state warfare and racial warfare. Lucy Dawidowicz described Hitler's war as a "war against the Jews,"[9] while Beatrice Heuser has rendered Auschwitz Hitler's "ultimate battle of annihilation."[10] Thus Germany's war in the east in 1941 signalled a radical departure from the hitherto (largely) conventional fighting of World War II. The Wehrmacht's military campaign in the east cannot therefore be defused from the parallel war of annihilation, while at the same time Nazi racial policy cannot be seen as distinct from the strategic context of the war, especially in the summer of 1941. As this collection of essays has shown, total war, genocide, and radicalization were all inherent aspects of Operation Barbarossa. They provided the foundations for Nazi policy, which not only led to mankind's largest clash of arms, but also instigated the most gratuitous destruction of human life in history.[11]

Notes

1. Wolfram Wette, *Die Wehrmacht: Feindbilder, Vernichtungskrieg, Legenden* (Frankfurt am Main: S. Fischer, 2002), pt. 1, "Feindbilder Russland, Sowjetunion, und Bolschewismus." In English: Wolfram Wette, *The Wehrmacht: History, Myth, Reality* (Cambridge: Harvard University Press, 2006), chapter 1, "Perceptions of Russia, the Soviet Union, and Bolshevism as Enemies."

2. Michael Howard, *Clausewitz* (Oxford: Oxford University Press, 1983), 47.

3. See Alex J. Kay, "A 'War in a Region beyond State Control'? The German-Soviet War, 1941–1944," *War in History* 18, no. 1 (2011): 109–22.

4. Geoffrey P. Megargee, *War of Annihilation: Combat and Genocide on the Eastern Front, 1941* (Lanham, MD: Rowman & Littlefield, 2006), 93.

5. For the most recent presentation of the "euphoria of victory" thesis, see Christopher R. Browning, with contributions by Jürgen Matthäus, *The Origins of the Final Solution: The Evolution of Nazi Jewish Policy, September 1939–March 1942* (Lincoln: University of Nebraska Press, 2004), 309–14.

6. See, for example, Jonathan Steinberg, "The Third Reich Reflected: German Civil Administration in the Occupied Soviet Union, 1941–4," *English Historical Review* 60 (1995): 620–51.

7. One examination of how this theoretical focus on total war played an important role in the planning for the war of annihilation is Babette Quinkert's study of the connection between psychological warfare and terror in the planning for hostilities with the Soviet Union. As Quinkert makes clear, the foundations for the Criminal Orders were laid during the 1930s as part of a larger project devoted to total war. See *Propaganda und Terror in Weißrußland, 1941–1944* (Paderborn: Ferdinand Schöningh, 2009), 43–70.

8. "Ereignismeldung UdSSR Nr. 90," Der Chef der Sicherheitspolizei und des SD, Berlin, September 21, 1941, R 58/217, fol. 215, Bundesarchiv Berlin-Lichterfelde. This particular comment was made by *Einsatzgruppe* B but is indicative of SS-Wehrmacht cooperation across the board.

9. Lucy Dawidowicz, *The War Against the Jews, 1933–45* (1975; London: Penguin, 1987).

10. Beatrice Heuser, *The Bomb: Nuclear Weapons in their Historical, Strategic, and Ethical Context* (Harlow: Longman, 2000), 112.

11. According to Peter Fritzsche, "in the first six months of Operation Barbarossa, German forces wiped out one in every five hundred people on the planet." See *Life and Death in the Third Reich* (Cambridge: Harvard University Press, 2008), 186.

Appendix

Comparative Table of Ranks for 1941

German Ministerial Bureaucracy[1]	SS[2]	German Army[3]	British Army[4]
Reichsminister	Reichsführer-SS	Generalfeldmarschall	Field Marshal
Staatssekretär	[no equivalent]	Generaloberst	General
Unterstaatssekretär	SS-Obergruppenführer	General	Lieutenant General
Ministerialdirektor	SS-Gruppenführer	Generalleutnant	Major General
[no equivalent]	SS-Brigadeführer	Generalmajor	Brigadier
Ministerialdirigent	SS-Oberführer	[no equivalent]	[no equivalent]
Ministerialrat	SS-Standartenführer	Oberst	Colonel
Regierungsdirektor	SS-Obersturmbannführer	Oberstleutnant	Lieutenant Colonel
Oberregierungsrat	SS-Sturmbannführer	Major	Major
Landrat	[no equivalent]	[no equivalent]	[no equivalent]
Regierungsrat	[no equivalent]	[no equivalent]	[no equivalent]
Amtsrat	SS-Hauptsturmführer	Hauptmann	Captain
Oberinspektor	SS-Obersturmführer	Oberleutnant	Lieutenant
Inspektor	SS-Untersturmführer	Leutnant	Second Lieutenant
Obersekretär	SS-Hauptscharführer	Oberfeldwebel	Warrant Officer Class I
Sekretär	SS-Oberscharführer	Feldwebel	Warrant Officer (Class II)
Verwaltungsassistent	SS-Scharführer	Unterfeldwebel	Staff Sergeant
Assistent	SS-Unterscharführer	Unteroffizier	Sergeant
Ministerialamtsgehilfe	SS-Rottenführer	Obergefreiter	Corporal
Amtsgehilfe	SS-Sturmmann	Gefreiter	Lance Corporal
[no equivalent]	SS-Mann	Soldat	Private

1. Michael Buddrus, *Totale Erziehung für den totalen Krieg: Hitlerjugend und nationalsozialistische Jugendpolitik* (Munich: K. G. Saur, 2003), 1:331. We are grateful to Martin Holler for bringing this work to our attention.
2. Buddrus, *Totale Erziehung*, 1:331; Ernst Klee, *Das Personenlexikon zum Dritten Reich: Wer war was vor und nach 1945*, 2nd rev. ed. (Frankfurt am Main: Fischer Taschenbuch, 2003), 718.
3. Buddrus, *Totale Erziehung*, 1:331; Klee, *Personenlexikon zum Dritten Reich*, 718.
4. George Forty, *British Army Handbook, 1939–1945* (Phoenix Mill: Sutton, 1998), 188–91.

Selected Bibliography

Achim, Viorel. "Romanian-German Collaboration in Ethnopolitics: The Case of Sabin Manuilă." In *German Scholars and Ethnic Cleansing, 1919–1945*, edited by Ingo Haar and Michael Fahlbusch, 139–54. New York: Berghahn, 2005.

Al'tman, Ilya. *Zhertvy nenavisti: Kholokost v SSSR, 1941–1945 gg.* Moscow: Kovcheg, 2002.

Altshuler, Mordechai. *Soviet Jewry on the Eve of the Holocaust: A Social and Demographic Profile.* Jerusalem: Maureen Mack, 1998.

Aly, Götz. *Hitler's Beneficiaries: Plunder, Racial War, and the Nazi Welfare State.* New York: Metropolitan, 2007.

Aly, Götz, and Susanne Heim. *Vordenker der Vernichtung: Auschwitz und die deutschen Pläne für eine neue europäische Ordnung.* Hamburg: Hoffmann & Campe, 1991.

Ancel, Jean. "The German-Romanian Relationship and the Final Solution." *Holocaust and Genocide Studies* 19, no. 2 (2005): 252–75.

Anderson, Truman. "A Hungarian *Vernichtungskrieg*?: Hungarian Troops and the Soviet Partisan War in Ukraine, 1942." *Militärgeschichtliche Mitteilungen* 58, no. 2 (1999): 345–66.

Angrick, Andrej. "The Escalation of German-Romanian Anti-Jewish Policy after the Attack on the Soviet Union, June 22, 1941." *Yad Vashem Studies* 16 (1996): 203–38.

———. *Besatzungspolitik und Massenmord: Die Einsatzgruppe D in der südlichen Sowjetunion, 1941–1943.* Hamburg: Hamburger Edition, 2003.

Angrick, Andrej, Martina Voigt, Silke Ammerschubert, Peter Klein, Christa Alheit, and Michael Tycher. "'Da hätte man schon ein Tagebuch führen müssen': Das Polizeibataillon 322 und die Judenmorde im Bereich der Heeresgruppe Mitte während des Sommers und Herbstes 1941: Mit einer Auseinandersetzung über die rechtlichen Konsequenzen." In *Die Normalität des Verbrechens: Bilanz und Perspektiven der Forschung zu den nationalsozialistischen Gewaltverbrechen. Festschrift für Wolfgang*

Scheffler zum 65. Geburtstag, edited by Helge Grabitz, Klaus Bästlein, and Johannes Tuchel, 325–85. Berlin: Edition Hentrich, 1994.

Arad, Yitzhak. *The Partisan: From the Valley of Death to Mount Zion*. New York: Holocaust Library, 1979.

———. *The Holocaust in the Soviet Union*. Lincoln: University of Nebraska Press, 2009.

Arad, Yitzhak, Shmuel Krakowski, and Shmuel Spector, eds. *The Einsatzgruppen Reports: Selections from the Dispatches of the Nazi Death Squads' Campaign against the Jews, July 1941–January 1943*. New York: Holocaust Library, 1989.

Ashworth, Gregory J. *War and the City*. London: Routledge, 1991.

Axworthy, Mark. *Axis Slovakia: Hitler's Slavic Wedge, 1938–1945*. New York: Axis Europa, 2002.

Baade, Fritz, Richard F. Behrendt, and Peter Blachstein, eds. *Unsere Ehre heisst Treue: Kriegstagebuch des Kommandostabes Reichsführer SS, Tätigkeitsberichte der 1. und 2. SS-Inf.-Brigade, der 1. SS- Kav.-Brigade und von Sonderkommandos der SS*. Vienna: Europa, 1965.

Backe, Herbert. *Um die Nahrungsfreiheit Europas: Weltwirtschaft oder Großraum*. 2nd ed. Leipzig: Wilhelm Goldmann, 1943.

Bähr, Walter, and Hans Bähr, eds. *Kriegsbriefe gefallener Studenten, 1939–1945*. Tübingen: Rainer Wunderlich, 1952.

Baldwin, Peter. *Reworking the Past: Hitler, The Holocaust, and the Historians' Debate*. Boston: Beacon Press, 1990.

Barkan, Elazar, Elizabeth A. Cole, and Kai Struve, eds. *Shared History—Divided Memory: Jews and Others in Soviet-Occupied Poland, 1939–1941*. Leipzig: Leipziger Universitätsverlag, 2007.

Bartov, Omer. *Hitler's Army: Soldiers, Nazis, and War in the Third Reich*. Oxford: Oxford University Press, 1992.

Bauer, Yehuda. *Rethinking the Holocaust*. New Haven: Yale University Press, 2001.

Beer, Mathias. "Die Entwicklung der Gaswagen beim Mord an den Juden." *Vierteljahrshefte für Zeitgeschichte* 35, no. 3 (1987): 403–17.

Benz, Wigbert. *Der Hungerplan im "Unternehmen Barbarossa" 1941*. Berlin: Wissenschaftlicher Verlag, 2011.

Benz, Wolfgang, Konrad Kwiet, and Jürgen Matthäus, eds. *Einsatz im "Reichskommissariat Ostland": Dokumente zum Völkermord im Baltikum und in Weißrußland, 1941–1944*. Berlin: Metropol, 1998.

Berkhoff, Karel. *Harvest of Despair: Life and Death in Ukraine Under Nazi Rule*. Cambridge: Harvard University Press, 2004.

Birn, Ruth-Bettina. *Die höheren SS- und Polizeiführer: Himmlers Vertreter im Reich und in den besetzten Gebieten*. Düsseldorf: Droste, 1986.

———. *Die Sicherheitspolizei in Estland 1941–1944: Eine Studie zur Kollaboration im Osten*. Paderborn: Ferdinand Schöningh, 2006.

Blood, Philip. *Hitler's Bandit Hunters: The SS and the Nazi Occupation of Europe*. Washington, DC: Potomac, 2008.
Bock, Fedor von. *Generalfeldmarschall Fedor von Bock: The War Diary, 1939–1945*. Edited by Klaus Gerbet. Atglen, PA: Schiffer Military History, 1996.
Boelcke, Willi. *Die Kosten von Hitlers Krieg*. Paderborn: Ferdinand Schöningh, 1985.
———. "Die 'europäische Wirtschaftspolitik' des Nationalsozialismus." *Historische Mitteilungen der Ranke-Gesellschaft* 5 (1992): 194–232.
Boog, Horst, Jürgen Förster, Joachim Hoffmann, Ernst Klink, Rolf-Dieter Müller, and Gerd R. Ueberschär. *Der Angriff auf die Sowjetunion*. Vol. 4 of *Das Deutsche Reich und der Zweite Weltkrieg*. Stuttgart: Deutsche Verlags-Anstalt, 1983. New ed., Frankfurt am Main: Fischer Taschenbuch, 1996.
———. *The Attack on the Soviet Union*. Vol. 4 of *Germany and the Second World War*. Translated by Dean S. McMurry, Ewald Osers, and Louise Willmot. Oxford: Oxford University Press, 1998.
Boog, Horst, Werner Rahn, Reinhard Stumpf, and Bernd Wegner. *Der globale Krieg: Die Ausweitung zum Weltkrieg und der Wechsel der Initiative, 1941–1943*. Vol. 6 of *Das Deutsche Reich und der Zweite Weltkrieg*. Stuttgart: Deutsche Verlags-Anstalt, 1990.
———. *The Global War*. Vol. 6 of *Germany and the Second World War*. Translated by Ewald Osers, John Brownjohn, Patricia Crampton, and Louise Willmot. New York: Oxford University Press, 2001.
Braham, Randolph. "The Kamianets-Podilskyi and Delvidek Massacres: Prelude to the Holocaust in Hungary." *Yad Vashem Studies* 9 (1973): 133–56.
———. *The Politics of Genocide: The Holocaust in Hungary*. New York: Columbia University Press, 1981.
———. *The Hungarian Labor Service System, 1939–1945*. New York: Columbia University Press, 1977.
Brandon, Ray, and Wendy Lower, eds. *The Shoah in Ukraine: History, Testimony, Memorialization*. Bloomington: Indiana University Press, 2008.
Browning, Christopher R. *Ordinary Men: Reserve Police Battalion 101 and the Final Solution in Poland*. 2nd rev. ed. New York: Harper, 1998.
———, with contributions by Jürgen Matthäus. *The Origins of the Final Solution: The Evolution of Nazi Jewish Policy, September 1939–March 1942*. Lincoln: University of Nebraska Press, 2004.
Bruder, Franziska. *"Den ukrainischen Staat erkämpfen oder sterben!": Die Organisation Ukrainischer Nationalisten (OUN), 1929–1948*. Berlin: Metropol, 2007.
Buggeln, Marc. "Währungspläne für den Großraum: Die Diskussion der nationalsozialistischen Wirtschaftsexperten über ein zukünftiges euro-

päisches Zahlungssystem." *Beiträge zur Geschichte des Nationalsozialismus* 18 (2002): 41–76.

Case, Holly. "Navigating Identities: The Jews of Kolozsvár (Cluj) and the Hungarian Administration, 1940–1944." In *Osteuropa vom Weltkrieg zur Wende*, edited by Wolfgang Mueller and Michael Portmann, 39–53. Vienna: Verlag der Österreichischen Akademie der Wissenschaften, 2007.

———. *Between States: The Transylvanian Question and the European Idea During World War II*. Stanford: Stanford University Press, 2009.

Chernoglasova, Raisa A. *Judenfrei! Svobodno ot evreev!: Istoriia minskogo getto v dokumentakh*. Minsk: Asobny Dakh, 1999.

Chiari, Bernhard. *Alltag hinter der Front: Besatzung, Kollaboration, und Widerstand in Weißrußland, 1941–1944*. Düsseldorf: Droste, 1998.

Cholawski, Shalom. *Be-Sufat Ha-Kilayyon: Yahadut Belorussia ha-mizrakhit be-Milkhemet ha-Olam ha-Shniyya*. Tel Aviv: Yiśro'el-bukh, 1988.

———. *The Jews of Bielorussia During World War II*. Amsterdam: Harwood, 1998.

Coox, Alvin D. *Nomonhan: Japan Against Russia, 1939*. Stanford: Stanford University Press, 1990.

Corum, James. *The Roots of Blitzkrieg: Hans von Seeckt and German Military Reform*. Lawrence: University Press of Kansas, 1992.

Creveld, Martin van. *Fighting Power: German and U.S. Army Performance, 1939–1945*. Westport, CT: Greenwood, 1983.

———. *Supplying War: Logistics from Wallenstein to Patton*. Cambridge: Cambridge University Press, 1984.

Cüppers, Martin. *Wegbereiter der Shoah: Die Waffen SS, der Kommandostab Reichsführer-SS, und die Judenvernichtung, 1939–1945*. Darmstadt: Wissenschaftliche Buchgesellschaft, 2005.

Curilla, Wolfgang. *Die deutsche Ordnungspolizei und der Holocaust im Baltikum und in Weißrußland, 1941–1944*. Paderborn: Ferdinand Schöningh, 2006.

Czollek, Roswitha. *Faschismus und Okkupation: Wirtschaftspolitische Zielsetzung und Praxis des faschistischen deutschen Besatzungsregimes in den baltischen Sowjetrepubliken während des Zweiten Weltkrieges*. Berlin: Akademie, 1974.

Dallin, Alexander. *German Rule in Russia, 1941–1945: A Study of Occupation Policies*. London: Macmillan; New York: St. Martin's Press, 1957.

Dean, Martin. *Collaboration in the Holocaust: Crimes of the Local Police in Belorussia and Ukraine, 1941–1944*. Basingstoke: Palgrave Macmillan, 2000.

———. *Robbing the Jews: The Confiscation of Jewish Property in the Holocaust, 1933–1945*. Cambridge: Cambridge University Press, 2008.

Department of the US Army, ed. *Small Unit Actions during the German Campaign in Russia*. Washington, DC: Center for Military History, 1953.
Documents on German Foreign Policy, series D, vols. 10–13. Washington, DC: US Government Printing Office, 1954.
Domarus, Max. *Hitler: Reden und Proklamationen, 1932–1945*. Wiesbaden: R. Löwit, 1973.
Dulić, Tomislav. *Utopias of Nation: Local Mass Killing in Bosnia and Herzegovina, 1941–1942*. Uppsala: Uppsala Universitet, 2005.
Edele, Mark, and Michael Geyer. "States of Exception: The Nazi-Soviet War as a System of Violence, 1939–1945." In *Beyond Totalitarianism: Stalinism and Nazism Compared*, edited by Michael Geyer and Sheila Fitzpatrick, 345–95. Cambridge: Cambridge University Press, 2009.
Eichholtz, Dietrich. *Geschichte der deutschen Kriegswirtschaft, 1939–1945*. 3 vols. Berlin: Akademie, 1969–96.
Epstein, Barbara. *The Minsk Ghetto, 1941–1943: Jewish Resistance and Soviet Internationalism*. Berkeley: University of California Press, 2008.
Erickson, John. *The Road to Stalingrad: Stalin's War with Germany*. New York: Harper & Row, 1975.
Even-Shoshan, Shlomo, ed. *Minsk: Ir ve-Em* [Minsk: Mother-city]. 2 vols. Tel-Aviv: Organization of the Former Minsk Inhabitants in Israel, 1988.
Förster, Jürgen. "Die Sicherung des 'Lebensraumes.'" In Boog et al., *Der Angriff auf die Sowjetunion*, 1030–78.
———. "Das Unternehmen 'Barbarossa' als Eroberungs- und Vernichtungskrieg." In Boog et al., *Der Angriff auf die Sowjetunion*, 413–47.
———. "Operation Barbarossa as a War of Conquest and Annihilation." In Boog et al., *The Attack on the Soviet Union*, 481–524.
———. "Hitler's Decision in Favour of War Against the Soviet Union." In Boog et al., *The Attack on the Soviet Union*, 13–51.
Forstmeier, Friedrich. *Odessa 1941: Der Kampf um Stadt und Hafen und die Räumung der Seefestung, 15. August bis 16. Oktober 1941*. Freiburg: Rombach, 1967.
Freymond, Jean. *Le IIIe Reich et la réorganisation économique de l'Europe, 1940–1942*. Leiden: Sijthoff, 1974.
Friedman, Philip. *Road to Extinction: Essays on the Holocaust*. New York: The Jewish Publication Society of America, 1980.
Frölich, Elke, ed. *Die Tagebücher von Joseph Goebbels*. 29 vols. Munich: K. G. Saur, 1996.
Ganzenmüller, Jörg. *Das belagerte Leningrad, 1941 bis 1944: Die Stadt in den Strategien von Angreifern und Verteidigern*. Paderborn: Ferdinand Schöningh, 2005.
Gartenschlaeger, Uwe. *Die Stadt Minsk während der deutschen Besetzung (1941–1944)*. Dortmund: Internationales Bildungs- u. Begegnungswerk, 2001.

Gellermann, Günther. *Der Krieg, der nicht stattfand: Möglichkeiten, Überlegungen, und Entscheidungen der deutschen Obersten Führung zur Verwendung chemischer Kampfstoffe im Zweiten Weltkrieg.* Koblenz: Bernard & Graefe, 1986.
Gerlach, Christian. "Deutsche Wirtschaftsinteressen, Besatzungspolitik, und der Mord an den Juden in Weißrußland, 1941–1943." In Herbert, *Nationalsozialistische Vernichtungspolitik, 1939–1945,* 263–91.
———. *Kalkulierte Morde: Die deutsche Wirtschafts- und Vernichtungspolitik in Weißrußland, 1941 bis 1944.* Hamburg: Hamburger Edition, 1999.
———. "Militärische 'Versorgungszwänge,' Besatzungspolitik, und Massenverbrechen: Die Rolle des Generalquartiermeisters des Heeres und seiner Dienststellen im Krieg gegen die Sowjetunion." In *Ausbeutung, Vernichtung, Öffentlichkeit: Neue Studien zur nationalsozialistischen Lagerpolitik,* edited by Norbert Frei, Sybille Steinbacher, and Bernd Wagner, 175–208. Munich: K. G. Saur, 2000.
———. "Die Ausweitung der deutschen Massenmorde in den besetzten sowjetischen Gebieten im Herbst 1941: Überlegungen zur Vernichtungspolitik gegen Juden und sowjetische Kriegsgefangene." In Christian Gerlach, *Krieg, Ernährung, Völkermord: Deutsche Vernichtungspolitik im Zweiten Weltkrieg,* 11–78. 2nd ed. Zurich: Pendo, 2001.
Geyer, Michael. "German Strategy in the Age of Machine Warfare, 1914–1945." In *Makers of Modern Strategy: From Machiavelli to the Nuclear Age,* edited by Peter Paret, 527–97. Princeton: Princeton University Press, 1999.
Glantz, David M. *Barbarossa: Hitler's Invasion of Russia, 1941.* Stroud: Tempus, 2001.
———. *The Battle for Leningrad, 1941–1944.* Lawrence: University Press of Kansas, 2002.
Glantz, David M., and Jonathan House. *When Titans Clashed: How the Red Army Stopped Hitler.* Lawrence: University Press of Kansas, 1995.
Görlitz, Walter, ed. *The Memoirs of Field-Marshal Keitel: Chief of the German High Command, 1938–1945.* Translated by David Irving. New York: Stein & Day, 1966.
Gorodetsky, Gabriel. *Grand Delusion: Stalin and the German Invasion of the Soviet Union.* New Haven: Yale University Press, 1999.
Gottwaldt, Alfred, and Diana Schulle. *Die "Judendeportationen" aus dem Deutschen Reich, 1941–1945: Eine kommentierte Chronologie.* Wiesbaden: Marixverlag, 2005.
Grossman, Vasily, and Ilya Ehrenburg, eds. *Chiornaia Kniga.* Jerusalem: Tarbut, 1980.
Haberer, Erich E. "The German Police and the Genocide in Belorussia, 1941–1944. Part 2, The 'Second Sweep': Gendarmerie Killings of Jews and

Gypsies on January 29, 1942." *Journal of Genocide Research* 3, no. 2 (2001): 207–18.

Halder, Franz. *Hitler als Feldherr*. Munich: Münchener Dom, 1949.

———. *Kriegstagebuch: Tägliche Aufzeichnungen des Chefs des Generalstabes des Heeres, 1939–1942*. Vol. 2, *Von der geplanten Landung in England bis zum Beginn des Ostfeldzuges (1.7.1940–21.6.1941)*. Edited by Hans-Adolf Jacobsen. Stuttgart: W. Kohlhammer, 1963.

———. *Kriegstagebuch: Tägliche Aufzeichnungen des Chefs des Generalstabes des Heeres 1939–1942*. Vol. 3, *Der Rußlandfeldzug bis zum Marsch auf Stalingrad (22.6.1941–24.9.1942)*. Edited by Hans-Adolf Jacobsen and Alfred Philippi. Stuttgart: W. Kohlhammer, 1964.

Hamburger Institut für Sozialforschung, ed. *Verbrechen der Wehrmacht: Dimensionen des Vernichtungskrieges, 1941–1944*. Hamburg: Hamburger Edition, 2002.

Hansmann, Claus. *Vorüber—Nicht Vorbei: Russische Impressionen, 1941–1943*. Frankfurt: Ullstein Sachbuch, 1989.

Hartmann, Christian, Johannes Hürter, and Ulrike Jureit, eds. *Verbrechen der Wehrmacht: Bilanz einer Debatte*. Munich: C. H. Beck, 2005.

Hartmann, Christian. *Wehrmacht im Ostkrieg: Front und militärisches Hinterland, 1941/42*. Munich: Oldenbourg, 2009.

Hartmann, Christian, Johannes Hürter, and Peter Lieb. *Der deutsche Krieg im Osten, 1941–1944: Facetten einer Grenzüberschreitung*. Munich: Oldenbourg, 2009.

Hass, Gerhart. "Deutsche Besatzungspolitik im Leningrader Gebiet." In *"Wir sind die Herren dieses Landes": Ursachen, Verlauf, und Folgen des deutschen Überfalls auf die Sowjetunion*, edited by Babette Quinkert, 64–81. Hamburg: VSA, 2002.

Hata, Ikuhiko. "Continental Expansion, 1905–1941." In *The Cambridge History of Japan*. Vol. 6, *The Twentieth Century*, edited by Peter Duus, translated by Alvin D. Coox, 271–314. Cambridge: Cambridge University Press, 1988.

Heer, Hannes. *War of Extermination: The German Military in World War II, 1941–1944*. New York: Berghahn, 2000.

Heer, Hannes, and Klaus Naumann, eds. *Vernichtungskrieg: Verbrechen der Wehrmacht, 1941–1944*. Hamburg: Hamburger Edition, 1995.

Herbert, Ulrich, ed. *Nationalsozialistische Vernichtungspolitik, 1939–1945: Neue Forschungen und Kontroversen*. Frankfurt am Main: Fischer Taschenbuch, 1998.

———. *National Socialist Extermination Policies: Contemporary German Perspectives and Controversies*. New York: Berghahn, 2000.

Herbst, Ludolf. *Der totale Krieg und die Ordnung der Wirtschaft: Die Kriegswirtschaft im Spannungsfeld von Politik, Ideologie und Propaganda, 1939–1945*. Stuttgart: Deutsche Verlags-Anstalt, 1982.

———. *Das nationalsozialistische Deutschland: Die Entfesselung der Gewalt: Rassismus und Krieg*. Frankfurt am Main: Suhrkamp, 1996.

Hilberg, Raul. *The Destruction of the European Jews*. 1961. 2nd ed. 3 vols. New York: Holmes & Meier, 1985.

Hill, Alexander. *The War behind the Eastern Front: The Soviet Partisan Movement in North-West Russia, 1941–1944*. London: Frank Cass, 2005.

———. *The Great Patriotic War of the Soviet Union, 1941–1945: A Documentary Reader*. London: Routledge, 2009.

Holler, Martin. *Der nationalsozialistische Völkermord an den Roma in der besetzten Sowjetunion (1941–1944): Gutachten für das Dokumentations- und Kulturzentrum Deutscher Sinti und Roma*. Heidelberg: Dokumentations- und Kulturzentrum Deutscher Sinti und Roma, 2009.

Hoth, Hermann. *Panzer-Operationen: Die Panzergruppe 3 und der operative Gedanke der deutschen Führung Sommer 1941*. Heidelberg: Kurt Vowinckel, 1956.

Hürter, Johannes, ed. 2001. *Ein deutscher General an der Ostfront: Die Briefe und Tagebücher des Gotthard Heinrici, 1941/42*. Erfurt: Sutton, 2001.

———. "Die Wehrmacht vor Leningrad: Krieg und Besatzungspolitik der 18. Armee im Herbst und Winter 1941/42." *Vierteljahrshefte für Zeitgeschichte* 49, no. 3 (2001): 377–440.

———. "Konservative Mentalität, militärischer Pragmatismus, ideologisierte Kriegführung: Das Beispiel des Generals Georg von Küchler." In *Karrieren im Nationalsozialismus: Funktionseliten zwischen Mitwirkung und Distanz*, edited by Gerhard Hirschfeld and Tobias Jersak, 239–53. Frankfurt am Main: Campus, 2004.

———. *Hitlers Heerführer: Die deutschen Oberbefehlshaber im Krieg gegen die Sowjetunion, 1941/42*. Munich: Oldenbourg, 2006.

International Military Tribunal, ed. *Der Prozess gegen die Hauptkriegsverbrecher vor dem Internationalen Militärgerichtshof, Nürnberg, 14. November 1945–1. Oktober 1946*. 42 vols. Nuremberg: Sekretariat des Gerichtshofs, 1947–1949.

Ioanid, Radu. *The Holocaust in Romania: The Destruction of Jews and Gypsies under the Antonescu Regime, 1940–1944*. Chicago: Ivan R. Dee, 2000.

Iriye, Akira. *The Origins of the Second World War in Asia and the Pacific*. New York: Longman, 1987.

Jackson, Julian. *The Fall of France: The Nazi Invasion of 1940*. New York: Oxford University Press, 2003.

Jacobsen, Hans-Adolf. "Der deutsche Luftangriff auf Rotterdam (14. Mai 1940): Versuch einer Klärung." *Wehr-Wissenschaftliche Rundschau* 5 (1958): 257–85.

Jahn, Peter. "Sowjetische Kriegsgefangene und die Zivilbevölkerung der Sowjetunion als Opfer des NS-Vernichtungskrieges." In *Dimensionen der Verfolgung: Opfer und Opfergruppen im Nationalsozialismus*, edited by Sibylle Quack, 145–66. Munich: Deutsche Verlags-Anstalt, 2003.

———, ed. *Blockade Leningrads—Blokada Leningrada*. Berlin: Ch. Links, 2004.

Kay, Alex J. "Germany's *Staatssekretäre*, Mass Starvation and the Meeting of 2 May 1941." *Journal of Contemporary History* 41, no. 4 (2006): 685–700.

———. *Exploitation, Resettlement, Mass Murder: Political and Economic Planning for German Occupation Policy in the Soviet Union, 1940–1941*. New York: Berghahn, 2006.

———. "Revisiting the Meeting of the *Staatssekretäre* on 2 May 1941: A Response to Klaus Jochen Arnold and Gert C. Lübbers." *Journal of Contemporary History* 43, no. 1 (2008): 93–104.

———. "Verhungernlassen als Massenmordstrategie: Das Treffen der deutschen Staatssekretäre am 2. Mai 1941." *Zeitschrift für Weltgeschichte* 11, no. 1 (2010): 81–105.

———. "A 'War in a Region Beyond State Control'?: The German-Soviet War, 1941–1944." *War in History* 18, no. 1 (2011): 109–22.

Kempowski, Walter, ed. *Das Echolot Barbarossa '41: Ein kollektives Tagebuch*. Munich: Albrecht Knaus, 2004.

Kenrick, Donald, and Gratton Puxon. *Sinti und Roma: Die Vernichtung eines Volkes im NS-Staat*. Göttingen: Gesellschaft für Bedrohte Volker, 1981.

Kershaw, Ian. *Hitler, 1936–1945: Nemesis*. New York: W. W. Norton, 2000.

———. *Fateful Choices: Ten Decisions that Changed the World, 1940–1941*. New York: Penguin, 2007.

Kiseleva, Tatiana F. "Tsygany evropeiskoi chasti Soiuza SSR i ikh perekhod ot kochevaniia k osedlosti." PhD diss., Moscow State University, 1952.

Klee, Ernst, Willi Dreßen, and Volker Rieß, eds. *"Schöne Zeiten": Judenmord aus der Sicht der Täter und Gaffer*. Frankfurt am Main: S. Fischer, 1988.

Klein, Peter, ed. *Die Einsatzgruppen in der besetzten Sowjetunion, 1941/1942: Die Tätigkeits- und Lageberichte des Chefs der Sicherheitspolizei und des SD*. Berlin: Edition Hentrich, 1997.

Klemp, Stefan. *"Nicht ermittelt": Polizeibataillone und die Nachkriegsjustiz: Ein Handbuch*. Essen: Klartext, 2005.

Kohl, Paul. *Das Vernichtungslager Trostenez: Augenzeugenberichte und Dokumente*. Dortmund: Internationales Bildungs- u. Begegnungswerk, 2003.

Kotze, Hildegard von, ed. *Heeresadjutant bei Hitler, 1938–1943: Aufzeichnungen des Majors Engel*. Stuttgart: Deutsche Verlags-Anstalt, 1974.

Krausnick, Helmut. "Kommissarbefehl und 'Gerichtsbarkeitserlaß Barbarossa' in neuer Sicht." *Vierteljahrshefte für Zeitgeschichte* 25, no. 4 (1977): 682–738.

———. *Hitlers Einsatzgruppen: Die Truppe des Weltanschauungskrieges, 1938–1942*. Frankfurt am Main: Fischer Taschenbuch, 1985.

Kroener, Bernhard, Rolf-Dieter Müller, and Hans Umbreit. *Organisation und Mobilisierung des deutschen Machtbereichs: Kriegsverwaltung, Wirtschaft, und personelle Ressourcen, 1939–1941*. Vol. 5, pt. 1, of *Das Deutsche Reich und der Zweite Weltkrieg*. Stuttgart: Deutsche Verlags-Anstalt, 1988.

———. *Organisation und Mobilisierung des deutschen Machtbereichs: Kriegsverwaltung, Wirtschaft, und personelle Ressourcen, 1942–1944/45*. Vol. 5, pt. 2, of *Das Deutsche Reich und der Zweite Weltkrieg*. Stuttgart: Deutsche Verlags-Anstalt, 1999.

———. *Organization and Mobilization of the German Sphere of Power: Wartime Administration, Economy, and Manpower Resources, 1939–1941*. Vol. 5, pt. 1, of *Germany and the Second World War*. Translated by John Brownjohn, Ewald Osers, Patricia Crampton, and Louise Willmot. Oxford: Oxford University Press, 2000.

———. *Organization and Mobilization of the German Sphere of Power: Wartime Administration, Economy, and Manpower Resources, 1942–1944/5*. Vol. 5, pt. 2, of *Germany and the Second World War*. Translated by Derry-Cook Radmore. Oxford: Oxford University Press, 2003.

Kühne, Thomas. *Kameradschaft: Die Soldaten des nationalsozialistischen Krieges und das 20. Jahrhundert*. Göttingen: Vandenhoeck & Ruprecht, 2006.

Kunz, Norbert. "Das Beispiel Charkow: Eine Stadtbevölkerung als Opfer der deutschen Hungerstrategie 1941/42." In Hartmann, *Verbrechen der Wehrmacht*, 136–44.

———. *Die Krim unter deutscher Herrschaft, 1941–1944: Germanisierungsutopie und Besatzungsrealität*. Darmstadt: Wissenschaftliche Buchgesellschaft, 2005.

Latzel, Klaus. *Deutsche Soldaten—Nationalsozialistischer Krieg?: Kriegserlebnis, Kriegserfahrung, 1939–1945*. Paderborn: Ferdinand Schöningh, 1998.

Laub, Thomas. *After the Fall: German Policy in Occupied France, 1940–1944*. Oxford: Oxford University Press, 2010.

Leeb, Wilhelm Ritter von. *Tagebuchaufzeichnungen und Lagebeurteilungen aus zwei Weltkriegen*. Edited by Georg Meyer. Stuttgart: Deutsche Verlags-Anstalt, 1976.

Lehnstaedt, Stephan. "Alltägliche Gewalt: Die deutschen Besatzer in Warschau und die Ermordung der jüdischen Bevölkerung." In *Besatzung, Kollaboration, Holocaust: Neue Studien zur Verfolgung und Ermordung der europäischen Juden,* edited by Johannes Hürter and Jürgen Zarusky, 81–102. Munich: Oldenbourg, 2008.

———. *Okkupation im Osten: Besatzeralltag in Warschau und Minsk, 1939–1944.* Munich: Oldenbourg, 2010.

Lemkin, Raphael. *Axis Rule in Occupied Europe: Laws of Occupation, Analysis of Government, Proposals for Redress.* Washington, DC: Carnegie Endowment for International Peace, 1944.

Levene, Mark. "The Experience of Armenian and Romanian Genocide, 1915–1916 and 1941–1942." In *Der Völkermord an den Armeniern und die Shoah,* edited by Hans-Lukas Kieser and Dominik Schaller, 423–62. Zurich: Chronos, 2002.

Lewy, Guenter. *The Nazi Persecution of the Gypsies.* New York: Oxford University Press, 2000.

Lieb, Peter. "Täter aus Überzeugung? Oberst Carl von Andrian und die Judenmorde der 707. Infanteriedivision, 1941/42." *Vierteljahrshefte für Zeitgeschichte* 50 (2002): 523–58.

Lower, Wendy. *Nazi Empire-Building and the Holocaust in Ukraine.* Chapel Hill: University of North Carolina Press, 2005.

Mallmann, Klaus-Michael, Volker Rieß, and Wolfgang Pyta, eds. *Deutscher Osten, 1939–1945: Der Weltanschauungskrieg in Fotos und Texten.* Darmstadt: Wissenschaftliche Buchgesellschaft, 2003.

Manoschek, Walter. *"Serbien ist judenfrei!": Militärische Besatzungspolitik und Judenvernichtung in Serbien, 1941/42.* Munich: Oldenbourg, 1993.

Mawdsley, Evan. *Thunder in the East: The Nazi-Soviet War, 1941–1945.* London: Hodder Arnold, 2005.

Mayer, Arno. *Why Did the Heavens Not Darken?* New York: Pantheon, 1988.

Mazower, Mark. *Hitler's Empire: How the Nazis Ruled Europe.* New York: Penguin, 2008.

Megargee, Geoffrey P. *Inside Hitler's High Command.* Lawrence: University Press of Kansas, 2000.

———. *War of Annihilation: Combat and Genocide on the Eastern Front, 1941.* Lanham, MD: Rowman & Littlefield, 2006.

Merridale, Catherine. *Ivan's War: Life and Death in the Red Army, 1939–1945.* New York: Metropolitan, 2006.

Meyer, Georg. *Adolf Heusinger: Dienst eines deutschen Soldaten, 1915 bis 1964.* Hamburg: Mittler & Sohn, 2001.

Müller, Norbert, ed. *Okkupation, Raub, Vernichtung: Dokumente zur Besatzungspolitik der faschistischen Wehrmacht auf sowjetischem Territorium, 1941 bis 1944.* Berlin: Militärverlag der DDR, 1980.

———. *Die faschistische Okkupationspolitik in den zeitweilig besetzten Gebieten der Sowjetunion (1941–1944).* Berlin: Deutscher Verlag der Wissenschaften, 1991.

Müller, Rolf-Dieter. "Industrielle Interessenpolitik im Rahmen des 'Generalplans Ost': Dokumente zum Einfluß von Wehrmacht, Industrie, und SS auf die wirtschaftspolitische Zielsetzung für Hitlers Ostimperium." *Militärgeschichtliche Mitteilungen* 29 (1981): 101–41.

———. "Von der Wirtschaftsallianz zum kolonialen Ausbeutungskrieg." In Boog et al., *Der Angriff auf die Sowjetunion*, 98–189.

———. "Das Scheitern der wirtschaftlichen 'Blitzkriegstrategie.'" In Boog et al., *Der Angriff auf die Sowjetunion*, 936–1029.

———. "Das 'Unternehmen Barbarossa' als wirtschaftlicher Raubkrieg." In Ueberschär and Wette, *"Unternehmen Barbarossa,"* 173–96.

———. "Die Mobilisierung der Deutschen Wirtschaft für Hitlers Kriegsführung." In Kroener et al., *Organisation und Mobilisierung des deutschen Machtbereichs*, pt. 1, 349–689.

———, ed. *Die deutsche Wirtschaftspolitik in den besetzten sowjetischen Gebieten, 1941–1943: Der Abschlußbericht des Wirtschaftsstabes Ost und Aufzeichnungen eines Angehörigen des Wirtschaftskommandos Kiew*. Boppard am Rhein: Harald Boldt, 1991.

———. "The Failure of the Economic 'Blitzkrieg Strategy.'" In Boog et al., *The Attack on the Soviet Union*, 1081–1188.

———. "From Economic Alliance to a War of Colonial Exploitation." In Boog et al., *The Attack on the Soviet Union*, 118–224.

———. "The Mobilization of the German Economy for Hitler's War Aims." In Kroener et al., *Organization and Mobilization of the German Sphere of Power*, pt. 1, 405–786.

———, and Gerd R. Ueberschär. *Hitlers Krieg im Osten, 1941–1945: Ein Forschungsbericht*. Darmstadt: Wissenschaftliche Buchgesellschaft, 2000.

Müller, Rolf-Dieter, and Gerd R. Ueberschär, eds. *Hitler's War in the East, 1941–1945: A Critical Assessment*. 1997; 3rd rev. ed. New York: Berghahn, 2008.

Müller, Rolf-Dieter, and Hans-Erich Volkmann, eds. *Die Wehrmacht: Mythos und Realität*. Munich: Oldenbourg, 1999.

Müller, Sven. *Deutsche Soldaten und ihre Feinde: Nationalismus an Front und Heimatfront im Zweiten Weltkrieg*. Frankfurt am Main: S. Fischer, 2007.

Müller-Hillebrand, Burkhart. *Das Heer, 1933–1945*. Vol. 3, *Der Zweifrontenkrieg: Das Heer vom Beginn des Feldzuges gegen die Sowjetunion bis zum Kriegsende*. Frankfurt am Main: Mittler & Sohn, 1969.

Mulligan, Timothy. *The Politics of Illusion and Empire: German Occupation Policy in the Soviet Union, 1942–1943*. New York: Praeger, 1988.

Munoz, Antonio, and Oleg V. Romanko. *Hitler's White Russians: Collaboration, Extermination, and Anti-Partisan Warfare in Byelorussia, 1941–1944*. New York: Europa, 2003.

Myllyniemi, Seppo. *Die Neuordnung der baltischen Länder, 1941–1944: Zum nationalsozialistischen Inhalt der deutschen Besatzungspolitik.* Helsinki: Vammalan Kirjapaino, 1973.

Neitzel, Sonke. *Abgehört: Deutsche Generäle in britischer Gefangenschaft, 1942–1945.* Berlin: Propyläen, 2005.

Neitzel, Sonke, and Daniel Hohrath, eds. *Kriegsgreuel: Die Entgrenzung der Gewalt in kriegerischen Konflikten vom Mittelalter bis ins 20. Jahrhundert.* Paderborn: Ferdinand Schöningh, 2008.

Oertel, Manfred. "Über die Reichsbank im Zweiten Weltkrieg." PhD diss., University of Rostock, 1979.

Ogorreck, Ralf. *Die Einsatzgruppen und die "Genesis der Endlösung."* Berlin: Metropol, 1996.

Ogorreck, Ralf, and Volker Rieß. "Fall 9: Der Einsatzgruppenprozeß (gegen Otto Ohlendorf und andere)." In *Der Nationalsozialismus vor Gericht: Die alliierten Prozesse gegen Kriegsverbrecher und Soldaten, 1943–1952,* edited by Gerd R. Ueberschär, 164–75. Frankfurt am Main: Fischer Taschenbuch, 1999.

Oldenburg, Manfred. *Ideologie und militärisches Kalkül: Die Besatzungspolitik der Wehrmacht in der Sowjetunion.* Cologne: Böhlau, 2004.

Otto, Reinhard. *Wehrmacht, Gestapo, und sowjetische Kriegsgefangene im deutschen Reichsgebiet, 1941/42.* Munich: Oldenbourg, 1988.

Overy, Richard. *Russia's War: A History of the Soviet War Effort, 1941–1945.* London: Penguin, 1997.

Philippi, Alfred, and Ferdinand Heim. *Der Feldzug gegen Sowjetrussland, 1941–1945.* Stuttgart: Kohlhammer, 1962.

Pinchuk, Ben-Cion. *Shtetl Jews Under Soviet Rule: Eastern Poland on the Eve of the Holocaust.* 2nd ed. Cambridge: Basil Blackwell, 1991.

Pohl, Dieter. *Die Herrschaft der Wehrmacht: Deutsche Militärbesatzung und einheimische Bevölkerung in der Sowjetunion, 1941–1944.* Munich: Oldenbourg, 2008.

Polian, Pavel. *Ne po svoej vole: Istoriia i geografia prinuditel'nykh migracii v SSSR.* Moscow: OGI-Memorial, 2001.

Puchert, Berthold. "Außenhandel und Okkupationswirtschaftspolitik, 1939 bis 1945." In *Wirtschaft und Staat in Deutschland, 1933 bis 1945,* edited by Lotte Zumpe, 366–406. Berlin: Akademie, 1980.

Quinkert, Babette. "Terror und Propaganda: Die 'Ostarbeiteranwerbung' im Generalkommissariat Weißruthenien." *Zeitschrift für Geschichtswissenschaft* 47 (1999): 700–21.

———. *Propaganda und Terror in Weißrußland, 1941–1944: Die deutsche "geistige" Kriegführung gegen Zivilbevölkerung und Partisanen.* Paderborn: Ferdinand Schöningh, 2009.

Rass, Christoph. *"Menschenmaterial": Deutsche Soldaten an der Ostfront: Innenansichten einer Infanteriedivision, 1939–1945.* Paderborn: Ferdinand Schöningh, 2003.

———. "Das Sozialprofil von Kampfverbänden des deutschen Heeres, 1939 bis 1945." In *Das Deutsche Reich und der Zweite Weltkrieg.* Vol. 9, pt. 1, *Die Deutsche Kriegsgesellschaft, 1939 bis 1945*, edited by Jörg Echternkamp, 641–741. Munich: Deutsche-Verlags Anstalt, 2004.

———. "Verbrecherische Kriegführung an der Front: Eine Infanteriedivision und ihre Soldaten." In Hartmann, *Verbrechen der Wehrmacht*, 80–90.

Redlich, Shimon. *Together and Apart in Brzezany: Poles, Jews, and Ukrainians, 1919–1945.* Bloomington: Indiana University Press, 2002.

Reinhardt, Hans. "Die 4. Panzer-Division vor Warschau und an der Bzura vom 9.–20.9.1939." *Wehrkunde. Zeitschrift für alle Wehrfragen* (1958): 237–47.

Ritschl, Albrecht. "Nazi Economic Imperialism and the Exploitation of the Small: Evidence from Germany's Secret Foreign Exchange Balances, 1938–1940." *Economic History Review* 54, no. 2 (2001): 324–45.

Röhr, Werner. "Forschungsprobleme zur deutschen Okkupationspolitik im Spiegel der Reihe *Europa unterm Hakenkreuz*." In *Europa unterm Hakenkreuz: Die Okkupationspolitik des deutschen Faschismus (1938–1945).* Vol. 8, *Analysen, Quellen, Register*, edited by the Bundesarchiv, 25–343. Heidelberg: Hüthig, 1996.

Romanovsky, Daniel. "Soviet Jews Under Nazi Occupation in Northeastern Belarus and Eastern Russia." In *Bitter Legacy*, edited by Zvi Gitelman, 230–52. Bloomington: Indiana University Press, 1997.

Römer, Felix. "'Im alten Deutschland wäre solcher Befehl nicht möglich gewesen': Rezeption, Adaption, und Umsetzung des Kriegsgerichtsbarkeitserlasses im Ostheer, 1941/42." *Vierteljahrshefte für Zeitgeschichte* 56, no. 1 (2008): 53–99.

———. *Der Kommissarbefehl: Wehrmacht und NS-Verbrechen an der Ostfront, 1941/42.* Paderborn: Ferdinand Schöningh, 2008.

Rossino, Alexander B. *Hitler Strikes Poland: Blitzkrieg, Ideology, and Atrocity.* Lawrence: University Press of Kansas, 2003.

Rutherford, Jeff. "Life and Death in the Demiansk Pocket: The 123rd Infantry Division in Combat and Occupation." *Central European History* 41, no. 3 (2008): 347–80.

Sahm, Christiane, ed. *Verzweiflung und Glaube: Briefe aus dem Krieg, 1939–1942.* Munich: Don Bosco, 2007.

Salisbury, Harrison. *The 900 Days: The Siege of Leningrad.* New York: Harper & Row, 1969.

Scherner, Jonas. "German Industrial Productivity and Exploitation of Occupied Europe During World War II: New Insights from Revised German

Import Statistics" (2008). http://economics.rutgers.edu/dmdocuments/Scherner_German.pdf.

Schramm, Percy Ernst, ed. *Kriegstagebuch des Oberkommandos der Wehrmacht (Wehrmachtführungsstab) 1940–1945*. Vol. 1, *1. August 1940–31. Dezember 1941*, edited by Hans-Adolf Jacobsen. Bonn, 1965. Reprint, Munich: Bernard & Graefe, 1982.

Schreiber, Gerhard. "Deutschland, Italien, und Südosteuropa: Von der politischen und wirtschaftlichen Hegemonie zur militärischen Aggression." In Schreiber et al., *Der Mittelmeerraum und Südosteuropa, 1940–1941*, 273–414.

——. "Germany, Italy, and Southeast Europe: From Political and Economic Hegemony to Military Aggression." In Schreiber et al., *The Mediterranean, Southeast Europe, and North Africa, 1939–1941*, 303–448.

Schreiber, Gerhard, Bernd Stegemann, and Detlef Vogel. *Der Mittelmeerraum und Südosteuropa, 1940–1941: Von der "non belligeranza" Italiens bis zum Kriegseintritt der Vereinigten Staaten*. Vol. 3 of *Das Deutsche Reich und der Zweite Weltkrieg*. Stuttgart: Deutsche Verlags-Anstalt, 1984.

——. *The Mediterranean, Southeast Europe, and North Africa, 1939–1941*. Vol. 3 of *Germany and the Second World War*. Translated by Dean McMurry, Ewald Osers, and Louise Willmot. Oxford: Oxford University Press, 1995.

Schüler, Klaus. "The Eastern Campaign as a Transportation and Supply Problem." In *From Peace to War: Germany, Soviet Russia, and the World, 1939–1941*, edited by Bernd Wegner, 205–22. Oxford: Oxford University Press, 1997.

Schulte, Theo. J. *The German Army and Nazi Politics in Occupied Russia*. Oxford: Oxford University Press, 1989.

Shepherd, Ben. *War in the Wild East: The German Army and the Soviet Partisans*. Cambridge: Harvard University Press, 2004.

Snyder, Timothy. *Bloodlands: Europe Between Hitler and Stalin*. New York: Basic, 2010.

Solonari, Vladimir. "Patterns of Violence: The Local Population and the Mass Murder of Jews in Bessarabia and Northern Bukovina, July–August 1941." *Kritika* 8, no. 4 (2007): 749–87.

Stahel, David. *Operation Barbarossa and Germany's Defeat in the East*. Cambridge: Cambridge University Press, 2009.

Streit, Christian. *Keine Kameraden: Die Wehrmacht und die sowjetischen Kriegsgefangenen, 1941–1945*. 1978. 4th rev. ed. Bonn: Dietz, 1997.

Stumpf, Reinhard. "Von der Achse Berlin-Rom zum Militärabkommen des Dreierpakts: Die Abfolge der Verträge, 1936 bis 1942." In Boog et al., *Der globale Krieg*, 127–43.

———. "From the Berlin-Rome Axis to the Military Agreement of the Tripartite Pact: The Sequence of Treaties from 1936 to 1942." In Boog et al., *The Global War*, 144–60.
Thomas, Georg. *Geschichte der deutschen Wehr- und Rüstungswirtschaft (1918–1943/45)*. Edited by Wolfgang Birkenfeld. Boppard am Rhein: Harald Boldt, 1966.
Tiaglyi, Mikhail, "Chingene—Zhertvy kholokosta?: Natsistskaia politika v Krymu v otnoshenii tsygan i evreev, 1941–1944." In *Odessa i evreiskaia tsivilizatsiia, sbornik materialov 4-oi mezhdunarodnoi nauchnoi konferentsii: Katastrofa, soprotivlenie, pobeda (31 oktiabria–2 noiabria 2005g., Odessa)*, edited by Evreiskii Obshchinyi Tsentr "Migdal," 140–75. Odessa: Studiia "Negotsiant," 2006.
———. "Were the 'Chingené' Victims of the Holocaust?: Nazi Policy Toward the Crimean Roma, 1941–1944." *Holocaust and Genocide Studies* 23, no. 1 (2009): 26–53.
Tönsmeyer, Tatjana. "Kollaboration als handlungsleitendes Motiv?: Die slowakische Elite und das NS-Regime." In *Kooperation und Verbrechen: Formen der "Kollaboration" im östlichen Europa, 1939–1945*, edited by Christoph Dieckmann, Babette Quinkert, Tatjana Tönsmeyer. Vol. 19 of *Beiträge zur Geschichte des Nationalsozialismus*, 25–54. Göttingen: Wallstein, 2003.
Tooze, Adam. *The Wages of Destruction: The Making and Breaking of the Nazi Economy*. London: Allen Lane, 2006.
Trevor-Roper Hugh R., ed. *Hitler's War Directives, 1939–1945*. London: Pan, 1966.
Ueberschär, Gerd R., and Wolfram Wette, eds. *"Unternehmen Barbarossa": Der deutsche Überfall auf die Sowjetunion, 1941; Berichte, Analysen, Dokumente*. Paderborn: Ferdinand Schöningh, 1984. New ed., *Der deutsche Überfall auf die Sowjetunion: "Unternehmen Barbarossa," 1941*. Frankfurt am Main: S. Fischer, 1991.
Umbreit, Hans. "Auf dem Weg zur Kontinentalherrschaft." In Kroener et al., *Organisation und Mobilisierung des deutschen Machtbereichs*, pt. 1, 3–328.
———. "Towards Continental Dominion." In Kroener et al., *Organization and Mobilization of the German Sphere of Power*, pt. 1, 9–404.
———. "Die deutsche Herrschaft in den besetzten Gebieten." In Kroener et al., *Organisation und Mobilisierung des deutschen Machtbereichs*, pt. 2, 4–274.
Ungváry, Krisztián. "Ungarische Besatzungskräfte in der Ukraine, 1941–1942." *Ungarn-Jahrbuch* 26 (2003): 125–63.
———. "Hungarian Occupation Forces in the Ukraine, 1941–1942: The Historiographical Context." *Journal of Slavic Military Studies* 20, no. 1 (March 2007): 81–120.

Volkmann, Hans-Erich. "NS-Außenhandel im 'geschlossenen' Kriegswirtschaftsraum (1939–1941)." In *Kriegswirtschaft und Rüstung, 1939–1945*, edited by Friederich Forsteimer and Hans-Erich Volkmann, 92–133. Düsseldorf: Droste, 1977.

Wegner, Bernd. "Der Krieg gegen die Sowjetunion." In Boog et al., *Der globale Krieg*, 759–1102.

———. "The War against the Soviet Union, 1942–1943." In Boog et al., *The Global War*, 843–1216.

Weinberg, Gerhard L. "Germany's War for World Conquest and the Extermination of the Jews." Washington, DC: US Holocaust Memorial Museum, 1995.

———. "Pearl Harbor: The German Perspective." In Gerhard L. Weinberg, *Germany, Hitler, and World War II: Essays in Modern German and World History*, 194–203. Cambridge: Cambridge University Press, 1995.

———. *A World at Arms: A Global History of World War II*. Cambridge: Cambridge University Press, 1994.

Weiss-Wendt, Anton. "Extermination of the Gypsies in Estonia during World War II: Popular Images and Official Policies." *Holocaust and Genocide Studies* 17, no. 1 (2003): 31–61.

Welzer, Harald. *Täter: Wie aus ganz normalen Menschen Massenmörder werden*. Frankfurt am Main: S. Fischer, 2005.

Westermann, Edward B. *Hitler's Police Battalions: Enforcing Racial War in the East*. Lawrence: University Press of Kansas, 2005.

Wettstein, Adrian. "Operation 'Barbarossa' und Stadtkampf." *Militärgeschichtliche Zeitschrift* 66, no. 1 (2007): 21–44.

Wilhelm, Hans-Heinrich. "Die Einsatzgruppe A der Sicherheitspolizei und des SD 1941/42." PhD diss., University of Munich, 1975.

Wippermann, Wolfgang. "Nur eine Fußnote? Die Verfolgung der sowjetischen Roma: Historiographie, Motive, Verlauf." In *Gegen das Vergessen: Der Vernichtungskrieg gegen die Sowjetunion, 1941–1945*, edited by Klaus Meyer and Wolfgang Wippermann, 75–90. Frankfurt am Main: Haag u. Herchen, 1992.

———. *"Auserwählte Opfer?" Shoah und Porrajmos im Vergleich: Eine Kontroverse*. Berlin: Frank & Timme, 2005.

Witte, Peter, Michael Wildt, Martina Voigt, Dieter Pohl, Peter Klein, Christian Gerlach, Christoph Dieckmann, and Andrej Angrick, eds. *Der Dienstkalender Heinrich Himmlers, 1941/42*. Hamburg: Christians, 1999.

Zbikowski, Andrzej. "Local Anti-Jewish Pogroms in the Occupied Territories of Eastern Poland, June–July 1941." In *The Holocaust in the Soviet Union: Studies and Sources on the Destruction of the Jews in the Nazi-Occupied Territories of the USSR, 1941–1945*, edited by Lucian Dobroszycki and Jeffrey S. Gurock, 173–81. New York: M. E. Sharpe, 1993.

Zeltser, Arkadi. "Interwar Ethnic Relations and Soviet Policy: The Case of Eastern Belorussia." *Yad Vashem Studies* 34 (2006): 87–124.

Ziemke, Earl F., and Magna E. Bauer. *Moscow to Stalingrad: Decision in the East*. Washington, DC: US Army Center of Military History, 1987.

Zimmermann, Michael. *Rassenutopie und Genozid: Die nationalsozialistische "Lösung der Zigeunerfrage."* Hamburg: Christians, 1996.

———. "The Soviet Union and the Baltic States, 1941–1944: The Massacre of the Gypsies." In *In the Shadow of the Swastika: The Gypsies During the Second World War*, edited by Donald Kenrick, 131–48. Hertfordshire: University of Hertfordshire Press, 1999.

Contributors

PAOLO FONZI was born in Naples, Italy, in 1973. He received a PhD in history from the University of Naples Federico II and the Humboldt University in Berlin with a thesis on German planning for the monetary New Order of Europe, published as a book entitled *La moneta nel grande spazio: La pianificazione nazionalsocialista dell'integrazione monetaria europea (1939–1945)*. From 2008 to 2010, Dr. Fonzi was a research fellow at the Istituto nazionale per la storia del movimento di liberazione in Milan, Italy, studying the occupation of Crete during World War II.

MARTIN HOLLER was born in 1972 and is a doctoral student in history at the Humboldt University in Berlin. He has studied in Moscow, Heidelberg, Warsaw, and Berlin, where he specialized in German and Eastern European history and Slavic (Polish and Russian) literature. He is currently completing his doctoral thesis, "Soviet Roma under Stalin and Hitler."

ALEX J. KAY was born in 1979 in Kingston upon Hull, England, and obtained his doctorate in modern and contemporary history in 2005 from Berlin's Humboldt University. His doctoral thesis appeared in 2006 in Berghahn Books's series Studies on War and Genocide under the title *Exploitation, Resettlement, Mass Murder: Political and Economic Planning for German Occupation Policy in the Soviet Union, 1940–1941*. Dr. Kay's articles have been published in several peer-reviewed journals, including the *Journal of Contemporary History*, *Transit: Europäische Revue*, the *Zeitschrift für Weltgeschichte*, *War in History*, and the *German Studies Review*. He received the *Journal of Contemporary History*'s George L. Mosse Prize in 2006.

THOMAS J. LAUB was born in Buffalo, New York. He completed his PhD at the University of Virginia in 2003 and was a finalist for the German Historical Institute's Fritz Stern Prize for best dissertation. He has taught modern European history at Sweet Briar College and James Madison University and currently directs an outreach education program for Longwood University. Dr. Laub is the author of *After the Fall: German Policy in Occupied France, 1940–1944*, published in 2010 by Oxford University Press, and is currently studying the laws of war during the twentieth century.

STEPHAN LEHNSTAEDT was born in 1980 and is research fellow at the German Historical Institute, Warsaw. He studied early modern and modern history at the Ludwig Maximilian University, Munich, and received his MA in 2004 and his DPhil in 2008. His doctoral thesis, *Okkupation im Osten: Besatzeralltag in Warschau und Minsk 1939–1944*, was published in 2010. From 2005 to 2009, Dr. Lehnstaedt was assistant researcher at the Institute for Contemporary History, Munich, in which capacity he edited documents for the project Flick During the Third Reich and furnished opinions for German social courts dealing with pensions for former ghetto inmates.

WENDY LOWER is a research fellow and lecturer in the history department at the Ludwig Maximilian University, Munich. She is the author of several publications on the Holocaust, including *Nazi Empire-Building and the Holocaust in Ukraine* (2005) and *Samuel Golfard's Diary and the Holocaust in Eastern Galicia* (2011). Dr. Lower is currently writing a book about perpetrator biographies in twentieth-century eastern and central Europe.

LEONID REIN was born in 1972 and has a PhD in history from Haifa University. He is currently a researcher at the International Institute for Holocaust Research Yad Vashem (Israel) and specializes in Nazi occupation policies, local collaboration, and the Holocaust in the Soviet territories. Dr. Rein's most recent publications include *The Kings and the Pawns: Collaboration in Byelorussia During World War II* (2011), "Untermenschen in SS Uniforms: 30th Waffen-Grenadier Division of Waffen SS," *Journal of Slavic Military Studies* 20 (April 2007): 329–45, and "Local Collaboration in the Execution of the 'Final Solution' in Nazi-Occupied Belorusia," *Holocaust and Genocide Studies* 20, no. 3 (2006): 381–409.

FELIX RÖMER was born in 1978 and received his PhD from the University of Kiel in 2007, after studying modern history in Kiel, Lyon, and Freiburg. Since 2008 he has been teaching in the Department of History at the University of Mainz, where his research focuses on the frames of reference of warfare in World War II. Dr. Römer's publications include the monograph *Der Kommissarbefehl: Wehrmacht und NS-Verbrechen an der Ostfront 1941/42*, as well as numerous articles on the German army during World War II and its involvement in war crimes.

JEFF RUTHERFORD was born in 1974 in Hudson, New York, and is assistant professor of history at Wheeling Jesuit University, West Virginia. He received his PhD from the University of Texas at Austin in 2007, and has contributed a chapter to a volume on German antipartisan warfare in Europe and also published an article in *Central European History* detailing the experiences of German troops in the Demiansk Pocket. Dr. Rutherford is currently working on a manuscript examining the combat and occupation practices of three German divisions in northwest Russia proper during World War II.

DAVID STAHEL was born in 1975 in Wellington, New Zealand. He completed an honors degree in history at Monash University (1998), an MA in the Department of War Studies at King's College London (2000), and a DPhil at the Humboldt University in Berlin (2007). His doctoral thesis was published in the series Cambridge Military Histories under the title *Operation Barbarossa and Germany's Defeat in the East*. Dr. Stahel has since written a second book on the battle of Kiev in September 1941, *Kiev 1941: Hitler's Battle for Supremacy in the East*. He is now working on a book about Operation Typhoon.

CHRISTIAN STREIT obtained his doctorate in history from the University of Heidelberg in 1977. He is the author of the standard work on the treatment and fate of Soviet POWs in German captivity during World War II, *Keine Kameraden: Die Wehrmacht und die sowjetischen Kriegsgefangenen, 1941–1945*, originally published in 1978 and most recently released in a revised edition in 1997. In 2000 he was a member of the commission set up by the Hamburg Institute for Social Research to appraise the exhibition *War of Annihilation: Crimes of the Wehrmacht*, and was coauthor of the final report.

ADRIAN E. WETTSTEIN was born in 1979 and is an academic assistant at the Department for Strategic Studies of the Swiss Federal Military Academy (MILAK). He wrote his PhD on the development of German urban warfare doctrine before and during World War II. Before joining MILAK, he researched at the University of Berne (Switzerland) on French visions of a future war between 1880 and 1914.

Index

An italicized page number indicates a figure or table.

Abetz, Otto, 293, 302
Abwehr, 199, 204
Africa, eastern, 190
Albania, 190
Alexander I, 20
Aleksandrovka, 277; murder of Roma in, 277–79
Alpers, Friedrich, 106
Alsace, 292, 293
Alushta, 271
Andrian, Carl von, 245, 246, 247, 250
Ansat, John, 80
antipartisan operations, 2–3, 5, 67n28, 93, 194–95, 208, 298–301; in Belarus, 242, 244–45, 254; in France, 301, 305. *See also* partisan warfare
Antonescu, Ion, 189–92, 198, 205–6, 208, 210
Antonescu, Mihau, 191
Ardennes forest, 291, 292
Argonne, 292
Armed Forces High Command (*Oberkommando der Wehrmacht*, or OKW), 22–23, 35, 74, 76, 103, 110, 132, 188, 190, 289–90, 294, 297, 301
Armies (German): Second Army, 28, 33, 36; Third Army, 45, 65n7; Third Panzer Army, 153n95; Fourth Army, 38; Sixth Army, 85, 138, 213n10, 226; Eighth Army, 45–46, 65n7; Ninth Army, 28, 33, 34, 36, 38, 88; Tenth Army, 45; Eleventh Army, 79, 189, 193, 213n10; Fourteenth Army, 45; Sixteenth Army, 135, 137; Seventeenth Army, 189, 200, 213n10, 302; Eighteenth Army, 49, 71n82, 79, 137, 139, 143–44, 151n62
Armies (Hungarian), Second Army, 193
Armies (Romanian): Third Army, 189; Fourth Army, 189
Armies (Soviet), Thirteenth, 52
Army Corps (German): 2nd Corps, 134–35; 3rd Motorized Corps, 235n29; 28th Corps, 137, 142; 38th Corps, 136; 50th Corps, 137
Army High Command (*Oberkommando des Heeres*, or OKH), 8, 22–25, 29–31, 34, 37, 39, 61, 63, 74–76, 139, 146, 194, 199, 216n40, 289–91, 294, 299
Army Group A, 291
Army Group B, 291
Army Group Center, 23–25, 28, 31, 33–34, 36, 38–39, 50, 61, 113, 136, 229–30, 276
Army Group North, 23, 29, 36–38, 50, 57, 61–63, 70n75, 131, 133, 136–37, 139–40, 143, 150n42, 152n78, 275

Army Group South, 23–24, 29, 34, 36–38, 50, 189, 193–94, 196, 213n10, 214n24
Artillery Regiments (German), 111th Mountain Artillery Regiment, 235n26
Atlantic Charter, 37
Auftragstaktik, 55
Auschwitz, 203, 214n22, 303–4, 319
Axis Powers, 3, 11, 186–93, 197–98, 203–5, 207–9, 211
Azov, Sea of, 192

Babi Yar, 56, 197
Bach-Zelewski, Erich von dem, 112–14, 125n70, 227, 229, 241
Backe, Herbert, 101–3, *104*, 106–12, 117n6, 117n7, 118n7, 124n60, 125n67
Backe, Ursula, 124n60
Baku, 113
Balkans, 131; campaign in, 1, 83
Baltic States, 134, 165, 231
Bandera, Stepan, 193, 204
Bar, 205
Barbarossa Martial Jurisdiction Decree, 8, 296; changes to, 80–82, 85–87; content, 74–76; distribution, 78–79; implementation, 83–87, 93; as reflection of Nazi ideology, 77, 94, 314
Barbarossa, Operation, 289, 290, 301, 302, 305, 306; as economic liability, 4; in English-language historiography, 4–6, 18n30; failure of, 8, 315; in German-language historiography, 5–7, 17n22, 18n30, 77–78; intelligence on Red Army, 23, 35, 40n8, 51; logistics of, 22–23, 33, 38, 59–60, 317; military planning for, 21–25, 40n9, 50–51; operational problems, 21, 26–29, 32–39, 53–54, 57; scale of, 2, 73 317, 320n11; strategic crisis, 23–25, 29–32, 34–37
Battalions (German): II Battalion, 135; 43rd Motorcycle Battalion, 55
Bayrhoffer, Walther, 164
Beamish, Henry Hamilton, 234n9
Becher (German district commissioner), 195–96
Bechtolsheim, Gustav Freiherr von, 230, 277, 279
Belarus, 11–12, 62, 113, 165, 187, 218n64, 220, 224–33, 236n30, 236n39, 240–43, 245, 247, 250, 252, 269, 275–77, 279–80, 316
Belgium, 48, 157, 160, 180n10, 290–91, 301
Belgorod, 276
Below, Nicolaus von, 24
Berezovka, 214n22
Berlin, 3, 39, 65, 74, 109, 115, 156–57, 203, 246, 289, 292–93, 297–99, 301, 307, 318
Bessarabia, 189, 191–92, 206, 208, 214n22
Bialacerkiev, 59
Bialowieza, 226
Bialystok, 166, 224, 226, 234n15, 236n30, 237n41
Bielsk-Podliaski, 236n39
Biiuk-Onlarskii, 272
Bircza, 235n26
Blitzkrieg, 1–2, 4, 8, 27, 53, 63–64, 77, 131, 164, 317
Bobruysk, 238n68, 276
Bock, Fedor von, 25, 36, 39
Bogdanivka, 197, 206, 208, 214n22
Bolekhov, 207
Bonaparte, Napoleon, 20–23, 26, 34, 40
Bordeaux, 299–300

Index 347

Borisov, 229, 238n65
Bormann, Martin, 124n60, 298
Borodino, battle of, 20
Borowka, 206
Borszcow, 193
Botanok, 286n54
Bousquet, René, 303
Brandenburg Division (German), 204
Bratslav, 193
Brauchitsch, Walter von, 23–25, 29–31, 36–37, 69n60, 76, 106
Brest, 224, 227–28
Brigade Pilfousek, 200
Brion, Fernand de, 297–98
British Expeditionary Force, 291
Brusilov, 235n29
Bryansk, 39, 134, 208, 276, 279
Bryansk Forest, 194
Buchach, 204
Bucharest, 189
Bukovina, 189, 191, 206, 208, 214n22, 214n24, 219n71
Bulba-Borovets, Taras, 205, 218n64
Bürckel, Joseph, 293
Bzura, battle of, 45

Cannae, battle of, 25
Carpatho-Ukraine, 196–97
Caucasus, 37, 50, 110, 114
Central Bank of Ostland, 10, 167, 173, 177
Central Bank of Ukraine, 10, 173, 175
Chamberlain, Neville, 290
Charles XII, 19–20, 40
Chernihiv, 195, 269
Chernovitz, 274
Cherovsty, 274
Choiniki, 200
Cholmy, 195
Chomsk, 228, 238n54
Churchill, Winston, 37, 210
Ciano, Galeazzo, 115, 128n88

Clausewitz, Carl von, 19–20, 315
Claussen, Julius, 109–10, 125n67
Cochenhausen, Conrad von, 45, 79
Cohrs, Alexander, 27
Cold War, 4
Commissar Order, 3, 8, 296; changes to, 80–82; content, 74–77; distribution, 78–79; implementation, 83–84, 87–93; as reflection of Nazi ideology, 77, 94
commissars, Red Army, 130, 221n7, 239n73, 274, 294–96, 318; Jewish Red Army commissars, 192
Companies (German), 7th Company (II Battalion, 407th Infantry Regiment), 135
coal, 101
Cologne, 244
Corps (Hungarian): Hungarian Mobile Corps, 59 (see also *Schnell* Corps); Carpathy Corps, 193
Corps (Italian), Italian Expeditionary Corps, 59, 189
Corps (German): 3rd Motorized Corps, 54–55, 58, 60; 7th Army Corps, 52; 9th Army Corps, 91; 10th Army Corps, 36; 24th Panzer Corps, 38; 29th Army Corps, 53, 86; 39th Army Corps, 49; 41st Motorized Corps, 61; 43rd Army Corps, 33; 44th Army Corps, 59; 46th Panzer Corps, 36; 47th Panzer Corps, 28; 57th Panzer Corps, 32, 37
Corps (Soviet), 34th Rifle Corps, 52
Crimea, 12, 200, 269, 271–72, 274, 279–80, 284n29, 285n37
Criminal Orders, 7, 9, 74, 77–83, 87, 89, 93–94, 95n13, 111, 296, 314–16, 320n7. *See also* Barbarossa Martial Jurisdiction Decree; Commissar Order

Croatia, 214n25, 267
Czechoslovakia, 199

Daladier, Éduard, 296
Dannecker, Theodor, 303
Darlan, Jean François, 302
Darré, Richard Walther, 102, 107, 117n7
De Gaulle, Charles, 300
Denmark, 157
Devkino, 277
Divisions, Infantry (German): 7th Infantry Division, 52; 8th Infantry Division, 86; 10th Infantry Division, 46; 15th Infantry Division, 52; 23rd Infantry Division, 52; 31st Infantry Division, 45, 65n3; 78th Infantry Division, 52; 87th Infantry Division, 48, 151n68; 102nd Infantry Division, 80; 120th Motorized Infantry Division, 55; 121st Infantry Division, 10, 130–31, 134–36, 141, 143–46, 153n95; 134th Infantry Division, 79; 198th Infantry Division, 56, 58–60; 292th Infantry Division, 91; 296th Infantry Division, 80; 707th Infantry Division, 230, 244–45
Divisions, Motorized (German): 3rd Motorized Division, 37–38; 29th Motorized Division, 28, 52; 60th Motorized Infantry Division, 55–56, 58, 60n45, 69n65, 70n67
Divisions, Mountain (German), 4th Mountain Division, 86
Divisions, Panzer (German): 3rd Panzer Division, 26; 4th Panzer Division, 26, 45; 7th Panzer Division, 26; 10th Panzer Division, 26, 29; 13th Panzer Division, 55, 68n46, 69n67, 70n71; 16th Panzer Division, 60; 17th Panzer Division, 26, 28; 18th Panzer Division, 27–28; 19th Panzer Division, 37; 20th Panzer Division, 26, 37–38
Divisions, Security (German): 213th Security Division, 217n53; 221st Security Division, 224, 230, 239n73; 281st Security Division, 275; 286th Security Division, 230
Divisions, *Waffen*-SS (German): SS *Das Reich*, 89; SS *Leibstandarte*, 60; SS *Viking*, 56
Divisions (Hungarian), 105th Infantry Division, 195
Divisions (Slovak): 1st (Mobile) Infantry Division, 200; 2nd Security Infantry Division, 200, 208, 217n53
Dnieper River, 25, 28, 51–52, 54–55, 59, 200
Dniester River, 191–92
Dnipropetrovsk, 68n40, 68n41; battle of, 8, 54–60, 63–64
Dno region, 286n54
Domanivka, 206
Don River, 193
Donets Basin, 23, 60, 101
Donner, Otto, 115
Dordrecht, 48–49
Drancy, French internment camp in, 303
Dreckmeier (gendarmerie station chief), 195
Drohobych, 200, 204
Dunkirk, 291
Dvina River, 25, 28, 51
Dzhankoi, 272

East Prussia, 45
Economic Command Staff East (*Wirtschaftsführungsstab Ost*, or Wi Fü Stab Ost), 107, 109, 171

Economic Staff East (*Wirtschaftsstab Ost*, or Wi Stab Ost), 10, 70n78, 106, 110, 130–33, 139–41, 144–45, 148n13, 150n53, 151n68, 164, 167

Einsatzgruppen, 75, 111, 186, 195, 200, 207, 222–23, 226, 231, 268–69, 291, 318; Advance Commando Moscow (*Vorkommando Moskau, Einsatzgruppe* B), 113, 276; *Einsatzgruppe* A, 108, 122n45, 136, 144, 269, 276, 280; *Einsatzgruppe* B, 113, 231, 236n39, 238n59, 241, 244, 276, 280; *Einsatzgruppe* C, 206–7, 269, 280; *Einsatzgruppe* D, 12, 269–74, 279, 280; *Einsatzkommando* 8 (*Einsatzgruppe* B), 228–30, 276–77; *Einsatzkommando* 9 (*Einsatzgruppe* B), 236n39, 276–77; *Sonderkommando* 4a (*Einsatzgruppe* C), 56, 194; *Sonderkommando* 10a (*Einsaztgruppe* D), 271; *Sonderkommando* 10b (*Einsaztgruppe* D), 274; *Sonderkommando* 11b (*Einsaztgruppe* D), 271

Einsatzstab Reichsleiter Rosenberg, 293

Einsiedel, Eugen, 175, 178

Egypt, 3

Engel, Gerhard, 35

Estonia, 231, 275, 276

ethnic German participation in mass murder, 11, 187, 206, 214n22

extermination camps, 2, 243

Extraordinary State Commission for the Investigation of German-Fascist Crimes (Soviet), 142, 268–69, 271, 276, 279

Faeckenstedt, Ernst Felix, 235n29
Fegelein, Hermann, 227

Feodosia, 272
Field Commands (*Feldkommandanturen*), 181; 181st Field Command, 277; 183rd Field Command, 196; 184th Field Command, 227
Filderman, Wilhelm, 192
Filippovschina, 276
"Final Solution," 10, 187, 188, 193, 195, 206, 209, 303, 305. See also Holocaust; Jews; Romania's "Final Solution"
financial crisis, German, 10
Finland, 3, 53, 62, 276
Fischböck, Hans, 174
Fischer (Hungarian Interior Ministry official), 198
Flanders, 292
Flottmann, Erich, 172
Foreign Armies East, 35
Foreign Office (German), 156, 198–99, 216n40, 297
Fortress Holland, 48–49
Four-Year Plan, Office of the (*Vierjahresplanbehörde*, or VJPB), 103, 107, 114–15, 118n13, 118n17, 132, 156, 171, 179n8
France, 12–13, 156, 160, 180n10, 222, 252, 290, 301, 305, 317; communist resistance in, 297–98; development of German hostage policy in, 294; German labor policy in, 304–5; German occupation policies in, 290–307; invasion and defeat of, 2–3, 22, 290–91; Ministry of the Interior in the occupied territories, 298; Popular Front government in, 296; Vichy regime, 292, 295, 297, 299, 302, 304, 305, 306
Franco-German Armistice, 292
Franco-German Armistice Commission, 301

Franco-Prussian War, 47–48, 82
Frank, Hans, 221
Frankfurt, 244
Free French, 300
Freikorps, 83
French colonial troops, massacre of, 3
French Communist Party, 296, 297
French police, 293–94, 297, 302–3, 306
Fromm, Fritz, 118n17
Fronts (Soviet): South-Western, 34, 37; Western, 25–26
Funk, Walther, 158, 164, 166–67, 169–71, 176

Galicia, 166, 198, 204, 207–8
gas vans, German use of, 11, 72, 231
Gauleiter, 103, 108–9, 174
Gautherot, Henri, 297
Gdov, 276
Geheime Feldpolizei Gruppe 647 (Secret Field Police Group 647), 273. See also Secret Field Police
General Commissariat for Jewish Questions (CGQJ), 302
General Government (*Generalgouvernement*), 195, 198, 221
Generalkommissariat Weißruthenien (General Commissariat White Ruthenia), 240, 246, 249
Geneva Convention, 289, 291
German military administration: in Belarus, 243; and France, 292–307; and murder of Roma in Soviet Union, 275–79
German radio, 250–51
German-Soviet Nonaggression Pact, 236n30, 296
German-Soviet trade agreement, 105
Goebbels, Joseph, 6, 108–9, 125n67, 171
Golta, 214n22
Gomel, 229, 239n68, 276

Göring, Hermann, 103, 105–8, 114–15, 118n17, 128n88, 132, 161, 165, 167–68, 171–78, 298, 300
Gottberg, Curt von, 241
grain, 101–3, 105–6, 109–10, 118n10, 123n53, 123n54, 123n55, 133, 137, 142
Gramsch, Friedrich, 107
Grand Mufti of Jerusalem, 213n12
Great Britain, 50, 131, 170, 222, 290, 292, 305; nationals in France, 292
Great Depression, 161
Greece, 1, 161
Green Folder (Guidelines for the Management of the Economy), 113–14, 126n78, 164, 167
Grodno, 224
Guderian, Heinz, 26–28, 51
Guidelines for the Conduct of the Troops in Russia, 296
Guidelines in Special Fields Concerning Directive No. 21, 296
Gulag, 272
Gypsies. *See* Roma
"Gypsy image," 274–75
Gyula Spitz, 197

Hague Convention, 157, 289–91, 295–96
Haisyn/Gajsin, 195, 209, 216n39
Halder, Franz, 22–25, 29–31, 34–37, 50, 61, 70n75, 70n76, 74, 106, 139, 193
Hamburg, 244
Hanneken, Hermann von, 106–7, 118n17
Hansmann, Claus, 28
Hasse, Gerhart, 139
Heinrich (Wehrmacht major), 195–96
Heinrici, Gotthard, 33
Henry, Harald, 33
Herr, Traugott, 55

Heuser, Georg, 241
Heusinger, Adolf, 29, 37
Heydrich, Reinhard, 222–23, 274
higher SS and police leaders (HSSPF), 112–13, 196–97, 223, 227, 229, 274, 290, 302, 306
Himmler, Heinrich (*Reichsführer-SS*), 107, 112–13, 125n70, 190, 194, 197, 203, 212n7, 226–27, 230–31, 237n41, 237n49, 246, 315
Hitler, Adolf, 101, 103, 105, 107–8, 111, 117n2, 124n60, 132, 163, 165, 169–71, 174, 187–90, *191*, 192–93, 199, 203, 208, 210–11, 212n7, 213n8, 213n12, 220, 222, 227, 232, 235n24, 305, 307, 315; declaration of war on the United States of America, 2; differences of opinion with OKH over Barbarossa's strategy, 8, 22–25, 29–31, 34–37, 50; instructions for war of annihilation, 73–75; at July 16 conference, 14n9; killing of Soviet Jews, 11; planning for Barbarossa, 22–25, 50; policy toward France, 289, 290, 291, 295, 297–99, 301–2, 306; strategic thinking, 27, 29, 33–34, 36, 60–61, 77; starvation plans for the Soviet Union, 9, 63, 111
Hitler Youth, 6
Hochhaus, Minsk, 242, 248
Hoepner, Erich, 37, 45
Hoffman, Ernst, 298
Holocaust, 318; and Axis collaboration in, 186–211; in Crimea, 269, 271–72, 279; in Belarus, 244–45, 253, 277, 316; in France, 303; in Ukraine, 316–17. *See also* "Final Solution"; Jews; Romania's "Final Solution"
Horodenka, 207
Horstenau, Edmund Glaise von, 108

Horthy, Miklós, 193
Hoth, Hermann, 24, 27–28, 31, 33, 67n29
Hotz, Carl Friedrich, 299
Hruska (Slovak commander), 200
Huch, Ricardo, 274
Hungary, 11, 188–89, 192–93, 196–98, 200, 209–10, 215n27, 317

Ilmen, Lake, 275
Imperial German Army, 305, 307
Ingrand, Jean, 298
International law, violations of, 2, 84, 93–94
Italy, 190
Ivangorod, 194
Ivano-Frankivs'k. *See* Stanyslaviv

Jeckeln, Friedrich, 112, 196–98, 216n40
Jelenowka, 219n69
Jelino, 194
Jewish labor battalions, Hungarian, 194, 208, 210, 215n31
Jews, 124n59, 189–90, 197–98, 211, 211n3, 213n12, 222, 224; Austrian, 196–97, 303; Czech, 196–97, 303; French, 13, 292–95, 301–6; German, 196–97, 243–44, 303; Hungarian, 193, 208, 215n27; Polish, 196–97, 221, 235n24, 256, 291, 303; Romanian, 192, 214n22; Serbian, 1–2; Slovak, 196–97; Soviet, 2–3, 10–12, 130, 135, 186, 192, 195–96, 198–200, *201*, 203–9, 213n18, 214n22, 218n57, 220, 222–33, 234n15, 234n17, 235n26, 235n29, 236n34, 236n39, 238n53, 238n54, 238n59, 238n68, 239n68, 239n73, 241–47, 253, 255–56, 267–69, 271–74, 277, 279–80, 296, 303, 316–19

Jodl, Alfred, 34, 62, 190
Joint Distribution Committee, 234n9

Kalinin, 287n58
Kaluga, 287n58
Kamianets-Podilskyi, 196–98, 208, 210
Karjukova, 194
Katlos, Ferdinand, 203
Kaunas, 148n20
Keitel, Wilhelm, 34, 61, 103, 105, 110, 113, 124n60, 297–301
Kerch, 12, 271, 272, 279
KGB (*Komitet gosudarstvennoy bezopasnosti*), 201
Kharkiv, 11, 60, 116, 129n95, 269
Kiev, 50, 53, 64, 116, 128n95, 189, 197, 200, 205; battle of, 21, 56
Kleinmischel, Bruno, 235n24
Kleist, Ewald von, 54
Kluge, Günther von, 38
Knuth, Hans, 151n62
Koch, Erich, 174–75
Kohl, Otto, 303
Kolaiskii, 272
Kolomyia, 207
Kommandeur der Sicherheitspolizei und der SS (Commander of the Security Police and the SS, or KdS), 241, 245
Komorovka, 194
Konotop, 195
Końskie, 235n24
Korenevshchina, 288n75
Körner, Paul, 106–7, 109, 118n13, 118n17
Korosten, 194
Kosov, 207
Krasnaia Gorka, 272
Krasnogvardeisk, 140–41
Krauch, Carl, 118n17
Kremenchuk, 56

Krimchaks, 12, 271–72, 279–80
Kremlin, 108
Krylova, Lidiia, 278
Kube, Wilhelm, 240–42, 248, 252, 254
Küchler, Georg von, 49, 79, 137–39, 143
Kupyshche, 215n31
Kursk, 276
Kurtuliarov, Jakub, 271
Kvaternik, Slavko, 193, 213n12

Lagarde, Paul de, 234n9
Lammers, Hans-Heinrich, 102, 124n60, 237n49, 298
Landau, Felix, 200, 217n56
Landessender Minsk, 250
Latvia, 231, 275
Laval, Pierre, 302–5
Le Paradis, massacre of British soldiers at, 291
Lebensraum, 77, 296, 314
Leeb, Wilhelm Ritter von, 62
Leese, Arnold, 234n15
Lemberg, 198
Lemkin, Raphael, 210–11
Leningrad, 10, 23–24, 29, 37, 50–51, 60, 70n72, 113, 116, 122n43, 130, 133–34, 136, 148n23, 275, 286n51; gassing of, 63–64; siege of, 4, 8, 57, 61, 68n52, 70n75, 71n83, 72n94, 138; starvation of, 61–62, 64, 70m78, 137, 139. *See also* St. Petersburg
Lenz, Wilhelm, 124n59
Lepel, 277
Libya, 190
Lieschke, Wolfgang, 244, 247, 254
Lipnja, 29
Lithuania, 275
Lohse, Heinrich, 166–67, 174, 176–78, 241

Index

Lombard, Gustav, 238n53
Loriet, French internment camp in, 303
Lorraine, 292
Lossberg, Bernhard von, 22
Low Countries, 291
Lublin, 221
Łubomir, Škrovina, 200
Ludin (German ambassador to Slovakia), 203
Luftwaffe, 25, 61, 64, 106, 131
Ludendorff, Erich, 6–7, 315, 318
Luga, 136, 276
Luky Hutor, 194
Lviv, 11, 204–5

Maas River, 48
Mackensen, Eberhard von, 55
Madagascar, 222
Magill, Franz, 227
Maly Trostenez, 243
Marchandeau Law, 302
Marcks, Erich, 22
Mauchenheim, Gustav von, 245
Measures to Prevent Sabotage directive, 293–94
meat, 103, 109, 112, 140, 142, 144
Mediterranean Sea, 170
Melitopol, 200
Melnyk, Andrij, 193, 204
Meyer, Alfred, 122n49
Michel, Elmar, 295
Militärbefehlshaber in Frankreich (military commander in France, or MbF), office of, 290, 292–95, 297–98, 301–2, 306
Minsk, 11–12, 26, 151n68, 224–25, 228, 231, 236n34, 240–57, 316; battle of, 21, 25–26, 28, 32; German everyday crime in, 252–53; German leisure time and activities in, 250–51; German living conditions in, 248–49, 252; German self-perception as occupiers, 256–57; German theft in, 248; German violence in, 255–56; German women in, 242; Ghetto, 242–43; Jews in, 243–44, 253 (*see also* Jews)
Minsk *Sondergericht*, 253
Minsker Zeitung, 246, 253, 255
Miropol, 200, *201*, 218n57
Mogilev, 51–52, 225, 228–31, 236n35, 269, 276, 277
Montua, Max, 226, 237n41
Moritz, Alfons, 117n6
Moscow, 4, 113, 133–34, 153n95, 220, 279; battle of, 11, 72n94, 211; German defeat at, 276; in German war plans, 23–25, 29–31, 34–35, 37, 39, 50–51, 60–61; as industrial center, 111; in previous wars, 19–20; in starvation planning, 70n78; as transport and armaments center, 101
Motol, 228, 238n54
Munich, 190
Munich Pact, 199
Murmansk, 133
Mushkin, Ilya, 236n34
Muslim Committee, 273
Musmanno, Michael Angelo, 274
Mussolini, Benito, 190, *191*

Nachtigal unit, 189, 204–5
Nagel, Gottlieb, 231
Nagel, Hans, 114, 132, 134
Nagy, Vilmos, 215n31
Nantes, 299–300
Narewka-Mala, 226
Narodnoe opolcheniye (Soviet militia units), 53
National Socialist Motor Corps (*Nationalsozialistische Kraftfahrkorps*, or NSKK), 228
Naval Group Command West, 298

Nebe, Arthur, 231, 236n39
Nehring, Walther, 27
Netherlands, 13, 48, 157, 290–91, 294
Neumann, Erich, 103, 118n17, 172–73, 179n8
Neva River, 62
New Order, Nazi, 7, 145, 156, 171
Night and Fog Decree (*Nacht und Nebel Erlass*), 300–1
Nikolayev, 12, 270–71
Nisko, 221–22
NKVD (*Narodnyy komissariat vnutrennikh del*), 52, 204, 272–73
Nogai steppe, 271
North Africa, 3
Norway, 157
Nosovsk, 194
Novgorod, 275
NSDAP, 103
Nuremberg, 113–14
Nuremberg *Einsatzgruppen* Trial, 269, 273, 280

Oberg, Carl, 302–3, 305–6
Obersalzberg, 111
Obertyn, 207
October Revolution, 277
Odessa, 192, 197, 205, 208, 214n22
Ohlendorf, Otto, 12, 269, 270, 273–75, 280, 285n45, 288n78, 317; and responsibility for radicalization of Nazi Roma policy, 279
oil, 115, 163, 170, 189, 190
oil crops, 113, 115
Oldenburg, Planning Staff, 106, 132. *See also* Economic Staff East
Olev'sk, 205
Opotschka, 140
Order Police (*Ordnungspolizei*) 186, 201, 222, 231, 233, 241; 303rd Order Police Battalion, 200; 309th Order Police Battalion, 223–25; 320th Order Police Battalion, 197; 322nd Order Police Battalion, 226, 228–31, 236n40, 238n59, 246; Order Police Regiment Center, 226, 238n62
Orel, 276
Organization of Ukrainian Nationalists (OUN), 204–5, 218n64
Organization Todt, 247, 249
Orsha, 51, 139
Ortskommandanturen, 276
Ostbahn, 248
Ostheer, 21, 31, 39, 41n10, 53–54
Ostland, 163, 165–68, 171–77. *See also* Reich Commissariat Ostland
OUN-B, 204–5. *See also* Organization of Ukrainian Nationalists
OUN-M, 205. *See also* Organization of Ukrainian Nationalists
Ovruch, 200

Panzer Groups (German): Panzer Group 1, 37, 54, 56, 59–60, 213n10; Panzer Group 2, 26, 29, 32, 37–38, 41n19, 51, 56, 84; Panzer Group 3, 24, 32, 36–37, 41n19, 67n29, 88; Panzer Group 4, 37
Paris, 105, 294, 297, 299, 306–7; and suburb of St-Denis, 297
partisan warfare, 2–3, 5, 82–85. *See also* antipartisan operations
Party Chancellery, Nazi, 124n60
Paulus, Friedrich, 24
Pavlovsk, 10, 130–31, 137, 141–43, 145–46, 316
Pearl Harbor, Japanese attack on, 2
Peipus, Lake, 275
Persterer, Alois, 274
Pétain, Philippe, 291
Phony War, 297

Poland, 2, 11–12, 19, 206–7, 221–23, 225–26, 231, 235n24, 236n30, 236n39, 247, 255, 294, 302; and German invasion, 2, 8, 45–47, 83, 290. *See also* Warsaw
Polissian Sich/Polis'ka Sich, 205, 218n64
Polonne, 217n53
Poltava, battle of, 19–20
Popov (chairmen of Smolensk branch of Extraordinary State Commission), 279
Popular Front, 296
Prague, 200, *201*
Pripet marshes, 205, 227–28
prisoners of war: French, 291; Jewish, 187; Soviet, 2–3, 115–16, 128n88, 242, 244
Pskov, 275, 287n56
Puhl, Emil, 167, 176
Pushkin, 137, 142, 145

Red Army, 23–26, 32, 34, 39, 53, 69n53, 152n79, 177, 192, 204, 269
refugees, in France, 291, 293; Austrian, 292; Czechoslovakian, 292; Dutch, 292; Norwegian, 292; Polish, 292
Regiments (German): 29th Infantry Regiment, 88; 66th Rifle Regiment, 55; 67th Infantry Regiment, 52; 350th Infantry Regiment, 239n73; 407th Infantry Regiment, 135
Regiments (Slovak): 101st Infantry Regiment, 200; 102nd Infantry Regiment, 200
Reich Chancellery, 74, 102
Reich commissar for price setting, 162, 168, 172, 174, 176
Reich Credit Offices, 156, 164, 166, 176

Reich Food Estate, 9, 102–3, 107, 110
Reich Forestry Office, 106
Reich Ministry for Food and Agriculture (*Reichsministerium für Ernährung und Landwirtschaft*, or RMEL), 9, 101–2, 107, 109–10, 117n6, 118n10, 186
Reich Ministry of the Interior, 124n59, 198
Reich Labor Service, 6
Reich Ministry for the Occupied Eastern Territories (*Reichsministerium für die besetzten Ostgebiete*), 166–67, 177, 194, 241, 275
Reich Security Main Office (*Reichssicherheitshauptamt*, or RSHA), 12, 75, 222–23, 272, 280
Reichenau, Walter von, 81, 138, 226
Reichsbahn, 157–58, 161–62, 164, 167, 169–70, 175, 178, 242, 245
Reich Commissariat Ostland (*Reichskommissariat Ostland*), 165, 168, 241, 275. *See also* Ostland
Reich Commissariat Ukraine (*Reichskommissariat Ukraine*), 174, 194–96. *See also* Ukraine
Reichsleiter, 108–9
Reichswehr, 47
Reinhardt, Fritz, 173–74
Reinhardt, Hans, 45, 61–62, 71n84
Relève Program, 304
Rentrop, Wilhelm, 176
Replacement Army, German, 118n17
reserve units: 45th Reserve Regiment, 239n73; 230th Reserve Battalion, 239n73
Reval. *See* Tallinn
Reynaud, Paul, 291
Richter, Friedrich, 114

Riecke, Hans-Joachim, 107, 110, 122n43, 167
Riga, 133
Rodt, Eberhard, 55
Rogatchev, 51
Roland unit, 189, 204
Roma: in France, 292; killing of in Yugoslavia, 1, 12; Romanian, 192; Soviet, 130, 267–80, 281n. 2, 316–17
Romania, 11, 188–89, 193, 198, 210, 213n8, 214n22, 317
Romania's "Final Solution," 189
Roosevelt, Franklin D., 37, 210
Roques, Franz von, 275
Rosenberg, Alfred, 109, 114, 122n49, 164, 167–68, 171–78, 182n34, 194, 196, 237n49, 241, 293, 298
Rostov, 56, 200
Rotterdam, 48–50
Royal Air Force (British), 131
Royal Hungarian Army, 189, 193
Rühl, Felix, 274
Russian Civil War, 83

Sahm, August, 33
Samra, Lake, 136
Sauckel, Fritz, 115, 289, 304–5, 306
Scandinavian campaign, 48
Schacht, Hjalmar, 171
Schaumburg, Ernst, 297
Schenckendorff, Max von, 230
Schiller, Friedrich, 274
Schlemann, Josef, 87–88
Schleswig-Holstein, 174
Schlotterer, Gustav, 167, 172, 175–76
Schmundt, Rudolf, 36
Schnell Corps, 193. *See also* Corps (Hungarian)
Schobert, Eugen Ritter von, 79

Schubert, Wilhelm, 106–7, 109
Schutzpolizei, 241
Schwerin von Krosigk, Lutz Count, 167–68, 172–73, 175–76, 178
Secret Field Police, 85, 195, 276. *See also Geheime Feldpolizei Gruppe* 647
Security Service (*Sicherheitsdienst*, or SD), 85, 111, 143, 196, 204, 206, 230, 233, 239n73, 273, 280
Security Police (*Sicherheitspolizei*, or Sipo), 111, 143, 206, 254, 274–76, 280
Semchenkov, Andrei, 278
Senegalese soldiers, massacred by Germans, 291
Serbia, 1, 193, 267
Seredina Buda, 194
Seret, 193
Sevastopol, 274
Shpykiv, 205
Siberia, 23, 111
Siménvalfy Sándor, 219n76
Simferopol, 12, 271–74, 280
Six, Franz Alfred, 113
slave labor, 6
Slovak Army Group, 200
Slovakia, 11, 189, 193, 199–200, 210
Smolensk, 28, 31, 134, 276–79; battle of, 21, 28–29, 32–33, 52
Sokol, 219n69
Sonderkommandos, 195, 279, 287n56, 302. *See also Einsatzgruppen*
Southern Bug River, 192
Soviet cities: destruction of, 108, 111–14, 116, 122n44, 129n95; starvation of inhabitants of, 111–12, 114, 116, 129n95, 134, 137, 139, 146, 186, 244, 248, 316. *See also* Kiev, Kharkiv, Leningrad, Minsk, Pavlovsk, and Smolensk

SS, 112–13, 130, 139, 148n13, 187, 190, 194, 197, 200, 203, 221, 224, 230–31, 233, 235n24, 306; SS Cavalry Brigade, 227, 237n50; 1st SS Cavalry Regiment, 228, 238n53; 2nd SS Cavalry Regiment, 227–28. *See also Waffen*-SS
SS- *und Polizeiführer* (SS and police leader, or SSPF), 241
St. Germain, 105
St. Petersburg, 111. *See also* Leningrad
Stadtkommissariat, in Minsk, 248
Staff Office of the Reich Farming Leader, 106–7, 110
Stahlecker, Franz Walter, 108, 122n45
Stalag 352, 244
Stalin, Joseph, 83, 190, 210, 297
Stalin Line, 28, 53
Stalingrad, 50, 194; battle of, 11, 66n16, 113
Stalino (Donetsk), 269
Stalin's Constitution (a Roma kolkhoz), 277
Stanyslaviv, 204, 207
Staraya Russa, 36
Staro-Bykhov, 228
Starokonstantinow, 217n53
starvation, German policy in Soviet Union for, 2, 4, 8–10, 61–62, 64, 70n78, 106–17, 129n95, 129n96, 131, 133–34, 137–39, 142, 146, 150n50, 186, 234n17, 246, 286n51, 316. *See also* Soviet cities; Kiev; Kharkiv; Leningrad; Pavlovsk; Minsk; Smolensk
starvation in Athens, 1
Staryi Krym, 272
Strasbourg, 205
Stemmermann, Wilhelm, 80
Strauch, Eduard, 241, 254
Strauss, Adolf, 36
Streccius, Alfred, 292–95, 305
Stuckart, Wilhelm, 124n59, 292

Subcarpathia, 193
Stülpnagel, Carl-Heinrich von, 301–2, 306
Stülpnagel, Otto von, 294–95, 298–301, 305–6
Sumy, 194, 269
Sweden, 61, 210
Syrup, Friedrich, 118n17
Szepetowka, 217n53

Tallinn, 133, 287n56
tanks: Kpfw 38 (t), 32, 42n26; 43n44; KV-1, 39; Mark I, 42n26; Mark II, 26, 32, 38, 42n26; Mark III, 26, 32, 38, 42n26; Mark IV, 26, 32, 38, 42n26; StuG III, 42n26; T-34, 39
Tatars, 269, 271–73, 280, 284n34
Teplyk, 196
Ternopil, 204
Tichvin, 63
Third Republic, French, 293
Thomas, Georg, 103, 105–9, 112, 114, 118n17, 132
Tiso, Jozef, 203, 210
Todt, Fritz, 118n17
total war: as a concept, 6; German adoption of, 6, 83, 314–19
Transnistria, 192, 208, 214n22
Transylvania, 193, 214n22
Treblinka, 246
Tver. *See* Kalinin
Typhoon, Operation, 37–39, 61
Tyszelman, Samuel, 297

Ukraine, 4–5, 11, 19, 23, 34–35, 36, 60, 102–3, 109, 123n54, 133, 134, 137–38, 164–65, 167, 173–76, 187–90, 194–98, 200, 202, 203–4, 206–10, 214n25, 218n64, 227, 231–32, 269, 280, 316. *See also* Kiev, Kharkiv, Reich Commissariat Ukraine

Uman, battle of, 21, 54, 60
United Nations, 210
United States of America, 37, 190, 210
Ural Mountains, 113
urban warfare doctrine (German), 47–48, 50–51
Ustascha, 267

Valenkamp (*Gefreiter* in 3rd Motorized Corps), 235n29
Vallat, Xavier, 302
Vatican, 203
Velekie Luki, 36–37, 275–76
Vergangenheitspolitik, 77
Viaz'ma, 39
Viborg, 53
Vienna, 200
Vilna. *See* Vilnius
Vilnius, 133, 148n20, 166
Vinnytsia, 196, 205
Vistula River, 45
Vitebsk, 67n29, 229, 269, 276
Vojvodina, 193
Volga River, 31, 66n16
Volhynia, 204
Volksdeutsche (ethnic Germans), 197, 210, 214n22, 242
Volkskrieg, 6

Waffen-SS, 186, 208. *See also* SS; Divisions, *Waffen*-SS (German)
Wagner, Eduard, 22–23, 105–6, 109, 136, 139–40, 222, 298–99, 301
Wagner, Josef, 174, 176
Wagner, Robert, 292
Wannsee Conference, 189, 198
War Directives, German: No. 21, 101–2, 110; No. 33, 29–31; No. 33a, 31; No. 34, 34
No. 34a, 36
War Economy and Armaments Office (*Wehrwirtschafts- und Rüstungsamt*, or Wi Rü Amt), 103, 106, 109, 114, 132
War of annihilation, 318–19; and antipartisan policy, 5; and criminal orders, 73–93; and Hitler, 190; and hunger strategy, 62; planning for, 50, 243, 320n7; radicalization of, 243; as reflection of Nazi ideology, 77, 94; scope of, 3; Wehrmacht's, 316–17
Warsaw, 207, 246, 247, 248, 251–53, 255–56; battle of, 45–46, 49, 64, 70n75; ghetto uprising in, 246–47
Wehrmacht, 107, 111, 139, 194–95, 197, 200, 275; and collaboration with Ukrainian nationalists, 204; and criminal activities of, 186, 207–8; and criminal orders, 73–93; discipline problems in, 245; in the historiography, 5–7, 77–78; March 30, 1941, conference, 73–74; and murder of Soviet Jews, 224; pre-Barbarossa, 2–3; and production for, 160; and relations with Soviet civilian population, 135, 141; and response to starvation of Soviet civilians, 138, 143–44, 153n95; and requisitioning from Soviet civilians, 135, 145–46, 153n96; and self-imposed logistical crisis, 141; and treatment of Soviet Jews, 225; and treatment of Soviet prisoners of war, 115, 153n96; and war of annihilation, 316–17. See also *Abwehr*; Armed Forces High Command; German military administration; Secret Field Police
Weiss (commander of 309th Order Police Battalion), 223
Weizman, Chaim, 238n54

Western Europe, 12–13, 225, 289, 292, 295, 303, 317
Wewelsburg, 112
White Ruthenia, 229–30. See also *Generalkommissariat Weißruthenien*
Winter (Reichsbank official), 177
Winter War, 51
Wolff, Karl, 125n70
World War I, 6, 22, 47–48, 72n97, 82–83, 122, 318

Yampil'/Yampol, 214n20
Yayla Mountains, 274
Yellow, Case (*Fall Gelb*), 290
Yel'nya, 29, 34, 36
Yevpatoria, 12, 271, 272, 280
Yugoslavia, 1, 193, 208, 215n31, 267

Zeitzler, Kurt, 69n60
Zhlobin, 27
Zhytomyr, 5, 194, 200, 203, 205, 207–8, 217n49, 217n53
Zolochiv, 204

www.ingramcontent.com/pod-product-compliance
Lightning Source LLC
Chambersburg PA
CBHW052056300426
44117CB00013B/2144